Unraveling the End

A balanced scholarly synthesis of four
competing and conflicting end time views

JOHN NOĒ, Ph.D.

Praise for
Unraveling the End

*From participant evaluation sheets
at the 13-week MPC seminar series*

"I am enthralled with Divine Perfection—it is so encouraging and invigorating."

"The question for me now is how do I demonstrate the beauty of this in my thinking and life?"

"I probably will have to go over this study more than three times!"

"The best Bible study I have ever had!"

"This has filled in the gaps that have been open for so long"

"Very thorough, highly scholarly, top-drawer presentation. Wouldn't trade it for anything!"

"I will never *JUST* read the Bible again."

"My faith is deepened. God blesses when we seek truth."

"I now read and understand the Bible in a whole new light."

"An eye-opener to me of our awesome Lord in his exactness of prophecy. I'm floored!"

"It has changed my whole outlook."

"Personally, I express profound appreciation to our Pastoral staff for making this watershed experience a reality."
— Rev. Dr. Ben Ruth, Facilitator

"A terrific and needed read . . . extremely interesting. . . .

Noē offers a detailed and superbly documented analysis of how the Bible's would-be defenders have mangled *sola scriptura* with presuppositions that cannot withstand objective analysis. He demolishes the walls constructed by the architects of faulty paradigms and constructs a synthesis that strongly validates biblical prophecy and offers great promise for strengthening Christian belief." — **John S. Evans, Ph.D., proofreader**

"This book could be your most significant . . . . I really liked the seminar series. . . I have used your synthesis of the four competing and conflicting end-time views in a few of my Sunday school lessons. . . . It is so well put together." — **Elder Mike**

"I thought I'd listen to the whole 13 weeks again. . . . I find your teaching and approach probably the one I most agree with and enjoy." — **Joe Perrott**

Pre-publication edition.
More comments, review excerpts, and blurbs
to be coming from readers of this pre-publication edition.
Additional pages to be added as needed (see contact info p. xi).

Official Publication Date: January 15, 2014

Unraveling the End

By John Noē, Ph.D.

Copyright © 2014 by John Noē.
All rights reserved.
Printed in the United States of America

No part of this publication may be reproduced, stored in a retrieval system or transmitted in any form by any means, electronic, mechanical, photocopy, recording, or otherwise, without the prior written permission of the author, except for brief quotations in critical reviews or articles.

Unless otherwise noted, all Scripture quotations are from the Holy Bible, *New International Version* © 1973, 1978, 1984 International Bible Society. Used by permission of Zondervan Bible Publishers.

Published by:

East2West Press
Publishing arm of the Prophecy Reformation Institute

5236 East 72nd Street
Indianapolis, IN 46250 USA
(317)-842-3411

Cover: Tom Haulter

ISBN: 978-0-9834303-5-3

Library of Congress Control Number: 2013947455

Jesus. Bible. End Times. Prophecy. New Testament Revelation.

Dedication

To David L. Turner, Th.D., Ph.D.,
Professor of New Testament, Grand Rapids Theological Seminary,
and Chairperson of my doctoral dissertation committee
for his encouragement and perseverance
in staying with me and getting me through
that challenging and demanding academic process.

And to the leadership of Madison Park Church of God,
Anderson, Indiana, and their seminar series participants
for your invitation and involvement in helping me make
this material accessible and acceptable.

Contact Us:

Pioneering the next reformation

www.east2westpress.org

Publishing arm of . . .

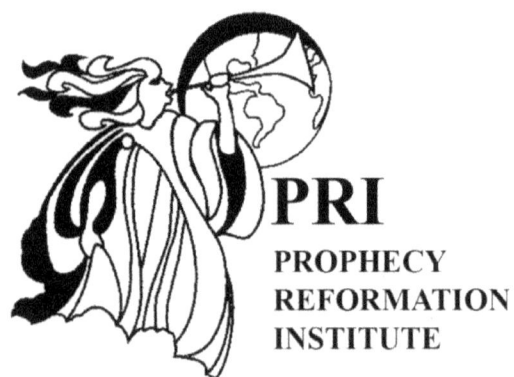

PROPHECY REFORMATION INSTITUTE

5236 East 72nd Street
Indianapolis, IN 46250
www.prophecyrefi.org
jnoe@prophecyrefi.org
Ph. # 317-842-3411

Contents

Prolegomenon – A Joke in the Eyes of the World *ix*

Introduction – Opening Night 1

Part I – So What? Who Cares?

Chapter 1 – 7 Reasons Your End-time View Is So Important 17

Chapter 2 – A Modern-day Parable 39

Part II – Presentation and Disputation of Views

Chapter 3 – The Soon-Coming Fulfillment View—Dispensational Premillennial 49

Chapter 4 – The Partial-Fulfillment View—Amillennial 63

Chapter 5 – The Distant-Fulfillment View—Postmillennial 71

Chapter 6 – The Precise Past-Fulfillment View—Preterist 93

Part III – Analysis of Strengths and Weaknesses

Chapter 7 – A More Comprehensive Approach 115

Chapter 8 – Discarding Four False Paradigms 141

Chapter 9 – A More Disciplined Methodology   185

Chapter 10 – God's Divinely Determined Timeline   213

Chapter 11 – Harmony in the New Testament   237

Chapter 12 – The Many Comings of Jesus   261

Chapter 13 – Reframing Jesus' Most Dramatic Prophecy   285

Chapter 14 – Revitalizing Revelation   331

Chapter 15 – More Countless Comings   363

Chapter 16 – Resurrection Reality   379

      <u>Part IV – Reconciliation of Views</u>

Conclusion – Recaps & Synthesis   417

Appendix A – Timeline Graphic of Divine Perfection   427

More Books from John Noē   428

Scripture Index   439

Prolegomenon

A Joke in the Eyes of the World

Time and again, over and over, for nineteen centuries and counting, the Church has been made to look like a joke in the eyes of the world as predictions of Christ's Second Coming or Return and other related end-time events have supposedly come and gone without fulfillment.[1] Adding to this humiliation is the reality that the biblical field of study of end-time views is termed "one of the most divisive elements in recent Christian history. . . . few doctrines unite and separate Christians as much as eschatology."[2]

As you begin reading this book, please be forewarned. You are about to embark on a journey of both discovery and upheaval. Some may find this experience unsettling since most people do not like change. Others will find it refreshing and enlightening. Hence, in the pages ahead, you will discover that many things are wrong, biblically and historically, with the way we Christian have been handling and trying to understand this branch or subset of theology we call eschatology.

Just as theology is the study of God (from the Greek *theos* meaning "God" and Latin suffix *–ology* meaning "a study of"), eschatology is the

---

[1] For listing of prominent examples, see the first chapter, "Clearly, Something Is Wrong," in my book: John Noē, *The Perfect Ending for the World* (Indianapolis, IN.: East2West Press, 2011), 21-47; also see cartoons, 56-62, 72-74.
[2] Kenneth S. Kantzer, ed., "Our Future Hope: Eschatology and Its Role in the Church," *Christianity Today*, 6 February 1987, 1-14 (I).

study of last things (from the Greek *eschatos* meaning "last"). And, as you will see, no one view or interpretative position has all the right answers. Each has blind spots and presuppositional biases that result in its proponents subscribing to erroneous concepts and flawed interpretative methodologies.

At times you may wonder why I am foolish enough to challenge the status quo and think that my presentations, disputations, analysis, and synthesis approach will ever be able to achieve a consensus, end the bitter debates, and resolve the complex issues that epitomize this most-divisive arena. Some may think that my unification attempt is impossible, as one of my critics wrote: "I have known John Noe since the beginning of the Full Preterist movement and his endeavors to 'synthesize' a bunch of contradictory eschatology paradigms is nothing but gibberish. It sounds intelligent, but it's just his way of not committing to any particular view at all."[3]

But the facts are, traditional answers and methodologies are not working. What is needed is a different approach for better understanding God's establishment and sustaining of his redemptive plan for this world. So help me God, I am this foolish to think I have found it. But you be the judge.

... please be forewarned. You are about to embark on a journey of both discovery and upheaval.

I am also well aware that the issues of eschatology are deeply embedded and their traditions fiercely defended. Moreover, I realize that my proposed synthesis solution for unifying of this field of knowledge has far-reaching implications, consequences, and ramifications that will be resisted. Perhaps, Basil Mitchell hit the proverbial nail on the head when he pointed out: "In politics, as in religion, men become committed to positions which they will not readily give up and which involve their entire personalities. On neither of these subjects are differences easily resolved by argument"[4]—especially for those professionally tied to their

---

[3] On a Facebook thread, "The Eschatological Forum, 7/20/13.
[4] Basil Mitchell, *The Justification of Religious Belief* (New York, NY.: A Crossroad Book, 1973), 1.

view. But I am willing to take this risk of argument and offer a solution of synthesis in order to face what others have chosen to ignore or avoid. I further accept the necessity to offend in order to break us out of our complacency. However, my overriding desire is not for this book to be controversial. It's for this book to be therapeutic, healing, and capable of making a meaningful contribution toward advancing discussions, resolving differences, and ending this divisive end-time dilemma.

"one of the most divisive elements in recent Christian history. . . . few doctrines unite and separate Christians as much as eschatology."

Surely, most of you know that the Church lacks a unified voice and is trumpeting an "uncertain sound" in the area of eschatology. Consequently, "who shall prepare himself for the battle?" (1 Cor. 14:8). But in the wise words of John Warwick Montgomery, "the search for truth can never be limited to the categories of a single modern school of thought."[5] Likewise, George Eldon Ladd recognized the wisdom of a multi-view and strategic perspective when he cautioned: "the easiest approach . . . is to follow one's own particular tradition as the true view and ignore all others, but intelligent interpreters must familiarize themselves with the various methods of interpretation that they may criticize their own views."[6] In the pages ahead, I have simply taken Montgomery's and Ladd's advice one step further—onto a solution of synthesis. This book is a by-product of that step. As you will also see, I originally took this step during my doctoral dissertation.

No one, however and in my opinion, has better epitomized our current eschatological dilemma and my hope for this synthesis approach than Frances A. Schaeffer with this profound insight: "The history of theology is all too often a long exhibition of a desire to win. But we should understand that what we are working for in the midst of our difference is a *solution*—a solution that will give God the glory, that will

---

[5] John Warwick Montgomery, *The Suicide of Christian Theology* (Newburgh, IN.: Trinity Press, 1970), 177.
[6] George Eldon Ladd, *A Theology of the New Testament* (Grand Rapids, MI.: Eerdmans, 1974, revised ed. 1993), 670.

be true to the Bible, but will exhibit the love of God simultaneously with his holiness."[7]

It is toward such a solution that this book is directed. At the least, I believe the solution of synthesis presented herein can be an effective catalyst for discussion. At the most, I believe it has massive potential for reconciliation (2 Cor. 5:18b). Flawed views of eschatology have menaced the world and discredited the Church long enough. But only God can bring about this unity of doctrine. If He so chooses, it could produce a reformation greater and more far-reaching than the Protestant Reformation spawned by Martin Luther and others in the 16th century.

My prayer, therefore, is you will wrestle with the issues and problems raised herein and, honestly and earnestly, approach the pages ahead with the willingness to sacrifice treasured traditions when they are proven biblically in error. After all, we are not called to follow tradition, but to follow God. Traditions should never become idols, even though they may have become comfortable. Likewise, we are not to blindly follow what we have been told and taught but to search the Scriptures like Bereans. Isn't that what being of "more noble character" is all about (Acts 17:11)?

Flawed views of eschatology have menaced the world and discredited the Church long enough.

My further hope is you will find this book to be a catharsis. It has been for me. It is also your opportunity to re-explore and unlearn many traditional interpretative practices and conclusions that will simply not stand up to an honest and sincere test of Scripture (1 Thess. 5:21; Acts 17:11). As we go forward, let us do so humbly and reaffirm what Scripture has said, "Let God be true and every man a liar" (Rom. 3:4). So, "Come now, let us reason together" (Isa. 1:18) as we mutually seek to correctly handle God's "word of truth." If you disagree with my presentations, my mode of argument, or even my conclusions, I trust, at the least, you will be afforded valuable insights into how and why proponents of the other views think and believe the ways they do.

---

[7] Frances A. Schaeffer, *The Great Evangelical Disaster* (Wheaton, IL.: Crossway Books, 1984), 176-177.

Three final points

First, I have written this book in a popular style but for an intelligent reader and at the level of a college text. It is not targeted for a scholarly readership or the academic world. Therefore, the use of foreign languages is minimal. Nevertheless, I have made liberal use of footnotes and placed them at the bottom of the page. The more casual reader can skip them and won't miss a thing. But the serious reader will find them helpful, supporting, and clarifying. They will also point you to other resources on particular topics.

Secondly, for the convenience of my first-time readers and for continuity-of-presentation and easy-of-comprehension reasons, I have incorporated some material from some of my other books. These portions are either excerpts and/or are condensed. For those of you who have read some of my other books, I trust you will not find this duplicity redundant but rather reinforcing and required in order to provide the flow of content and logic this book demands.

Thirdly, much of the material contained herein was originally presented and recorded during a 13-week church seminar series. But it has been significantly enhanced and expanded for this book. To listen to the podcasts from that seminar series, go to PRI's website at www.prophecyrefi.org. Click on "About Us," "In the Media," and "Unraveling the End Teaching Series."

So, if you are ready for a grand adventure of discovery, upheaval, and reconciliation, read on, enjoy, and be encouraged as we unravel the end, straighten out its maze and mess in an orderly manner, and untangle the paradigms and beliefs of four competing and conflicting end-time views (see picture on the front cover)!

But only God can bring about this unity of doctrine. And if He so chooses, it could produce a reformation greater and more far-reaching than the Protestant Reformation . . . ."

Introduction

Opening Night

It was with a degree of apprehension that I entered the large Madison Park Church of God facility in Anderson, Indiana, for the opening night of my new, 13-week seminar series billed as: *Unraveling the End: A Biblical Synthesis of Competing Views*. This evening would begin the first public presentation of materials that comprised the topic of my doctoral dissertation. But this time my audience would not be the three professors on my doctoral committee, or academics, or biblical scholars. I would be facing a group of regular church people in their auditorium.

Then why my apprehension, you may wonder? It's because of the divisive nature of the arena of eschatology, or end-time prophecy, and the highly emotional and negative reactions it often elicits, especially when one's view is called into question.

Welcome to the Divisive Arena

I use this word "arena" advisedly because eschatology is not only termed "one of the most divisive elements in recent Christian history... few doctrines unite and separate Christians as much as eschatology,"[1] as we have seen.

---

[1] Kantzer, ed., "Our Future Hope: Eschatology and Its Role in the Church," 1-14 (I).

It has also been . . .

. . . declared a "war zone"[2] that's comprised of four "armed camps."[3]

. . . lamented as "a highly complex subject" that's filled with "disagreement"[4] and "a variety of . . . theories."[5]

. . . and dismissed by many as "a complex spectrum of beliefs" upon which "no labeling system will capture everything" since "the boundary lines here . . . are vague."[6]

Others have characterized this divisive arena as a mine field—one false step and you can get blown away by your opposition.

Perhaps Jerry Newcombe best captures this present state of hostility by summarizing: "When we consider the various views on the Second Coming within the evangelical camp, we see such division we almost wonder whether anybody agrees on anything."[7]

Over the course of Church history the arena of eschatology has become a complex maze of four confusing, conflicting, and competing views in which everything is contested, often hotly so. Each camp has its experts who are armed to the teeth and prepared to defend their position against all others. Consequently, no consensus has ever existed.

This lack of consensus has led to major disarray and widespread division. Premillennialists say the amillennialists are wrong. Amillennialists say the premillennialists are wrong. Postmillennials say they are right and everybody else is wrong, Few scholars are familiar with and even fewer lay people are aware that there is another comprehensive end-time view that claims all prophetic fulfillment is past and over; behind us and not ahead of us. It's called the preterist view. Shockingly for some, it's a legitimate and scripturally grounded view that needs to be heard and considered.

---

[2] Gordon J. Spykman, *Reformational Theology* (Grand Rapids, MI.: Eerdmans, 1992), 531.
[3] Robert M. Grant with David Tracy, *A Short History of Interpretation of the Bible* (n.c.: Fortress Press, 1963. 1984), 165.
[4] Henry A. Virkler, *Hermeneutics* (Grand Rapids, MI.: Baker Books, 1981), 190.
[5] Ibid., 201.
[6] Vern S. Poythress, *Understanding Dispensationalists* (Phillipsburg, NJ.: P&R Publishing, 2d ed., 1994), 13.
[7] Jerry Newcombe, *Coming Again But When?* (Colorado Springs, CO.: Chariot Victor Publishing, 1999), 275.

Ironically, at different times and places in Church history, each of the first three views has held sway as the dominant view. Yet each has also taken its turn as the chief recipient of heresy charges. Not surprising, many Christians avoid end-time prophecies like the proverbial plague, thinking, "when you experts get it all figured out let me know, then I'll consider it."

> **... the arena of eschatology has become a complex maze of four confusing, conflicting, and competing views in which everything is contested, and often hotly so.**

Since I only knew a few people in the audience—their end-time beliefs, backgrounds, and personalities—some degree of apprehension on my part was justified. Naturally, I was concerned about possible negative reactions and wondered what type of eschatological "hornet's nest" I might be entering. But this church's leadership had invited me to come and present this seminar series. They were most supportive of having this discussion, were recording it, and would be posting it on their website for those who could not attend, or could not attend all the sessions.

So I pondered, how would be the best way for me to start that opening night's session?

My Personal Story—How I Got Involved

I began rather predictably by thanking them for coming and recognizing the uniqueness of their church's leadership in sponsoring this 13-week teaching and discussion seminar series on this topic. Sad to say, most churches with whom I was familiar would never allow such an event of this scope, magnitude, and risk. For those churches, allowing an open and honest exploration of other eschatological views is not considered "safe." If this topic is ever addressed, it's only to expound on their particular end-time view and ignore or disparage the others. So I emphasized how exceptional this opportunity truly was and how much I appreciated this church's willingness to entertain this discussion. (Once again, to listen to some or all of the recorded sessions, go to www.prophecyrefi.org and click on "About Us," "In The Media" and "Unraveling the End Teaching Series.")

Next, I shared some of the above quotes that demonstrate the divisive and confusing nature that most Christians associate with the arena of eschatology. Then, after admitting to them my degree of apprehension, I related my personal story of how I first got involved in this divisive field of end-time prophecy.

Actually, it was by accident.[8]

For you see . . . a strange thing happened when I became a Christian for sure in 1980. My family and I became victims of the end-saying tradition (saying, "The end is near!"). Back then, all that we were hearing was, "Time is short. We don't have much time left."

"How do you know?" I asked.

"We are living in the 'last days!'" they exclaimed. "These are the end times. Soon it will be all over. Jesus is coming back. We're leaving this world."

It was the heyday of Hal Lindsey's book, *The Late Great Planet Earth*. And this end-times gospel was everywhere, at least everywhere in the circles I was traveling. For me, however, this was not good news.

I remember thinking at the time, "Oh, no!" I had just become a Christian. The business my wife and I started five years earlier was starting to make money. Our two children were attending grade school. I wanted to see them grow up. I didn't want everything to end, at least not yet.

When my daughter, Elise, transferred to a Christian school, she was hearing so much of this end-saying message that for several years she was convinced she would never have to make plans to go to college and would never get married. Today, she is happily married, has four wonderful children, and has earned a both a bachelor's and master's degree. How sad, in retrospect, that she had to undergo all this confusion and needless anxiety when she was young.

---

[8] The following account is taken from my book: Noē, *The Perfect Ending for the World*, xi-xiv.

As a new Christian, I was also being told and taught to read and study my Bible. That's when another strange thing started happening. Verses began popping out, like these two from the New Testament book of Hebrews 1:1-2: "In the past God spoke to our forefathers through the prophets at many times and in various ways, but in these last days he has spoken to us by his Son."

So I started asking more questions of those I deemed to be in the know like . . . "Doesn't the writer of Hebrews state here that the biblical timeframe known as the 'last days' was taking place, back then and there—i.e., during the earthly ministry of Jesus and during the time he was writing? And if that is true, how can we possibly say that we are now living in the 'last days?'"

"Well, we just are! Look around," I was bluntly informed. "It doesn't take a genius to figure this out. Just look at the moral decay in society and world events—especially those in Israel. How could anyone come up with any other conclusion? Everybody knows we are living in the 'last days'."

But I found this response quite unsatisfying. The answer of another Christian leader, however, seemed to make more sense. He assured me that the "last days" were, indeed, present in the 1st century. But they stopped.

"When and how?" I queried.

"When the Jews rejected the kingdom Jesus was bringing and crucified Him, God's prophetic time clock stopped ticking and everything—the kingdom and 'these last days'—was postponed and put on hold" he replied with confidence. "But the 'last days' started up again."

"When was that?" I followed up.

"In 1948 when Israel was re-birthed as a nation. And soon, Jesus will return and set up his kingdom here on earth, in Jerusalem," he further explained.

His answers seemed plausible, until I got home. Then it hit me. The writer of Hebrews was writing some 35 years after Jesus' crucifixion and this claimed postponement of the kingdom and interruption of the "last days." But I discovered that other inspired Scriptures, written some 20 to 30 years after Jesus' crucifixion, were still presenting the kingdom as a then-present and viable reality. For example, the Apostle Paul, after his three missionary journeys, was "boldly and without hindrance" preaching "the kingdom of God" and teaching "about the Lord Jesus Christ" (Acts 28:31 – also see Acts 1:3; 19:8; Heb. 12:28). Furthermore, and fifty days after Jesus' resurrection, the Apostle Peter proclaimed that the outpouring of the Holy Spirit at Pentecost was "in the last days" (Acts 2:17).

Apparently, if what I was being told was correct, somebody, like the Apostle John or the Holy Spirit, forgot to clue in either Paul or Peter that the kingdom had been postponed and the "last days" put on hold. Besides, I pondered, how are Christians today supposed to follow Jesus' admonition to "But seek first his kingdom and his righteousness" (Matt. 6:33), if God has placed the kingdom in a postponed status and it's not even here anymore?

A few months later, I discovered another view. "Sure, they were living in the 'last days' back then," one pastor agreed. "And we have been living in them ever since."

This view seemed much more credible, until I started asking questions like: These are the lasts days of what? "The end of the world, the end of time," they told me. Yet in almost every Sunday worship service we dutifully either sang or recited in unison this famous doxology and confessional of the historic Church:

> Glory be to the Father, and to the Son, and to the Holy Ghost.
> As it was in the beginning, is now and ever shall be.
> World without end, Amen.
> *(Gloria Patri)*

Once again, I was confused. A lot of things weren't matching up.

Needless to say, the more questions I raised about "these last days" and other related topics, the more I began to sense that most of my Christian leaders and friends did not appreciate my inquisitiveness. One other thing was for sure. I was not being viewed or treated as being of "more noble Character" like the Bereans when they went to the Scriptures to question if what the Apostle Paul was teaching them "was true" (Acts 17:11).

"If you keep this up," my Bible study leader warned me, "you'll only get more confused and confuse many others."

I confess his warning intimidated me. Maybe, I was being too critical. After all, I was a new Christian and, at the time, had no formal theological training. What did I know? And everyone I knew believed this end-time-gospel message. All the popular Christian books proclaimed it. The TV preachers preached it. It seemed that almost everything I heard or read was proclaiming a message of an impending global cataclysm. We must be living in the "end times," the "last days." It seemed so logical. But I also knew that the answers I was getting simply did not match up to what the Bible actually said.

> **. . . somebody, like the Apostle John or the Holy Spirit, forgot to clue in either Paul or Peter that the kingdom had been postponed and the "last days" put on hold.**

What's more, the imminent destruction teaching I was being fed seemed to poke holes in other teachings I was expected to accept. I wondered, for example, why I should be such a good steward over my possessions and invest my time and resources in future generations when I was living in the "final generation" and when everything I owned and invested in was going to be wiped out anyway? Why should I be concerned about spreading the gospel around a world that was soon going to be blown out of existence? And how could I live in joy, peace, and hope when people I dearly loved were about to be annihilated?

When I asked these questions, I got all the trite answers most Christians have come to accept without challenge. "Just do it because God's Word commands it," "You just can't worry about all those things," and so on. But my curiosity continued on, unabated, for over thirty years now in my quest for truth and understanding.

Meeting My Mentor

"Thirteen years later," as I further related to the Madison Park group, "I met your Dr. James Earl Massey." At that time, Dr. Massey was dean of their School of Theology, Anderson University, and much respected and beloved. He was also one of seven Senior Editors of *Christianity Today* magazine.

Dr. Massey had either heard about or saw my appearance on CNN's *Larry King Live* program on March 9, 1993 and in the midst of David Koresh's apocalyptic ravings at the peak of the Waco, Texas crisis. And since I was the author of a recent book titled, *The Apocalypse Conspiracy*[9] King's producers had asked me to come on the show to refute the additional end-time ravings of radio evangelist and founder of Family Radio network, Harold Camping. In 1993, Camping's latest book was simply and fittingly titled, *1994*. He was proclaiming the return of Christ and the end of the world for September 1994. I opposed his position for some of the reasons you will read in this book. Guess who was right.

After I returned home, Dr. Massey and I got connected. He expressed interest in what I was doing and invited me to lunch in Anderson. Thus, began our two-year mentoring relationship (he of me, not me of him), and which I valued highly. At the time, I was working on a new book. So every month or so, at his request, I'd send Dr. Massey the first draft of a new chapter. He'd read it, I'd drive up to Anderson, and we'd go out to lunch and discuss it. Never once during our discussions was he ever adversarial. But he was always challenging, thought-provoking, and encouraging.

Those times were very special and important for me in my theological development. Dr. Massey even endorsed that new book. His quote appears on the back cover and reads: "Noē's book just could be the spark that ignites the next reformation of Christianity."[10] If that quote was prophetic, this book (the one you presently hold in your hands) could fan that spark into a flame and flame into a blaze.

Several months later, when I asked him about the wisdom of entering a Ph.D. program, he candidly responded, "Why? What you've already done is equivalent to two PhDs. Besides, they will ruin your writing style. And who would you be willing to submit to, anyway?" So I put that idea aside. A year or so later, Dr. Massey retired, moved to Alabama, and our lunches ceased.

But when 2000 arrived, Y2K was a bust, and the world didn't end, I found a credible and conservative doctoral program and entered it. Oh,

---

[9] John Noē, *The Apocalypse Conspiracy* (Brentwood, TN.: Wolgemuth & Hyatt/Word, 1991 – out of print).
[10] His quote in now on: Noē, *The Perfect Ending for the World*, back cover, *ii*.

yes, Dr. Massey's admonitions against doing this were still on my mind. But I had begun working on the concept and materials for my synthesis approach to eschatological views. And because of the seriousness of the topic and weightiness of its implications, I felt that I should not undertake it as just another book project. Rather, for scholarly and credibility reasons, it deserved being developed, written, and tested under the discipline of Ph.D. program, if possible.

> **Why? What you've already done is equivalent to two PhDs. Besides, they will ruin your writing style. And who would you be willing to submit to, anyway?**

True to Dr. Massey's warnings, and twice—once during my course work and once during my dissertation, professors who were opposed to my synthesizing approach tried to run me out of the program. Yes, Dr. Massey's poignant question of, "Who would you be willing to submit to, anyway?" proved prophetic. Thankfully, I was able to appeal to the dean and the academic committee. They came to my defense. Three-and-a-half years after entering my doctoral program I completed my dissertation, defended it, and received my Ph.D. degree in Theology.

My Beliefs and Two Guidelines

The next item I wanted to cover with the MPC group on that opening night, and so there would be no misunderstandings about me and my so-called "radical" notions and "unconventional" if not "unorthodox" ideas, I shared my foundational beliefs. I assured them that everything I would be presenting and we would be discussing over these next thirteen weeks would be solidly and biblically based. Then I shared this brief belief statement.

I believe we must fully honor the inspiration and authority of Scripture, the Trinity, and the deity of Christ (He's God's only provision for and only way of salvation). But also we need to "Test everything, hold on to the good" (1 Thess. 5:21) and to be of "more noble character" by examining "the Scriptures . . . to see" if what these four confusing, completing, and conflicting end-time views are telling us is "true" or not (Acts 17:11).

Next, we engaged in a lively group discussion surrounding this question: "Why do you think some Christians avoid the tough eschatological issues we will be addressing in this seminar?" Some in the audience felt it was due to fear or insecurity that if one aspect of their faith is proven wrong, other "non-negotiable" beliefs may also be proven wrong. In other words, it was a knee-jerk, paranoia-type of reaction—if that's wrong, what else is wrong? Needless to say, the easiest defense is to avoid any discussion at all. Others mentioned bad past experiences and how they had been turned off by the bitterness and divisiveness that these type of discussions oftentimes incite.

Lastly, I asked them in a rhetorical fashion, if we evangelical Christians are all regenerated and illuminated by the Holy Spirit, then why do we have so many different, contradictory, and divisive beliefs—especially in this arena of eschatology? We concluded that what we are largely dealing with are emotions in conflict with facts. Actually, it's a form of self-deception wherein many of us dearly want to believe what we've been told and taught regardless of the facts.

Sadly, the bottom line from my experience, and as I further shared with the group, has been that most Christians just sit in their pews and never question or test anything they hear, see, or read. And yet the Bible admonishes all Christians to do just that. Hence, and as we shall increasingly see throughout this book, the field of eschatology is arguably the most deficient area in Christian academia. Additionally, many Christians have a distain for theologians, viewing them with suspicion, if not as a threat. In other words, we are talking about an anti-intellectual bias that does not want to get involved in detailed and comprehensive exegesis or engage in nauseating arguments over complex but relevant matters. Instead, as Brian McLaren points out, most church people "simply want to hear what they already know and agree with."[11] But make no mistake, as we shall see in Chapter 1, the stakes for Christianity are enormous!

Naturally, the question next became, how can shall we proceed? I proposed the following two simple guidelines for our group to agree

---

[11] Brian D. McLaren, *a Generous Orthodoxy* (Grand Rapids, MI.: Zondervan, 2004), 23.

upon in advance and follow during the next thirteen weeks, as we sought to question and test the four major end-time views and pursue truth.

1). <u>Sola Scriptura</u>

I explained my simplistic definition of this Latin phrase this way. It's not what I think or you think that's important, nor what you or I may have been told and taught. What's paramount is what do the Scriptures say and not say! Period. It's not how do you or I interpret them or understand them, but what do they actually say and don't say. Yes, the Bible is, with a few exceptions, that easy to understand. I have proven that this definition works at the highest level of scholarship. Now I want to prove it to you. Therefore, this first guideline was our standard and plumb line throughout that seminar series (and now this book). But as we shall see many times in the weeks (pages) ahead, this is exactly what has been missing. Interestingly, our first guideline perfectly matched one of Madison Park's Core Values statements on their website. I displayed it on a PowerPoint slide and quoted it. It was placed under their heading of "TRUTH:"

> <u>The Bible is our ultimate guide and authority, the standard</u> by which we live.
>
> Our world is filled with <u>competing ideas</u> and values, voices everywhere demanding attention and allegiance. Sometimes, it's easy to become <u>confused</u>. Are there absolutes? Is anything absolutely right or absolutely wrong? <u>How can I sort things out and make sense out of all the confusion?</u> We believe <u>the Bible</u> is God's written word. It helps us understand our world and ourselves. From beginning to end, it reveals the heart of God and His way of life. The Bible introduces us to Jesus Christ, God's Living Word. The Bible explains God's love and His desire to be in a life-giving relationship with us.[12] (<u>underlined emphasis mine</u>)

---

[12] www.madisonparkchurch.org/about/corevalues.

2). In Love

Secondly, I emphasized that we are on a mission of discovery of truth and understanding. We are not on a mission of "gotcha," "one-upsman-ship," or "I-know-more-about-this-than-you" arrogance. And while we need to be careful how we explore, question, and unravel truth, we need not be afraid to do so when we proceed in "Sola Scriptura" and "in love."

If, for instance, I step on your eschatological toes, or you on mine, we will agree to disagree in love and not bad mouth, despise, leave in a huff, talk behind the other's back, or speak negatively of each other in any way. Can we agree on this? I asked them. They shook their heads in the affirmative. But I well knew I would have to remind them of these two agreed-upon guidelines at some point or points in the weeks ahead.

After all, I expounded, a group like this would be comprised of people from different levels of interest, knowledge, feelings, and, most likely, beliefs. My hope for them, as it also now is for you my reader, is they would find my "unraveling" approach exciting, rewarding, stimulating, perhaps like a breath of fresh air, and yet challenging. But I also knew from past experience that some might find this process uncomfortable, upsetting, or even threatening.

Lastly, I presented the three-fold purpose of this unique seminar series and laid out an overview of where we are headed in our re-exploration of eschatology/end-time prophecy:

1) To acquaint the participants with the strengths and weaknesses of the four major eschatological views of the historic, evangelical, and conservative Church.
2) To expose each view's principle yet unscriptural hermeneutic.
3) To offer a solution of synthesis.

Next, to accomplish all this, we must first define some basic terms.

Secondly, we'll answer the question "What difference does it make what I believe or don't believe?"

Thirdly, we'll contrast what I call the "end-time fiasco" with God's plan of divine perfection in two creations.

Fourthly, we'll present and dispute the four major, confusing, conflicting, and competing end-time views—highlighting the principle strengths and weaknesses associated with each.

Fifthly, in the remaining 10-11 weeks (chapters 7 - 16), we'll commence the unraveling process. When I use the word "unraveling" I'm thinking of a maze or mess of something that needs to be undone, carefully and systematically. Certainly, that is not the way my thirteen grandchildren open their Christmas or birthday presents. For me, the word "unraveling," reminds me of times when my dad and I would go fishing and cast our lures out into the water using open faced reels. If you weren't careful, or good at controlling and stopping the spinning reel with your thumb before your lure hit the water, the reel would backlash and create a mess of knotted up fishing line. The only thing you could then do was stop fishing, sit down, and painstakingly pull out the knots, one by one and little by little, and rewind the line neatly back onto the reel (see again picture on front cover).

Likewise, in unraveling this divisive arena of eschatology, we first and foremost need to survey the playing field and gain a basic understanding of the mess of knotted-up problems we're up against and dealing with before making any diagnosis of what's wrong or offering a solution to fix it.

Please be assured, this approach is exactly what we shall do. And, in the conclusion of this book, I shall offer a solution of synthesis for your consideration. It's a solution that will embrace and encompass all four of the major, competing, and conflicting end-time views. If you are ready to begin, let's define some terms.

Some Basics Terms

Definitions

Eschatology is not an appendix to Christianity, a divisive afterthought in the mind of God, or a defeatist mentality for the current future of humankind and destiny of planet Earth. Here are two better and more scholarly definitions:

1). <u>Technical</u>: A subset of Theology (Gr. *theos* = God + Latin suffix-*logy* = study of God and his relations with man and the universe)

Eschatology = (Gr. *eschatos* = last + *logy* = study of last things)

2). <u>Practical, less technical, easier to grasp and remember</u>:
Eschatology = is the study of the progressive completion or fulfillment of God's plan of redemption (salvation)

Hence, the whole Bible can be contextualized as eschatological and (as I'm holding up my Bible and quickly fan-thumbing through the pages from Genesis to Revelation at the MPC seminar session) characterized as the story of "man's problem and God's solution. Isn't that the ultimate context for everything in the Bible," I asked them?

Four Chief Moments

Eschatology's "four chief moments,"[13] or four end-time events are:

    1) The Second Coming/Return of Christ
    2) The Judgment
    3) The Resurrection of the Dead
    4) The Consummation – or "end of the world"
    5) Some also include the afterlife—what happens to you after you die.

The pivotal event is #1. It is the most anticipated event in all of history. Everything else is tied to its occurrence.

During the course of this book, we shall address each of these four chief moments/events and much more. But the 800-pound gorilla in the room that absolutely must first be recognized and explained before we get into any of this unraveling content is the all-to-common question or retort: So What? Who Cares? Why does it matter to me? These questions bring us to PART I and our first two chapters.

---

[13] J.N.D. Kelly, *Early Christian Doctrines* (New York, NY.: Harper & Row, 1959), 462.

Part I – So What? Who Cares?

Arguably, the divisive arena of eschatology has become like old saw says:

> Two men looked through prison bars;
> One saw mud the other saw stars.

Chapter 1

7 Reasons Your End-time View Is So Important

If asked, many Christians would say your eschatological view is not important. After all, we are saved by grace through faith, and not by works or one's eschatological view (Eph. 2:8-9). So they've come up with terms like: <u>Pan</u>-millennialist – "However it pans out that's fine with me." <u>Pro</u>-millennialist – "Whatever happens, I'm for it." Actually, these labels are copouts from people who simply do not want to follow scriptural injunctions, such as 1 Thessalonians 5:21: "Test everything, hold on to the good."

Others are simply confused by the current complexity and contradictions of views. Or they are turned off by the arguing. Hence, they dismiss the importance of eschatology, claiming:

- If the experts cannot agree, why should I bother trying to figure it out?
- It is a non-essential for salvation.
- It's only an appendix to the Christian faith and, therefore . . .
- It's not significant for my daily life.
- It's majoring on minors, etc.

This is why I want to share with you, as I did with the MPC seminar group that opening night, the seven key reasons and pertinent issues for why your eschatological view or non-view is so important. As you will see, eschatology's influence and impact is vast. It touches, encompasses, and has implications for many other significant areas of theology, practical living, and the nature and mission of the church. And there are broad differences of understanding and opinion within Christianity in each of these areas. See if you agree or disagree. Perhaps, you can think of more reasons?

1. How much of the Bible is involved? According to R.C. Sproul, "It has been argued that no less than two thirds of the content of the New Testament is concerned directly or indirectly with eschatology."[1] Some experts have estimated that 25 to 30 percent of the whole Bible is so concerned. So we are not dealing with a fringe issue. As Brian Daley aptly understands, there is "an eschatological dimension to every aspect of Christian faith and reflection . . . . because it touches so many of the central themes of faith."[2] The fact is, your view or non-view of eschatology dramatically affects your understanding, misunderstanding, or lack of understanding of many other important aspects of the Christian faith. For instance, it impacts reasons #2 through #7 below.

2. How much salvation do we currently have? As we've seen, the whole of the Bible is concerned with and can be characterized as man's problem and God's solution. The final outworking of that redemptive solution for both those alive and those dead is what salvation and eschatology are both all about. Hence, the fields and subjects of soteriology and eschatology are inseparable.

But depending upon your eschatological view, your answer to this above question will vary from "some," to "most," to "all." A classic example is contained in one of Dr. Billy Graham's newspaper columns. Here, this most renown and respected evangelist assures his readers that "Christ's work is complete . . . . God's plan for our salvation was finished through Christ's death and resurrection for us."[3] But will Dr. Graham's completion statement stand up to an honest and sincere test of Scripture, as we've been commanded to do?

---

[1] R.C. Sproul, "A Journey Back in Time," *Tabletalk*, January 1999, 5.
[2] Brian E. Daley, *The Hope of the Early Church* (Cambridge, MA.: Cambridge University Press, 1991), 2.
[3] Billy Graham, "My Answer," *The Indianapolis Star* (5/6/08), E-5.

One of the classic evangelism questions many of us were taught to ask when witnessing to someone we didn't think or know if he or she was a Christian or not is, "If you were to die tonight, do you know for sure that you would go to heaven and be with God?" Most evangelicals automatically assume that the answer to this question for them is, "of course." That's what they have been told many times. But don't be so sure. Let's test this commonly held belief for biblical accuracy. Please keep in mind that our salvation is an eschatological issue.

It has been argued that no less than two thirds of the content of the New Testament is concerned directly or indirectly with eschatology."

At the beginning of his earthly ministry Jesus told Nicodemus, "No one has ever gone into heaven except the one who came from heaven – the Son of Man" (John 3:13). How many is Jesus' "no one?"

Critical Objection and My Response: There are two possible exceptions or, if they are true, contradictions to Jesus' statement here.

1) Enoch, (who later may or may not have seen death) was taken away by God (Gen 5:24, Heb 11:5). But to where he was taken is not stated.

2) Elijah, who "went up to [into] heaven in a whirlwind" (2 Ki 2:11). The preposition "to" does not exist in the original Hebrew. It's only implied and is rendered as either "to" or "into." If its meaning was "to," that does not necessitate going "into." If it was "into," then it may only refer to a temporary experience like the man Paul said he knew who was caught-up to the third heaven (2 Cor. 12:2-4). Or, it could mean "into" the outer courts of the heavenly realm (see in Rev. 6:9 – the souls under the altar) and not into the Presence of God in the Holy of Holies, if we follow Jewish temple typology. Another possible explanation is, the Hebrew word *shamayim*, which is translated as "heaven," also means "to be *lofty*; the *sky* (as *aloft*); alluding to the visible arch in which the clouds move, as well as to the higher ether where the celestial bodies revolve): – air, astrologer, heaven" (-s)

> [#8064 – *Strong's Exhaustive Concordance of the Bible*]. Or, this instance is a scripturally cited exception / contradiction to Jesus' John 3:13 statement.

Given both of these above possibilities and explanations, I'll still stick with what Jesus said, "no one." Three follow-up questions then arise: Has this "no one" situation changed since Jesus spoke those words? If so, when and how? If not, is John 3:13 still in effect? Yes, Jesus did have more to say on this issue. He also told his first followers: "Where I am going, you cannot come. . . . Where I am going you cannot follow now, but you will follow later. . . . I am going there to prepare a place for you. And if I go and prepare a place for you, I will come again and take you [receive you – *KJV*] to be with me that you also may be where I am [in heaven]" (John 13:33b, 36; 14:2-3; also see 8:21-22).

So far so good, or so it may seem. But most Christians have been told, taught, and believe that this prerequisite and eschatological event of Jesus' coming again has not taken place, even yet in our day and time. Therefore, if this eschatological belief is correct, then why isn't John 3:13 is still in effect? And at death today, why doesn't a Christian still go somewhere else to await this coming again of Jesus and does not yet go to be with the Lord in heaven? Is not this scriptural and historical conclusion that simple, straightforward, and inescapable?

Unfortunately, I've found that most Christian pastors, teachers, leaders, and even scholars do not like these kind of questions being raised, nor people like me who raise them. Why so? It's because they don't know how to answer them without being inconsistent with their particular eschatological position. So, dismissal, ignoring, or defaming the questioner are the most common responses, sad to say. And most Christians, I believe, have never stopped to honestly consider, or have never quite grasped, the truth and ramifications of this highly consequential, eschatological, and nonoccurrence conundrum. Therefore, when comforting the family and mourners at a Christian funeral, the presiding pastor commonly and casually tells them that the dearly departed is better off than we are today because he or she is now with Jesus in heaven. Oh, no he or she isn't if this prerequisite and eschatological event of Jesus coming again, after having finished preparing that place, has not yet occurred.

Nevertheless, Dr. Graham, continues to inconsistently maintain that "by his death and resurrection he opened Heaven's door..."[4] Others explain that some or all of Jesus' post-resurrection appearances or his sending of the Holy Spirit at Pentecost fulfilled his John 14:1-3 promise to come again and take/receive them to where He is. But there are three more insurmountable scriptural problems with accepting these popular explanations:

1) No verse of Scripture written twenty or thirty or more years afterwards ever confirms either of these notions.

2) During one of his post-resurrection appearances Jesus informed Mary of Magdala that He hadn't yet returned to heaven (see John 20:17).

   Critical Objection: What about Jesus' statement to thief on the cross: "I tell you the truth, today you will be with me in paradise" (Luke 23:43)?

   My Response: Paradise was not heaven. Most likely, it was the righteous compartment of the dead ones in Hades awaiting resurrection. Arguably, that's where Jesus went on the literal "day" on which He was crucified (see Acts 2:31; Eph. 4:9; 1 Pet. 3:18-20; 4:6) and for "three days and three nights" (Matt. 12:40). (More on this in Chapter 16.)

3) Inspired New Testament epistles written twenty- or thirty-some years later were still anticipating this coming as yet-future and yet-unfulfilled, although quite imminent (see Rom. 13:11; Heb. 9:28; 10:36-37; 1 Pet. 1:5; Luke 21:28).

Critical Objection: What about what Paul said about departing and going to be with Christ in Philippians 1:21-24 and 2 Corinthians 5:8?

My Response: In Paul's first passage, he was only expressing his desire, a yearning, or a preference about dying and being present with the Lord. He only said, "I *desire* to depart and be with Christ," not "I *know* I

---

[4] Billy Graham, "My Answer," *The Indianapolis Star* (5/14/99).

can depart and be with Christ." Likewise, in 2 Corinthians 5:8, he only said "would prefer," not that he "could." Let's not make more of these verses than what Paul did. Furthermore, his latter words must be understood within his previously stated futuristic context of "a deposit, guaranteeing what is to come" (2 Cor. 5:5). Hence, and at best, it's a stretch to claim that Paul was teaching a then-present reality that if he died, right then, he would immediately go to heaven. Most plainly and bluntly, Jesus told his 1st-century disciples that where He was going they could not follow "now" but would "later"—i.e. upon his coming again to take/receive them (John 13:33, 36; 14:1-3)—and not upon their deaths as is also sometimes assumed. (All but one of the original twelve died before A.D. 70.) Once again, we must emphasize, inspired Scripture written twenty- or thirty-some years later was still anticipating this coming again of Jesus as yet-future. And based upon our first and agreed upon guideline of "Sola Scriptura," we must honor the clear and emphatic teachings of Jesus as taking precedence over how we understand Paul's two "preference" statements above. Would you agree?

Further notable, only one of the four eschatological views, the preterist view, believes that Jesus did come again as He said and for this purpose. But it occurred after the New Testament books were written. Thus, for preterists, heaven's door is open today. If correct, isn't this is extremely good news? Obviously, the other three views are inconsistent, at best, between their soteriology and their eschatology. Agree?

Another theological tidbit to throw into the mix at this point is, many but not all proponents of the other three views do not believe that the heaven in existence today is a believer's eternal dwelling place. They believe this heaven is temporary and will only last until God creates a new heaven and a new earth. Three prominent examples are:

- Randy Alcorn in his best-selling book, *Heaven*, in which he writes: "God never gave up on his original plan for human beings to dwell on Earth. In fact, the climax of history will be the creation of new heavens and a New Earth, a resurrected universe inhabited by resurrected people living with the resurrected Jesus (Revelation 21:1-4)."[5]

---

[5] Randy Alcorn, *Heaven* (Wheaton, IL.: Tyndale House Publishers, 2004), xx.

- Another popular writer, N.T. Wright, in an article in *Christianity Today* magazine titled "Heaven Is Not Our Home," starts off with the weighty and telling admission that "There is no agreement in the church today about what happens to people when they die." But because of his eschatological position, Wright puts down "the traditional picture of people going to either heaven or hell as a one-stage, postmortem journey." Instead, he declares that this view "represents a serious distortion and diminution of the Christian hope." He does cite Paul's Philippians 3 expression "citizens of heaven" but then interprets it to mean that Paul here "doesn't mean that we shall retire there when we have finished our work here."[6]
- A third example comes from Anthony Hoekema's book, *The Bible and the Future*. Regarding "the final state of those who are in Christ," he insists about the believers who are currently in heaven that: "They will be happy during the intermediate state between death and resurrection . . . . But their happiness will be provisional and incomplete. For the completion of their happiness they await the resurrection of the body and the new earth which God will create as the culmination of his redemptive work."[7]

So given the divergence of views within the Church, how much salvation do we currently have? Some? Most? Or all? Your answer depends on your eschatological view.

3. How much of the kingdom do we currently have? Once again, and according to your eschatological view, your answer will be: "none," "some," "most," "all," or "all minus some major parts taken back by God."

The hardcore scriptural fact is this. The kingdom of God was the central teaching of our Lord Jesus Christ and at the heart of his earthly

---

[6] N.T. Wright, "Heaven Is Not Our Home," *Christianity Today* (posted 3/24/08 on www.christianitytoday.com).
[7] Anthony A. Hoekema, *The Bible and the Future* (Grand Rapids, MI.: Reformed Free Pub, 1966), 274.

ministry. It was also the very essence of New Testament Christianity. Today, however, the kingdom is no longer the central teaching of his Church, at the heart of its ministry, nor Christianity's very essence. For me, this kingdom deficiency in our day and time is an automatic "red flag." Something is wrong, seriously wrong.

So what has happened? What has changed?

Another question I like to ask church leaders and attendees is, When was the last time you heard a sermon on the kingdom? Or, attended a Sunday School class whose topic was the kingdom? Or, signed up for a conference or seminar whose theme was the kingdom of God? I've also found that the kingdom has been written out of most biblical and Christian worldviews. Again, what has happened? What has changed?

Sadly, what has happened and changed is: the kingdom of God that Jesus was presenting as a then-and-there, present reality has gotten caught up in eschatological mid air. Why so? It's because the coming of the everlasting form of the kingdom of God is an eschatological event.

The most popular Christian view (dispensational premillennialism) claims that the kingdom Jesus presented was postponed and withdrawn by God when the Jews refused to receive the type of kingdom Jesus was presenting, reject Him as king, and crucified Him. But if that view is correct, why does inspired Scripture—written some twenty- or thirty-some years later—continue talking about this kingdom as a then-and-there present reality (see for example Acts 1:3, 6; 8:12; 14:22; 19:8, 20; 20:25; 28:23, 31; Rom. 14:17; 1 Cor. 4:20; 15:24; Col. 1:13; 4:11; ; 1 Thess. 2:12; 2 Thess. 1:5; Heb. 12:28; and more). Doesn't this list of scriptures solidly make our point?

The next most-popular view (amillennialism) is one of uncertainty. Its proponents cannot decide what to do with the kingdom. To illustrate this scriptural absurdity, here's a true and personal story. The amillennial speaker at one of the few conferences on the kingdom that I've ever heard about or attended was addressing the kingdom and rightly proclaiming how Jesus during his earthly ministry presented the kingdom as a then and there present reality. He also rightly proclaimed that the kingdom was at the very heart of Jesus' ministry and the very essence of New Testament Christianity. So far so good. Then he dropped the other shoe, so to speak.

"But," he continued, "all we have today is a foretaste of the kingdom . . . It's here but only in an already/not yet sense . . . in some sense." At which point I raised my hand and he called on me.

"I agree with you on Jesus' presentation of the kingdom as a then and there present reality and with its significance in New Testament Christianity. But where did Jesus or any New Testament writer ever say that the kingdom was only there in a foretaste, an already/not yet, or only in some sense?"

. . . the kingdom of God that Jesus was presenting as a then-and-there, present reality has gotten caught up in eschatological mid air.

You could have heard pins drop around the room as the speaker stood there in silence, slowly but nervously stroking his beard, and after a few awkward moments of contemplation nodded his head and responded, "Okay, that was George Eldon Ladd."

Whether you know who Dr. Ladd was or not, one thing is sure. Ladd is not Jesus or any New Testament writer. Not only are those expressions about the kingdom both non-scriptural and un-scriptural, amillennialists cannot define in what sense the kingdom is only here in a foretaste, already/not yet, or in some sense.

A third view (postmillennialism) assures us that while the kingdom is mostly here and it is each individual's responsibility to advance it, it will only come fully in the future at Christ's return. But, once again, what did Jesus or any New Testament writer say about the kingdom being only mostly here or would only come fully in the future. Again, nothing! Zero! Nada! Not once!

A fourth view (preterist cessationism) professes a consummated, present, and spiritual kingdom, here and now, but says little about it in their writings—except some who maintain that significant parts of the kingdom (miraculous charismatic gifts of the Spirit) have been withdrawn by God (cessation theology). Then how do they explain that the kingdom to be brought in by the Messiah would only increase (Isa. 9:6-7; Luke 1:33)? Wouldn't this withdrawal of such an intrinsic and supernatural component be a decrease? And what does Scripture say about the kingdom being only a "spiritual kingdom?" Again, nothing!

In my opinion, when the evangelical Church in America lost its kingdom orientation and worldview—post A.D. 1948 when the prominent eschatological view changed from postmillennial to premillennial—we started losing the culture. As we have increasingly lost the culture, we have also increasingly lost our children raised in the Church, and in droves. In my opinion, once again, the only way to stop and begin reversing this downward trend is by reclaiming and restoring the kingdom reality and worldview Jesus brought, taught, and manifested to the Church and the world. This reclamation would also necessitate a reclamation of the full gospel.

To their credit, Fee and Stuart are right on target regarding the consequences of our confused understandings of the kingdom.

> One dare not think he or she can properly interpret the Gospels without a clear understanding of the concept of the kingdom of God in the ministry of Jesus[8] . . . . [however] the major hermeneutical difficulty. . . lies with understanding 'the kingdom of God.'[9]

Several other prominent theologians have also bemoaned the kingdom's denigration from the gospel and the gospel being reduced to only individual salvation by much of the modern-day Church:

- Dallas Willard terms this kingdom deficiency, "the great omission" in his most recent book by this title and the primary reason "why . . . today's church [is] so weak."[10]
- Darrell Guder calls it "reductionism of the gospel."[11]
- Robert Lynn laments that "the gospel we proclaim has been shrunk."[12]

---

[8] Gordon D. Fee and Douglas Stuart, *How to Read the Bible for All Its Worth* (Grand Rapids, MI.: Zondervan, 1981), 131.
[9] Ibid., 113.
[10] Dallas Willard, *The Divine Conspiracy* (New York, NY.: HarperSanFrancisco, 1997), 40f.
[11] Darrell L. Guder, *The Continuing Conversion of the Church* (Grand Rapids, MI.: Eerdmans, 2000), *xiiif*.
[12] Robert Lynn, "Far as the curse is found" in *Breakpoint Worldview* magazine, Oct. 2006, 14.

- Scot McKnight worries that "we have settled for a little gospel, a miniaturized version that cannot address the robust problems of our world."[13]
- N.T. Wright in his most recent book consequently asks, "Where is the gospel in the Gospels?" He answers by "interweaving four themes: Christ is the climax of the story of Israel, is Jehovah in the flesh, founds a new community, and attacks the kingdom of Caesar with the kingdom of God. Through Jesus' work, God reigns now on earth as in heaven . . . that truth is the best news of all."[14]

Today, as I write, this kingdom-deficiency problem is beginning to change in a few circles. But we have a long way to go to restore it to centrality as it was in Jesus' earthly ministry and in the New Testament.

Another eschatological and kingdom-related problem we must also expose is this. Jesus proclaimed that "the kingdom of God" would be "taken away" from the Jews and "given to a people who will produce its fruit" (Matt. 21:43). This would happen "when the owner of the vineyard *comes*" (Matt. 21:40). The Jews back then knew from the prophet Isaiah that this owner was God (see Isa. 5:1-7; also see John 5:22). This portion of Scripture from Matthew's Gospel also reveals that the chief priests and Pharisees listening to Jesus "knew he was talking about them" (Matt. 21:45). All of which brings up two pertinent questions: 1) If this coming has not yet taken place, why doesn't the kingdom still belong to the Jews and not to us Gentiles? 2) Subsequent to Jesus' words here, or anywhere in Scripture, where is the kingdom ever promised to be given back to the Jews someday? Notably, Revelation 20, the renowned millennium chapter, never mentions the kingdom, Jerusalem, or Israel.

Sadly but not surprisingly, with these kinds of popular and kingdom-deficient beliefs floating around, is it any wonder why so few Christians today take seriously Jesus' basic admonition to "seek ye first the kingdom of God . . ." (Matt. 6:33)? Likewise, is it any wonder that so much of the modern church is "far from being a manifestation of the

---

[13] Scot McKnight, "The 8 Marks of a Robust Gospel" in *Christianity Today*, March 2008, 36.

[14] Review of N.T. Wright's new book, *How God Became King: The Forgotten Story of the Gospels* by Caleb Nelson, "Notable Book," *World*, 12/1/12, 27.

kingdom of God." Rather, as Gerald Bray further notes, it has largely "retreated into private life where it does whatever it can to protect its members from the onslaughts of the aggressive secularism that is increasingly dominant in secular society."[15]

So, how much of the kingdom do we currently have? Again, your answer depends upon your eschatological view. At the least, would you now agree that there are major problems with how we are handling, or mishandling, this central teaching of Jesus? There is more.

4. What do you do with the modern-day nation of Israel? In November of 2000, at the 52nd Annual Meeting of the Evangelical Theological Society, I presented a theological paper titled "The Israel Illusion: 13 Popular Misconceptions about This Modern-day Nation and Its Role in Bible Prophecy." Needless to say, it created quite a stir. Below are its opening three paragraphs:

Perhaps no more volatile or politically charged issue has exploded onto the front page of the world scene and into the Church than that of the contemporary role, or non-role, of the modern-day nation of Israel in fulfillment of end-time Bible prophecy.

Ever since its re-birth in 1948, an end-time obsession has characterized popular Christianity. Prophecy charts, rapture movies, best-selling books, and Antichrist speculations abound. Apparently, the stage is set. Israel is ground zero. How do Israeli Jews feel about their upcoming prophetic role and the pending Battle of Armageddon? Their wooing of Christians and prophecy popularizers has paid off handsomely.

America is passionately pro-Israel. And more than anything else, this end-time obsession has shaped our stance. It has also conditioned an almost uncritical support for Israel's existence and actions in world affairs. But while Zionist Christians are longing for a rebuilt temple in Jerusalem and anticipating the soon-arrival of other disastrous end-times events, they do not believe peace in the Middle East is possible, or even desirable. Meanwhile, other Christians claim that God is finished with

---

[15] Gerald Bray, "The Kingdom and Eschatology" in Christopher W. Morgan and Robert A. Peterson, eds. *The Kingdom of God* (Wheaton, IL.: Crossway, 2012), 219.

the Jews and that the Bible should not be used to advance or detract from the position of any of the three main religious groups whose origin are in the Holy Land.[16]

So does the modern-day nation of Israel still have a biblical entitlement to possess the land promised them by God? Once again, your answer depends on your eschatological view.

Many Christians, as well as some non-Christian political leaders, believe that if we don't support Israel, we'll be biblically cursed, individually and nationally, (a la Gen. 12:3; Zech. 2:8-9). Well, will we or won't we? Regardless of your answer, these biblical verses are the hammer used to pressure the American government to comply with an Israel-first theology and support, politically and financially, the modern-day nation of Israel.

Other Christians, believe that biblical Israel has been replaced by the Church. Most, however, simply don't know what to think, believe, or do about Israel. Or, they don't care.

Perhaps no more volatile or politically charged issue has exploded onto the front page of the world scene and into the Church than that of the contemporary role, or non-role, of the modern-day nation of Israel in fulfillment of end-time Bible prophecy.

On September 5, 2003 I had the privilege of meeting briefly with then President George Bush regarding Israel and his "Road Map for Peace" initiative that he was pursuing in the Middle East. He was signing autographs. But instead of getting his autograph, I presented him with a copy of my ETS paper, "The Israel Illusion."

I began by saying, "I want to encourage you, Mr. President, and your 'Road Map for Peace' for Israel and the Middle East."

---

[16] John Noē, "The Israel Illusion: 13 Popular Misconceptions about This Modern-day Nation and Its Role in Bible Prophecy," a theological paper presented at the 52nd Annual Meeting of the Evangelical Theological Society, November 2000, Nashville, TN, 1-2.

He thanked me. Then I pleaded, "Please do not be influenced by some Christians who do not think that peace is possible." (It had been reported that several high-level and influential Zionist Christian leaders had been meeting with him at the White House.)

He shook his head in agreement and assured me, "Oh, I believe peace is possible."

I next mentioned that my ETS paper biblically supports his belief that peace is possible and a worthy undertaking. As we concluded, I twice encouraged him with these words from Jesus' beatitudes, "Blessed are the peacemakers, Mr. President. Blessed are the peacemakers."

He looked up, smiled, and moved on down the line signing more autographs.

I have no idea how influential our brief conversation or my paper might have been, or even if he read it. But I did receive a nice thank you note back from him.

Today, Israel is as volatile and vulnerable as ever, if not more so. It remains to be seen how President Obama will handle Israel and the Middle East during his second term. But one thing is for sure. Pressure from the pro-Israel-first lobby will be hot and heavy. How effective is this pressure, you may ask?

Dan Carpenter in an editorial titled, "Obama's missed moment," in my local newspaper during President Obama's first term capsulated this pressure thusly: "Indeed, there is no more sacrosanct a subject to American politicians than the 'security' of this Middle Eastern ally, far and away the supreme beneficiary of our foreign aid."[17]

And while we're talking about Israel. Didn't Jesus instruct his followers in his longest and most dramatic prophecy the Olivet Discourse, "When you see Jerusalem surrounded by armies . . . .flee to the mountains . . ." (Luke 21:20-21)? Have you watched the nightly news lately? Israel is surrounded by armies today, isn't it? So why shouldn't we Americans be making plans to go to the Rockies or the Smokies? Does that question sound ridiculous? It should. But those are Jesus' instructions aren't they? Then what do you do with the modern-day nation of Israel? Your answer depends on your eschatological view, or non-view.

---

[17] Dan Carpenter, "Obama's missed moment," *The Indianapolis Star*, 1/7/09, News-8.

5. It's the focal point of the liberal-skeptic attack on the Bible and Deity of Christ. R.C. Sproul lays out this problematic reason quite accurately from his own personal experience.

> In seminary I was exposed daily to critical theories espoused by my professors regarding the Scriptures. What stands out in my memory of those days is the heavy emphasis on biblical texts regarding the return of Christ, which were constantly cited as examples of errors in the New Testament and proof that the text had been edited to accommodate the crisis in the early church caused by the so-called parousia-delay of Jesus. . . .[18] It is my fear that evangelicals today tend to underplay the significance of the problems . . . .[19]

This perceived weakness was, and still is, the crack that let the liberals in the door to begin their systematic criticism and dismantling of Scripture, along with its inevitable bankrupting of the faith. Consequently, in America over the past 50 to 100 years, seminary after seminary, denomination after denomination, church after church, and believer after believer have departed from the conservative faith.

The fundamental and foundational problem behind all this is, skeptics and critics have hit Christianity at its weakest point—the embarrassing statements of Jesus to return within the lifetime of his contemporaries and the "failed," Holy-Spirit-guided expectations of the New Testament writers that He would do just that (John 16:13). It is called the "battle for the Bible." The focal point of this battle has been and continues to be the eschatological statements of Jesus and the imminency expectations of the New Testament writers.

The fact is, Jesus made several, clear, concrete, and future predictions about his coming in glory that seemingly did not come to pass, or so we have been told and taught. Liberal criticism especially concentrates on that point. These critics are more than aware of the dilemma that nonoccurrence presents for the Christian Church and the impossibility of escaping it without being disloyal to Christ.

---

[18] R.C. Sproul, *The Last Days According to Jesus* (Grand Rapids: Baker Books, 1998), 14-15.
[19] Ibid., 17.

Their weighty criticism truly should be a "cause for pause" for anyone who believes in the inspiration and authority of Scripture. After all, the integrity of Christ and all the New Testament writers are at stake.

Robert P. Carroll, for example, in his book titled, *When Prophecies Failed,* discussed: "the phenomenon of disconfirmed expectation." He charged that this tendency was not "particular to Marxian thought or limited to modern political structures." To the contrary, it went "back much further in time and thought to the early centuries of Christianity when various Christian communities struggled to come to terms with the failure of the parousia . . . ." This then "gave rise to the need for interpretation of the traditions so as to justify them in light of what had *not* happened."[20]

Kurt Aland began by confirming that "it was the definite conviction, not only of Paul, but of all Christians of that time, that they themselves would experience the return of the Lord."[21] Later, he disclosed that "around the middle of the second century . . . the Shepherd of Hermas thinks he has found a solution . . . the Parousia—the Lord's return—has been postponed for the sake of Christians themselves . . . . At first, people looked at it as only a brief postponement, as the Shepherd of Hermas clearly expresses. . . . But soon . . . it was conceived of as a longer and longer period, until finally—this is today's situation . . . ."[22]

This perceived weakness was, and still is, the crack that let the liberals in the door to begin their systematic criticism and dismantling of Scripture, along with its inevitable bankrupting of the faith.

Brian E. Daley rationalized that eschatology is often seen as a "by-product of failed eschatological hope – a way of coping intellectually with the non-fulfillment of first-century apocalyptic fantasies." And

---

[20] Robert P. Carroll, *When Prophecies Failed* (New York: A Crossroads Book, 1979), 2.
[21] Kurt Aland, *A History of Christianity* (Philadelphia: Fortress Press, 1980), 87.
[22] Ibid., 91-92.

since "the fulfillment of their early hopes was surely delayed," it "required" a "reorientation of the time-line of its eschatological hope."[23]

Jaroslav Pelikan saw it this way, "When the consummation was postponed," this necessitated "the reinterpretation of biblical passages that had carried eschatological connotation . . . toward a more complex description of the life of faith . . . in the development of Christian eschatology."[24]

Atheist Bertrand Russell, in his book *Why I Am Not A Christian*, discredits the inspiration of the New Testament:

> I am concerned with Christ as He appears in the Gospels . . . there one does find some things that do not seem to be very wise. . . . For one thing, He certainly thought that His second coming would occur in clouds of glory before the death of all the people who were living at the time. There are a great many texts that prove that. . . . He believed that His coming would happen during the lifetime of many then living. That was the belief of his earlier followers, and it was the basis of a good deal of his moral teaching.[25]

Russell further reasoned that it would be fallacious to follow a religious leader (such as Jesus) who was mistaken on so basic a prediction as his parousia.

Liberal Albert Schweitzer, in his 19th-century book *The Quest of the Historical Jesus*, summarized this problem of "Parousia delay" as follows:

> The whole history of 'Christianity' down to the present day . . . is based on the delay of the Parousia, the nonoccurrence of the Parousia, the abandonment of eschatology, the process and completion of the 'de-eschatologizing' of religion which has been connected therewith.[26]

---

[23] Daley, *The Hope of the Early Church*, 3.
[24] Jaroslav Pelikan, *The Christian Tradition: A History of Development of Doctrine* (Chicago: The University of Chicago Press, 1971), Vol. 1, "The Emergence of the Catholic Tradition," 123-124.
[25] Bertrand Russell, *Why I Am Not A Christian* (New York: A Touchtone Book by Simon & Schuster, 1957), 16.
[26] Albert Schweitzer, *The Quest of the Historical Jesus* (New York: The Macmillan Company, eighth printing, 1973), 360.

But as we shall see, Scripture teaches "no delay" (Hab. 2:3; Ezek. 12:21-28; Heb. 10:37). Yet the Church has been preaching "delay" for nineteen centuries and counting. In the meantime, during this unscriptural delay period, they contend that someday Jesus will return and finish the job. This excuse of a delay only proves the liberal/skeptic point. So who should we believe? Again, it depends on your eschatological view.

6. It makes a difference in your worldview. Our forefathers in the faith came to this country under a particular historical and optimistic worldview to expand the kingdom of God (postmillennialism). They believed that the world would become a better and better place as it became more and more Christianized, and that each Christian was responsible to do his or her part to help make it happen. Hence, they came and founded the great institutions of our country—the government, the schools, the universities under Judeo-Christian principles—and Christianity was the moral influencer in our society.

But 50 to 75 years ago all this began to change. Today, the hard reality is, we Christians have given away almost everything our forefathers came to this country and founded. And we have done so almost without a fight. The facts are, we didn't get pushed out by a more powerful and evil force. We simply withdrew. And into the vacuum gladly swept the ungodly forces.

Why did this happen?

Arguably, the prime reason was the dominant eschatological view here in America changed from one of historical optimism to one of historical pessimism—i.e., the belief that the world is supposed to get worse and worse before Christ returns. As a result, many believe that the modern-day Church's obsession with the "Rapture" and the "end times" has led Christianity here in America into a period of cultural paralysis and impotence. They see this period stretching back several decades—particularly to 1948 and the rebirth of Israel, which is viewed as the "super sign" authenticating this negative, earthly view. Incidentally, or not incidentally, this "last days madness," as one author terms it,[27]

---

[27] Gary DeMar, *Last Days Madness* (Brentwood, TN: Wolgemuth & Hyatt, 1991).

perfectly coincides, is statistically significant, and correlates with societal decline statistics.

Perhaps, Edmund Burke, the 18th-century British statesman foresaw this decline when he wrote, "The only thing necessary for evil to triumph is for good men to do nothing." Yes, eschatological ideas do have consequences.

Today, many, if not most, American Christians feel overwhelmed by events in our world. They have also been led to believe there is absolutely little if anything they can do about it. Dallas Willard aptly points this out and elaborates on one of the psychological and practical implications of this popular but negative worldview, which is held by many evangelicals:

> If we think we are facing an irresistible cosmic force of evil, it will invariably lead to giving in and giving up - usually with very little resistance. If you can convince yourself that you are helpless, you can then stop struggling and just "let it happen." That will seem a great relief - for a while. . . . But then you will have to deal with the consequences. And for normal human beings those are very severe.[28]

Seriously, ask yourself, is it any wonder American culture no longer values the Church the way it did? Is it any wonder why the Church is no longer automatically accepted as a player at the table of public life? The facts are, the values of Christianity no longer dominate the way Americans believe or behave. And today much of American culture has become downright hostile to the Church and Christianity (or at least to the type or brand of Christianity we are presenting).

Yes, one's eschatological view dramatically affects one's worldview. And beliefs have consequences

7. It makes a difference in your life and family. If you have bought into the popular concepts that Christ will soon return and/or the world is going to end, these beliefs will affect how you and your family think, pray, work, save, plan, invest, and commit or don't commit to do things in the present—especially things that have long-term payouts.

---

[28] Willard, *The Divine Conspiracy*, 343.

As someone once put it . . .

"Your view of the future determines your philosophy of life."

"If there's no faith in the future, there is no power in the present."

Again, eschatological beliefs and ideas do have consequences. Sad to say, for most evangelical Christians in America, their worldview is something like this:

"We are living in the "last days."

"Why fight, we're on the next flight."

In concluding this chapter on why your end-time view is so important, let's get quite practical and very graphic about the consequences of belief. The following is a transcription of Bill O'Reilly's memo on Fox News' "The O'Reilly Factor." It aired March 4, 2004 (italic emphasis is mine):

> It's a fact. Special interests in the USA are now dominating the cultural debate.
> For example, all the polls say most Americans don't want to change the traditional definition of marriage. Yet, the will of the people is being battered by a media sympathetic to gays, by activist judges, and well-financed special interest groups. Thus, *the battle may be won by the minority.* And, this is happening in many different areas.
> *Right now, religious people are the ones speaking out for traditional values. But America doesn't forge public policy based on religion. Thus, as soon as God enters the debate, the secularists win.*
> Think about your own life in this country. How many changes have you seen in the past twenty years? Gangster rap would have been unthinkable in 1984. Ditto on taking God out of the Pledge of Allegiance. Gay marriage? Not even on the radar screen.
> So what has changed in America?
> #1 – The media has shifted dramatically to the left as network news and powerful urban newspapers promote secular causes all day long. And these entities often demonize those who oppose them with labels like "fundamentalists." The powerful media is aided by people like billionaire George Soros who pumps tens of millions of dollars

into special interest groups allowing those groups to file lawsuits to change local standards. That's why you're seeing the words "Christmas Holidays" being taken off some school calendars. The school districts can't afford the legal fight.

But most importantly, traditional Americans lack a strong leader on social issues. I mean think about it. You have a conservative leader in the White House who rarely engages in these issues. So, the secularists have the bully pulpit. And, they are using it very effectively.

What kind of a country to you want? Denmark—where pretty much any conduct is acceptable? Do you want gay marriage? Do you want legalized drugs? Do you want vile entertainment mainstreamed by powerful media companies? Do you want your kids taught about all kinds of sexual activity in the 2nd grade? *Well, those things may well happen in America and soon, because the forces that want them are well-financed, well-organized, and extremely aggressive. All the things the traditionalists are not.*

And, that's a memo.

So what kind of America do you want your children and grandchildren growing up in? Yes, one's eschatological view will dramatically affect one's life and family. If we are seeing "a world that is winding down . . . our response has been the equivalent of painting the house of a dying man, or performing CPR on a corpse." Likewise, if we view ourselves as "temporary citizens of a temporary kingdom on this temporary earth," we will take little, if any, responsibility for its improvement.[29] Those are the hard and basic human facts.

In sum, these seven reasons are why a proper understanding of eschatology will prompt a proper understanding of God's plan for humanity. An incorrect view, on the other hand, will create confusion, conflict, ignorance, and error. Perhaps you can think of other reasons why your eschatological/end-time view or non-view is so important? Or, you may not agree with all or any of my seven reasons. But this one thing I believe we can agree on. The much-discussed ineffectiveness of much of the Church in the world today—especially in the United States, Canada, and Western Europe— should cause us to stop and ponder if we

---

[29] Cal Thomas and Ed Dobson, *Blinded By Might* (Grand Rapids, MI.: Zondervan, 1999), 177-178.

truly and properly are understanding our faith and our role as Christians. Or, have we missed the mark and gotten caught up in eschatological, mid-air confusion, if not schizophrenia, and have consequently invalidated much of our witness to a watching world? What do you think? Here again are our seven reasons and pertinent issues:

#1 – How much of the Bible is involved?

#2 – How much salvation do we currently have?

#3 – How much of the kingdom do we currently have?

#4 – What do you do with the modern-day nation of Israel?

#5 – It's the focal point of the liberal-skeptic attack on the Bible and Deity of Christ.

#6 – It makes a difference in your worldview.

#7 – It makes a difference in your life and family.

Chapter 2

A Modern-day Parable

Before we can adequately assess the eschatological problems we are up against, make an accurate diagnosis of what's wrong, or propose a solution, we must also better understand the playing field on which we stand.

One of the best ways I've discovered for introducing the millennial maze of competing, conflicting, and confusing end-time views and more of the difficulties most Christians face as they attempt to understand, interpret, and explain end-time prophecy is by using this modern-day parable and application. After all, Jesus frequently used parables to teach and convey complex truths. So why shouldn't we?

This parable also illustrates how many of our eschatological views have been selectively formed and artificially evolved.

They say, "Become like us."
And I say, "Well, who are you?"
They say, "We're a particular denomination."
I say, "What is that?"
And they say, "We believe the dragon's purple."
I say, "Oh, I see. How do you know?"
They say, "Someone told us."
And I say, "A real dragon?"
And they say, "No, it's spiritual stuff. The dragon's a symbol of something or other."

I say, "Well, what about the purple? Could that be spiritual also?"

They say, "Not a chance. As far as we've been informed, purple is purple."

Conclusion: a purple spiritual thing.[1]

Smile if you may, laugh if you must. But no reasonable or responsible principle of hermeneutics will allow such a dichotomous treatment. The mindset that produces this kind of interpretation is not only folly, it is also frightening. To treat Scripture with this much disrespect and in such a manner is not only cavalier, it is also abusive. Wouldn't you agree?

Yet to bend Scripture to one's own liking or advantage is not unusual. It is a *modus operandi* utilized by all four views.

Did you catch the four abuses this parable illustrates? Here they are:

1) The tendency to import and add things not in the text.
2) Selectively and inconsistently applying literal or symbolic meanings.
3) Accepting a belief because it was simply "told us."
4) Stubborn resistance to change when confronted with scriptural evidence.

Next, let's take a very practical look at a millennial application of the above parable. The terms millennium, millennial, and millennialism are not found in the Bible. In only one place in the Bible is a 1,000-year reign ever mentioned—in the ten verses of Revelation 20:1-10. Morris terms these ten verses "one of the most difficult parts of the entire book"[2] of Revelation. Yet this single and small portion of Scripture is the centerpiece for three of the four major views of eschatology we will be addressing in this book. As Sproul emphasizes, "whole systems of eschatological thought have been labeled, defined, and indentified in

---

[1] I'm indebted to Kim Rees from Pottstown, PA who is the author of this parable titled, "The Deeper Things." She shared it with me back in the 1990s over the phone and in response to my book, *The Apocalypse Conspiracy*, which she had just read. I use it here, adapt, and rephrase it later with her permission.
[2] Leon Morris, *Revelation* (Leicester, England & Grand Rapids, MI: InterVarsity & Eerdmans, 1987, reprinted 2000), 227.

accordance with the place the millennium holds within each system."[3] Those three views are: premillennialism, amillennialism, and postmillennialism. The lone exception is the preterist view. Although millennial is not part of its name, it, too, has a millennium position.[4]

Of course, the idea of a so-called "thousand-year reign of Christ" has been the subject of vast eschatological speculation and investigation throughout Church history. Today, it is a highly volatile subject that is "hotly debated"[5] and a large part of the "war zone"[6] of eschatology. Disputed are its timing, duration, and nature. And many books have been written denouncing and ridiculing opposing millennial views.

Hence the position of the millennium within each view divides believers, sets the precedent for one's worldview and view of the future, and also greatly affects how Christians understand the current role or non-role of the Church and individual Christians in society, as well as their responsibilities in living the Christian life in the present. Once again, ideas and beliefs do have consequences.

So here's another modern-day parable I created for your consideration. It illustrates how the thousand years in Revelation 20:1-10 is similarly mishandled by the most popular, prominent, and dominant eschatological view today (dispensational premillennialism):

They say, "Become like us."
And I say, "Well, who are you?"
They say, "We're millennialists."
I say, "What is that?"
And they say, "We believe the thousand years in Revelation 20 are literal."
I say, "Oh, I see. How do you know?"
They say, "Someone told us."
And I say, "A literal thousand years with a real literal chain, lock, key, pit, beheading, and thrones?"

---

[3] Sproul, *The Last Days According to Jesus*, 193.
[4] Due to space limitations, I will not be addressing this issue in this book. I do, however, plan on presenting it in my future book on the kingdom of God.
[5] G.K. Beale, *The Book of Revelation* (Grand Rapids, MI: Eerdmans, 1999), 972.
[6] Spykman, *Reformational Theology*, 531.

They say, "No, some of that stuff is spiritual. They are symbols of something or other."

I say, "Well what about the thousand years? Could that be spiritual or a symbol also?"

And they say, "Not a chance. As far as we've been informed, a thousand is a thousand."

Conclusion: a literal thousand-year, (purple) spiritual thing.

Again, smile if you may, laugh if you must. But let's reread this highly contested passage together (Revelation 20:1-10, *NIV*). Then, I want to ask you some direct and factual questions about it (a la 1 Thess. 5:21). So, please pay close attention as you read through this passage below:

The Thousand Years

20:1 And I saw an angel coming down out of heaven, having the key to the Abyss and holding in his hand a great chain. ² He seized the dragon, that ancient serpent, who is the devil, or Satan, and bound him for a thousand years. ³ He threw him into the Abyss, and locked and sealed it over him, to keep him from deceiving the nations anymore until the thousand years were ended. After that, he must be set free for a short time.

⁴ I saw thrones on which were seated those who had been given authority to judge. And I saw the souls of those who had been beheaded because of their testimony about Jesus and because of the word of God. They had not worshiped the beast or its image and had not received its mark on their foreheads or their hands. They came to life and reigned with Christ a thousand years. ⁵ (The rest of the dead did not come to life until the thousand years were ended.) This is the first resurrection. ⁶ Blessed and holy are those who share in the first resurrection. The second death has no power over them, but they will be priests of God and of Christ and will reign with him for a thousand years.

⁷ When the thousand years are over, Satan will be released from his prison ⁸ and will go out to deceive the nations in the four corners of the earth—Gog and Magog—and to gather them for battle. In number they are like the sand on the seashore.⁹ They marched across the breadth of the earth and surrounded the camp of God's people, the city he loves. But fire came down from heaven and devoured them. [10] And the devil, who deceived them, was thrown into the lake of burning sulfur, where the beast and the false prophet had been thrown. They will be tormented day and night for ever and ever.

My Questions:

- Where in this passage is any mention of a Second Coming, a temple, a re-built temple, re-institution of animal sacrifices, or Jesus sitting on an earthly throne?
- Where does this passage speak of Israel, an earthly Jerusalem, a gathering of the Jews back to Palestine, a revived Jewish kingdom, an earthly utopian paradise, or material prosperity on the earth?
- Where does this passage even speak of a "1,000-year reign of Christ?" Doesn't it only speak of the saints reigning *with* Him a thousand years? Nowhere does it limit Christ's reigning to only a thousand years. Big difference.

Conspicuously, these popular elements are totally absent from this passage. They are also totally absent from the entire New Testament and the whole Bible. And yet they are vital elements of the most popular millennial view. How has this happened? Simple and sadly, they have been fabricated and imported into the text.

First and foremost, this all-to-common tendency to import and add *things not in the text* is specifically warned against in the Book of Revelation, along with major consequences for those violating this warning (see Rev. 22:18-19). And yet this practice of adding content in Revelation 20 (and elsewhere) is a disturbing and distorting phenomenon that has developed during the course of Church history. Today, it is commonly and casually done and has become an accepted practice—much to our detriment.

Secondly, we must face up to the problem of selectively and inconsistently applying literal or symbolic meanings. The fact is, as Mel White argues in his book, *Religion Gone Bad*, "most literalists are really selective literalists . . . . they pick and choose what verse (or parts of a verse) they want to take literally and then ignore the rest."[7] Seriously, how do we decide what and when a text, or a portion of it, is to be taken literally or spiritually, symbolically or figuratively?

One of my favorite questions to ask a dispensational premillennialist is, "Are you planning on reigning and ruling with Christ during his future and literal 1,000-year reign here on earth?"

"Oh, yes," he or she will confidently answer.

"Then when do you literally plan on getting beheaded?" Isn't that what this passage literally says?

The fact is, I know of no definite guideline(s). Therefore, many, who promote interpreting the Scriptures literally—an intuitively appealing ideal—consistently fail to do so, and at some very critical but convenient points. Others, who insist certain passages are to be take spiritually, likewise deviate at whim. What results is a pick-and-chose hermeneutic called cherry picking or proof texting. Practitioners simply vacillate whenever and wherever necessary to comply with the demands of their eschatological view and/or personal feelings.

Even more blatant, most interpreters are more interested in defending and maintaining their position than in rightly dividing the word of God and seeking truth. Thus, they hold on tightly to whatever interpretative methodology enables them to do so. As a result, we shall find these type of deficiencies in each of the four views:

- Basic principles or rules of general hermeneutics being violated and broken whenever and wherever it suits one's purposes.

- These accepted hermeneutical violations producing a self-perpetuating stalemate in the divisive arena of eschatology.

The bottom line is, in the Church's quest to interpret what the Bible teaches, especially in the arena of eschatology, sound hermeneutics have been subordinated to emotions, opinions, and traditions. So, with these pervasive abuses in mind, let's turn our attention to PART II and the four confusing, conflicting, and competing end-time views themselves.

---

[7] Mel White, *Religion Gone Bad* (New York, NY.: Jeremy P. Tarcher / Penguin, 2006), 108.

Part II – Presentation and Disputation of Views

As I shared with you in the Introduction, when I became a Christian for sure back in 1980, I did not know there were four major end-time views (and several minor ones). For many years thereafter, I only thought there was one—the one I was hearing about all the time. I've also found that I'm not alone in this regard. Many, if not most, Christians in churches every Sunday, do not know that there are other end-time views beside the one they and/or their church holds and/or they've been told and taught.

Three of those views are futurist—i.e., the fulfillment of eschatology's four chief moments, or four key end-time events, are still in the future (see again p-14). Each of these views is defined and differentiated by when the central and pivotal chief moment/event of the Second Coming/Return of Christ, which will be personal, physical, and visible worldwide, and occurs in relationship with to the 1,000-year time period mentioned only in Revelation 20:1-10. The fulfillments of the other three chief moments or events are attached to its occurrence. The fourth view stands in dramatic contrast to the other three. It is not futurist but preterist—i.e., fulfillment of all four chief moments/events is in the past.

Therefore, the four major competing and conflicting end-time views we shall present, dispute, analyze, and synthesis in this book are (in order of their popularity and prominence in America, and perhaps the rest of the world as well):[1]

#1 – Dispensational Premillennial View of soon-coming fulfillment – Christ has not come again or returned, nor have any of the other associated end-time events taken place. But his Second Coming/Return is very near and will occur before his literal 1,000-year reign on earth—i.e., *pre – millennial*.

#2 – Amillennial View of partial fulfillment and an unknowable, future, final fulfillment – Christ's Second Coming/Return is future. It will happen within human history and during the symbolic/figurative 1,000-year millennium, which lasts longer than a literal thousand years and in which we are currently living. But no one can know when this pivotal and climactic event will occur. Other comings of Jesus, however, have already occurred, and some associated end-time events have been partially fulfilled, in some sense, but await a final future fulfillment—i.e., *a – millennial*.

#3 – Postmillennial view of partial fulfillment and distant-future, final fulfillment – This was the view of our forefathers in the faith who came to and founded America. Postmillennialists believed that Christ's Second Coming/Return is a long way away, perhaps a 100, a 1,000 or even 5,000 years away. But first, the world must become more Christianized. Then, after a future golden age of special blessings, which will last a thousand or more years, Christ will return—i.e., *post – millennial*. In the meantime, many but not all end-time events already have been fulfilled and/or partially fulfilled. Also, they acknowledge many comings of Jesus Christ throughout history. But his future return will be his *final* coming.

#4 – Preterist view of precise past fulfillment – This view is the least known of the four views. But it is the view creating the most conversation and controversy nowadays. The term preterist is derived

---

[1] These four are not Preterism, Historicism, Futurism, and Idealism as some have suggested.

from the Latin word *praeter*, which means "past"). Hence, Christ's Second Coming/Return is past and occurred circa A.D. 70. He came again exactly *as* and *when* He said He would and was expected. It was a coming in judgment, in a day of the Lord, and in association with the destruction of Jerusalem and the Temple. The fulfillment of all other end-times events, including his millennial reign, also happened at or before that time. Therefore, all fulfillments are behind us and not ahead of us; are past and not future. Many preterists also believe that there are no more comings of Christ after A.D. 70—i.e., He came "in finality."

Before you dismiss the preterist view out of hand, allow me to demonstrate a simple reason why it is not as unorthodox as it may first sound. For example, do you believe the following?

- Jesus of Nazareth was and is the promised Messiah come in human flesh.
- Jesus was born, lived, crucified, bodily resurrected, and ascended to heaven to sit at the right hand of God Almighty.
- All these events were prophesied of the Messiah hundreds of years beforehand in the Old Testament.
- All these events are now past in fulfillment.

If you answered yes to any or all four of these above bulleted statements, that makes you a preterist, at least in these beliefs for they are past in fulfillment. The question next becomes, "How much fulfillment is past and how much is still future?" Once again, the answer depends on your eschatological view.

With this brief overview in mind, let's take a fresh and further look at the key distinctives and major problems associated with each view. Please be aware that during these presentations, we shall be asking some tough and practical theological questions. As we proceed, some of you may feel as if you are swimming in a sea of confusion and perplexity. Let me assure you that it is quite okay to feel this way because that is indeed what we shall be doing. My purpose in doing this throughout these presentations and disputations is to give you a hands-on feel for the fiasco that these four confusing, conflicting and competing views have produced.

For others of you, and as I've mentioned previously, this presentation and disputation of views may be an uncomfortable experience, even upsetting or threatening—especially when we start exposing some of the problems of your particular view. Hopefully, however and for most of you, this experience will be cathartic. So let's begin with the most popular and prominent view in evangelical Christianity today.

Chapter 3

The Soon-Coming Fulfillment View— Dispensational Premillennial

This most popular view was the first view I encountered when I became a Christian for sure. At that time I didn't know there were other views. It's the view most Christians hear and see on Christian radio, TV, and in best-selling books. It places Christ's Second Coming/Return in the very near future and happening before a literal 1,000-year millennium period.

Today this view is held by such well-know proponents as Tim LaHaye, co-author of the "Left Behind" series fictional books, and author and TV personality Hal Lindsey, whose blockbuster book, *The Late Great Planet Earth*, is one of the all-time bestsellers. It is also held by most TV evangelists such as Jack Van Impe, John Hagee, Paul Crouch, Pat Robertson, and Billy Graham.

Another adherent is former (and disgraced) radio evangelist, Harold Camping, who once again famously predicted the end of the world would occur in May 2011. But the only thing that ended was his radio network's financial stability. Camping also misled the world in 1993 with the same prediction that the world was to end in 1994. I appeared with Camping on CNN's *Larry King Live* on March 8, 1993 to refute his contention and book titled *1994*. Guess who was right back then?

The historical fact is, this view has been the main Christian source of a sad trail of proclaimed and false predictions. Over many centuries, especially the last fifty to seventy-five years, these repeated failures have taken a huge toll on the credibility and viability of the Christian faith. As a result, *Charisma* magazine, which editorially holds this view, recently lamented that "most young believers no longer uphold Bible prophecy and eschatology as key components of the faith. . . . young people not only don't care about our topics, they are somewhat offended by them." In the same article, former pastor and sought-after speaker, Brian McLaren, explains, "I think a lot of people—those my age along with younger people—have been turned off by the 'cry-wolf' scenario."[1]

On the aggressive side, another of this view's popular authors is John MacArthur. Categorically, he terms the premillennial anticipation of Christ's soon-coming return: "the hope of every true believer."[2] Unfortunately, his terminology implies that those who do not hold to this view are not "true believers," whatever that might mean? He further charges that "those who abandon the hope of Christ's bodily return have in effect abandoned true Christianity."[3]

Three Varieties of Premillennialism

The three varieties of Premillennialism are:

1) Dispensational Premillennialism or Classic Dispensationalism
2) Classic or Historic Premillennialism
3) Progressive Dispensationalism

For our purposes, we will focus primarily on the dispensational premillennial variety. The other two do not add anything extra. They present more a softening of the sharp distinctions drawn by traditional

---

[1] Jim Fletcher, "Can Prophecy Be Saved?" *Charisma*, June 2013, 52-53.
[2] John F. MacArthur, *The Second Coming* (Wheaton, IL.: Crossway Books, 1999), 81.
[3] Ibid., 9.

dispensationalists. However, in the two sections below highlighting these latter two varieties, I shall take the text straight from my doctoral dissertation. I do so to give you a direct feel and hands-on flavor for the confusion, conflict, and evolving dynamics taking place within this complex view itself. As you will hear in their own words, these internal squabbles among premillennialists are not only significant but also, in my opinion, quite enlightening and positive. For one thing, they demonstrate a movement of thought in a direction of a synthesis.

Dispensational Premillennialism or Classic Dispensationalism

Today, this dispensational version of the premillennial view is the dominant view in conservative, evangelical circles in America. Even Playboy magazine has recognized the explosion of its popularity. In a sidebar article titled, "Apocalypse Now," Playboy acknowledged that this "peculiar brand of Christian fundamentalism has invaded mainstream America." Citing a Gallup poll, Playboy reports that "44 percent of Americans now believe in the premillennial version of rapture."[4]

Yet, historically speaking, this most popular premillennial variety is a fairly recent development. Arguably, its origins only go back to John Nelson Darby in the 1830s, who seems to have been the first to systematically articulate this view and system of interpretation. Later, it was popularized by C.I. Scoffield (1900s) in his Scoffield Bible. Since then, this view has gained wide acceptance within evangelical circles. But many find it confusing and overly complex. If you do, don't worry about it. Even premillennialists themselves find it so, and for reasons that shortly will become evident.

All premillennialists, however, are in agreement about two things. The fulfillment of all four chief eschatological moments/events lie in the future. And secondly, in contrast to both the amillennial and postmillennial views, they see the Lord returning *within* human history and not at the end of history. Therefore, Jesus' Second Coming/Return

---

[4] Nancy Garascia, "Apocalypse Now," *Playboy*, November 2004, 96.

occurs after a 7-year, or perhaps 3 ½-year, or some period of time called the "Great Tribulation," after which the millennium begins.

Upon his Second Coming/Return, Christ will destroy the end-time Antichrist, who many dispensationalists believe is alive today. This will happen at the battle of Armageddon, after which Satan will be bound for a literal thousand years. Those believers who died during the tribulation period will be resurrected at this time. Christ will set up his earthly, millennial kingdom on earth, headquartered in Jerusalem, for a literal 1,000 years. During this time, the Jews will reign with Him in supremacy over everyone else—i.e., over the Gentiles (that's us). At the end of the 1,000 years, a final rebellion of evil will take place, followed by God's final victory, resurrection of the wicked, and the beginning of the eternal state.

Yet, historically speaking, this most popular premillennial variety is a fairly recent development.

While most premillennialists are in agreement that we moderns are living in "the last days in which the evils of this age are perennial, and the only hope is for rapture out of this evil life and into the realm of a bodiless, spiritual heaven, by and by,"[5] not all premillennialists are in agreement on what precedes all this—i.e., the 7-year Great Tribulation period and the Rapture (a secret and non-visible coming of Jesus). For instance, they argue over the time of the Rapture, whether it's before, during, or after this Great Tribulation. Hence, they have developed these subcategories of pre-trib, mid-trib, 2/3s-trib (pre-wrath), and post-trib.

By far the largest subgroup are the pre-tribers. They are sure the Rapture will occur very soon since they believe everything is in place—especially Israel being back in the Promised Land (1948), which is termed the "super sign." Following this Rapture is the 7-year tribulation period that will be ruled over by the end-time Antichrist.

Recently, the mega-bestselling and most-popular author for this view, Tim LaHaye, was quoted in *Charisma* magazine regarding the current status of "Israel is the super sign." Once again he emphasized that "the Jews were scattered to almost every country in the world for

---

[5] Mark Galli, "Incredible Journeys," *Christianity Today,* December 2012, 29.

1,900 years, and in the last 100 years they have been brought back to their homeland. The whole world's focus is on this super-sign that we prophetic teachers have been talking about for 150 years, and now it's gaining momentum."[6]

Thus, pre-tribers, mid-tribers, and 2/3s (pre-wrath)-tribers foresee two future returns/comings of Jesus: 1) the secret, non-visible one termed the Rapture. 2) The every-eye-will-see public one. But they argue not only over when it will occur, but also over how many believers will be removed in the Rapture. Some subscribe to a partial Rapture view, claiming it all depends upon how faithful believers have been—the more faithful removed before the less faithful. Post-tribers, on the other hand, are expecting only one future coming of Jesus at the end of the tribulation period.

Let's also note that pre-trib, dispensational premillennialists are expecting three future resurrections of the dead:

1) The first resurrection comes prior to the Great Tribulation and involves the resurrection of all the righteous dead of history along with those believers alive who will be raptured off the surface of planet Earth.

2) A second resurrection at the beginning of 1,000 years for all the righteous who died during the Great Tribulation.

3) A third resurrection at the end of 1,000 years for all the wicked.

But here's a troublesome question for dispensationalists to ponder. How many future resurrections was Paul talking about and expecting when he voiced this prophetic proclamation at his trial before Felix: "and I have the same hope in God as these men, that there will be a resurrection of both the righteous and the wicked" (Acts 24:15)?

Interestingly, the Greek words translated "will be" here literally reads, "to be about to be." It's a double intensification of imminence (nearness) missed by the translation in most Bibles.

Below is a listing of some other embarrassing problems to ponder: (Before proceeding, please recall, again, from the Introduction our agreed upon guideline of *Sola Scriptura*)

---

[6] Troy Anderson, "America at the End," *Charisma*, December 2012, 38.

1) What does the Bible say about a future 7-year or 3 ½-year period of tribulation?
   Nothing!
2) The Antichrist making a 7- or 3 ½-year covenant with the Jews?
   Nothing!
3) God withdrawing Jesus' kingdom because most of the Jews rejected Him.
   Nothing!
4) The world getting worse and worse.
   Nothing!
5) Jesus coming back and setting up his kingdom in Jerusalem and giving it back to the Jews?
   Nothing!
6) A rebuilding of a third Jewish temple?
   Nothing!
7) A reinstitution of animal sacrifices?
   Nothing!
8) What did Jesus say about the Rapture idea of a removal of believers (or a group of) from planet Earth?
   Careful here! Actually, Jesus prayed against it. In his prayer for all believers, Jesus prayed not only for his followers, then and there present with Him. He also prayed for those "who will believe in me through their message" (John 17:20). I believe that includes you and me. And He prayed that they and we would "not" be taken "out of the world but that you protect them from the evil one" (John 17:15). What do you do with Jesus' prayer here?
   Notably, post-tribers ask this same question and cite this same verse, as well as John 16:33 (*KJV*) where Jesus assures his followers that in the world they will face tribulation. Especially note that Jesus does not place a time frame on tribulation, here or anywhere else—nor do any New Testament writers.
9) An end-time Antichrist or The Antichrist?
   One searches in vain to find an or the "antichrist" in the Book of Revelation, in the Gospels, in Paul's or Peter's letters, or in the Old Testament. The only two places in the

Bible where you will find antichrist mentioned are in 1 and 2 John. But here John puts down this idea of a single future Antichrist (see 1 John 2:18). Most likely, the Jews had heard about this Antichrist from the religion of Zoroastrianism (with a good god and evil god) when they were in Babylonian captivity. But John emphatically states that there are "even now many antichrists" (note the plural). Then, in three other scriptures, he defines what makes one an antichrist—"any such persons is . . . the antichrist" (see 1 John 2:22; 4:2-3; 2 John 7). Please check out John's definitions in these verses. They applied back then, since then, and today as well. John's words here are the full scriptural teaching regarding antichrist. They certainly do not align themselves at all with the dispensational premillennial view.

10) So without any tribulation timeframe being stated in Scripture, how do we know that a so-called "rapture" is pre-, mid-, or post- anything?

Nevertheless, these above ten problems are ten pillars of this most popular view. And there are more problems. But most of the proponents of this view are so deeply committed to these above notions that they cannot imagine that they may be in error on any of this. Realistically, however, it seems that once we begin building upon the silence of the scriptures, there is no limit to where we may end up. Is it any wonder, therefore, why many non-dispensational theologians consider dispensational premillennialism to be not only unscriptural, but also heretical?

For example, Henry A. Virkler in his classic book, *Hermeneutics*, records that classic dispensationalism has been called "the most dangerous heresy currently to be found within Christian circles."[7] One of

---

[7] Virkler, *Hermeneutics*, 122. For more charges of heresy see: Millar J. Erickson, *A Basic Guide to Eschatology* (Grand Rapids, MI.: Baker Books, 1998), 61; Larry Spargimino, *The Anti-Prophets: The Challenge of Preterism* (Oklahoma City, OK.: Hearthstone Publishing, 2000), 12, 37-38; R.C. Sproul, Jr., in Foreword to C. Jonathin Seraiah, *The End of All Things: A Defense of Futurism* (Moscow, ID.: Canon Press, 1999), 9.

its chief distinctives, the dichotomy between Israel and the Church, produces two different peoples of God, with two different plans of salvation, and two different destinies. This further produces a dichotomized hermeneutic forcing its interpreters and followers to divide all Scripture into two different columns and time periods—one that applies to Israel, the other that applies to the Church (more of this in Chapter 8).

> **... classic dispensationalism has been called "the most dangerous heresy currently to be found within Christian circles."**

Are you confused yet? If so, you are not alone. Many premillennialists are confused among themselves. For validating evidence of this internal confusion and conflict, we need look no further than into the two other varieties of premillennialism. Since these next two subsections below are excerpted directly from my dissertation, those of you not accustomed to a more academic style of presentation may want to skip them and proceed directly to our presentation of the amillennial view in our next chapter.

Classic or Historic Premillennialism

This variation is not dispensational. It holds that the rapture and the second coming are not a two-stage event or two separate events. They occur together and are indistinguishable as part of one event. Furthermore, this single, climactic event takes place at the end of the tribulation period. Hence, the Church will go through the great tribulation of the Antichrist before Christ returns, fights the battle of Armageddon, witnesses the raising of dead believers, and begins his millennial reign on the earth. This reign, however, is not seen as Jewish-oriented but will include both Jews and Gentiles. The millennium will be followed by the loosing of Satan, the final rebellion, resurrection and judgment of the wicked, and the final state in which sin, evil, and death will no longer exist. Additionally, historic premillennialists do not hold to the traditional classic dispensational distinction between Israel and the Church, nor to the idea that the kingdom was postponed or put on hold.

Progressive Dispensationalism

Because "even those within dispensationalism are seeing the need to rethink much of what has been taught for years now,"[8] there has arisen, "since about the middle of the twentieth century," a third variation called "progressive dispensationalism."[9] Its introduction has "made the theological picture . . . still more complex."[10] Classic dispensationalist Master summarizes the current situation in dispensationalism in this manner:

> Until the advent of "progressive dispensationalism," the sine qua non of dispensationalism, as stated by Ryrie (literal interpretation, distinction between the church and Israel, and the unifying theme of the glory of God) was widely accepted as providing the critical identifying markers. At this point, however, all of these criteria have been questioned as essential to dispensationalism . . . . Crossovers on every point make it difficult to distinguish a dispensationalist.[11]

Blaising, one of the chief progressive proponents, describes his emerging variation as "various modifications."[12] While Blaising and

---

[8] Seraiah, *The End of All Things*, 12.
[9] Erickson, *A Basic Guide to Eschatology*, 120. In a personal conversation (11/21/02 at ETS' Annual Meeting), Darrell Bock credited Robert Saucy for initiating the tenets of this variation in the 50s. But he indicated that the concepts of "progressive dispensationalism" originated during ETS meetings in the mid 80s. The term was "introduced" in 1991 "at the national ETS meeting" [Craig A. Blaising and Darrell L. Bock, *Progressive Dispensationalism*, (Grand Rapids, MI.: Baker Books, 1993), 23]. The name is taken from the "progressive relationship of the dispensations to one another" [Ibid., 49].
[10] Poythress, *Understanding Dispensationalists*, 12.
[11] John Master, "The Future of Dispensationalism" (Toronto, Canada: Evangelical Theological Society, 2002, paper), 1.
[12] Craig A. Blaising, "Changing Patterns in American Dispensational Theology," *Wesleyan Theological Journal* 29 (Spr.-Fall 1994): 150.

Bock together recognize that "it is not easy to classify all the differences between various dispensational theologians,"[13] they distinguish these "three phases of dispensational thought: classical, revised, and progressive"[14] as a movement of "gradual modification."[15] They further characterize progressives as "rethinking and reinterpreting" the beliefs of dispensationalism.[16] But basically, progressive dispensationalism seems only to be a blending or amalgamation between the above two premillennial varieties just covered.

Erickson's analysis of this new movement is that "while redefining or even abandoning some of the tenets of traditional dispensationalism, they maintain that they preserve the distinctive features of that system of thought."[17] Key for progressives is their attempt to soften, or modify, as they say, the two major dispensational distinctives of a dichotomy, or dualism, between Israel and the Church regarding redemption and a literal interpretation of the Bible. At the same time, however, they retain some of each.[18]

> **"it is not easy to classify all the differences between various dispensational theologians."**

Hoch explains that progressives, like historic premillennialists and amillennialists, retain "the emphasis of one people of God," "the distinctive nature of Pentecost" as the establishment of the Church, and "the non-Jewish millennium."[19] At the same time, they embrace the classic dispensational idea that "Israel always refers to physical descendants of Abraham," and yet reject its "radical discontinuity between Israel and the church" and "rigid definition of the kingdom."[20]

---

[13] Blaising and Bock, *Progressive Dispensationalism*, 22.
[14] Ibid., 7, 22.
[15] Ibid., 34.
[16] Ibid., 9.
[17] Erickson, *A Basic Guide to Eschatology*, 120.
[18] Ibid., 120-122. Also see: Blaising and Bock, *Progressive Dispensationalism*, 47, 49-50.
[19] Carl B. Hoch, Jr., *All Things New* (Grand Rapids, MI.: Baker Books, 1995), 260.
[20] Ibid., 261.

Hence for progressives, "Israel and the church are distinct in some ways" while they "also overlap to a significant degree." The result is, the Church is now "on an equal basis with Israel." But "Israel has a priority in terms of privilege, but not a priority in terms of program."[21]

In keeping with this mediation, the classic dispensational periods are viewed as a progression of grace rather than as separate and distinct. Likewise, the progressive views of the biblical covenants and the Church have also been modified to a more already/not yet perspective.[22] Hence, they see "present blessings" as "a *partial* . . . fulfillment" with "complete fulfillment" coming at Christ's return.[23]

Hock further elaborates that progressives believe "all of God's covenants will be fulfilled eschatologically both in the church and in ethnic Israel who turn to Christ in faith."[24] But he confesses that unlike classic dispensationalists, progressives just are "not quite as certain how the whole process works out eschatologically."[25] The bottom line is, progressives have moved toward the historic premillennial and amillennial positions. Thus, they "can allow fulfillment of Old Testament promises and covenants (at least partially) to the church without making Israel and the church synonymous." Hoch adds that "the key is the remnant of Israel [Jewish believers] within the church."[26]

While Blaising and Bock admit that there has been a "gradual revision of early dispensationalism's dualism,"[27] Master notes that "some measure of distinction between the church and Israel has been maintained."[28] But Blaising and Bock have also proposed an "eventual abandonment . . . of the two divine purposes/two peoples theory" of classic dispensationalism.[29] Again, this is in line with historic premillennialism. They also have discarded the classic idea of different "kingdoms" in favor of "one promised eschatological kingdom which

---

[21] ibid.
[22] Blaising and Bock, *Progressive Dispensationalism*, 48-53, 127.
[23] Ibid., 53.
[24] Hoch, *All Things New*, 261-262.
[25] Ibid., 262.
[26] ibid.
[27] Blaising and Bock, *Progressive Dispensationalism*, 19.
[28] Master, "The Future of Dispensationalism," 1.
[29] Blaising and Bock, *Progressive Dispensationalism*, 7.

has both spiritual and political dimensions."[30] But they are unsure how the full establishment of the kingdom on earth in its intermediate "millennial" form and a thousand years later in its "everlasting" form will be revealed or fulfilled in the future.[31] Meanwhile, the Church is the "mystery form of the kingdom,"[32] as well as a "phase of the eschatological kingdom" and "a new manifestation of grace."[33] A future tribulation period still forms the setting of the return of Jesus.[34]

Additionally, the famed "literal hermeneutic for all Scripture, including prophecy" has been called into question and is in a state of flux. As Master concludes, "today the situation is not nearly so simple or clear cut."[35] For instance, he argues that "a 'consistent literal hermeneutic' does not determine, in prophecy, when something is a real metaphor and when it is not, if something is a metaphor, failure to interpret it as such would not be using a 'normal' or 'literal' hermeneutic."[36] Adding to these difficulties, in his opinion, is the realization that "differences may emerge concerning the amount of metaphor in OT prophecy."[37]

Not surprisingly, criticism of this new variation comes from both inside and outside of the premillennial view. From the inside, classic dispensationalist Thomas condemns this new approach. He states that it is "a system that attempts to combine preterism, idealism, and imminence into itself." He believes it "creates a complex mixture of hermeneutical principles."[38] In his opinion, this mixture "runs counter to what traditional grammatical-historical principles dictate."[39]

From the outside, postmillennialist and partial preterist DeMar chides this new variation in writing, "when will the dispensationalists

---

[30] Ibid., 54.
[31] Ibid., 54, 228, 270. (They also see no difference between the terms kingdom of heaven and kingdom of God as held by classic dispensationalists (ibid.).
[32] Ibid., 262.
[33] Ibid., 285.
[34] Ibid., 294.
[35] Master, "The Future of Dispensationalism," 1.
[36] Ibid., 2.
[37] Ibid., 3.
[38] Thomas, "The Place of Imminence in Recent Eschatological Systems," in Baker, *Looking into the Future*, 205.
[39] Ibid., 213.

deal with the time texts that point to the near coming of Christ in judgment in the first century? Until this question is answered, the new dispensationalism is still the old dispensationalism."[40] Moore, on the other hand, is quite lenient when he cites its "chief weakness" as being its "newness." He feels that it offers "opportunities for exploration and perhaps implementation."[41]

Erickson speaks of "problems"[42] because progressives have so modified "the dispensational hermeneutic that they are in danger of slipping into amillennialism."[43] Amillennialist Poythress agrees and "can imagine a [further] transition all the way into an amillennial position."[44] Bock feeds this influx perception in an article tellingly titled "Why I Am a Dispensationalist with a Small 'd.'"[45]

Not surprisingly, criticism of this new variation comes from both inside and outside of the premillennial view.

As a result of progressive dispensationalism, "dispensationalism today is in a state of fluidity."[46] Even Blaising and Bock admit that they have not "solved all interpretative problems," that the work of progressives is "ongoing,"[47] and that "much more work remains."[48] In

---

[40] Gary DeMar, "Sola Scriptura Our Badge of Authority," *Biblical World View*, Vol. 9 #12, December 1993, 3.
[41] Russell D. Moore, "Till Every Foe Is Vanquished: Emerging Sociopolitical Implications of Progressive Dispensational Eschatology," in David W. Baker, ed., *Looking into the Future: Evangelical Studies in Eschatology* (Grand Rapids, MI.: Baker Academic, 2001), 361.
[42] Erickson, *A Basic Guide to Eschatology*, 123.
[43] Ibid., 124.
[44] Poythress, *Understanding Dispsensationalists*, 38.
[45] Darrell L. Bock, "Why I Am a Dispensationalist with a Small 'd'" *Journal of the Evangelical Theological Society* Vol. 41, No. 3 (Sept 1998): 383.
[46] Stanley J. Grenz, *The Millennial Maze* (Downers Grove, IL.: InterVarsity Press, 1992), 122.
[47] Blaising and Bock, *Progressive Dispensationalism*, 284.
[48] Ibid., 285.

light of this fluidity, Master asks, "What is the future of dispensationalism?" He answers, "I do not know."[49]

In conclusion, confusion and conflict certainly reign within this most-popular view of itself.

---

[49] Master, "The Future of Dispensationalism," 10.

Chapter 4
The Partial-Fulfillment View— Amillennial

Amillennialism is the second most popular or prominent view among conservative evangelicals in America. But it is "the majority view of organized Christendom,"[1] That is "primarily because Roman Catholics and Lutherans generally hold it."[2] It also "has long been considered the principle rival to dispensationalism"[3]

Ironically, the word and name "amillennial" is both misleading and a misnomer. Normally, the prefix "a" means "no" or "not." But in this case that is not what it means because amillennialists do believe in the millennium and that we are currently living in that 1,000-year reign. They just do not do not believe in a literal or visible 1,000-year reign. Some see the 1,000 years as an earthly reign but only in the hearts of believers. They believe it started in the 1st century and lasts longer than a literal 1,000 years. Consequently, the amillennial millennium has been underway for over 1,900 years and counting. They also see their millennium as synonymous with "these last days" (Heb. 1:2). Other

---

[1] Renald Showers, *There Really Is A Difference* (Bellmawr, NJ.: The Friends of Israel Gospel Ministry, 1990), 151.
[2] Kenneth L. Gentry, *He Shall Have Dominion* (Tyler, TX.: Institute for Christian Economics, 1992), *xxvi*.
[3] Poythress, *Understanding Dispensationalists*, 39.

amillennialists believe the millennium is a heavenly reign with Christ for Christians who have died. And some amillennialists believe it's both.

But one thing all amillennialists are known for is avoiding getting bogged down in or disagreeing over details. Therefore, it is often difficult to know exactly what they believe and not easy to generalize this system of eschatological thought.

The one element that amillennialism does share with both dispensational premillennialism and postmillennialism is the future coming and fulfillment of Christ's Second Coming/Return, which will be personal, visible, physical, bodily, and glorious. The other three chief moments/events, of course, are tied to that pivotal future event.

What amillennialists don't share with these two other views is, all four chief moment/events happen at one time during the 1,000 years period, in which we are now living. But their uniqueness lies in their insistence that no one can know when all this will occur. In support, amillennialists cited Jesus' several statements regarding how "No one knows about that day or hour, not even the angels in heaven, nor the Son, but only the Father," (Matt. 24:36, 44; 25:13) or "times and dates" (Acts 1:7). Hence, "amil" can humorously but seriously be said to stand for "Ahhh (I) . . . don't know, you don't know, and no one can know when all these things will occur."

Two Major Problems

Two major problems arise with the amillennial ignorance-pleading stance:

1) None of the other three views buys this argument. Their proponents are sure we can know the time. Dispensationalists claim Jesus' coming is very soon. And as we shall see, postmillennialists are sure it is not near or soon but far away. And preterists are sure it has already happened long ago circa A.D. 70. So amillennialists stand alone with this ignorance stance and are ridiculed for it. Proponents of the other three views see this avoidance argument as a copout. Hence, the amillennial ("Ahhh-don't-know, you-can't- know, no-one-can-know") view has proven rather

impotent in competing against the other three views—especially against the dominant dispensational premillennial view.
2) Thirty-seven to thirty-eight years after Jesus' death, burial, resurrection, and ascension, the Apostle John knew the "hour." Twice, in one verse he exclaimed, "this is the last hour . . . it is the last hour." How could he say that? Hadn't Christ forbidden it? No, something major had changed, as we shall explore later in this book.

Amillennialists Emasculate Their Own View

Some well-known amillennialists include: my mentor James Earl Massey, R.C. Sproul, D. James Kennedy, and theologian Anthony Hoekema. Hoekema, humbly and rightly, characterizes his own eschatological view as being one of "ambiguity"[4] and "uncertainty"[5] because the Scriptures are just not clear.

And given their ignorance-pleading caveat, amillennialists readily admit they just do not know many other things as well, such as:

- How long their millennium is.
- Just what Old Testament prophecies and blessings for Israel remain unfulfilled.
- While they deny that the kingdom was postponed, they do not know now much of it is a present reality or to what degree it does or does not operate in the world today.
- They only know that Christ's kingdom is here "in some sense," "already / not yet," "in a foretaste," "but not yet completely here nor realized." Notably, none of these is expressions found in the Bible.
- Its location is also in doubt, whether it is in the hearts of those who believe, in heaven, or elsewhere.
- They are also uncertain about what age we are living in—"this age" or in "the age to come" in some sense.

---

[4] Hoekema, *The Bible and the Future*, 34-35.
[5] Ibid., 121, 136.

- They disagree over the meaning of the reigning of the saints with Christ. Some hold that it refers to the Church on earth. Others think it only applies to deceased saints in heaven during the so-called intermediate state (another expression never used in the Bible).
- Nor do they know in what bodily or disembodied form deceased saints currently exist in, in heaven.
- Many amillennialists believe heaven is temporary and the final destination for Christians is to live throughout eternity on a new earth, which isn't here yet.

As you can see, Hoekema characterized his view quite accurately. Little is well defined and their spiritualizing methodology is not easy to regulate. So, in general, amillennialists are simply ambiguous and uncertain about what most prophetic passages mean. Not surprisingly, most don't even care and dismiss the whole field of eschatology as not important. While they are definitely awaiting the Lord's return, the final judgment, the end of the Christian age, the general and bodily resurrection of the dead, and the eternal state, there is little sense of urgency as the Lord's return may still be far into the future. Therefore, for most amillennialists, Christ's coming has had little impact on "more practical matters" of faith.

> **Hoekema, humbly and rightly, characterizes his own eschatological view as being one of "ambiguity" and "uncertainty."**

Despite these weaknesses, a few amillennilists do attempt to contend against the other views. One such writer is Jerry Newcombe. He warns that "those who think they know will in all likelihood soon join the ranks of those who thought they knew in times past and lead others down that same misguided path."[6] And for 19-centuries and counting, Newcombe makes a good point here. He further chides other views, claiming that "the details of His return are not fully clear in Scripture."[7]

---

[6] Newcombe, *Coming Again But When?*, 23.
[7] Ibid., 28.

Like most other amillennialists, Newcombe is also uncertain whether "the world may get both better and/or worse before the end comes." He suggests that "it may get better and worse simultaneously."[8] He further believes that "time seems to be of little importance in God's kingdom."[9] But the one thing "we can agree on [is] this: Jesus is coming back one day. That will be the climax of history as we know it."[10] He does admit, however, that "the postmil and amil views of the end times are much more difficult to peg than the premil view because prophecies aren't taken literally."[11]

The one thing many amillennialists think they do know *for sure* is the Church has replaced Israel in the plan of God. The one huge problem, however and once again, with this belief is the Bible never says anything about replacement—nothing. To the contrary, Paul teaches that we Gentiles were and are grafted into the "holy root" (Rom. 11:11-24). There is no replacement in being grafted into something.

In summary, and in dramatic contrast to the other three views. Amillennialists . . .

- Generally have the weakest interest in prophecy.
- Like premillennialists, do not emanate the joy or confidence necessary for changing the world.
- Deemphasize the importance of eschatology in the life of the believer.
- Differences among them are not as precise or categorical as within the other views.
- Their end-time beliefs are more difficult to pin down.

But one positive aspect of amillennialism bears special mentioning. Amillennialists take an idealist (ongoing) view of the relevancy of the prophecy of the Book of Revelation. We shall address this aspect in Chapter 14.

---

[8] Ibid., 33.
[9] Ibid., 43.
[10] Ibid., 44.
[11] Ibid., 64.

A Dichotomized Hermeneutic

Most amillennialists also believe that the four chief moment/events have been partially fulfilled. This partial fulfillment occurred during the Jewish-Roman War of A.D. 66-70 and in association with the destruction of Jerusalem and the Temple. It is called a "partial preterist" position. This partiality produces a dichotomized hermeneutic that forces amillennialists to divide Scripture into two different columns—i.e., what happened circa A.D. 70 and what is yet-to-happen at their so-called "end of time."

R.C. Sproul explains his dichotomizing hermeneutic like this:

> I am convinced that the substance of the Olivet Discourse was fulfilled in A.D. 70 and that the bulk of Revelation was likewise fulfilled in that timeframe. . . . While partial preterists acknowledge that in the destruction of Jerusalem in A.D. 70 was *a* parousia or coming of Christ, they maintain that it was not *the* parousia. That is, the coming of Christ in A.D. 70 was a coming in judgment on the Jewish nation, indicating the end of the Jewish age and the fulfillment of a day of the Lord, Jesus really did come in judgment at this time, fulfilling his prophecy in the Olivet Discourse. But this was not the final or ultimate coming of Christ. . . . [which will be] universal in scope and significance. It will come . . . at the end of human history as we know it. It will be, not merely a day of the Lord, but the final and ultimate day of the Lord."[12]

While recognizing many comings of Christ throughout Church history, this "final" and "ultimate" coming event takes places at the defeat of the end-time Antichrist at the "end of history" or "end of time." The huge problem here, once again, for amillennialists is, the Bible says nothing about an "end of time" or "end of history." The Bible discusses the "time of the end." As we shall see, there is a big difference.

Adherence, however, to this non-biblical "end-of-time" paradigm leads amillennialists to advocate other non-biblical expressions as biblical concepts and/or anticipated events, such as:

---

[12] Sproul, *The Last Days According to Jesus*, 158.

- a "final return" – How many returns are there?
- a "final consummation" – How many consummations are there?
- a "final resurrection" – How many resurrections are there?
- a "last judgment" or "final judgment" after which there will be no more judgment.

Once again, what does the Bible say about all this? Nothing. The Bible never uses these expressions and for a good reason. That reason will become apparent when we begin the unraveling process in PART III—utilizing our two guidelines of *Sola Scriptura* and *In Love*. But we still have two more important views to cover. They are the least known today. And for that reason they need to be given more attention. I believe you will find them fascinating, scripturally and historically.

A Muddling Caveat

Unfortunately, our next view has frequently been muddled together with amillennialism. As amillennialist Newcombe concedes, this comingling is because "there is not uniformity in how postmillennialism and amillennialism are defined or differentiated." Foundationally, "neither holds to a literal thousand-year Millennium." Consequently, he reports that "these two schools of thought sometimes get lumped together."[13] Erickson agrees that the differences between these two views have been "blurred" and cites the fact that men such as Augustine, Calvin, and Warfield "have been claimed by both groups."[14] Virkler even terms amillennialism "conceptually a form of postmillennialism."[15] Turner allows that "chronologically the two systems are similar."[16] Both emphasize "the presence, not the future, of the millennium (God's reign)."[17]

---

[13] Newcomb, *Coming Again But When?*, 192.
[14] Erickson, *A Basic Guide to Eschatology*, 73.
[15] Virkler, *Hermeneutics*, 201.
[16] Turner, "The Continuity of Scripture and Eschatology: Key Hermeneutical Issues." *Grace Theological Journal*, 283.
[17] Ibid., 284.

> "there is not uniformity in how postmillennialism and amillennialism are defined or differentiated.... these two schools of thought sometimes get lumped together."

Chapter 5
The Distant-Fulfillment View— Postmillennial

Even though I'm not a postmillennialist, *per se*, I find this view fascinating and stimulating. I think you will, too.

Once again, Postmillennialism is the view that motivated our forefathers in the faith to come to America, not just to escape religious persecution, but to expand the kingdom of God and help Christianize the world. They believed the world would become a better and better place as society was transformed by becoming more and more Christianized. They further believed that it was each Christian's individual responsibility to do his or her part to make this happen and that their combined activity and involvement would hasten the coming of the millennium, and subsequently return of the Lord. But those Christians who remained selfish and non-involved hindered and delayed these most-anticipated, eschatological events.

Hence, postmillennial-empowered and emboldened believers came to America and founded the great institutions of our country—the government, the schools, the universities—under Judeo-Christian principles. And Christianity was established as the moral influencer in our society. This end-time view and worldview dominated the eschatology of conservative Protestantism from the 17th through the late 19th centuries. But one hundred years ago or so this all began to change.

Today, and sad to say, the one word that best characterizes postmillennialism is "discredited." It was discredited by world events, such as: World War I, World War II, the atom Bomb, the threat of a nuclear Armageddon and annihilation, moral decline and decay of society, and the rebirth of the nation of Israel in 1948. All of this and more, according to Grenz, "appeared to confirm the dispensational interpretation of prophecy"[1] and its dramatically opposite worldview that things are supposed to and will get worse and worse before Christ returns.

This end-time view and worldview dominated the eschatology of conservative Protestantism from the 17th through the late 19th centuries.

Hence, the positive influence of postmillennialism has greatly waned since its domination of the American millennial scene from the colonial days through the early part of the 20th century. It seems most Christians became convinced that the world was indeed not standing on the verge of the "golden age" of peace and prosperity known as "the millennium," at least not one that would come slowly and gradually. They were now looking for one that would come someday, catastrophically and cataclysmically.

Consequently, the well-known prophecy populazier of dispensational premillennialism, Hal Lindsay, was prompted to conclude in his 1970s best seller *The Late Great Planet Earth* that:

> ... there used to be a group called 'postmillennialists.' ... World War I greatly disheartened this group and World War II virtually wiped out this viewpoint. No self-respecting scholar who looks at the world conditions and the accelerating decline of Christian influence today is a 'postmillennialist.'[2]

---

[1] Grenz, *The Millennial Maze*, Ibid., 62.
[2] Hal Lindsey, *The Late Great Planet Earth* (Grand Rapids, MI.: Zondervan, 1970, 1979), 164-165. Also see, Ryrie, *The Basis of the Premillennial Faith*, 13.

Today, postmillennialism is held by only a small minority of scholars. And we Americans have managed to give away almost all the institutions and societal influence our postmillennial forefathers in the faith came to this country to found—the government, the schools, the universities, etc.—and almost without a fight. But we didn't get beat or pushed out by a superior or more powerful anti-God force. We simply withdrew from the public square. And into the vacuum gladly swept in the ungodly crowd.

Once again, why and how did all this happen?

A, if not the, prime reason was, the dominant eschatological view here in America changed from one of historical optimism to one of historical pessimism. Thus, in the 20th century, postmillennialism was discredited and "overshadowed" by dispensational premillennialism and amillennialism.[3]

Some postmillennialists today are fighting back. Mathison, for instance, argues "the Scriptures of the Old and New Testament, not newspapers, are our doctrinal authority."[4] Besides, as Gentry challenges, "who won World Wars I and II? Was the world made a more dangerous place for Christianity because of the defeat of Japan in Asia and Germany in Europe?"[5]

What Do Postmillennialists Believe Today?

Postmillennialists today are sure that Christ's Second Coming/Return is future and will happen after the 1,000 years mentioned in Revelation 20 when He returns personally, visibly, bodily, and in great glory to end history at the "end of time." They are also sure that this climactic event will not occur any time soon because society has not advanced far enough, righteous wise, nor have we entered the "golden age" for which many of them are looking. Hence, "postmillennialists are alone in the Futurist camp in denying the New Testament doctrine of imminence in

---

[3] Keith A. Mathison, *Postmillennialism: An Eschatology of Hope* (Phillipsburg, NJ.: P&R Publishing, 1999), 175.
[4] Ibid., 203.
[5] Gentry, *He Shall Have Dominion*, 428-429.

the present day"—i.e., "that the Lord could return virtually at any time."[6] (The preterist view also denies this imminence, but for a different reason.) Therefore, postmillennialists also see the fulfillment of the other three of the four chief moments/events as still being in the distant future.

For many Christians today, postmillennialism's optimistic worldview and view of the future may sound radical or even strange. Then why do postmillennialists believe this way? The plain and simple reason is, and in stark and dramatic contrast to our other two end-time views we've covered, they have strong scriptural support for it.

Optimistic Kingdom Orientation

Postmillennialism can also be characterized by another word, "optimism." Even Grudem, a dispensational premillennialist, credits postmillennialists for being "very optimistic about the power of the gospel [of the kingdom] to change lives, transform societal institutions, and bring about much good in the world."[7] Actually, this view forecasts a redemption of the entire created order.

Notably, postmillennialism is rarely, if ever, charged with heresy. And why not? Once again, it's because, unlike the other two views we've presented, it has a lot of Scripture to back it up:

- for the earthly and historical success of the gospel.
- for the growth of the present and earthly kingdom of God in this present age.
- for this victory occurring within history, spiritually, and in terms of converting a sizeable portion of humankind to Christianity.

According to this view, all of the above bulleted points must take place before Christ can return. And we Christians are the instruments God has chosen to carry out this work—i.e., his full plan of redemption and Christ's kingdom becoming universally realized. Then, and only

---

[6] Thomas, "The Place of Imminence in Recent Eschatological Systems," in David W. Baker, ed., *Looking into the Future*, 200.
[7] Wayne Grudem, *Systematic Theology* (Grand Rapids, MI.: Zondervan, 1994), 1111.

then, will Christ return. Therefore, in the postmillennial mindset, we've got a long way yet to go before this climactic and history-ending event will happen.

So let's take a quick look at some of the scriptures postmillennialists use to make their case. Starting at the very beginning in Genesis with the dominion mandate (Gen. 1:28; 9:7), they say this is where the Bible first tell us that "those who are redeemed by God's grace are assigned a task: to extend His dominion in history."[8]

Next, skip ahead to Isaiah 9:6-7, where Isaiah prophesied of the arrival of the Messiah and his unending, ever-increasing kingdom to which there will be no end. Postmillennialists believe the arrival of this form of God's kingdom was a major expansion, or if you prefer enhancement, of the original dominion mandate. They see similar representations of this ever-increasing kingdom in Ezekiel 47:1-12, where a small stream grows into a large river; in Daniel 2:35, where the stone that struck the statue becomes a great mountain and fills the whole earth; likewise in Daniel 2:44, where this same never-to-be-destroyed, world-crushing, endure-forever kingdom was to be established "in the days of those kings"—i.e., the days of the old Roman Empire. During that same time period, this kingdom would be handed over "to the saints of the Most High. His . . . everlasting kingdom that all rulers will worship and obey him" (Dan. 7:27-28a). All of which brings postmillennialists to the New Testament and the angel in Luke 1:33 proclaiming to Mary the arrival of "his kingdom" that "will never end." Then we have Jesus in Mark 1:15 at the very beginning of his earthly ministry announcing "the time has come . . . . The kingdom of God [long awaited] is at hand."

For further scriptural support, postmillennialists point to the growth parables. They claim these illustrate the "progressive growth" and "victory of Christ's kingdom during this present age."[9] So we read of seed scattered on the ground that produces a harvest (Mark 4:26-29); a mustard seed that grows into a tree (Matt. 13: 31-32; Mark 4:30-32; Luke 13:18-19); and yeast spreading throughout the dough (Matt. 13:33; Luke 13:20-21).

---

[8] Gary North, *Rapture Fever* (Tyler, TX.: Institute for Christian Economics, 1993), *xxiii*.
[9] Mathison, *Postmillennialism*, 242.

Similarly cited is Christ's Great Commission (Matt. 28:18-20). Here Jesus proclaims that all authority has been given to Him in heaven and on earth (especially note the past tense of the verb). Based on that information and foundation, we, his followers ever since then, are to make "disciples," not just converts, of the "nations." According to postmillennialists, the scope of this "nations" mandate is not limited to soul winning. Rather, it includes the transformation of lives, laws, institutions, and relationships—i.e., the government, education systems, the legal system, financial markets, businesses, entertainment industry, media, everything.

If that worldview and version of Christianity isn't mind-blowing enough, look at what Jesus next commanded his disciples to do. In Matthew 28:20, we read that He commanded them (his disciples) "to obey everything I have commanded you." Was Jesus kidding? Do you know some of the things that Jesus had commanded them to do? The most dramatic examples of Jesus commanding his disciples to do things were when He sent out the twelve and the seventy (see Matt 10:5-15f; Luke 10:1-12). Look what He commanded them to do: "preach this message: 'The kingdom of heaven is at hand.' Heal the sick, raise the dead, cleanse those who have leprosy, drive out demons. Freely you have received, freely give" (Matt. 10:7-8). Seriously, is this the type of Christianity we see being preached, practiced, and perceived today? If not, why not? If not, are we really obeying Jesus' Great Commission command to "teach them to obey everything I've commanded you to do" (Matt. 28:20)?

Admittedly, not all postmillennialists are preaching and practicing this brand of "radical" Christianity either. But they do see the increase of Christ's kingdom as being a long-term process as it conquers cultures and nations. Yes, they argue, we've come a long way during this present age. But we obviously have a long if not longer way yet to go. Thus, they challenge the inadequacies of the other two futuristic views in that neither premillennialism nor amillennialism can "do justice to these and other texts that describe the gradual growth of the messianic kingdom and the subjugation of all other kingdoms."[10]

Certainly, the historical optimism of postmillennialism stands in stark contrast to the earthly pessimism of both the premillennial and

---

[10] Ibid., 180.

amillennial views. This unique distinctive of postmillennialism, in my opinion, deserves careful reconsideration.

One More Key Scripture

Another reason postmillennialists claim that Jesus' Second Coming/Return is not imminent in our day and time is Matthew 24:14: "And this gospel of the kingdom will be preached in the whole world as a testimony to all nations, and then the end will come." But Postmillennialists point to the fact that the gospel of the kingdom is not being preached in most churches today. Dallas Willard in his book, *The Divine Conspiracy* pinpointed this glaring deficiency, thusly:

> During the past sixteen years I can recollect only two occasions on which I have heard sermons specifically devoted to the theme of the Kingdom of God. . . . I find this silence rather surprising because it is universally agreed by New Testament scholars that the central theme of the teaching of Jesus was the Kingdom of God.[11]

As we covered in Chapter 1, the kingdom of God was the central teaching of our Lord Jesus Christ, at the heart of his earthly ministry, and the very essence of New Testament Christianity. Today, however, the kingdom is no longer the central teaching of his Church, at the heart of its ministry, nor Christianity's very essence—an automatic "red flag."

What has happened? What has changed?

When, for instance, was the last time you heard a sermon or sermon series on the kingdom? Or attended a Sunday school class whose topic was the kingdom? Or signed up for a conference or seminary whose theme was the kingdom of God? The kingdom also has been written out of most biblical and Christian worldviews.

Again, what has happened? What has changed? Please see the kingdom-deficiency quotes again in the Chapter 1, pp. 26-27. But let's switch gears and do something different.

---

[11] Willard, *The Divine Conspiracy*, 59 – in quoting Dr. I. Howard Marshall of the University of Aberdeen.

Could You Be an Operational Postmillennialist and Not Know It?

I utilized this little exercise in the seminar series at Madison Park Church and they found it most helpful. So, I'm replicating it here. It's a series of ten excerpts from pastor Myles Munroe's book, *Rediscovering the Kingdom: Ancient Hope for Our 21st Century World*.[12] In it, Dr. Munroe makes some candid observations about Jesus' kingdom-preaching prerequisite in Matthew 24:14 and the kingdom of God in general. Hence, I picked these ten excerpts from his book and asked each participant, by a show of hands, if they would agree or disagree with his statements. I'll ask you, my reader, to do the same. Of course, if you don't have an opinion or don't care to participate, that's okay. I still believe you will glean quite a bit of value from this little exercise.

1) Munroe claims: "Fulfilling the assignment of preaching the Kingdom is the key to the timing of the return of Christ. Jesus said that the end will come after the gospel of the Kingdom is preached to all nations. . . . The fact that Jesus has not come back yet is proof that His assignment, which He delegated to His followers in every generation, has not yet been fulfilled." (p.121)

Agree or disagree?

2) He asks: "How many churches today are actively and conscientiously preaching the gospel of . . . . the Kingdom of God? Not just any message will do. . . . Jesus will return only when the message of the *Kingdom* has been proclaimed in all the earth, and that proclamation is the Church's responsibility." (pp.110-111)

Agree or Disagree?

3) He writes: "[In] Africa, many African believers have never heard the gospel of the Kingdom of God. They know Jesus, but they have

---

[12] Myles Munroe, *Rediscovering the Kingdom* (Shippensburg, PA.: Destiny Image Publishers, 2004).

never been taught about their status and rights as sons and daughters of God and citizens and heirs of His Kingdom. . . . Even in Europe and the West . . . few people have heard the gospel of the Kingdom. [Yet] Many have heard about Jesus. . . ." (p.122)

Agree or disagree?

4) He warns: [Some] "have heard the wrong message of the Kingdom. . . . that is perhaps the most serious [deficiency] of all. . . . The gospel of the Kingdom of God . . . must be carefully defined so that there are no ambiguities. . . ." (p.145)

Agree or disagree?

5) He goes on to say: "One of the reasons the Church is not more effective at reaching the nations is because we are not preaching the message they need to hear. . . . Unfortunately many in the Church have discovered the King but they have no clue about the Kingdom that He came to bring to mankind." (pp.146-147)

Agree or disagree?

6) He adds: "So much time today we get the message wrong by preaching the good news of *heaven*. The two are not the same. We tell people to put their faith in Jesus for salvation and then we focus on heaven as our goal and destination. Jesus never preached heaven. The disciples never preached heaven, and neither should we. There may be a lot of appeal to the idea of going to heaven . . . but people struggling with daily life on earth . . . . need to hear the good news of the Kingdom of heaven—the rule of God has come to earth and all can experience the reality of that world." (p.155)

Agree or disagree?

7) He feels: "People everywhere are looking for the Kingdom, even if they don't recognize it by that name. . . . People are not looking for religion; they are looking for power, and the Kingdom offers power. . . .

If we preach the gospel of the Kingdom of God, people will respond." (pp.113-114)

Agree or disagree?

8) He notes: "When we preach Christ without preaching also about the Kingdom of God, we do people a great disservice. . . . Jesus preached the Kingdom, but the Church preaches so many other things rather than the Kingdom. . . . It's the lost message of Jesus that needs to be resurrected in our times." (pp.149, 162)

Agree or disagree?

9) He cautions: "The gospel of the Kingdom is the only true gospel. Anything else we preach is not the true gospel, or at least, not the complete gospel. Preaching about Jesus Christ is a vital and essential part of preaching the gospel of the Kingdom, because He is our way into the Kingdom. Just because we place our faith in Christ, however, does not mean that we automatically understand either what it means to be a citizen of the Kingdom or how to live like one." (p.157)

Agree or disagree?

10) He concludes: "Every one of the 7 billion people on planet earth is seeking the Kingdom of God, which is their ultimate fulfillment. Every religion and activity of mankind is man's attempt to find the Kingdom. It is the pearl that out-values all pearls, and the only treasure that is worth all the other treasures of life. The Kingdom is life itself. . . . [and] The king is the central component of a kingdom and embodies the essence of the kingdom." (p.215)

Agree or disagree?

Whether you agreed with Dr. Munroe or not, one thing is for sure. The above excerpts are a valid presentation of the postmillennial view of the kingdom. The irony of ironies here, however, is Dr. Munroe is not a postmillennialist. He's a premillennialist. Then how could he believe this way, you may wonder? The answer is, Dr. Munroe is merely properly reading the Scriptures.

Two More Demising Factors

Two more factors that contributed to postmillennialism's demise in popularity, besides the negative world events we mentioned at the beginning of this view, were:

1) Absorbed into the Social Gospel Movement. As Koester relates, "by the late nineteenth century, the ideals associated with postmillennialism were absorbed into the social gospel movement."[13] This absorption turned off and drove away millions of evangelicals. But postmillennialists to their credit argue back that postmillennialism's optimism "was [not] born out of any misconceptions concerning the innate goodness of humankind or of the ability of the church to convert the world by its own power." To the contrary, it "was born out of a belief in the triumph of the gospel in the world and of the work of the Holy Spirit in bringing in the kingdom."[14]

2) Drew charges of being "triumphalistic."[15] Dispensational premillennialists, particularly, rail against the "triumphalistic rhetoric" of postmillennialists. They term as "unrealistic [their] expectation of a worldwide conversion of the nations." One dispensationalist further jumped on the critical bandwagon by charging, "after fourteen years of study it is my belief that there is not one passage anywhere in Scripture that would lead to the postmillennial system. The best postmillennialism can come up with is a position built upon an inference."[16] Another critic

---

[13] Craig R. Koester, *Revelation and the End of All Things* (Grand Rapids, MI.: Eerdmans, 2001), 13-14.
[14] Grenz, *The Millennial Maze*, 66.
[15] Ibid., 147.
[16] Wayne H. House and Thomas Ice, *Dominion Theology: Blessing or Curse* (Portland, OR.: Multnomah Press, 1988), 9.

contends that the growth parables "do not tell us the *extent* to which the kingdom will grow."[17]

More Modern-day Attacks

Some amillennialists take a different tack against the postmillennial position. They argue the world is becoming both more Christian and more evil. In so doing they cite a few New Testament passages "that seem to explicitly deny the postmillennial position." These include:

- Jesus' wide and narrow gate comments in Matthew 7:13-14 and that "only a few find it."
- Jesus' question about finding faith on the earth when He comes in Luke 18:8.
- Several of Paul's apostasy statements in 2 Thessalonians 2:1-11; 2 Timothy 3:1-5, 12-13; 4:3-4.
- Jesus' dire predictions in Matthew 24:21-30.[18]

Postmillennialists, who are also partial preterists, as are most amillennialists, counter that these verses "refer specifically to the first-century conditions at the time of Christ's coming in judgment upon Jerusalem [circa A.D. 70]." To remove these verses from that historical, time-frame context requires that "exegetical violence be done to the text."[19] But premillennialists jump back into attack mode insisting that Matthew 24 "talks about his coming just *after* a period of great tribulation, not after a millennium of peace and righteousness has been established on the earth." These premillennialists also see the kingdom "as the eschatological event, which is utterly independent of all human effort."[20]

In defense, amillennialist Newcombe comes across as conciliatory. While he concedes "there are still many other evils in the world yet to vanquish," he recognizes "there has been considerable progress over the

---

[17] Grudem, *Systematic Theology*, 1123.
[18] Ibid., 1124-1125.
[19] Mathison, *Postmillennialism*, 183.
[20] Ladd, *A Theology of the New Testament*, 101.

centuries." He cites "Christian influence" in the abolition of slavery, works of charity, building of hospitals, the reading of the Bible around the world, and improved literacy. He notes that "Jesus Christ has exerted a greater influence on human history than any other person who ever lived" and that "approximately, two billion souls the world over claim to be Christians."[21]

But premillennialists do not buy this defense. They are hard and fast in their pessimism and claim that "for the postmillennial hope to materialize . . . a rather radical reversal of current trends would be required." They focus their major criticism, however, on postmillennialists basing their doctrine "on very carefully selected Scripture passages." The one passage they particularly allege postmillennialists have "neglected" is Matthew 24:9-14, which they believe portrays "spiritual and moral conditions as worsening in the end times."[22]

Other postmillennial opponents believe such thinking completely ignores what the Bible says about human depravity and the negative outcome of history they believe is prophesied in Scripture. They cite the parable of the wheat and the tares (Matt. 13:24-30, 36-43) as biblical proof that "the world will not be Christianized during this age."[23] Hence, they steadfastly oppose "the belief that the gospel will pervade society and change society for the better" claiming it is erroneous and "has no basis in Scripture."[24]

Opponents further charge that postmillennialism "allegorizes large portions of prophecy and consequently has the Church inheriting Israel's promises."[25] Even worse, if possible, they accuse this optimistic view of "divert[ing] . . . efforts from the salvation of individuals to the salvation of society" and condemn the idea of the kingdom now in opposition to "a future theocratic kingdom to be established in person by Jesus Christ." Not surprisingly, they attributed this perversion "of the true gospel" to

---

[21] Newcombe, *Coming Again But When?*, 75.
[22] Erickson, *A Basic Guide to Eschatology*, 72.
[23] Spargimino, *The Anti-Prophets*, 196.
[24] Ibid., 197.
[25] Ibid., 12.

Satan.[26] Hence many futurists are not persuaded by postmillennial claims and see this view as discredited. Instead, they are determined to stick tenaciously to their view that a glorious future on earth is promised only after Jesus returns, and not before.

Postmillennialists Fight Back

But a small band of modern-day postmillennial scholars continues fighting back. They counter that "the parable of the wheat and the tares [only] demands . . . that evil will remain until the end. It does not demand that evil be dominant until the end." Furthermore, "the Son returns to a field of *wheat*, not a field of tares."[27] They also contend that if the amillennial millennial view is true, "then the life and death of Christ had virtually no effect . . . or [no] positive effect on the growth of Satan's kingdom."[28]

Pragmatically, on the other hand, postmillennialists recognize that "it is difficult to cast off one's eschatology in order to adopt a new one"[29]—i.e., unlearning. They propose, however, that "when postmillennialism is properly defined, it expresses the glorious hope of all Scripture." Yet they complain that "the modern Church, sapped of the power of hope, largely through poor exegesis and a lack of an understanding of Church history, is weaker for it."[30]

They also directly challenge "both the amillennialist and the premillennialist insist[ence] that the world is evil" and "the fullness of the kingdom will come only with the coming of the King."[31] The reason they pinpoint for why Christianity is rarely "considered . . . to be a remedy for the mess the world is in" is because of "the general pessimistic and fatalistic worldview that seems to be inherent in much of

---

[26] Renald Showers, *What On Earth Is God Doing?* (Neptune, NJ.: Loizeaux Brothers, 1973), 88.
[27] Mathison, *Postmillennialism*, 211.
[28] Ibid., 181.
[29] Gentry, *He Shall Have Dominion*, 47.
[30] Ibid., 93.
[31] George Eldon Ladd, *The Blessed Hope* (Grand Rapids, Eerdmans, 1956), 141.

modern-day fundamentalism and evangelicalism."[32] So, they castigate premillennial dispensationalist Tim LaHaye for "wasting the precious, unrecoverable time of a generation of psychological retreatists."[33]

Another ironic factor in play in this great debate is that many Christians love to sing hymns written from a postmillennial, kingdom-present-and-expanding perspective. Below are a few well-known examples (underlined emphasis is mine):

- *Onward, Christian Soldiers* (1865)

    > Onward, Christian soldiers, <u>marching as to war</u>,
    > With the cross of Jesus going on before.
    > Christ, the royal Master, leads against the foe;
    > <u>Forward into battle</u> see His banners go!

    Question: Who are they/we supposed to be fighting?

    > At the sign of triumph Satan's host doth flee;
    > On then, Christian soldiers, <u>on to victory!</u>
    > Hell's foundations quiver at the shout of praise;
    > Brothers lift your voices, loud your anthems raise.

- *Stand Up, Stand Up for Jesus* (1858) . . . whose first stanza proclaims:

    > Stand up, stand up for Jesus,
    > Ye soldiers of the cross,
    > Lift high His royal banner,
    > <u>It must not suffer loss</u>;
    > From victory unto victory His army shall He lead,
    > <u>Till every foe is</u> vanquished
    > And Christ is Lord indeed.

---

[32] DeMar, *Last Days Madness*, 209.
[33] Gary North, letter to ICE Subscribers, January 30, 2002, email, 7.

- *Joy to the World!* (1719)

(My comments in parentheses.)

> Joy to the world, the Lord is come!
> Let earth receive her King;
> Let every heart prepare Him room,
> And heaven and nature sing,
> And heaven and nature sing,
> And heaven, and heaven, and nature sing.

(But Jesus is not King yet, the most popular view tells us. He and we are still waiting for this to happen.)

> Joy to the world, the Savior reigns!
> Let men their songs employ;
> While fields and floods, rocks, hills and plains
> Repeat the sounding joy,
> Repeat the sounding joy,
> Repeat, repeat, the sounding joy.

(The Savior reigns? Not according to many Christians. They believe Satan reigns now.)

> No more let sins and sorrows grow,
> Nor thorns infest the ground;
> He comes to make His blessings flow
> Far as the curse is found,
> Far as the curse is found,
> Far as, far as, the curse is found.

(He comes to what, to whom? Most think He's up in heaven waiting to come again. And, how far in our world is the curse found?)

> He rules the world with truth and grace,
> And makes the nations prove
> The glories of His righteousness,

And wonders of His love,
And wonders of His love,
And wonders, wonders, of His love.

(Again, does Jesus rule the world today? Or does Satan?)

- Do you know what hymn this Refrain comes from?

<u>For the darkness shall turn to dawning</u>,
And the dawning to noonday bright,
And Christ's great kingdom shall come to earth,
The kingdom of peace and light

(Is this a futuristic, "Second Coming" message and hymn? No. It comes from the hymn, *We've a Story to Tell to the Nations* (1896), and carries forth the same, postmillennial kingdom-expansion and gospel-optimistic message.)

Ironically, nevertheless, many premillennialists and amillennialists enjoy singing these hymns in their churches without ever thinking about or realizing that their musical message conflicts with their eschatological view and worldview—not to mention our massive failures to "let men their songs employ."

Not to be outdone, one postmillennial writer maintains that "when Christians seek to make permanent, meaningful, Bible-based changes in the world outside the local Christian ghetto, they become *operational postmillennialists*."[34] Hence we find the likes of a Dr. Myles Munroe that we cited above.

Obviously, the bottom-line question here is this: "Is God willing to put up with the triumph of sinners over his Church in history? Yes, say premillennialists and amillennialists. No, say postmillennialists."[35] What say you?

So is it true as Rushdoony asks that "the world is ruled by Satan, and therefore postmillennialism is impossible?" Is it true "the Christian hope has been turned into flight and despair?" What about Psalm 24:1—"The

---

[34] North, *Rapture Fever*, 119.
[35] Ibid., 68.

earth is the Lord's, and everything in it, the world, and all who live in it?"

Today's small band of postmillennialists are convinced that "postmillennialism will again prevail . . . because it is the truth of God . . . . . an eschatology of victory . . . [that] will inspire men and women with the power of God . . . as it did with the great saints of old and the Puritans of yesteryears and lead again more enduringly to the triumph of Christ in every area, bringing every sphere of thought and action into captivity of Christ."[36] They also believe this revival of interest began "in the late 1960s and early 1970s"[37]

One formidable amillennialist, Oswald T. Allis, has even conceded that "the most serious error in much of the current 'prophetic' teaching is the claim that the future of Christendom is to be read not in terms of revival and victory, but of growing impotence and apostasy."[38]

But the bottom line reason why the postmillennial view is so despised nowadays is, their view of exercising "dominion in history . . . . teaches responsibility. This is why its message is so hated. Today's Christians have been taught that they must flee responsibility. . . . This is why they believe the Church is so weak in our day."[39]

So who's right? Once again, it seems everyone thinks their view is the right one.

Duration of the Millennium

"Both premillennialism and postmillennialism . . . anticipate a future kingdom era on this earth."[40] But as was true in each of the two other views we've covered so far, there is not uniformity among postmillennialists in how they define their millennium.

---

[36] Rousas John Rushdoony, in Introduction to Marcellus J. Kik, *An Eschatology of Victory* (Phillipsburg, NJ.: Presbyterian and Reformed Publishing Co., *ix*.
[37] Mathison, *Postmillennialism*, 52.
[38] Oswald T. Allis, in Foreword to Roderick Campbell, *Israel and the New Covenant* (Philadelphia, PA.: Presbyterian and Reformed, 1954), *ix*.
[39] Gentry, *He Shall Have Dominion*, back cover.
[40] Grenz, *The Millennial Maze,* 70.

Some, like the amillennialists, believe this period of time should be taken figuratively, that it lasts longer than a literal thousand years, and we are living in it now.[41] Therefore, this millennium is not something to come cataclysmically in the future.

Other postmillennialists do not believe we are now living in the millennium. They see it as a special and future "golden age" of peace and prosperity, of unsurpassed gospel success, and the triumph of good over evil. And, it may or may not be a literal thousand years in length.[42]

For most postmillennialists, this unprecedented time will be "a further dimension of the advance of the kingdom during the present age that will lead to the age to come."[43] In other words, "the present age will gradually merge into the millennial age as an increasingly larger proportion of the world's inhabitants are converted to Christianity through the preaching of the gospel."[44] Consequently, social institutions are transformed by becoming more Christianized.

The difficulty here, however, is in trying to determine the length of the postmillennial millennium since it has no clear point of beginning and the kingdom advances by degrees. Thus, no postmillennialist knows for sure or can say how far it must advance before Christ can return.

End of the Millennium

In common with amillennialism, postmillennialists envision the end of time and the end of history coming after the millennial period and at Christ's visible Second Coming/Return—hence *"post-millennium."* Preceding this end will be a brief period of apostasy and conflict between Christian and evil forces headed up the end-time Antichrist. So what does the Bible say about this timing for his coming or an end-time Antichrist? As was true with several other end-time claims in the other two views, nothing.

---

[41] Keith A. Mathison, *Dispensationalism* (Phillipsburg, NJ.: P&R, 1995), 129-130.
[42] Gentry, *He Shall Have Dominion*, 53-54.
[43] Grenz, *The Millennial Maze*, 183.
[44] Hoekema, *The Bible and the Future*, 175.

Simultaneous with Christ's visible Second Coming/Return will be his taking the Church away to be with Him, as well as the resurrection of the righteous and the wicked dead, an end to all earthly existence and to the earth itself, the final judgment, and the beginning of "the eternal state,"[45] along with a totally new or renewed earth—the new heavens and new earth.[46]

Therefore, our eternal destiny and home as believers will not be in the heaven that exists today. But in another location. However, postmillennialists do not see any of these future realities coming any time soon and are careful to clarify:

> This does not mean that there ever will be a time on this earth when every person will be a Christian, or that all sin will be abolished. But it does mean that evil in all its many forms eventually will be reduced to negligible proportions, that Christian principles will be the rule, not the exception, and that Christ will return to a truly Christianized world.[47]

Concluding Condemnations

C.S. Lewis, among many others, condemned postmillennialism as "the idea which here shuts out the Second Coming from our minds." He further decried its "idea for the world slowly ripening to perfection" as "a myth . . . which distracts us from our real duties and our real interest"[48]— i.e., saving souls. Others condemn postmillennialism for "postponing any hope of Christ's imminent appearing for a minimum of a thousand-plus years"[49]

---

[45] Loraine Boettner, *The Millennium* (Philadelphia, PA.: Presbyterian and Reformed, 1987), 18.
[46] John Jefferson Davis, *Christ's Victorious Kingdom: Postmillennialism Reconsidered* (Grand Rapids, MI.: Baker Book House, 1986), 11.
[47] Boettner, *The Millennium*, 14.
[48] C.S. Lewis, essay, "The World's Last Night" (1960), in *The Essential C.S. Lewis*, Lyle W. Dorsett, ed. (New York, NY.: A Touchstone Book, Simon & Schuster, 1996), 388.
[49] J. Barton Payne, *The Imminent Appearing of Christ* (Grand Rapids, MI.: Eerdmans, 1962), 27.

But a small band of postmillennialists press on and argue back that "watchfulness and preparedness do not demand the doctrine of imminence."[50] They insist that "Scripture simply does not teach the dispensational doctrine of the 'imminent' return of Christ . . . . [Therefore] We do not know how many generations remain before Christ comes again."[51] One historical fact remains in their counterclaiming favor: "His return has not been imminent since the Ascension."[52] The reason for this delay, postmillennialists further contend, is that it "allows time for the advancement and victory of Christ's kingdom in the world and encourages a future-orientation to the labors of God's people."

Furthermore, Christ's return will not be "datable." In support, postmillennialists cite the verse: "of that day and hour no one knows, no not even the angels of heaven, but My Father only" (Matt. 24:36; also see 23:44; 25:13).[53] Sadly, they also observe that "the Christian public has more interest in the tribulation woes than in the millennial glory."[54]

The Many Comings of Jesus

Postmillennialists attempt to resolve, or at least soften, their lack-of-imminence issue—that Christ's Second Coming/Return is not near—by advocating numerous comings of Christ. This includes his "return in judgment" coming circa A.D. 70 and his future final coming in glory and consummation at the end of time. Therefore, postmillennialists, like amillennialists, are partial preterists.

In the meantime, between these two comings, they claim there have been, are, and will be many comings of Christ in various ways. They feel, and rightfully so, that this realization is an "important qualification . . . that needs to be understood."[55] (We shall address the many comings of

---

[50] Mathison, *Postmillennialism*, 204.
[51] Ibid., 206.
[52] Gentry, *He Shall Have Dominion*, 331.
[53] Ibid., 332.
[54] Ibid., 337.
[55] Ibid., 271.

Jesus and the various ways in which He comes in chapters 12, 13, and 15.)

One More Big Problem

To close our overview presentation and disputation of this view and transition into our fourth and final view, the preterist view, there is one more big problem that postmillennialists must face.

As we have seen, the prerequisite reality that must occur before the end and Christ's final coming is the "world-wide" preaching of the gospel of the kingdom: "And this gospel of the kingdom will be preached in the whole world as a testimony to all nations, and then the end will come" (Matt. 24:13). Arguably, and just twenty-one verses later, Jesus appears to time-restrict this occurrence to happen within his "this generation:" "I tell you the truth this generation will certainly not pass away until all these things have happened" (Matt. 24:34).

Yes, this passage of Scripture termed the Olivet discourse is highly and hotly contested. But what is more difficult to contest is, and according to the following and inspired scriptures, the gospel was preached (past tense) to all nations and to the world in that 1st century time period and within the time-restriction of "this generation" that Jesus had placed upon it (see Col 1:6, 23; Rom. 1:8; 10:18; 16:26; Acts 1:8 2:5; 24:5; also Luke 2:1).

Most notably, the Greek word translated as "world" in Matthew 24:14 is *oikoumene* and means "land . . . specifically the Roman Empire." It was commonly used in this restrictive sense back then to refer to the then-known Roman world, or the civilized world of the Roman Empire. For instance, it is used this way in Luke 2:1 for where the census that Caesar Augustus decreed was to be taken prior to Jesus' birth. It was not the word, *kosmos*, meaning the entire global earth.

Consequently, and according to inspired and authoritative Scripture, Jesus' prerequisite for the end to come—i.e., the "world-wide" preaching of the gospel of the kingdom—was met, fulfilled, and satisfied over 1,900 years ago. This past-fulfillment and scriptural perspective brings us to our fourth and final view.

Chapter 6
The Precise Past-Fulfillment View—Preterist

The preterist view is the least known of our four views. Nowadays, it is also the chief recipient of heresy charges. Surprisingly, it's the easiest view to present but the hardest for most Christians to accept.

The word preterist is derived from the Latin word *praeter*—which means "past." It's used in verb form for past tense. In eschatology it means "past in fulfillment."

The two basic types of preterism are full preterist and partial preterist. Full preterists are sometimes called preterists, consistent preterists, or radical, hyper, and extreme preterists by their opponents. Partial preterists are also often called "preterists" (the dual use of this terms creates confusion), moderate, or orthodox preterists. As we have seen, partial preterism is comprised mostly of amillennialists and postmillennialists. But it does include some premillennialists. All Christians, however, who subscribe to the past fulfillment of some prophecies are partial preterists. The degree of partialness depends on the degree of fulfillment already accomplished.

Full preterists believe that all four chief moments/events are past in fulfillment. Most of them today say these events occurred during the Jewish-Roman War of A.D. 66-70 and in association with the events surrounding the destruction of Jerusalem and the Temple. They are sure this was Christ's Second Coming and Return. And while it was a non-visible coming in judgment, it was, nevertheless, personal and glorious.

Many, if not most, full preterists, however, do not believe in many comings of Jesus prior to his birth, following his resurrection, or post A.D. 70. Rather, they subscribe to two advents, with Jesus coming "in finality" circa A.D. 70.[1]

Under Heavy Attack

This past-fulfillment view has increasingly come under attack from proponents of the other three views. This attack has become especially heavy following the release of R.C. Sproul's book, *The Last Days According to Jesus* (Baker 1998). In that book, Sproul explored the resurgence of interest in both the full and partial preterist views. Subsequently, several high-profile opponents have fired off highly critical comments in their denunciations of the full preterist view.

Dispensational premillennialist John MacArthur, for one, finds preterism preposterous and rejects it out of hand, claiming that "the position sounds so bizarre that some may wonder if it seriously deserves to be refuted."[2] He accuses preterists of sacrificing "the plain sense of every other prophecy about the return of Christ and end-times events."[3] Worst of all, he concludes that preterism is *"heresy* of the worst stripe"[4] and a "sub-Christian heresy."[5] Not surprisingly, he is quite upset that it

---

[1] On April 6, 2002, a public debate was held in New York City between two preterist leaders and two amillennialist scholars. The debate topic illustrates this point: "Did Jesus Come In Finality In A.D. 70?" The two preterists took the affirmative position. (International Preterist Association, "Did Jesus Come In Finality In A.D. 70?" debate between Edward E. Stevens and Don K. Preston (preterists) and Gray George and Kevin Hartley (amillennialists), Bayside, NYC, April 6, 2002, audio cassette.)
[2] MacArthur, *The Second Coming*, 11.
[3] ibid.
[4] Ibid., 13.
[5] Ibid., 223.

"is currently overthrowing the faith of many."[6] Many of MacArthur's colleagues concur with his anti-preterist assessment.[7]

Interestingly, and once again, let's recall that the preterist view is not the only end-time view stigmatized by some as being heretical. Each of the four views has taken its turn as being the enemy of the day at some point in Church history. But today most full preterists do not consider any of the other three views to be heretical—mistaken, yes, but not heretical.

Thomas Ice captures the essence of this recent motivation to gang-up against the preterists when he points out that "the debate is shaping up as a showdown between preterism and futurism."[8] In another book, he writes:

> Until recently, futurism has enjoyed an unobstructed field. But over the last decade, preterism, the polar opposite of futurism, has grown to provide a challenge to the futurist dominance. . . . In the absence of any perception of a challenger, the futuristic position has been taken for granted with almost no need to learn how to defend it. But with the rise of preterism, futurists are now required to think more about the basis for their position.[9]

Ice also puts modern-day preterism in perspective and pays it a back-handed compliment by acknowledging that beginning back in the 17th

---

[6] Ibid., 13.
[7] For further heresy assessments of preterism see: Grant R. Jeffrey, *Triumphant Return: The Coming of the Kingdom of God* (Toronto, Ontario: Frontier Research Publications, 2001), 10, 76, 78. Spargimino, *The Anti-Prophets: The Challenge of Preterism*, 9. Sproul, Jr., in Foreword to Seraiah, *The End of All Things: A Defense of Futurism*, 9, 10, 15. Mathison, *Postmillennialism*, 240, 244, 248. Gary North, letter to ICE subscribers, subject "Preterism Revisited," September 29, 2001. email. Kenneth L. Gentry, Jr., "A Brief Theological Analysis of Hyper-Preterism," www.chalcedon.edu/report/97jul/s10.htm., 1. Newcombe, *Coming Again But When?*, 35. Hank Hanegraaff, "Bible Answer Man," December 28, 2001, radio program.
[8] Thomas Ice and Kenneth L. Gentry, Jr., *The Great Tribulation: Past or Future?* (Grand Rapids, MI.: Kregel Publications, 1999), 6.
[9] Thomas Ice and Tim LaHaye, *The End Times Controversy: The Second Coming Under Attack* (Eugene, OR.: Harvest House Publishers, 2003), 62.

century and forward "early forms of preterism were mild and undeveloped by today's standards."[10]

LaHaye, on the other hand, is not so generous in condemning preterism:

> When all the evidence is considered, we are forced to conclude that the case for a past fulfillment of the prophetic Scriptures is untenable. Too many unanswered questions still exist to make the rapture of the church, the Tribulation period, the second coming of Christ, the establishing of His kingdom on earth, and other significant events be anything but future—just as the Bible teaches.[11]

Likewise, but even more so, postmillennialists are quite concerned by the recent "rapid spread" of full preterism. Keith A. Mathison, an associate of R.C. Sproul on the staff of Sproul's Ligonier Ministries, derogatorily calls it "hyper-preterism."[12] His stated motivation for serving as editor of a multi-contributor, anti-preterist book titled, *When Shall These Things Be? A Reformed Response to Hyper-Preterism*, is simply because "hyper-preterists have presented a significant challenge to orthodox Christian doctrine, and it cannot be ignored. The purpose of this book is to introduce the basic issues and to provide church leaders and laymen alike with a tool to help them deal with hyper-preterism."[13]

> ## "early forms of perterism were mild and undeveloped by today's standards."

In the Foreword of Mathison's book, R.C. Sproul, Jr. (not Sr.), labels hyper-preterists "an aberrant group"[14] and "enemies of Christ."[15] His

---

[10] Thomas Ice & Timothy Demy, gen. eds., *When the Trumpet Sounds* (Eugene, OR.: Harvest House, 1995), 14.
[11] Ice and LaHaye, *The End Times Controversy,* 10-11.
[12] Keith A. Mathison, ed., *When Shall These Things Be? A Reformed Response to Hyper-Preterism* (Phillipsburg, NJ.: P&R Publishing, 2004), *xiii*.
[13] Ibid., *xviii*.
[14] Ibid., *viii*.
[15] Ibid., *ix*.

prayer is "that those who have been ensnared by this error will, in reading this book, come under conviction, and so be set free."[16]

Mathison concludes his attack book by noting that "hyper-preterists have come along and thrown down a theological gauntlet." Yet he finds it "almost laughable" that anyone would "suggest that the church is not merely mistaken about a few secondary eschatological issues" but "that the church's entire eschatological outlook has been backwards for almost two thousand years." He asks, "How could anyone possibly believe this?"[17] Reluctantly, he laments that preterism "is a doctrine that some are finding persuasive."[18]

Not to be outdone, dispensational prophecy expert Jack Van Impe, on his June 22, 2005 television show, vowed to deal with preterism, once and for all. He announced that "next week I'm going to take this thing apart. Tell others about it. I'm going to show you that one of the propagators of this blasphemous teaching is Hank Hanagraaff—the Bible Answer Man. Well, this is one Bible question he has wrong. It teaches that every sign happened by 70 A.D. and the extreme preterists believe that Jesus came back then, and my question is, 'If so, where is He and what day did He arrive?' How come the Mount of Olives didn't split in two, according to Zechariah 14:4? Come on now! Next week I'm really going to deal with this."

When next week's show came, Van Impe credited "too many headlines" for preempting his time to discuss preterism. On his July 2nd show, he only devoted half of his half-hour show to denouncing the "false teaching" and "nonsense" of "preeeterism," as he derogatorily pronounces it. But he did not use Scripture to refute it. He only used "signs" from recent newspaper articles as proof that Jesus did not come back in A.D. 70.

The bottom line reason, however, for all these recent attacks is, the preterist view is gaining traction and momentum. Across the country and around the world serious Bible students and intelligent readers, alike, are taking a serious or second look at preterism and questioning and reconsidering some of the futuristic concoctions they have been led or told to believe.

---

[16] Ibid., x.
[17] Ibid., 353.
[18] Ibid., 354.

Of course, the preterist view rubs hard against the grain of Christian tradition and popular futuristic thought. So, not every inquirer comes to the same conclusions. More often than not, the preterist view is confronted with hostility, and not rationality. After all, unlearning is the hardest form of learning. But as one young lady from a large fundamentalist Baptist church in Florida wrote me and volunteered, "I can't believe how clear the Word of God is on the subject when read in context . . . . Of course, I still have questions." But she is right. Context is the main issue, the ultimate question, and the hermeneutical key. So, whose context do we trust? The preterist context? Or, one of the futurist view's context?

What is not being questioned is, no longer can the adherents of the three futurist views dismiss the preterist view out-of-hand or let it go unanswered. Preterism is gaining too much ground and moving forward. Of course, not all futurists are as hostile or demeaning of the preterist view as are some of the above opponents. Many inquirers are gracious and willing to take a look, or a second look, given preterism's recent theological development and rise in prominence. They admit that preterism, or parts of it, makes sense. So they are open to listen and are inviting preterists to the table to discuss what exactly did or did not take place, eschatologically, in the destruction of Jerusalem and the Temple in the 1st century.

A notable example occurred in April, 2007 when ThomasNelson, the largest Christian publishing house in the world and No. 6 overall, at that time released Hanegraaff's non-fiction book titled, *The Apocalypse Code*. In it, Hanegraaff, an amillennial partial preterist, scripturally scolds *Left Behind* series author, Tim LaHaye, for major biblical inconsistencies in his dispensational premillennial view, while pointing out many strengths of this least-known view of precise past-fulfillment. Sadly, he ignored or simply overlooked major biblical inconsistencies in his own amillennial view.

The plain fact today is, the preterist view has replaced the amillennial view as the most threatening to the prominence of the premillennial view. Another factor is, preterism's past-fulfillment distinctive is a direct and opposing challenge to each of the three futuristic views. That's why the proponents of the other three views are ganging up together, writing books, and attacking preterism, and not each other.

In the face of such mounting pressure one might wonder how anyone could legitimately believe in or continue to hold to the preterist view? Conspicuously, the Evangelical Theological Society does not consider preterism to be heretical. For more than twelve years, it has allowed the International Preterist Association to exhibit its books and materials at its annual meetings and both preterists and anti-preterists to present theological papers—sixteen papers by yours truly.

The plain fact today is, the preterist view has replaced the amillennial view as the most threatening to the prominence of the premillennial view.

So what makes full preterism so guilty of heresy charges and spurred this recent onslaught of vicious attacks? See what you think.

In a Nutshell—The 9.5 Theses

At the 53rd Annual Meeting of the Evangelical Theological Society in Colorado Springs, Colorado, on November 14-16, 2001 a full-preterist document titled the "9.5 Theses for the Next Reformation" was handed out to over 800 of the 1400 attendees. Admittedly, it was patterned after Martin Luther's famous "95 Theses." Below are its "9.5" propositions. See what you think of them:

1. *Everything* Jesus said would happen, *happened* exactly *as* and *when* He said it would—within the lifetime of his contemporaries.
2. *Everything* every New Testament writer expected to happen, *happened* exactly *as* and *when* they expected it would—within their lifetime—as they were guided into all truth and told the things that were to come by the Holy Spirit (John 16:13).
3. Scholars across a broad spectrum are in general agreement that this is *exactly how* every NT writer and the early Church *understood* Jesus' words. If they were wrong on something this

important, how can we trust them to have conveyed other aspects of the faith accurately, such as the requirements for salvation?
4. *No* inspired NT writer, writing twenty or more years later, *ever corrected* their Holy-Spirit-guided understanding and fulfillment expectations (John 16:13). Neither should we. Instead, they intensified their language as the "appointed time of the end" (Dan. 12:4; Hab. 2:3) drew near—from Jesus' "this generation" (Matt. 24:34), to Peter's "the end of all things is at hand" and "for it is time for judgment to begin" (1 Pet. 4:7, 17), and John's "this is the last hour . . . . it is the last hour" (1 John 2:18).
5. Partial fulfillment is *not satisfactory*. 3 out of 5, 7 out of 10, etc., won't work. Partial does not pass the test of a true prophet (Deut. 18:18-22). Again, Jesus time-restricted *all* of his end-time predictions to occur within the 1st-century time frame.
6. God is faithful (2 Pet. 3:9) and "not a man that he should lie" (Num. 23:19). Faithfulness means not only doing *what* was promised, but also doing it *when* it was promised.
7. 1st-century fulfillment expectations were the *correct ones* and everything happened, right on time—no gaps, no gimmicks, no interruptions, no postponements, no delays, no exegetical gymnastics, and no changing the meaning of commonly used and normally understood words. Such manipulative devices have only given liberals and skeptics a foothold to discredit Christ's Deity and the inerrancy of Scripture.
8. What needs adjusting is our understanding of both the *time* and *nature* of fulfillment, and not manipulation of the time factor to conform to our popular, futuristic, and delay expectations.
9. The *kingdom of God* was the *central teaching* of our Lord Jesus Christ, is a present but greatly under-realized reality, and must again become the central teaching of his Church.
9.5. We have been guilty of proclaiming a *half-truth*—a partially delivered faith to the world and to fellow Christians. We must repent and earnestly "contend for the faith that was once for all delivered to the saints" (Jude 3). If Christianity has been as effective as it has by proclaiming that Jesus Christ, the Messiah, came, died for our sins, bodily arose from the dead, and ascended to Heaven "at just the right time" (Rom. 5:6; Dan. 9:24-27), how much more effective might it be if we started

preaching, teaching, and practicing the ***whole truth***—i.e., a faith in which everything else also happened "at just the right time," exactly ***as*** and ***when*** Jesus said it would and every NT writer expected (John 16:13). Dare we continue to settle for less?

Seven Big Problems

Simply put, the seven biggest problems full preterists face in their attempts to advance their view, and in the words of their opponents, are:

1) "I just can't believe everything is fulfilled and over."
2) "My eyes aren't seeing what your words are saying!"
3) "If Jesus has already returned, why didn't anyone see Him do it?"
4) "Where is He today—I don't see Him?"
5) "Why are sin and evil still here?"
6) "Is *this* the New Heavens and New Earth and the New Jerusalem? You've got to be kidding!"

And the biggest problem of all.

7) "If all was fulfilled, where's our hope?"

In defense, amillennialist R.C. Sproul, and unlike many others, does not castigate the full preterist view as heretical. Instead, he suggests that preterism performs a "great service" by focusing "attention on two major issues:"

> The first is the time-frame references of the New Testament regarding eschatological prophecy. The preterist is a sentinel standing guard against frivolous and superficial attempts to downplay or explain away the force of these references.
>
> The second major issue is the destruction of Jerusalem. This event certainly spelled the end of a crucial redemptive-historical epoch. It must be viewed as the end of some age. It also represents a significant visitation of the Lord in judgment and a vitally important "day of the

Lord." Whether this was the *only* day of the Lord about which Scripture speaks remains a major point of controversy among preterists.[19]

Even with his ending qualification, Sproul certainly attributes more to circa A.D. 70 than do the creeds or confessions of the historic Church in which there are no mentions of the events of A.D. 70 whatsoever. But Sproul is a partial preterist. And as we've seen, the adjective "partial" is a qualifying term. For most Christians it means some end-time prophesies were fulfilled. For others it means most were fulfilled, but not all. For a few it means all, or most, of the four chief moments/events were fulfilled in some sense but await a more complete, final, or ultimate fulfillment—e.g., when the Lord returns in the future at the "end of time."

The best way I've found to explain partial preterism is the way R.C. Sproul himself explained it to me during a private meeting in a small conference room in the mid 90s at a convention of the Christian Booksellers Association, where we were both exhibitors.

"John," R.C. politely began to clarify, "I have two columns for fulfillment: A.D. 70 and the End of Time. I put the fulfillment of some scriptures in the A.D. 70 column and others in my End of Time column. I will tell you this, however. As I have been evolving in my understanding of eschatology, I find that I keep pulling more scriptures out of my End of Time column and put them into my A.D. 70 column. But (as he wagged his index finger in my direction) I still have some things in my End of Time column."

To Sproul's further credit and objectivity, he is quite complimentary of the preterist view. Check out this additional insight that he placed in a Foreword for another book:

> The modern revival of preterism represents an interesting and important paradigm shift in eschatology. The advantage of preterism is that is "saves the phenomena" of the New Testament time-frame references; it interprets biblical prophecy according to the images used in Scripture itself; and it offers a framework for consistent interpretation of the difficult apocalyptic literature of the Bible, such as that found in Daniel and Revelation. . . . Serious study and dialogue are needed if we are to reach agreement as to how far preterism is to go and what remains for

---

[19] Sproul, *The Last Days According to Jesus*, 202-203.

the hope of the church's and the cosmos' future in the full plan of redemptive history.[20]

Preterist Views of Early Church Fathers

In further support of this little-known view, history shows that at least four early-Church fathers subscribed to a preterist (past fulfillment) understanding that at least some of Jesus' "all these things" (Matt. 24:34) had indeed occurred within the time span of "this generation" as Jesus had specified.

Eusebius, a 4th-century Christian leader and writer who is often called "the father of Church history"

- Understood that the "great tribulation" of Jesus' Olivet prophecy was fulfilled in the events leading up to and culminating circa A.D. 70:

    > It is fitting to add to these accounts the true prediction of our Saviour in which he foretold these events . . . ."For there shall be great tribulation . . . ." These things took place in this manner, in the second year of the reign of Vespasian [A.D. 70], in accordance to the prophecies of our Lord and Saviour Jesus Christ . . . .[21]

    > . . . the abomination of desolation, proclaimed by the prophets [Dan. 9:27], stood in the very temple of God . . . which was now awaiting its total destruction by fire.[22]

- Confirmed that both the worldwide preaching of the gospel and the end of biblical Judaism were fulfilled:

---

[20] R.C. Sproul, in Foreword, *And It Came To Pass: The Third Annual C.E.F. Symposium: Preterism,*
(Moscow, ID.: Cannon Press, 1993), *vii*.
[21] Eusebius, *Ecclesiastical History*, Book 3, Ch.7, in The Nicene and Post-Nicene Fathers, Vol. 1 (Grand Rapids, MI.: Eerdmans, 1979), 141.
[22] Ibid, Book 3, Ch.5., 138.

Moses had foretold this very thing and in due course Christ sojourned in this life, and the teaching of the new covenant was borne to all nations, and at once the Romans besieged Jerusalem and destroyed it and the Temple there. At once the whole of the Mosaic law was abolished, with all that remained of the Old Covenant. . . . [23]

- Recorded that in obedience to the Lord's Olivet Discourse instructions, 1st-century Christians fled from Jerusalem to Pella in Transjordan around A.D. 68 after the first siege and before the second one, and no Christians were trapped and destroyed in the siege of Jerusalem, which concluded in A.D.70.[24]

- Affirmed that Jesus "came" in the fall of Jerusalem and in fulfillment of Zechariah's end-time prophecy.[25]

> For so it was prophesied concerning the destruction of the royal glory of the Jewish nation . . . . Yea, in return for their insults to the Lord who thus prophesied, there has not failed for them lamentation, mourning and wailing. And it was only after our Saviour came . . . . laying their Temple low, and driving them from their country, to serve their enemies in a hostile land;[26]

> When, then, we see what was of old foretold for the nations fulfilled in our own day, and when the lamentation and wailing that was predicted for the Jews, and the burning of the Temple and its utter destruction, can also be seen even now to have occurred according to the prediction, surely we must also agree that the King who was prophesied, the Christ of God,

---

[23] Eusebius, W.J. Ferrar, ed., *Proof of the Gospel*, Book. I, Ch. 6 (Grand Rapids, MI.: Baker Books, 1981) 35.
[24] Eusebius, *Ecclesiastical History*, Book 3, Ch. 5, 86, 138.
[25] Eusebius, *The Proof of the Gospel*, Book 8, Ch. 4, 143-6 – his discussion on Zechariah 14:1-5.
[26] Eusebius, W.J. Ferrar, ed., *The Proof of the Gospel*, Book 7, Ch. 4, 144, 146 – his discussion on Zechariah 14:1-5.

has come, since the signs of His coming have been shewn in each instance I have treated to have been clearly fulfilled.[27]

Clement of Alexandria, writing in the 3rd century, placed the abomination of desolation of Daniel's 70th week prophecy in the time of Nero (A.D. 37-68):

> " . . . in the one week," was He Lord. The half of the week Nero held sway, and in the holy city Jerusalem placed the abomination; and in the half of the week he was taken away, and Otho, and Galba, and Vitallus. And Vespasian rose to the supreme power, and destroyed Jerusalem, and desolated the holy place.[28]

Athanasius, writing in the 4th century,

- Declared that Christ came again and fulfilled all of Daniel's 70 weeks prophecy (Dan. 9:24-27):

> And Jerusalem is to stand till his coming, and thenceforth, prophet and vision cease in Israel. . . . And this was why Jerusalem stood till then—namely that there they might be exercised in the types as a preparation for the reality . . . but from that time forth all prophecy is sealed and the city and temple taken, why are they so irreligious and so perverse as to see what has happened, and yet to deny Christ, Who has brought it all to pass? . . . What then has not come to pass, that the Christ must do? What is left unfulfilled, that the Jews should now disbelieve with impunity?[29]

---

[27] Ibid., 147.
[28] Clement of Alexandria, *The Stromata, or Miscellanies*, Vol. 2, Book 1, in The Ante-Nicene Fathers (Grand Rapids, MI.: Eerdmans, 1979), 329.
[29] Athanasius, *Incarnation of the Word*, Section 39 Verse 3, Section 40 Verses 1-7 in The Nicene and Post-Nicene Fathers (Grand Rapids, MI.: Eerdmans, 1978) 57-58.

- Further he wrote:

  > For no longer were these things to be done which belonged to Jerusalem which is beneath…the things pertaining to that time were fulfilled, and those which belonged to shadows had passed away.[30]

Tertullian (A.D. 145-220), presumed by some modern scholars to have been a premillennialist, also wrote of the coming of Christ during the destruction of Jerusalem and how this was a fulfillment of predictions made in Daniel 9:26:

> Accordingly the times must be inquired into of the predicted and future nativity of the Christ, and of His passion, and of the extermination of the city of Jerusalem, that is, its devastation. For Daniel says, that 'both the holy city and the holy place are exterminated together with the coming Leader, and that the pinnacle is destroyed unto ruin.' And so the times of the coming Christ, the Leader, must be inquired into, which we shall trace in Daniel; and after computing them, shall prove Him to be come, even on the ground of the times prescribed, of the consequences which were ever announced as to follow His advent; in order that we may believe all to have been as well fulfilled as foreseen.
>
> In such wise, therefore, did Daniel predict concerning Him, as to show both when and in what time He was to set the nations free; and how, after the passion of Christ, that city had to be exterminated![31]

These writings of four early Church fathers more than suggest a preterist understanding of at least some past fulfillment of end-time prophecy and Jesus' coming circa A.D. 70. Amazingly, once again, no creed or confession of the undivided or divided Church, mentions, teaches, or even recognizes that any kind of judgment, or coming, or

---

[30] Athanasius, *The Festal Letters*, Letter IV, in The Nicene and Post-Nicene Fathers, Vol. 4, 1978, 516-517.
[31] Tertullian, *An Answer to the Jews*, in The Ante-Nicene Fathers, Vol. 3 (Grand Rapids, MI.: Eerdmans 1979) 158.

anything of eschatological significance occurred in association with the destruction of Jerusalem and the Temple circa A.D. 70. Also remarkable, the creedal councils never discussed eschatological issues and their eschatological sections only employed vague and fragmented language.

On the other side of this eschatological issue, other early Church fathers believed differently. These included: Justin Martyr, Papias, Tertullian, Irenaeus, Hippolytus, Methodus, Commodianus, and Lactantius. They thought they were still living in the last times, that Christ's return was still imminent, and it would occur prior to a coming millennium period. Apparently, they had no notion of any end-time fulfillment as having occurred in A.D. 70. But they were also "classic" or "historic premillennialsits" and not dispensational. That means they were not looking for a Rapture, the kingdom being restored to Israel, or a 7-year tribulation period as dispensational premillennialists are today. Those ideas had not yet been discovered, or "invented," as you prefer.

These writings of four early Church fathers more than suggest a preterist understanding of at least some past fulfillment of end-time prophecy and Jesus' coming circa A.D. 70.

But one thing we can safely conclude at this point is, from the very beginning of Church history there has been quite a difference of opinion regarding eschatological issues. The early-Church fathers were divided. We are divided today. So who was or is right? Were the expectations of the New Testament writers and the early Church the right ones? Or, are our delayed and futuristic expectations today the right ones?

A Spiritualizing Tendency

Some leading preterist writers and spokespersons believe that following the fulfillment of all things circa A.D. 70, the kingdom Jesus came presenting, modeling, and conferring is now a spiritual kingdom. So what does the Bible say about a spiritual kingdom. Again, nothing! The kingdom is never qualified as being only spiritual.

They further claim that the nature of resurrection is also spiritual. It's termed the "Collective Body View" verses the "Individual Body View." CBV preterist adherents teach that the eschatological resurrection, which occurred in A.D. 70, consisted of the "collective body" (the Church) being raised out of the dead "body" of biblical Judaism and into the new "body" of Christ. The nature of this resurrection, therefore, is seen as a change in covenantal mode of existence. This view arises from two primary sources: Ezekiel's prophecy and the new use of the word "body."

The resurrection from the dead depicted in Ezekiel's prophecy of dry bones (Ezek. 37:1-14) had both an immediate historical fulfillment and a future spiritual application. The text says that the "bones" are "the whole house of Israel" (vs. 11), a collective group. What happened to those bones was they symbolically pictured national Israel's literal return to their land from Babylonian/Assyrian captivity in the 6th and 5th centuries B.C. Their captivity and separation from their land and their Temple was considered by God's prophet as being dead. Consequently, their return is seen as a resurrection.

This historic fulfillment is also seen as a portrait, a type, a shadow of Israel's ultimate, and once again collective, resurrection. Prophetically, it was timed to coincide with the time God would "put my Spirit in you and you will live" (vs. 14). This refers to Israel's "last days" in the 1st century when the Spirit is poured out (Acts 2:1-21; Joel 2:28-32). But the collective group resurrected at this time was the new Israel of God, the Church. It arose out of the "graves" of a "ministration of death" and out of captivity within the law system of Old Covenant, biblical Judaism. It arose into a resurrection of new covenantal existence, "the ministration of the spirit" and "righteousness" (2 Cor. 3:7-9 *KJV*) in a new age of grace, freedom and power (Heb. 6:5).

Paul's numerous singular uses of the word "body" is likewise understood in a collective and covenantal sense, instead of its usual meaning of a physical human body. This application seems appropriate in some of his writings. But the difficulty here is the Greek word *soma*, translated "body," is used in a wide variety of literal and figurative applications in Scripture. Thus it cannot be exclusively interpreted only one way in all texts. In some instances, it may even have a dual meaning. Wherever it is used, its meaning must be determined by context. For example (see if you agree):

Collective "body"
1 Cor. 12:12-27;
Eph. 4:4; 5:23, 30;
Col. 1:18, 24

Individual "body"
Rom. 6:12; 8:23; 1 Cor. 6:18, 19: 7:4;
11:24; 15:35, 37, 38; 2 Cor. 7:1;
Phil. 1:20; Jas. 2:26; Matt. 6:22; 10:28;
26:12; 1 Thess. 5:23

Possible collective and/or individual "body"
Rom. 6:6; 7:4, 24; 1 Cor. 15:44; 2 Cor. 5:6, 8; Ph 3:21

Those preterists favoring the collective body view equate Paul's "body of death" (Rom. 7:4) with the "law of sin and death" (Rom. 8:12). During the time of Paul's writing, the Old Covenant mode of existence, the "ministration of death," was on its way out. It was being superseded and replaced by the Torah-free, New Covenant "ministration of the spirit" (2 Cor. 3:7-9) and "law of life" (Rom. 8:2). In contrast, this new mode of existence was collectively imparted to the "body of Christ" (1 Cor. 12:12-27; Eph. 4:4; 5:23, 30; Col. 1:18). Thus, the "covenant with death" inherent in the old way of existence was being "annulled" by the new mode of covenantal life and righteousness (Isa. 28:18).

This contrast between covenants is further illustrated by Paul in the allegory of Abraham's two sons—respectively, one *of the flesh* and the other *of the spirit*— as represented two covenants (Gal. 4:21-31). Thus, Paul's use of the term "flesh" is connected to death and "spirit" to life. They are antithetically interpreted to mean living under two different covenant modes of existence (see John 3:6; Rom. 6-8). Hence, a collective spiritual resurrection occurred when God's people—who are also determined by covenant—moved from the old "flesh" system into the new "spirit" system.

The "creation" (Rom. 8:18-23) is collectively viewed as being Old Testament saints living under the law awaiting and groaning to be delivered from that bondage and into the new, as adopted sons. A covenantal identity is ascribed to the two contrasting houses in Hebrews 3:2-6. The two covenants are said to serve as the "clothing" for the two different corporate bodies (Ezek. 16:8; 2 Cor. 5:2-4).

Although the collective body view of resurrection may be hard to grasp, that's no reason to reject it. Paul told us, "The letter [of the Law] kills, but the Spirit gives life" (2 Cor. 3:6b). Passing from death to life is resurrection. Perhaps the Old Covenant Jewish system was the "body of death" from which Paul longed for deliverance (Rom. 7:24; 8:2; also see all of Rom. 11; 2 Cor. 3-6). If it's true that human beings do not live in isolation, but in relation to the world(s) around them, then this change of covenant worlds is a valid perspective on spiritual resurrection—from the "old order" to "the time of new order" (Rev. 21:4; Heb. 9:10).

Consequently, collective body proponents conceive an individual believer's spiritual transformation of dying and rising with Christ within this same covenantal-change framework. One dies to the old Judaic law system and is raised with Christ into a new "more glorious" mode of life. "Death has no more dominion" (Rom. 6:7-9; 7:4) and people can live in a new, death-free way (1 John 3:14; Rom. 8:6).

As viable as the collective body view may be, it's only one perspective on the greater and multifaceted nature of resurrection reality. Therefore, in Chapter 16, we shall explore the individual body view. Yet some preterist authors and leaders advocate this spiritualized collective body view as the only aspect of biblical resurrection. The most recognized such advocate is Max R. King.[32]

Two Concluding Questions

1) How much end-time prophecy (like Jesus' Olivet Discourse, Book of Revelation, etc.) was relevant to his original audience?

- <u>Premillennialists</u> say – "none of it" or "little of it" was.
- <u>Amillennialists</u> say – "some of it" was.
- <u>Postmillennialists</u> say – "most of it" was.
- <u>Preterists</u> say – "all of it" was relevant and fulfilled, right on time.

What do you say?

---

[32] Max R. King, *The Cross and the Parousia of Christ* (Warren, OH.: Writing and Research Ministry, The Parkman Road Church of Christ, 1987), 429-666.

2) Who's right?

<u>Premillennialists</u> – who are looking for the future fulfillment of all things very soon in our day and time?
<u>Amillennialsists</u> – who honor some partial and/or past fulfillment but foresee mostly future fulfillment at a time we cannot know at the end of time?
<u>Postmillennialists</u> – who honor much partial and/or past partial fulfillment but believe consummatory fulfillment lies in the far-away future at the end of time?
<u>Preterists</u> – who see the precise past fulfillment of all things having happened right on time circa A.D. 70?

So which view is the right view? Is it the one most evangelicals subscribe to? Or, is it the one the least evangelicals subscribed to? Or, perhaps, it's one of the others? Most Christians tend to stick with whatever view they've been told, taught, or heard. But what do you now think? Or, are you more confused than ever?

Perhaps you are wondering what view I hold or favor? Do you think you know? You may be surprised because it is not any one of the four we've discussed. Rather, and as you will begin to see in the pages ahead, it's parts of all four.

Of course, when I first became a Christian, for sure, I was a dispensational premillennialist by default. After all, that view was the only view I was hearing (see again the Introduction). Then I gravitated into the amillennial view because it seemed to make more sense. Next, I was drawn into the postmillennial view due to its compelling concept of the kingdom of God and the many comings of Christ. But then I became aware of the preterist view. It quickly grabbed my attention when I recognized the significance of and started honoring the time statements in both the Old and New Testaments, as well as the Holy-Spirit-guided expectations of the New Testament writers (John 16:13).

Today, however, I have further evolved into what I am calling a P.I.P.S. That's an acronym for Preterist / Idealist / Postmillennial Synthesis. After all my study and research, I now realize that each view has captured a portion of the truth. But each view has also added a significant amount of error.

Therefore, with these four views presented and disputed, it's time for us to begin the unraveling process. Please be assured, you are in for quite a ride in the pages ahead. So buckle up, take a deep breath, and read on.

So which view is the right view? . . . Most Christians tend to stick with whatever view they've been told, taught, or heard. But what do you now think?

Part III – Analysis of Strengths and Weaknesses

I believe it was the Lord God Almighty Himself, eighteen years ago or so, Who planted in my heart, mind, and spirit the idea that it was time for new thinking and a new approach to the divisive maze of competing and conflicting, end-time views presented, expressed, and disputed in our last four chapters and that this area of theology could be unraveled, its problems solved, and conflicts resolved. This foundational belief propelled my pursuit of my synthesis concept into becoming the topic of my doctoral dissertation. Much that I already have and will be sharing with you comes from the research and writing that went into that work.

This new approach was the idea I discussed with Dr. Massey (see again the Introduction). Even back then, I felt that this writing project should not be undertaken as just another book. If possible, it deserved to be carried out under the discipline of a doctoral dissertation committee. However, when he advised me against pursuing a doctoral degree, I put this notion aside for a few years.

Then, after Y2K came and went and the world was still here, I reconsidered and found a conservative, evangelical seminary with a Ph.D. program with which I thought I could work. Even more, they were willing to accept me. It was a joint Ph.D. program in Theology between Trinity Theological Seminary and the University of Liverpool.

So I visited with the dean here in the United States. During our three-hour lunch I told him about my synthesis idea for my dissertation, that I believed God had planted it in me, and this was my motivation for seeking this a doctoral degree. He responded positively and shared with me how unusual it was for a Ph.D. candidate to know their dissertation topic prior to entering the program. Later, I found out that only ten percent of those who enter Trinity's doctoral programs ever complete them (I was also told is the national average is only one percent). He said the reasons for this sharp drop off vary but range from numerous life issues interfering with progressing through the program to the inability to finally present an approvable dissertation topic, proposal, and a finished and defendable document.

I also shared with him Dr. Massey's and my concerns about my entering this program and submitting my idea to others, and some of the problems I might run into. He assured me that he didn't think it would be a problem. But if I encountered any, I should contact him. I will spare you the details but I had to call on him twice. And true to his word, he came to my defense. Yes, more than once, Dr. Massey's question came back to haunt me, "Whom would you be willing to submit to, anyway?"

Therefore, during my course work the prime motivation that drove me, day by day, was getting to my dissertation. Two years into my program, I had completed most of my course work and was then allowed to begin the dissertation process.

Chapter 7

A More Comprehensive Approach

The first hurdle I had to clear during my dissertation process was to secure the formal approval from my doctoral committee for my topic. The high academic standard that a Ph.D. dissertation must meet to be both approved and completed is, it must be an "addition to the body of knowledge." In other words, it cannot merely be a report, a survey, or even a master's level thesis. It must add to the body of knowledge in its field and have at least three doctoral-level professors willing to sign their names that it does. It all starts with the approval of your topic.

In other words, I had to offer something new, unique, and significant. And the burden of proof for convincing the three professors serving on my dissertation committee (two dispensational premillennialists and my chairperson, a progressive dispensationalist) rested solely on me. Therefore, I knew I had to propose a more comprehensive approach for addressing this most divisive arena of confusing, conflicting, and competing end-time views than anything that had ever been tried or done before, and I had to prove that to them.

My first step was to submit a formal statement of my topic and an overview of my approach. My initial topic was "An Evaluation and Synthesis of the Four Major Evangelical Views of the Return of Christ." And my premise was simple, straightforward, and fourfold:

1. **God is not the author of our confusion in eschatology (1 Cor. 14:33, *KJV*)—we are.** I assumed that it was not and is not God's character or nature to have included in his Word any content that would create the amount of confusion, conflict, divisiveness, and/or ambivalence we see among Christians in this arena of eschatology. Personal interpretations have "muddied the waters" for everyone. I further assumed that we are the ones who have misconstrued the whole thing, and that this impasse could be resolved—scripturally.

2. **Each of the four major views focuses on the Second Coming/Return of Christ as the central, pivotal and controlling end-time event.** So get this one right and the other events will fall readily into place. The four views in order of their prominence today are: dispensational premillennialism, amillennialism, postmillennialism, and preterism.[1]

3. **Each view has principal strengths and weaknesses that can be identified through a scripturally disciplined approach grounded upon what the text actually says and does not say.** Eschatology is an area filled with problems caused by both additions and subtractions to the text. These are necessitated by the traditions of men and will not stand up to an honest and objective test of Scripture. Yet more often than not, we are unaware of the weaknesses inherent in our own view, until someone points them out to us. They are blind spots. *And unlearning is the hardest form of learning.* I also knew I'd have to be both objective and gracious in exposing these weaknesses for each view.

4. **The solution would be a solution of synthesis—discarding the weaknesses, keeping the strengths, and synthesizing the strengths into one meaningful, coherent, and cogent view that is more Christ-honoring, Scripture-authenticating, and faith-validating than any one view in and of itself.** Since each view has grasped a portion of the biblical truth regarding the end times, I proposed a synthesis treatment that would meet all hermeneutical and exegetical demands, and not contradict itself. This was significant because no one had ever done this

---

[1] They are not Preterism, Historicism, Futurism, and Idealism, as some suggest.

before to the degree and scope I was proposing and none of the four views themselves meet this criterion.

My next task was to conduct an extensive literature review to convince them that no comprehensive synthesizing work of the type or magnitude I was proposing had ever been conducted in Church history. After several months of researching, I was unable to locate any book, study, article, paper, or dissertation which offered such a comprehensive evaluation or synthesis—i.e., one that spanned the entire spectrum of the four, major, evangelical, and eschatological views. I found only a few scant books, journal articles, theological papers, and dissertations which even hinted at or made a partial attempt—i.e., they only compared and/or contrasted selected aspects of two or three of the four views and left the other view(s) and issues untouched.

But I did uncover credible documentation from several well-know scholars supporting my premise that no comprehensive works of synthesis are known to exist.

Back in 1937, Louis Berkhof in his book, *The History of Christian Doctrines*, viewed "the doctrine of the last things . . . [as] one of the least developed doctrines." He further believed that "it may be . . . we have now reached that point in the history of dogma in which the doctrine of the last things will receive greater attention and be brought to further development.[2] Berkhof also concluded that "eschatology is even now the least developed of all the loci of dogmatics."[3]

In 1973, in the preface of J. Barton Payne's *Encyclopedia of Biblical Prophecy*, Payne quotes Dwight Pentecost in noting that "there has been little attempt to synthesize the whole field of prophecy . . . and there is a great need for a synthetic study and presentation of Biblical prophecy."[4]

In 1984, Frances A. Schaeffer chimed in with these words in his book, *The Great Evangelical Disaster*:

---

[2] Louis Berkhof, *The History of Christian Doctrines* (Grand Rapids, MI.: Eerdmans, c1937, 1959), 267.
[3] Louis Berkhof, *Systematic Theology* (Grand Rapids, MI.: Eerdmans, 1939), 664.
[4] J. Barton Payne, *Encyclopedia of Biblical Prophecy* (Grand Rapids, MI.: Baker Books, 1973), *vi*. From J. Dwight Pentecost, *Things to Come* (Findlay, OH.: Dunham Pub. Co. , 1958), *viii*.

The history of theology is all too often a long exhibition of a desire to win. But we should understand that what we are working for in the midst of our difference is a solution—a solution that will give God the glory, that will be true to the Bible, but will exhibit the love of God simultaneously with his holiness.[5]

Such a solution was exactly what I was proposing and would be pursuing. I was also encouraged by comments from more recent scholars. Below are a few examples.

In 1998, Millard Erickson in his book, *A Basic Guide to Eschatology*, was still recognizing that eschatology is "the one remaining undeveloped topic of theology."[6] He also referred to J. Barton Payne's previous attempt "to synthesize the major strengths of the three methods of prophetic interpretation: historical, futurist, and preterist."[7] Payne's treatment, nevertheless, was cursory and shallow. Even Payne himself admitted:

> . . . any of the three methods if used rigorously . . . is productive of confusion. Actually, there are not a few alleged antecedents to Christ's return that may better be understood as having attained their fulfillment in the ancient past and hence as of no continuing prophetic significance whatsoever. Space forbids an exhaustive treatment of Biblical prophecy in reference to these three methods of approach.[8]

Unfortunately, Payne's book did not accomplish much of a synthesis. Hence eschatology remains "an object of criticism."[9] But in my proposed dissertation, and in this subsequent book, "space" would not and is not "forbidding" doing what Payne proclaimed but fell far short of accomplishing.

Conspicuously, I also discovered that no creedal council during the early centuries of Christianity ever debated or discussed eschatology.

---

[5] Frances A. Schaeffer, *The Great Evangelical Disaster* (Wheaton, IL.: Crossway Books, 1984), 176-177.
[6] Erickson, *A Basic Guide to Eschatology*, 11.
[7] Ibid., 179.
[8] Payne, *The Imminent Appearing of Christ*, 106.
[9] Geerhardus Vos, *Biblical Theology: Old and New Testaments* (Carlisle, PA.: The Banner of Truth, 1948, 1975), 287.

Even the 16th-century Reformers spent little time with it and paid it scant attention.

Nowadays, growing numbers of theologians are feeling that the embarrassing and perplexing arena of end-time biblical prophecy, or eschatology, is the next major area of Christianity ripe for reform. For instance, and as I cited in the Prolegomenon, the renowned theologian George Eldon Ladd maintained: "the easiest approach . . . is to follow one's own particular tradition as the true view and ignore all others, but intelligent interpreters must familiarize themselves with the various methods of interpretation that they may criticize their own views."[10] John Warwick Montgomery further and wisely advised that "the search for truth can never be limited to the categories of a single modern school of thought."[11]

Even the chairperson of my dissertation committee, David L. Turner, a progressive dispensationalist, in a 1989 article in the *Grace Theological Journal* titled, "The Structure and Sequence of Matthew 24:1-41," advocated that "some combination of the two (preterist-futurist views)" offers "the most promising solution to the exegetical difficulties of this passage."[12]

Nowadays, growing numbers of theologians are now feeling that the embarrassing and perplexing arena of end-time prophecy, or eschatology, is the next major area of Christianity ripe for reform.

In a 1999 *Christianity Today* magazine article titled, "Is Revelation Prophecy or History?", Dr. David S. Dockery, President of Union University in Jackson, TN, recommended that the Book of Revelation be approached on a synthesis basis. Here's how he put it:

---

[10] Ladd, *A Theology of the New Testament*, 670.
[11] John Warwick Montgomery, *The Suicide of Christian Theology* (Newburgh, IN.: Trinity Press, 1970), 177.
[12] David L. Turner, "The Structure and Sequence of Matthew 24:1-41: Interaction with Evangelical Treatments," *Grace Theological Journal* 10.1 (1989): 3, 26.

> Both the futurist and preterist views have their strengths and weaknesses. Instead of choosing only one or the other, a 'both/and' approach that applies the strengths of each is a better option. . . . Combining the preterist and futurist views allows us to understand both that the message of Revelation spoke directly to John's own age and that it represents the consummation of redemptive history. . . . The preterist position by itself fails to understand that Revelation confronts the modern reader with promises, challenges, and choices that are similar, if not identical to those faced by the book's original readers. The futurist position by itself is prone to see Revelation as a crystal ball with a literal timetable of events that will happen in the future.[13]

We will do exactly this and more later on in Chapter 14.

Lastly, Stanley J. Grenz, in another *Christianity Today* article certainly grasped the validity of a synthesis concept. Although he did not mention the preterist view, he did discern that "we would be mistaken if we merely weighed the evidence, chose one, and ignored the other two. The Spirit has something important to tell us in each of the three traditional views of the millennium."[14]

While I have basic agreements and disagreements with each of the above synthesis suggestions, they are, indeed, steps in the right direction. For that I applaud them. But they all are too limited in scope.

So what do you think my premillennial-dominated, dissertation committee thought of my proposed topic and synthesis approach? After mandating three revisions, they found it interesting, felt it had possibilities, and finally approved my topic and proposal. But they were highly skeptical that I could pull it off and develop it into a full-blown, approvable, and defendable dissertation.

Two years later, I completed and defended that dissertation, and my three premillennial professors signed off on it. In actuality, the solution of synthesis I presented and defended was and is not my solution. For it was clearly in God's Word all along. It only awaited our discovery and humbly receiving it. Now, it serves as the basis for this book.

---

[13] David S. Dockery, "Is Revelation Prophecy or History?" *Christianity Today*, 25 October 1999, 86.

[14] Stanley J. Grenz, "The 1,000-year Question: Timeless truths behind the debates over Christ's return," *Christianity Today*, 8 March 1993, 35.

I believe, with all my heart that the presentations and approach contained in my dissertation and in this book is *that* all-encompassing, longed-for, and bold step of synthesis these above scholars have been awaiting. No doubt, I shall be vilified by some for this "arrogance."

Ten Guiding Assumptions

Given that the present-day field of eschatology is a maze of four competing and conflicting views that seem hopelessly stalemated, it is also important for us to be cognizant of the ten assumptions that guided me in my quest for truth and understanding and produced my solution of synthesis. They still guide and motivate me as I have taken this bold step of synthesis:

1. The Bible is the inspired and authoritative Word of God. By it, and not by creeds, confessions, or traditions, we are to be of "more noble character" like the Bereans (Acts 17:11) and "Test everything. Hold on to the good" (1 Thess. 5:21). This we do in the interest of seeking truth and understanding so that all humankind may be benefited. After all, if truth sets one free, as Jesus announced (John 8:32), what do you think error does? It puts us in bondage.

2. We are not as gullible as we have been in previous times. Today, many Christians are more open than ever for a better way to understand and explain the meaning and fulfillment of end-time prophecy. The historical fact is, for twenty centuries, God has been leading the Church into a better understanding of the faith on such matters as the Trinity, the two natures of Jesus Christ, sin, grace, atonement, and justification by faith. Eschatology is the next major area ripe for reform—*Ecclesia Reformata [et] Semper Reformanda*—"The Church is reformed and always reforming."

3. This is the time that God has decided for his great plan of redemption—i.e., eschatology—to be better understood via a synthesis of views that is more faithful to his Word than any of the four views on its own, as the basis for the next reformation.

4. Since eschatology is an arena filled with very real problems and inconsistencies, such as the use of artificial and arbitrary interpretative devices that are necessitated by traditions and will not stand up to an honest and objective test of Scripture, these flaws/weaknesses can and will be identified and their lack of scriptural support demonstrated. This identification procedure provides the basis and exegetical rationale for breaking through the current impasse and offering a solution of synthesis.

5. Others can and should judge whether I have succeeded or failed and was objective or biased in my identification of strengths and weaknesses. Above all in this endeavor, a hermeneutic of humility is certainly in order.

6. Not only is eschatology a hermeneutical (interpretive) issue, it is also a philosophical (worldview) and psychological (emotional) issue that has become a paradigm (mindset) problem. We tend to believe what we want to believe and to adjust our hermeneutic(s) accordingly. In my opinion, this is the root-source of most, if not all, of our conflict and confusion in this area of study. It is why volumes have been written attempting to dilute, water down, or explain away clear and concise, textual statements. It is why some have ascribed errors of perspective to Jesus and the inspired New Testament writers. It is also why others have postulated failure, delay, or postponement notions, or contrasted God's time clock in comparison to man's, or taken a fulfilled-and-over stance. Many have redefined "iminency" to mean "certainty" and stretched out its timeframe for nineteen centuries and counting. This stretch has been "justified" with hidden gaps, necessitated intervals, foreshortened perspectives, blending of things near and far, etc., etc. Others have overly spiritualized some real events and consummated realities. These are just some of the interpretive techniques being employed in one or more of the four eschatological views we shall be addressing. But they are not supportable by Scripture or by sound hermeneutics. They are simply artificial and arbitrary devices that have been imposed upon the text without scriptural warrant but in support of a particular eschatological tradition. They have caused major damage and are weaknesses to be discarded prior to synthesis.

7. I believe our understanding of hermeneutics, and of Scripture, is getting better and better all the time. If we do not believe we can make progress in our understanding of God's Word, why bother studying hermeneutics and trying to refine our methodology? Iain Murray is right on target regarding our progressive development in understanding. "The constant business of the Church [is] to seek a larger knowledge of Scripture . . . 'We are but touching the fringes of the mystery of God's will . . . .'"[15] Surely, we have come to the point in Church history where we can sense that something is severely wrong in the field of eschatology. And while we want to build on the understandings of the past, we should also want to learn from its failures. Now the time may be right to come together around the purity of God's Word and to provide a better biblical view of the end—one that makes sense, and is more Christ-honoring, more Scripture-authenticating, and more faith-validating than any of the four views by and of itself.

8. While I believe this synthesis treatment meets all hermeneutical and exegetical demands and does not contradict itself, it does not, for length and depth of treatment reasons, address all the aspects in the eschatological schema. Of course, these unaddressed aspects are related and interconnected. They, too, are brought into the discussion where and when appropriate. But when brought in, they do not receive extensive treatment or development. Likewise, I do not attempt to answer every question, solve every issue, address every difficulty, or explain every nuance, passage, or verse. Unfortunately, critics often assail a work based on what was not addressed. The implication is that the author avoided those things that would not agree with his thesis. Hence, this book's scope and focus must only be viewed as a first step in the greater endeavor of fully synthesizing these four eschatological views.

9. I now believe the whole divisive arena of eschatological views can be fully synthesized, harmonized, reconciled, and unified. If my dissertation and this resultant book have begun the process, then it is my hope that a tremendous joy and excitement will accompany more input

---

[15] Iain Murray (1977) said about John Murray in the Preface to Vol. 2 of the *Collected Writings of John Murray* (Edinburgh, Carlisle, PA.: Banner of Truth Trust, 1976), Preface.

from others and/or a more comprehensive resolution. Surely, a divine solution of synthesis offers a fresh, viable, and never-before-offered alternative to the categorization system of eschatological views that has greatly divided the Church and caused much harm for far too long.

10. Allowance must be made for Deuteronomy 29:29: "the secret things belong to the Lord." There will always be things we humans will never completely understand or agree upon. However, the second half of this verse is just as relevant: ". . . but the things revealed belong to us and to our children, forever, that we may follow all the words of this law." Even though God's Word has been totally and perfectly revealed, God is still revealing things from his Word. Hence, we should continue to pray for God's "Spirit of wisdom and revelation" (Eph. 1:17).

So with these ten guiding assumptions in mind, let's proceed with our unraveling the end by next comparing and contrasting what I term "the great end-time fiasco" with God's demonstrated attribute of "divine perfection in two creations."

The Great End-time Fiasco

A fiasco is defined as being "a complete or ridiculous failure, humiliating breakdown." And the essence of "the great end-time fiasco" is twofold:

Element #1) Things that were supposed to happen didn't happen as New Testament expectations proved false.
Here's how the much-revered C.S. Lewis framed these "fail expectations" in his essay, "The World's Last Night" (1960):

> "Say what you like," we shall be told [by the skeptic], "the apocalyptic beliefs of the first Christians have been proved to be false. It is clear from the New Testament that they all expected the Second Coming in their own lifetime. And, worse still, they had a reason, and one which you will find very embarrassing.

"Their Master had told them so. He shared, and indeed created, their delusion. He said in so many words, 'this generation shall not pass till all these things be done.' And He was wrong. He clearly knew no more about the end of the world than anyone else."

It is certainly the most embarrassing verse in the Bible. Yet how teasing, also, that within fourteen words of it should come the statement "but of that day and that hour knoweth no man, no, not the angels which are in heaven, neither the Son, but the Father." The one exhibition of error and the one confession of ignorance grow side by side.[16]

Did you hear what C.S. Lewis said? He said Jesus was *literally wrong* when He made numerous time-restrictive predictions and statements regarding his coming again, his return. But as we shall see, the embarrassment belongs to C.S. Lewis.

Element #2) The Church invented "delay theory" in direct contradiction of Scripture.

If you have never heard of this sidestepping, excuse-providing theory, I'm not making it up. The *Dictionary of Biblical Prophecy and End Times* contains this topic and section:

> **Delay of the Parousia**
> The term *Parousia* refers to the second coming of Christ. The delay of the Parousia refers to the assumption by some New Testament scholars that the first generation of Christians (A.D. 30-70) believed that Christ would return before their deaths. When that didn't happen (i.e., when the Parousia was delayed), the early believers were supposedly thrown into a crisis of faith[17]. . . . The delay reveals God's patience and desire that many will come to repentance and faith . . . ."[18]

It further claims that . . .

---

[16] Lewis, essay "The World's Last Night," 385.
[17] J. Daniel Hays, J. Scott Duvall, and C Marvin Pate, *Dictionary of Biblical Prophecy and End Times* (Grand Rapids, MI.: Zondervan, 2007), 114.
[18] Ibid., 410.

Jesus provides strong hints that there could indeed be a delay between some of the immediate, partial fulfillment of his prophecies and the ultimate final fulfillment of his prophecies, particularly in regard to the Parousia.

Finally, the early church developed the already – not yet eschatological perspective in order to deal with the delay of the Parousia . . . . [between] Christ's first coming . . . . [and] his second coming, however short or long a time that entailed.[19]

Below are three significant scriptural problems for this "invented" delay theory, which—as we saw in Chapter 1, p. 32—was probably first espoused "around the middle of the second century by the Shepherd of Hermas."[20]

Problem #1 – If God's plan of redemption was, indeed, delayed, you would hope and expect that this "delay" would show up somewhere in the Bible, if for no other reason than this revealed truth: "Surely the Sovereign Lord does nothing without revealing his plan to his servants the prophets" (Amos 3:7). So where did God ever reveal a "delay" of something as big as his plan of redemption to one of his prophets, to Jesus, or to any New Testament writer?

Problem #2 – In three places the Bible emphatically declares there would be no delay. (Bold and italics emphasis mine.)

- "For the revelation awaits an appointed time; it speaks of the end and will not prove false. Though it linger, wait for it; it will certainly come and will ***not delay***" (Hab. 2:3).
- "The word of the Lord came to me: 'Son of man, what is this proverb you have in the land of Israel: 'The days go by and every vision comes to nothing'? Say to them 'This is what the Sovereign Lord says: I am going to put an end to this proverb, and they will no longer quote it in Israel.' Say to them, 'The days are near when every vision will be fulfilled. For there will be no more false visions or flattering divinations among the people of Israel. But I the Lord will speak what I will, and it shall be fulfilled ***without delay***. For in your days, you rebellious house, I

---

[19] Ibid., 115.
[20] Aland, *A History of Christianity*, 91-92.

will fulfill whatever I say, declares the Sovereign Lord'" (Ezek. 12:21-25).
- "For in just a very [very] little while, 'He who is coming will come and will *not delay*'" (Heb. 10:37).

Sadly, the Church has been preaching delay for nineteen centuries and counting. Whom should we believe—the uninspired Church or the inspired writers of Scripture?

Problem #3 – It was the "wicked" or "evil" servant in Jesus' parable in Matthew 24:42-51 who said, "My lord delayeth his coming" (Matt. 24:48, *KJV* – also see: Matt. 18:32; 25:26; Luke 19:22).

First, let's notice that this "delay" in the parable was only within that servant's lifetime, and not 1,900 years and counting. Secondly, let's ask this question – Has the Church become a "wicked servant" for inventing, preaching, and teaching "delay theory" for 19 some centuries and in blatant contradiction of Scripture? I'll let you contemplate the answer to that question.

In our next section, let's compare and contrast this "great end-time fiasco" with God's attribute of divine perfection in two creations. Your recognition and appreciation of this attribute of God is absolutely crucial and foundational for everything else we shall be covering throughout this book. However, the material in our next section was not part of my dissertation. I developed it later and presented it to the MPC group. It was so well received, I decided to include it herein. The following is a condensed version taken from the Introduction of my book, *The Perfect Ending for the World*. For the more extensive presentation, see that book.

Sadly, the Church has been preaching delay for nineteen centuries and counting. Whom should we believe—the uninspired Church or the inspired writers of Scripture?

Divine Perfection in Two Creations

Proposition #1

The God of the Bible is the God of order and design. Everything He created He did so with a plan, purpose, timeframe, and mathematical precision. For those who have eyes to see, his guiding hand is evident in every part of his creation—from macro to micro, the largest to the smallest. This attribute of God has been called the stamp or fingerprint of divinity. I choose to call it simply divine perfection.

So how do you feel when you gaze up into clear, star-studded night sky with no man-made light to obscure the view? What do you think about when you contemplate this dazzling array, its immensity, its complexity, its beauty, and all that's up there and beyond—a hundred-billion-trillion stars, the planets, the Milky Way, the sun, the moon, and multiple galaxies? They aren't just up there twinkling and floating around. All are in motion spinning through the vastness of space at astronomical speeds, and with such mathematical precision and in such intricate and predictable patterns that people all over the world set their clocks by it.

The word *cosmos* literally means "order." The dependability of this order and its mathematical perfection is totally rational. That's the only reason space flight is possible. It allows us moderns to calculate a trajectory, launch a space craft, and land it on the moon or Mars, or fly it past other planets, precisely at the right time. But if the universe was a product of unintelligent, unguided, random forces and chance, what would be rational and dependable about that?

To the contrary, this part of creation is so perfect and dependable that Albert Einstein said, "I cannot believe that God plays dice with the cosmos."[21] And the ancient psalmist was inspired to write in awe:

> The heavens declare the glory of God;
> the skies proclaim the work of his hands.

---

[21] Albert Einstein on quantum mechanics, published in the *London Observer*, April 5, 1964; also quoted as "God does not play dice with the world." in *Einstein: The Life and Times*, Ronald W. Clark, New York: World Publishing Co., 1971, p. 19.

> Day after day they pour forth speech;
> night after night they display knowledge.
> (Psalm 19:1)

Not only do the heavens spin in mathematical precision, so do the smallest subatomic particles. And they comprise everything created: the chair you sit on, this book you hold in your hands, and the clothes you are wearing, even your own body.

Tremendous advancements in scientific technology over the past one hundred years have enabled scientists of all kinds to discover and study the breadth and depth of the perfection that exists all around us. One of the realities they have increasingly discovered is that physical matter is not solid and still. It only appears that way. Everything material is made out of atoms, and inside each atom is ceaseless, mathematically precise order and motion.

Powered by rapidly improving technology, it has become increasingly more difficult to defend the notion that anything or everything in the universe and on the earth just evolved from chaos, over billions of years, through millions of mutations, via natural selection, random chance, and unintelligent forces.

Not only do the heavens spin in mathematical precision, so do the smallest subatomic particles.

Let's briefly look at some dramatic examples of hard, empirical, and scientific evidence of this perfection from both the macro and micro creations.

Macro Evidence

Launched into orbit in 1990, the Hubble telescope has provided scientists an unprecedented opportunity to search our solar system, the universe, and distant stars and galaxies. Increasingly, they have discovered that we humans, indeed, live on a very privileged planet.

The two scientist-authors of the book, *The Privileged Planet* (2004) assure us that in our now more widely observable universe "mounting evidence suggests that the conditions necessary for complex life are exceedingly rare, and that the probability of them all converging at the same place and time is minute."[22]

Astrophysicist, Hugh Ross, calculates that, to date, 128 finely tuned, interdependent conditions or constants have been identified.[23] Each is necessary for life as we know it to exist on planet earth. Others agree and have calculated that "just a slight variation in any one of these values would render life impossible."[24] These finely tuned constants encompass the earth's location in the universe, in our galaxy, and in our solar system, along with the conditions present on the earth itself.

Here is a small sample of areas and factors which must be just right in order for life to exist on earth: the unique properties of water, the composition of earth's atmosphere, its magnetic field, its axis tilt, its rotation speed, its density and size, its crust, its distance to the sun and moon, its oceans-to-continents ratio, its nuclear force that holds atomic nuclei together, its electromagnetic force, the color/size/heat of our sun, and size of our moon, etc. No other planet or star in our observable universe possesses even a few of these 128 constants.[25]

Some scientists affectionately call this convergence of finely tuned constants the "Goldilocks" story. Why? For the reason that "alone among planets, earth supports human life, because it is 'not too hot and not too cold, not too hard and not too soft, but just right.'"[26] In contrast, "most of the Universe is too cold, too hot, too dense, too vacuous, too dark, too bright, or not composed of the right elements to support life."[27]

What must be emphasized, once again, is this fine-tuned realization was only recently and increasingly made possible by "the unprecedented

---

[22] Guillermo Gonzalez and Jay W. Richards, *The Privileged Planet: How Our Place in the Cosmos Is Designed for Discovery* (Washington, DC.: Regnery, 2004), xii.

[23] Hugh Ross, *The Creator and the Cosmos* (Colorado Springs, CO.: NavPress, 2001), 194.

[24] William Lane Craig, "The Teleological Argument and the Anthropic Principle," www.leaderu.com/offices/billcraig/docs/teleo.html, 1/15/08, 3.

[25] For an elaboration of some of these constants familiar to most of us non-scientists, see **Exhibit A** in my book, *The Perfect Ending for the World*, 3-6.

[26] www.aish.com/societywork/sciencenature/The_Anthropic_Principle.asp, 1/16/08, p-1.

[27] Peter D. Ward and Donald Brownlee, *Rare Earth: Why Complex Life Is Uncommon in the Universe* (no c.s.: Copernicus Books, 2000), 35.

scientific knowledge acquired in the last century, enabled by equally unprecedented technological achievements . . . [that] when properly interpreted, contribute to a deeper appreciation of our place in the cosmos."[28]

Another factor recently discovered, according to Jonathan Wells who holds two Ph.D.s—one in biology and one in theology, is:

> Not only is Earth especially suited for life, but it is also well situated for scientific discovery. Because the Milky Way is a spiral galaxy [most galaxies are elliptical], it is relatively flat, so we can observe distant galaxies that would otherwise be obscured by dust and stars in our own galaxy. And Earth's position in the Milky Way, about halfway between the galactic center and its visible edge, is just about ideal for making astronomical observations, giving us a fairly clear view of nearby stars as well as distant galaxies.[29]

Hence, and more and more, scientists are discovering that "the conditions necessary for complex life . . . . takes a lot of factors to have a habitable planet."[30] "The probability that all [this] would exist today *for any planet in the universe* has been calculated at 'one chance in 10 to the 138th.'"[31] In other words—almost if not totally impossible.

Get the picture—the big picture? We live in the midst of a vast and hostile universe that is finely tuned and mathematically precise. And our earth is perfectly located in the only place in our solar system, galaxy, and perhaps the universe, suited for life and tailor-made for our existence. What's the best explanation?

The Privileged Planet scientist-authors reckon that all this perfection strongly suggests a "conspiracy . . . the product of a mind . . . an

---

[28] Gonzalez and Richards, *The Privileged Planet*, x.
[29] Jonathan Wells, *Darwinism and Intelligent Design* (Washington, DC.: Regnery Publishing, 2006), 123-124.
[30] Gonzalez and Richards, *The Privileged Planet*, x. For more, I recommend the two books and DVD referenced above: *The Privileged Planet* and *Rare Earth*, along with the DVD, Illustra Media's DVD: *The Privileged Planet*. Also you can search the Internet under the expressions "the anthropic principle" or teleology," which is a recently formed field of study (from Greek: *telos*: end, purpose is). Teleology is "the philosophical study of design, purpose, directive principle, or finality in nature or human creations."
[31] www.inplainsite.org/html/anthropic_principles.html., 1/16/08.)

intelligent being . . . a supremely good and orderly Creator . . . for our sake . . . . the universe is ordered in an intelligent way."[32] And, intuitively, most us know that design requires a designer. But there's more hard evidence for us to consider.

Micro Evidence

Let's now turn our gaze for divine perfection from upward through a telescope to downward through an electron microscope (invented in 1930). As with telescopes, recent advancements in microscopic technology have also opened up new vistas of study and discovery for scientists.[33] But whether one peers up or looks down, intricate order, design, plan, purpose, and mathematical precision are readily evident. Thus, scientists are increasingly finding that divine perfection is exhibited throughout all creation.

In 1996, Michael Behe (Ph.D. in Biochemistry from the University of Pennsylvania and Professor of Biological Sciences at Lehigh University) challenged the scientific community and its Darwinian theory of evolution on purely scientific grounds. With the publication of his best-selling book, *Darwin's Black Box*, Behe popularized the concept of and term "irreducible complexity."[34] In defense of his book's title, Behe correctly pointed out that "to Darwin . . . as to every other scientist of the time, the cell was a black box" (i.e., its contents were unknown) and Darwin was only able to try and make sense of "biology above the level of the cell."[35] And as was true for the macro evidence cited above, "the black box of the cell could not be opened without further technological improvements."[36]

---

[32] Illustra Media, *The Privileged Planet*, DVD.
[33] "For the last four years biochemists have possessed X-ray scanning electron microscopes so powerful they can map complex biological molecules down to the level of the individual atoms that make up the molecules." Ross, *The Creator and the Cosmos*, 140.
[34] Michael Behe, *Darwin's Black Box: The Bio-chemical Challenge of Evolution* (New York: Free Press, 1996).
[35] Ibid., 9.
[36] Ibid., 10.

Behe launched his challenge by quoting Darwin's own admission that his theory of gradual evolution by natural selection carried a heavy burden:

> If it could be demonstrated that any complex organ existed which could not possibly have been formed by numerous successive, slight modifications, my theory would absolutely break down.[37]

Behe then proceeded to do just that with his concept of *"irreducible complexity"* and by going all the way down into the micro, single cell level. He presented numerous examples of irreducibly complex biological, biochemical life systems in which evolution is an impossible explanation for their formation. He documented scientific reasons why the whole system had to have been created all at once, which, again, is impossible in Darwin's theory of gradualism. And he emphasized that his conclusion of *"irreducible complexity"* "flows naturally from the data itself—not from sacred books or sectarian beliefs."[38]

Therefore, "over [just] the past four decades modern biochemistry has uncovered the secrets of the cell . . . . The result of these cumulative efforts to investigate . . . life at the molecular level—is a loud, clear, piercing cry of *"design!"* In his opinion, "the result is so unambiguous and so significant that it must be ranked as one of the greatest achievements in the history of science."[39] Behe called it, "intelligent design."[40]

He documented scientific reasons why the whole system had to have been created all at once, which, again, is impossible in the Darwin's theory of gradualism.

---

[37] Charles Darwin, *Origin of Species* (New York , NY.: New York University, 11872, 1998), 154.
[38] Behe, *Darwin's Black Box*, 193.
[39] Ibid., 232.
[40] Ibid., 193.

So what has been the response of the scientific and educational communities? The bulk have roundly denounced Behe and his book in order to discredit his conclusion of intelligent design. Writing ten years later in his book's new edition, Behe notes that "the scientific argument for design is stronger than ever" because of "the enormous progress of biochemistry in the intervening years.[41]" He prognosticates that "as science advances relentlessly . . . . the case for intelligent design of life becomes exponentially stronger."[42]

In other words, and like a simple mouse trap, or a more sophisticated wrist watch or computer, complex living organisms could not have functioned until all their intricately interwoven components were all assembled. Also during these ten intervening years, Behe records that the scientific community has done little, if anything, to refute his claim of "intelligent design" or "to show that the Darwinian process really can do [explain] what its boosters claim it can do . . . account for the functional complexity of the molecular foundation of life"[43] and how such systems "could have evolved . . . by random mutation and natural selection, with each tiny mutational step improving on the last, without causing more problems . . . and without veering off into temporarily-advantageous-but-dead-end structures."[44] So today, "the situation remains unchanged from what it was ten years ago."[45]

In retrospect and fairness, however, let's note that Darwin did not have the advantage of the great advances in scientific technology for understanding life that we have today. And yet, today, evolution theory has an almost stranglehold on scientific and educational circles. But it is in crisis because the plausibility of its core concept of random, unguided, natural processes grows more and more implausible as scientists continue to discover more and more about "irreducible complexity" and "intelligent design."

Once again, I like to call all this micro, hard, physical, empirical evidence for what it truly is, in my opinion—more proof of divine perfection.

---

[41] Ibid., 255.
[42] Ibid., 256.
[43] Ibid., 266.
[44] Ibid., 267.
[45] Ibid., 270.

So Who's the Fool?

In the midst of overwhelming evidence—found not only in the largeness of the universe but throughout its smallness—and given the insurmountable odds of all this perfection occurring without design and a designer, an atheistic folly prevails in most scientific and educational communities. In these circles, people who believe the "god-myth" are ridiculed as hopelessly ignorant and outmoded.

But, once again, most of us when we see design, we infer—via everyday logic—a designer. Who of us when we visit a place like Mount Rushmore would assume these carved faces are actually the result of unguided, unintelligent, and random forces?

Of course, the existence of God cannot be proved or disproved. But the precision in the sky, in the cell, in biochemical systems, and at the subatomic level is hard, rational, stunning, and compelling evidence. Scientifically, it can be rationally viewed and weighed. Even so, some are compelled to believe that "nothing times nobody plus random change over billions of years equals everything in perfection."

Practically speaking—and in my opinion—it takes less faith to believe that "In the beginning God created the heavens and the earth." (Gen. 1:1; also see Isa. 40:26-28).

> **In the midst of overwhelming evidence . . . an atheistic folly prevails in most scientific and educational communities.**

Those, of course, who feel no need of God will always find ways to ignore, discount, and explain away the view of a supernatural creation as they grope around for alternative explanations to avoid the "god-myth." They want no part of God. Therefore, they must disassociate Him from *both* the plainest hard evidence up in the sky as well as all that's around us here on the earth.

So how, you may ask, can two scientists look at the same evidence and come up with radically divergent conclusions? Perhaps, it's like the old saw says:

> Two men looked through prison bars;
> One saw mud; the other saw stars.

But I believe there is a greater and more basic answer. Since everything that exists does so in a vast storehouse of order, knowledge, precision, perfection and even beauty; and since design inspires most of us people to infer if not seek its Designer, those who despise God must distort this truth. And so they have. In my opinion, to believe that all this perfection circling around us in mathematical precision just happened by chance is the folly of the fool who "says in his heart 'there is no God'" (Psa. 14:1a; Isa. 53:1).

To the contrary, this evidence of divine perfection is one of the most powerful arguments for the existence of God. Once again, the ancient Psalmist is right on as he proclaims, "the earth is the Lord's and everything in it" (Psa. 24:1). And it shows. "For since the creation of the world God's invisible qualities—his eternal powers and divine nature—have been clearly seen, being understood from what has been made, so that men [and women] are without excuse" (Rom. 1:20).

Even more amazing, if that is possible, this Lord of creation allows and encourages us humans to explore, study, and discover how incredibly wise, powerful, skillful, and purposeful He was in creating it all. Moreover, He did so within a fixed and specified timeframe of "six days" (Gen. 1:1-2:3).[46]

In our continually enhanced and advancing explorations, however, an ever-increasing irony keeps manifesting itself. The more explainable the universe has become, the more amazing and baffling its innermost workings appear. This irony reinforces the probable involvement of an all-knowing, all-powerful, creative being—as opposed to some vague or mysterious cosmic force(s) operating by chance.

Many scientific giants of history, such as Bacon, Boyle, Copernicus, Descartes, Einstein, Faraday, Galileo, Kepler, Mendel, Newton, Pascal, and Planck, believed in an infinite and personal God, Who created a uniform universe and earth with pattern and purpose. They felt their task as scientists was to observe, discover, and explain his handiwork, not to invent it, create it, or deny it.

---

[46] I will not get into the debate here of how long these days may have been.

Today, some are terming this new and increasingly being uncovered perfection in creation "the new apologetic" (defense of the faith). They see it as the best hope for the resurgence or revival of Christianity in the face of recent and bold atheistic challenges.[47] But there is another venue of order and mathematical precision for us to re-explore that also exhibits God's attribute of divine perfection.

> **The more explainable the universe has become, the more amazing and baffling its innermost workings appear.**

And now, you are about to find out why I spent this time at the MPC seminar and in this book on *this* attribute of divine perfection in the physical creation at both the macro and micro levels. It's because this objective realization brings us to our second proposition.

Proposition #2

The God of order and design in creation is the same God of order and design in redemption. As He did in the physical creation, He created his plan of redemption with a design, purpose, and a fixed and specified timeframe leading up to and culminating with its goal. Then, He progressively completed it with timely and mathematical precision. As we shall see in the pages ahead, every event in the orderly unfolding of his plan falls with exactness in its proper time and place—no delays, no postponements, no unexpected interruptions, as we have been traditionally told and taught. This is what end-time prophecy or eschatology is all about.

This is also why the Apostle Paul was prompted by God's Spirit to write these time-sensitive words: Jesus Christ was born "when the time had fully come . . . to redeem those under the law" (Gal. 4:4); that He

---

[47] See: William Lang Craig, "God Is Not Dead Yet," *Christianity Today* (July, 1008): 22-27. Troy Anderson, "A New Day for Apologetics," ibid., 28-29. Dinesh D'Souza, *What's So Great about Christianity* (Washington, DC.: Regnery, 2007).

died "at just the right time" (Rom. 5:6); and "who gave himself as a ransom for all men – the testimony given in its proper time" (1 Tim. 2:6). The Greek word translated "time" in the first verse is *chronos* and denotes a space or span of time. But in the latter two verses the word is *kairos* and is more specific. It means a fixed, definite, or set time.

According to God Himself, the timely and precise fulfillment of prophecies foretold long ago "from the distant past"—and not the perfection in the physical creation—is how we humans can know Who the one true God truly is. This demonstrated factor of divine authenticity is so important that the God of the Bible inspired the Old Testament prophet Isaiah to write about it six times and in various ways (see Isa. 41:21-24; 42:8-9; 44:6-7; 45:20-22; 46:9-11; and 48:3-6).

The God of order and design in creation is the same God of order and design in redemption.

The fact is, the God of the Bible foretold—many times and in many ways—what was going to happen in the future. And it all happened. No other god, faith, religion, or ideology in the world can claim this phenomenon of predictive and prophetic precision. Nor do they have anything to compare with the subsequent validating evidence of fulfilled prophecies.

As I shall present for your consideration throughout the rest of this book, everything else the God of the Bible promised and prophesied via his prophets regarding his plan of redemption (saving us human beings from sin and restoring our fellowship with Him) *also* happened "at just the right time" and "in its proper time." One thing this perfection provides is to allow the Christian faith to be more defensible and not as easily disregarded or dismissed by skeptics and critics. It should be taken more seriously by everyone.

Unfortunately, this reality of timely, mathematical, and precise past-fulfillment has been largely ignored, resisted, or denied by most Christian and non-Christian traditions. But as was true with the physical creation, evidence of divine perfection in this other venue abounds. How can this be, you may ask? It is because in the Bible there is such a thing as . . .

The Appointed Time of the End

We are a time-oriented people. God is time-oriented, too. After all, He created time—the "two great lights" in the sky, the sun and moon, to "serve as signs to mark seasons and days and years" (Gen. 1:14, 16). They travel across the sky with mathematical precision. God also knows how to tell time. And He has communicated to us human beings in time-restrictive language we can easily understand. We can rest assured in the revelation, as the Hebrew prophet Amos announced long ago, "Surely the Sovereign Lord does nothing without revealing his plan to his servants the prophets" (Amos 3:7). That is why, seven centuries before Christ, the God of the Bible inspired the ancient prophet Habakkuk to write:

> For the revelation awaits an appointed time; it speaks of the end and will not prove false. Though it linger, wait for it; it will certainly come and will not delay.
> (Habakkuk 2:3)

When was this appointed time of the end appointed? God did not say. I suspect it was from or before "the creation of the world" since Jesus was "slain from the creation of the world" (*NIV*) / "slain from the foundation of the world" (*KJV* – Rev. 13:8; also see: 1 Pet. 1:20; Eph. 1:4). And, once again according to Scripture, He died "at just the right time" (Rom. 5:6)

Then when was this appointed time of the end to happen? God did not tell Habakkuk.

But one century later, and in keeping with Amos 3:7 above, God gave another Old Testament prophet Daniel, two specific time prophecies that pinpointed the exact time in human history for this "appointed time . . . of the end." Daniel also perfectly foretold the end's historical setting and defining characteristic. We shall cover these prophecies and their precise fulfillments in Chapter 10. But in our next chapter we must expose and discard four big objections in the form of four false and misleading paradigms that prevent most Christians from being able to receive the divine perfection we'll be presenting throughout the rest of this book.

> **God also knows how to tell time. And He has communicated to us human beings in time-restrictive language we can easily understand.**

Chapter 8

Discarding Four False Paradigms

Not only do we live on a privileged planet, we are a privileged people. To be living at this time in human history with the great advances in technology and scientific knowledge that have taken place over the past one hundred years allows us to live lives our ancestors would never have dreamed possible. They also have enlightened many of us with a greater and deeper appreciation for the divine perfection that exists all around and above us.

In our continuing re-exploration of divine perfection we shall be unraveling, unveiling, and documenting the reality of a timely, mathematical, and precise past-fulfillment of all end-time prophecies—a reality ignored, resisted, or denied by most Christian traditions. But as was true with the physical creation, evidence of divine perfection in this other creation venue abounds.

How can this be, you ask? It's because seven hundred years before Christ the God of the Bible announced there was such a thing as the "appointed time . . . of the end." He also decreed through his prophet Habakkuk that this end would "not prove false," would "certainly come," and would "not delay" (Hab. 2:3).[1]

One century later, and in keeping with his pattern revealed in Amos 3:7, God gave another Old Testament prophet, Daniel, two specific time

---

[1] Some scholars argue that in Habakkuk 2:3, that which would come was the vision of the end and not the end itself. Daniel's two time prophecies concerning this time and event, however, cannot be so construed.

prophecies that perfectly pinpointed the exact time in human history for this "appointed time . . . of the end." Daniel also perfectly foretold the end's historical setting and defining characteristic.

This "appointed time . . . of the end" is a paradigm, a divinely provided paradigm. But as we shall see, there are other contending and misleading paradigms born of human traditions that conflict with God's "appointed time . . . of the end" paradigm.

What Is a Paradigm?

As I have explained more fully in another book,[2] the word paradigm comes from the Greek *pardeigma* (*para*, side by side + *deiknynai*, to show, point out). A paradigm is a model, a pattern, a frame of reference, a worldview, or simply a way of thinking for understanding and interpreting external reality. It's the way we "see" the world, not visually but by perception. It is the mental framework by which we construe reality, process information, make decisions, and determine actions. For individuals, it brings order and meaning to our experiences. It's also at the very heart of any culture

Our paradigm answers our most basic question: what is real? If one's paradigm is the correct way of seeing the world, then one's judgments, decisions, and actions will be correlated and productive. If it's distorted or incorrect, they will be skewed. In practice, a person may not live what he or she professes, but that person will always live in accordance with his or her paradigm. In other words, we live out what we truly believe and think. Consequently, when our paradigm shifts, many things will change.

Our view of the world and particularly the future is a paradigm. As we shall see, multiple millions, if not billions, have been programmed into believing paradigms that are not in harmony with God's revealed Word. Most of them are simply following the way they have been raised and are comfortable parroting what they've heard others say. But many are in bondage to these paradigms, almost venerating one or more of them to iconic status. They are afraid to raise questions. Few have bothered to check the Scriptures for themselves. Consequently, most

---

[2] Noē, *The Perfect Ending for the World*, 102-103.

Christians and non-Christians alike are unaware of the Bible's clear and concise promises to the contrary.

... billions, have been programmed into believing in paradigms that are not in harmony with God's revealed Word.

Therefore, this chapter is designed to help us begin breaking out of these old mindsets and transition away from unscriptural and false paradigms that have led so many astray for far too long. My hope is that you will find my methodology and logic here clear and convincing.

A Sneak Preview

In Daniel's second time prophecy, Daniel 12:1-13, God revealed many aspects about his coming "time-of-the-end" paradigm. Before you read it anew, however, I want to reiterate that for some of you this unraveling process will be a major unlearning and relearning experience. Hence it may be uncomfortable, upsetting, or even threatening. For others of you, it will be exciting, rewarding, and like a breath of fresh air. In this undertaking, please remember, once again, our agree-on Guideline #1 of *Sola* Scriptura—what does the Bible actually say and not say. (Bold emphasis below is mine.)

> "At that time Michael, the great prince who protects **your people**, will arise. There will be **a time of distress such as has not happened from the beginning of nations until then.** But at that time **your people** – everyone whose name is found written in the book – will be delivered. **Multitudes who sleep in the dust of the earth will awake:** some to everlasting life, others to shame and everlasting contempt. Those who are wise will shine like the brightness of the heavens, and those who lead many to righteousness, like the stars for ever and ever. But you, Daniel, **close up and seal the words of the scroll until the time of the end.** Many will go here and there to increase knowledge."

Then, I Daniel, looked, and there before me stood two others, one on this bank of the river and one on the opposite bank. One of them said to the man clothed in linen, who was above the waters of the river, **"How long will it be before these astonishing things are fulfilled?"**

The man clothed in linen, who was above the waters of the river, lifted his right hand and his left hand toward heaven, and I heard him swear by him who lives forever, saying, "It will be for a time, times and half a time. **When the power of the holy people has been finally broken, all these things will be complete."**

He replied, "Go your way, Daniel, because the words are **closed up and sealed until the time of the end.** Many will be purified, made spotless and refined, but the wicked will continue to be wicked. None of the wicked will understand, but **those who are wise will understand.**

From the time that the daily sacrifice is abolished and the abomination that causes desolation is set up, there will be 1,290 days. Blessed is the one who waits for and reaches the end of the 1,335 days.

"As for you, go your way **till the end.** You will rest, and then at **the end of the days** you will rise to receive your allowed inheritance."

Critical Questions to Begin Asking Yourself

Seeking truth and understanding is often initiated by asking right and critical questions. Therefore, in our unraveling-the-end endeavor, let's proceed in this manner.

Who were "the holy people" and Daniel's "your people" when Daniel was writing down these prophetic words during his Babylonian captivity? Was it not the Jews/Israel?

What was their "power?" Was it not the greatest power God has ever given any particular people on Planet Earth—an exclusive relationship with Him as manifested by the Temple complex (see Isa. 2:2-5; 56:7)?

What did Jesus say would happen to the Temple? Was it not, "Not one stone will be left on another; every one will be thrown down" and "your house is left to you desolate' (Matt. 24:2; 23:38)?

When did Jesus say this would happen? Was it not, "I tell you the truth, this generation will certainly not pass away until all these things have happened" (Matt. 24:34)?

When did it happen? Was it not forty years later, circa A.D. 70, and within Jesus' specified timeframe of "this generation?"

Then what was going on when "the tombs broke open and the bodies of many holy people who had died were raised to life?" Did they not come "out of the tombs, and after Jesus' resurrection they went into the holy city and appeared to many people" (Matt. 27:52-53)? Were these "many" the fulfillment, or first fruits of the fulfillment (see Chapter 16) of Daniel's prophecy that "multitudes who sleep in the dust of the earth will awake" (Dan. 12:2a)?

Was Jesus quoting Daniel's prophecy when He claimed that "For then there will be great distress, unequaled from the beginning of the world until now – never to be equaled again" (Matt. 24:21; Dan. 12:1)?

Was Jesus' "this generation" the time of intensified distress, trouble, or tribulation Daniel wrote about that was to be poured out upon his people (the Jews/Israel) and "in the latter days" (Dan. 10:14 *KJV*)?[3]

Was this prophesied time the time of divine judgment for their continual breaking of covenant, rebellion against God, and rejection of his plan of redemption via the coming of the Messiah and their killing of Jesus?

Was "the power" of those "holy people . . . finally broken"—i.e., biblical Judaism—with the total destruction and desolation of Jerusalem and the Temple in that 1st-century time period (Dan. 12:7)?

Was that the time when "all these things" concerning the "time of the end" was "completed" (Dan. 12:7)?

Was the resurrection of the dead actually taking place back, then and there?

---

[3] "In the future . . . a time yet to come" (*NIV*); "in the future of the days" (literal Hebrew).

Was this 1st century A.D. chain of events the final breaking of "the power of the holy people" and the *historical setting* and *defining characteristic* for Daniel's "time of the end" and Habakkuk's "appointed time . . . of the end?"

Were these the biblical "last days," as the writer of Hebrews stated circa A.D. 65, "But in these last days he has spoken to us by his Son" (Heb. 1:2)?

Are we "those who are wise" and "understand" or not (Dan. 12:10b)?

Most Christian scholars and leaders object to that 1st-century time and the destruction of Jerusalem and the Temple as being the end and the end-time paradigm the Bible consistently proclaims. They maintain that back then was not the end of the world, the end of time, or the end of history as we know it. Nor was it the Rapture, the restoration of Israel, Christ's 1,000-year reign, or any of the other, familiar, and traditional end-time paradigms that have been popularized in the Church.

Four Other Contending Paradigms

Contending Paradigm #1). What about the "End of the World" or "End of Time?"

In 2006, I was able to fulfill a long-held dream. My wife and I joined a group of confessing Methodists on a tour of Greece and the Greek Isles. It was billed as "In the Footsteps of St. Paul." But the prime attraction and high point for me was this trip's scheduled half-day visit to the island of Patmos "on the Lord's day"—a Sunday morning (see Rev. 1:10), and which the Apostle Paul never visited.

Around nine o'clock in the morning we disembarked from our cruise ship onto small tender boats that ferried us to shore. There, we boarded buses that took us to the Monastery of the Apocalypse, which was built around the 11th century. It surrounds the cave, or the Sacred Grotto as the Greeks refer to it, in which St. John supposedly received the Book of Revelation.

By the time our group arrived, several other buses had already unloaded. So while we waited in line to get into the monastery a young Greek lady and our tour guide told us that "during the reign of the

Roman Emperor Domitian in A.D. 95 the Apostle John was banished to Patmos, where he was held for two years. Here he received the inspiration for the Book of Revelation from his professor, Jesus Christ. It contains prophecies about the cataclysmic end of the world."

When she finished her prepared spiel, I stepped out of line, worked my way over to her, and asked this question, "How do you know the prophecy of Revelation is about the end of the world?"

"This is the interpretation I was told," she casually replied.[4]

You may or may not believe this, but some people in our world actually want it to end. They imagine this end as a wondrous happening. Call it a termination wish, if you will. They see "the End" as God's and their own final vindication, and their best opportunity to escape from the toils and responsibilities of this life, even from death itself. For them the idea that "the world's going to end" sounds so good and so right.

But what does the Book of Revelation literally say about the end of the world? The answer is *nothing*! What does the whole Bible say about the end of the world? Again, the answer again is *nothing*! What about the historic creeds? *Nothing*!

Many Bible teachers, scholars, and even the much-respected Dr. Billy Graham like to qualify "the End" by telling us that the world and human history will certainly end in its present form or, "as we know it."[5] What do these qualifying phrases mean? They don't know. Nobody knows. Yet they keep saying them and expect us to believe it.

The fact is, the world is always changing or coming to an end in its present form or as we know it, and a new one is continually coming in existence. Ask your parents or grandparents if the world as they knew it hasn't changed. Or perhaps, you have seen the world change "as you knew it."

So, and in keeping with our Guideline #1, what does the Bible say about the world ending "as we know it" or in its present form? Again, *nothing*! What did Jesus say about it? *Nothing*!

What does the Bible say about an "end of time" or "end of human history? Again, *nothing*!

---

[4] For the full account of what all happened to me that morning see: Appendix A in John Noē, *The Greater Jesus* (Indianapolis, IN.: East2West Press, 2012), 397-411.

[5] Billy Graham, "My Answer," *The Indianapolis Star*, 11/17/07, E-7.

Not a single text, taken in context, declares the world will ever end. As unpleasant as this truth may be for some, the end of the world is simply a false and pagan doctrine that has been dragged into the Church and read into the Bible.

What does the whole Bible say about the end of the world? Again, the answer is *noting*! What about the historic creeds? *Nothing*!

Question: "Doesn't the Bible say that God is someday going to destroy the world and set up a new heaven and earth?" We'll deal with this objection and contending paradigm next. But this "end-of-the-world" or "end-of-time" paradigm is, by far, the #1 reason so many have been hamstrung in their understanding of end-time prophecy.

"But wait a minute!" you protest. "I've been reading Billy Graham's newspaper column for years and he frequently says the Bible says 'the world will definitely end some day[6] . . . . When Christ comes again[7] . . . . [and] this world is only temporary[8] . . . . Jesus warned that someday this world as we know it *will* come to an end – not because of a war or natural disaster. The future is in God's hands, and he alone will bring an end to the world.'"[9]

With all due respect to this revered man of God, and one with whom I agree on so many points of faith, the emphatic answer to that assertion is, *it does not!* Moreover, relying on who says what will not settle this matter. Only specific statements from Scripture will do as we agree to "test everything. Hold on to the good..." (1 Thess. 5:21). Nothing is exempt from this scriptural admonishment. And the fact is that there is no clear statement that teaches an end of the world, an end of time, or an end of human history. *None*! It's the "time of the end." Big difference!

One clarification, however, is in order here. The original King James Version of the Bible mistranslates the Greek word *aion* as "world" rather than "age" in the phrase "the end of the world (age)" in Jesus' longest

---

[6] Ibid., 6/17/98, 12/12/96 and 11/25/94, for example.
[7] Ibid., 10/7/05, E-2.
[8] Ibid., 4/20/05, E-6.
[9] Ibid., 1/7/13, E-4.

and most dramatic prophecy (see Matt. 12:32; 13:22, 39, 40, 49; 24:3; 28:20, for instance). Most modern Bible translations, including the New King James Version, clear up this confusion and render it properly as "age." Those who like to use fear to hold on to and/or control people hesitate to give up this mistranslation weapon, however.

Likewise, not one iota of evidence exists that 1st-century Jews, the early Christians, or any New Testament writer (men guided by the Holy Spirit, according to John 16:13) were anticipating an end to the human race or the demise of the planet. It is simply not, as some believe, a profound and glorious doctrine of the Church.[10]

The biblical truth about the proverbial "end of the world" is contained within the biblical phrase "world without end, Amen." The Bible says that the world had a beginning, but is without end. "From the beginning of the world . . . . throughout all ages, world without end. A-men. (Ephesians 3:9, 21, *KJV*). And as we've seen in our Introduction, the Gloria Patri, the famous doxology and confessional of the historic Church, emphasizes and confirms this same biblical truth:

> Glory be to the Father, and to the Son, and to the Holy Ghost.
> As it was in the beginning, is now and ever shall be.
> World without end, Amen.

A pastor friend of mine declared in astonishment to me one day, "I've said this doxology so often in church and never stopped to realize what it meant." He added, "it's tragic that so many of us, so often, have said or sung this biblical phrase in our church services without ever stopping to consider what it means."

So what does "world without end, Amen" mean, anyway?

It means exactly what it says: the world (or age) is not going to end! In the original Greek, the phrase translated as "world without end" in the King James Bible is an idiom and is translated differently in other, more modern translations. Some versions read, "throughout all generations (ages) for ever and ever!" Literally, it's "into all generations of the age of the ages." As an idiom the actual meaning of the phrase is greater than,

---

[10] For a more extensive treatment, see my book, Noē, *The Perfect Ending for the World*, 81-106.

and cannot be directly understood, from its literal words. But every translation of this Greek idiomatic phrase contains the same basic truth.

The meaning of the word translated as "age" (*olam* in Hebrew and *aion* in the Greek) is "a long indefinite period of time." In this idiom, however, both the singular age and the plural ages are used. This double use intensifies the meaning of an unending future. Therefore, "world without end," and all the other translations, emphasize the concept of permanence, eternalness, endlessness, everlastingness, perpetuity. It clashes with any idea of an end of the world or of human history.[11] The world simply does not have an end.

The translation "world without end" is also a contra positive. In literary style, a contra positive is used to make the meaning more emphatic, like John F. Kennedy's famous phrase, "ask not what your country can do for you . . . ." Biblical statements, too, are sometimes made more powerful by using a negative. Are they not? Instead of strengthening a point by using a superlative, the statement is emphasized by using a negative. "I am not ashamed of the gospel of Christ" (Rom. 1:16 *KJV*) is an example. What it really means is, I am exulting in it, I am proud of it.

So what does "world without end, Amen" mean, anyway? It means exactly what is says:

The "amen" following "world without end" makes the phrase even more emphatic. Amen affirms the contra-positive proclamation and adds the meaning, "so may it be in accordance with the will of God." What we end up with, then, is a double strengthening and emphasis of the certainty of this idiom that the world (or age) is without end. Other Bible verses emphatically and directly support the world's continuing forever and ever by telling us that:

---

[11] Compare with similar idiomatic uses in Heb. 1:8, Rev. 11:15, and Isa. 45:17. A few scholars feel that this double use in the idiom does not speak of eternity or endlessness, but of aggregated or compounding periods of time—until all ages have run their course. Most, however, do agree with the explanation given here.

- "Generations come and generations go, but the earth endures [remains] forever" (Eccl. 1:4).[12]
- The Psalmist confirms that the earth is established forever (Psa. 78:69)
- And that the earth, the world, and its foundations "can never be moved (Psa. 104:5; see also Psa. 93:1; 96:10; 119:90).
- This applies to the whole material universe that God created, as well as to both moon and sun that are eternally established as faithful witnesses in the sky (Psa. 89:36-37), and to the highest heavens (Psa. 148:4, 6).

Eternalness is not only an attribute ascribed to God and his glory, it's also an attribute ascribed to his creation. That's one reason why Psalm 19:1 states, "The heavens declare the glory of God; the skies proclaim the work of his hands."

Critical Objection: What about God *only* promising never again to destroy the world by water?

My Response: Twice, since the flood in Noah's day, God has promised not to destroy the world. He made these two promises to Noah on behalf of all humanity for all time. They are recorded in the Old Testament and the Torah book of Genesis as a record of his faithfulness and trustworthiness:

Promise 1: "Never again will I [God] curse the ground because of man, even though every inclination of his heart is evil from childhood. And never again will I destroy all living creatures, as I have done. As long as the earth endures [remains], seedtime and harvest, cold and heat, summer and winter, day and night will never cease." (Gen. 8:21b-22)

---

[12] Some Bible scholars maintain that the book of Ecclesiastes cannot be relied on because the arguments it contains are man's, and not God's. The New Testament book of 2 Timothy, however, asserts that "All Scripture [including Ecclesiastes] is useful for teaching, rebuking, correcting, and training in righteousness" (2 Tim. 3:16).

Promise 2: "Never again will all life be cut off by the waters of a flood; never again will there be a flood to destroy the earth." (Gen. 9:11b)

For centuries, theologians have debated what these two promises really mean. Most agree they are eternal promises and depend solely upon the reliability of God. But most also surmise that the second one is a disclaimer or qualifier of the first. They assume God placed this later restriction on his first promise and argue that since God "destroyed" the world once by a flood, the sum total of these two promises is that He has only limited Himself by how He can destroy it the next time. That is, He is supposedly free to use any method other than water (such as: fire, colliding planets, nuclear bombs, or even bowling balls) to destroy it all or end it all as we know it. Or, is He free to do this? After all, what is the value of a promise?

What is at stake here is the fundamental question of the reliability of God. Nowhere else in the Bible does God take away from any of his other eternal promises. Let's think about this for a moment. If God or you or I can make a promise and then come back a little while later and diminish what we said, can this be considered trustworthy? Faithful?

Let me illustrate this point by being absurd. Suppose I go on a mad rampage and destroy my house by hacking up some or all the furniture and chopping holes in the walls with a long-handle ax. Then I promise my wife and kids that "Never again will I destroy all the furniture and the walls, as I have done. As long as the house endures [remains]." A few days later, however, I tell them, "Never again will all the furniture be cut to pieces and holes poked in the walls by a long-handle ax; never again will there be a long-handled ax to destroy the house."

What will I have promised? Would my second promise reduce the commitment of the first? Would the greater promise be diminished by the lesser? Would the first one then be null and void, freeing me to choose any other method (fire, bulldozer, bombs, chainsaw, or bowling balls)? If so, how could my wife and kids ever again trust one of my promises if all I had to do was come back a little later and change things by making a lesser promise or issuing a qualifying disclaimer? My family would never buy it, neither would yours, and neither should we. God is trustworthy and faithful. He is not playing games with his promises. We can rely fully on both of them.

Why not just take God's Word at face value here? If we do, his second promise does not compromise his first. He simply made two independent promises about the same topic separated by ten verses of scripture—not one promise plus a disclaimer. Each one stands on its own merits and is subject to its own contingencies.

Granted, God's second promise is contingent upon a flood method. There is no question about that. Special notice should be given, however, to the fact that planet Earth remained intact both during and after the flood; nor did time end, even though the world was said to have been destroyed.

God's first promise, conversely, is not contingent upon the phrase, "as I have done," but upon the conditional phrase, "as long as the earth endures [remains]." God did not say "as long as I allow the earth to endure." So how long does the earth endure [remain]? As we have already seen, the Bible tells us, "Generations come and generations go, but the earth endures [remains] forever" (Eccl. 1:4).

It is important to note again that God has never diminished any of his promises in the Bible, but only enhanced them. Likewise, no scripture can be used to negate or diminish another. They all fit together in harmony and consistency. This is part of God's divine perfection. And, we have many corroborating scriptures stating that not only is the world without end, but so are the moon, the sun, and the heavens—they endure [remain] forever, as well.

The second stanza of the classic hymn of the Church, "Great Is Thy Faithfulness," picks up on a portion of this great enduring truth from God's first promise to never again destroy the world:

> Summer and winter, and springtime and harvest,
> Sun, moon and stars in their courses above.
> Join with all nature in manifold witness,
> To Thy great faithfulness, mercy and love.
> Great is Thy faithfulness, Great is Thy faithfulness...[13]

---

[13] "Great Is Thy Faithfulness" by Thomas O. Chisholm (1866-1960) and William M. Runyan (1870-1957).

The Psalmist further writes, "Your faithfulness continues through all generations; you established the earth and it endures [forever]" (Psa. 119:90; also see Lam. 3:22-23).

In this regard, Moses, in the 14th century B.C., wrote by inspiration, "Know therefore that the Lord your God is God; he is the faithful God, keeping his covenant of love to a thousand generations of those who love him and keep his commands" (Deut. 7:9; also 1 Chron. 16:15-17; Psa. 105:7-10).

This passage is to be understood figuratively and as an understatement. But even if we reduce Moses' thousand generations to a literal level and assume that a generation is forty years, then that equals 40,000 years. Approximately 3,400 years have transpired since God directed Moses to write these words in the book of Deuteronomy. If my mathematics are correct, that leaves us with at least 36,600 years yet to go. So, what do you think people 100, 200, 5,000, 7,000 and 10,000 years from now will think of our 21st-century, end-of-the-world musings? Someday future generations may view our 21st century as a primitive and unenlightened time—especially on this topic of the end of the world.

Let's recap. God's plan since the flood has not been to deal with human sin by eliminating the human race or by destroying his creation. If we think otherwise, we've misunderstood his plan of redemption. "For God so loved the world that he gave his one and only Son . . .   For God did not send his Son into the world to condemn the world . . ." (John 3:16a, 17a). And neither should we condemn it by saying it's going to end, when inspired Scripture clearly states that it's without end and therefore not ever going to end.[14]

So why can we rest assured that the future stability and everlasting nature of the earth and the cosmos are secure? It's because they are grounded in the trustworthiness of the Almighty God who created the universe in the first place. As the Creator and Controller of the Universe, He has personally pledged to forever sustain and protect all life from total destruction by his grace and his great faithfulness? This promise includes all animal life, as well. So, in whom shall we believe? In God's

---

[14] The Greek word translated as "world" here is *kosmos*. In a narrow or wide sense, it can mean the earth, and/or by metonymy, the human race.

promises, grace, and great faithfulness? Or, in Hal Lindsey, Harold Camping, Nostradamus, the Mayans, and other endsayers who prophesy, predict, peddle, and merchandise worldwide catastrophe and destruction of all living things, even the entire universe, which certainly isn't contaminated by sin, is it?

Contending Paradigm #2). What about the "New Heaven and a New Earth?"

Doesn't the Book of Revelation's prophecy of a coming new heavens and a new earth teach or at least imply that this world is going to end someday (Rev. 21 & 22)? Likewise, what about Jesus' similar words, "Heaven and earth will pass away, but my words will never pass away" (Luke 21:33; Matt. 24:35)? "See," many exclaim, "that's a clear prediction that the earth is going to pass away!"

Something, however, that most Christians do not know is—*three different entities* in the Bible are called "heaven and earth." One of those entities would never pass away. Another had already passed away. A third would soon pass away and be made new. So which "heaven and earth" was the one that Jesus said would "pass away" and Revelation said would be made new?

Before you answer too quickly, let's take a closer look at these three different "heaven and earth" entities.[15]

Entity #1 – planet Earth and the cosmos creation (Gen 1:1; also Acts 4:24; 14:15-17). The first entity is the physical creation—the cosmos and terra firma—which God eternally created with divine perfection. As we have seen, this entity is without end—i.e., endures/remains forever.

Entity #2 – the old empire of Babylon (Isa. 13:13, 1, also 19-22). The second biblical entity called "heaven and earth" was the sixth-century-B.C empire of Babylon. It's destruction in 539 B.C. was depicted by the prophet Isaiah as a trembling and shaking of heavens and earth, respectively. "Therefore I will make the heavens tremble; and the earth will shake from its place at the wrath of the Lord Almighty, in the

---

[15] For a more extensive treatment, see my books, Noē, *The Perfect Ending for the World*, 279-319 and Noē, *The Greater Jesus*, 339-389.

day of his burning anger" (Isa. 13:13). How do we know this prophecy was speaking of Babylon, back then and there? Isaiah told us in the first verse of this chapter: "An oracle concerning Babylon that Isaiah son of Amoz saw:" (Isa. 13:1).

Entity #3 – the Old Covenant creation (Deut. 32:1; Isa. 1:2-3; 51:13, 15-16). For the proper and scriptural identification of this third entity termed "heaven and earth," let's utilize the Bible's own admonition, which is mentioned several times throughout Scripture: "Every matter must be established by the testimony of two or three witnesses" (2 Cor. 13:1; Deut 17:6; 19:15; Matt. 18:16; also see John 8:17 re "two witnesses").

Our *first witness* is labeled in the subheading of most Bibles, "The Song of Moses" (see Deut. 32:1-43). Specially notice how Moses begins his prophetic exhortation: "Listen, O heavens . . . Hear, O earth" (Deut. 32:1). To whom or what is Moses talking? In his introduction to this prophecy, Moses tells them and us it's for "all the elders of your tribes and all your officials" whom Moses had assembled before him "so that I can speak these words in their hearing and call heaven and earth to testify against them." (Deut. 31:28). Moses also tells them and us what this prophecy is about. It's about what will happen to Israel "in their latter [or last] days" (Deut 31:29, *KJV*).

Something, however, that most Christians do not know is – *three different entities* **in the bible are called "heaven and earth."**

For our *second witness*, turn to the book of Isaiah, chapter 1. Once again, the prophet starts his Old Testament exhortation with the very same words: "Hear, O heavens! Listen, O earth." (Isa. 1:2a). To whom or what is Isaiah directing his message? Seriously, did these two ancient prophets really expect the physical stars and planets to hear, and the global Earth (inanimate dirt, rocks, water, trees, etc.) to listen, take need, and be obedient? Of course not. Like Moses, Isaiah tells them and us that "O heavens" and "O earth" are simply other names for God's "children," or "my people" of Israel (Isa. 1:2b-3). They were the ones who could hear, listen, heed, and obey or not.

God also used this same symbolism in simile form in his promises to Abraham:

- "I will make your offspring like the dust of the earth" (Gen. 13:16).
- "Look at the heavens and count the stars . . . so shall your offspring be" (Gen. 15:5; also 22:17; Dan. 12:3).

Our *third witness* also comes from a short passage in the Book of Isaiah. In Isaiah 51:13-16 the prophet contrasts God's establishment of two different entities represented by "heaven and earth" terminology. We shall use the *KJV* here because it is more graphic and revealing than some other translations:

"And forgettest the Lord thy maker, that hath stretched forth the heavens, and laid the foundation of the earth; and hast feared continually every day because of the fury of the oppressor, as if he were ready to destroy? and where is the fury of the oppressor? The captive exile hasteneth that he may be loosed, and that he should not die in the pit, nor that his bread should fail. But I am the Lord thy God, that divided the sea, whose waves roared: The Lord of hosts is his name. And I have put my words in thy mouth, and I have covered thee in the shadow of mine hand, that I may plant the heavens, and lay the foundation of the earth, and say unto Zion, Thou art my people."

When Isaiah writes by inspiration: "And forgettest the Lord thy maker, that hath stretched forth the heavens, and laid the foundations of the earth," God, through his prophet, uses the past perfect form of the verbs translated "stretched" (*natah*) and "laid" (*suwm*) in recounting his creation of the physical heavens and *terra firma* Earth. Then verse 14, which begins with "the captive exile," speaks of bringing them out of exile in Egypt. But notice what happens in the next two verses when the verb form switches to the infinitive: "But I am the Lord thy God, that divided the sea, whose waves roared: The Lord of Hosts is his name. And I have put my words in thy mouth; I have covered thee in the shadow of mine hand, that I may plant the heavens, and lay the foundations of the earth, and may say unto Zion, 'Thou art my people'" (Isa. 51:15-16 *KJV*).

What a difference! It's a totally different "world" in meaning. In the second portion of this passage, God is still speaking to Israel. But here He says He gave them his Law ("words in thy mouth") and his covenant protection ("covered thee in the shadow of mine hand"). Next, He uses the infinitive form of the verbs (to "plant" [*nata*] and to "lay" [*suwm*]) to speak of forming a "heavens and earth" different from the ones mentioned in first verse 13. This latter "heavens and earth" He forms by the process of delivering his people, the Jews, from Egyptian slavery by parting the Red Sea, giving them the Mosaic Covenant on Mt. Sinai, and protecting them from their enemies.

It's important to emphasize that this second portion of the passage could not be referring to the physical creation (it is improperly translated by the *NIV* [4]), because the material heavens and earth existed long before the first Jewish exodus out of Egypt and the giving of the Mosaic Law on Mt. Sinai. Neither is God saying through Isaiah that He created the *terra firma* Earth for Israel to occupy since Gentiles occupied it as well. What God is saying in these two infinitive purpose clauses is He gave them the Law to establish a theocratic "heavens and earth." He gave his covenant to the Israelites to create their "world" of biblical Judaism—the Jewish religious system. That's how the Jews became God's covenant people.

God later confirmed this establishment process through another prophet using the same infinitive verb forms: "And at what instant I shall speak concerning a nation, and concerning a kingdom, to build and to plant it" (Jer. 18:9 *KJV*; see also Jer. 1:10; Eccl. 3:2).

The Jewish historian Josephus corroborates this 1st-century Jewish understanding. In his book *The Antiquities of the Jews*,[5] he describes how the Jews of Jesus' time looked upon their Temple as "a Heaven and

---

[4] *KJV, AMP* and *NAS* translate it properly. Perhaps the grammatically correct way didn't make sense to the *NIV* translators. But the more difficult and correct rendering does make sense when we understand what God is actually conveying here.

[5] Josephus, *The Antiquities of the Jews,* In William Whiston, trans. *The Works of Josephus* (Peabody, MA.: Hendrickson Publishers, 1987), book 3, chapter 6, paragraph 4, lines 122-126; also see Book 1, chapter 7, paragraph 7, lines 180-182.

earth." They believed their Temple was at the very center of the earth, and saw it as the place where heaven and earth came together, and where God met man. Josephus calls its outer tabernacle "an imitation of the system of the world" and "sea and land, on which men live." He terms the inner, Most Holy Place "a Heaven peculiar to God." The veil that separated the two "was very ornamental, and embroidered with all sorts of flowers which the earth produces."

In summary, two of these three "heavens and earth" entities proclaimed in the Bible have already ended. The other, as we've seen from Scripture, never ends.

Question: Which "heaven and earth" do you now think Jesus was talking about when He prophetically declared near the beginning of his earthly ministry, "Do not think that I have come to abolish the Law or the Prophets; I have not come to abolish them but to fulfill them. I tell you the truth, until heaven and earth disappear, not the smallest letter, not the least stroke of a pen, [one jot or one tittle – *KJV*] will be any means disappear [pass] from the Law until everything is accomplished" (Matt. 5:17-18)?

If we are sincere about seeking truth and understanding by unraveling the end, we cannot ignore or sidestep the plain meaning of Jesus' words here. Undeniably, He conjoined the disappearing/passing of the Law with two contingency clauses: 1) "Until heaven and earth disappear." 2) "Until everything is accomplished." Until then, not "the smallest letter" or "least stoke of a pen" (*NIV*) or not a "one jot" or a "one tittle, " (*KJV*) could pass away.

Another question: If the destruction of Babylon was called a shaking of "heavens . . . and the earth," why not also the destruction of Jerusalem and the Temple circa A.D. 70-73?

But if Jesus was referring to the physical universe and the *terra firma* Earth, which has not passed away, and/or if everything hasn't been accomplished and fulfilled yet, the inescapable conclusion must be—the Law of Moses is still in effect! That would mean God's people, or at least the Jews, are still under its authority! And if that is so, shouldn't they and/or we be performing animal sacrifices, celebrating Jewish feasts and rituals, observing Jewish dietary laws, and honoring the Jewish priesthood? Neither orthodox Jews nor the Christian Church have practiced these parts of the Law in over 1,900 years. But doesn't such a literal interpretation make complete sense?

Also consider this awkward conundrum. If as the Bible declares the physical earth and material universe were and are eternally established; and if Jesus was referring to *that* heaven and earth in this above passage, didn't He just contradict the Bible? Seriously, Jesus left no wiggle room. It is a case of all or nothing. Either *all* was accomplished (fulfilled), or *nothing* was accomplished (fulfilled). *All* passed away, or *nothing* passed away. If there is a single Old Testament promise or prophecy that's unfulfilled, or if the old heaven and earth did not disappear, then the Old Covenant and its Law system are still in effect. There is no legitimate escape from this simple conclusion and straightforward consequence.

If the destruction of Babylon was called a shaking of "heavens and the earth," why not also the destruction of Jerusalem and the Temple circa A.D. 70-73?

The scriptural conundrum disappears, however, when we understand that the "heaven and earth" Jesus was referring to was the Old Covenant Temple system, and not the physical earth and material universe. So, if that system did passed away, then the "heaven and earth" Jesus named also had to have pass away and all is accomplished. Would you agree, yet?

Moreover, the demise of the Temple and desolation of its vital institutions of the Law circa A.D. 70 was much more than "the smallest letter" or "least stoke of a pen" or a "one jot" or a "one tittle." It was the entire system of biblical Judaism—with one exception as we shall see shortly.

So in concluding the discarding of this second contending paradigm, let's see if we can find more New Testament confirmations or witnesses—via a quick Bible drill—that the heaven and earth Jesus was talking about was covenantal and not cosmic, did pass away, and was superseded by a new heaven and a new earth, a covenantal reality. And it all came to pass precisely *as* and *when* He had said it would—within the generation of his contemporaries.

Ten New Testament confirmations of a covenantal, not cosmic, nature of the end:

#1 – Paul wrote around A.D. 57 – *"Time is short"* **(1 Cor. 7:29) . . . . "The world in its present form is passing away" (1 Cor. 7:31).** If Paul was inspired and not deluded, whose time was short? What world was passing away back then? The answer to these two questions is key for determining the proper paradigm for eschatological fulfillment. Do you really believe he was referring to the end of the material universe or the destiny of the physical planet? How were they ending or "passing away" back then? One thing is for sure. A great crisis was nearing. And if Paul was referring to the Old Covenant "heaven and earth" Law system, then what he was saying did not fail to materialize.

#2 – The writer of Hebrews wrote around A.D. 65 – "By calling this covenant 'new,' he [God] has made the first one obsolete; and what is obsolete and aging will soon disappear" (Heb. 8:13).[16] *KJV* translates this as "ready to vanish away." Sounds familiar, doesn't it? And the writer here (probably Paul) is certainly talking in covenantal terms and not cosmic. History records that within five to seven years that "obsolete and aging" Old Covenant system (the world of biblical Judaism) did "soon disappear."

#3 – This writer again wrote – "The Holy Spirit was showing by this that the way into the Most Holy Place had not yet been disclosed as long as the first tabernacle was still standing. This is an illustration for the present time, indicating that the gifts and sacrifices being offered were not able to clear the conscience of the worshipper. They are only a matter of food and drink and various ceremonial washings—external regulations applying until the time of the new order" (Heb. 9:8-10). In other words, the new could not fully come until the old was fully removed. If this, too, is speaking of God destroying the Old Covenant "heaven and earth"—the world of biblical Judaism—would He not establish a new one to replace the old? Or would

---

[16] The writer of the Book of Hebrews is not identified in the text, or elsewhere in Scripture. And while there are differing opinions, I agree with many, if not most scholars, that, most likely, it was Paul.

He leave a multi-century void? As we shall see, the old "heaven and earth," which God had "planted," prefigured and linked directly into the new. And, indeed, the old did pass away and was changed. How did this happen?

#4 – The writer again wrote – "At that time his voice shook the earth, but now he has promised, 'Once more I will shake not only the earth but also the heavens' (Haggai 2:6). The words 'once more' indicate the removing of what can be shaken – that is created things – so that what cannot be shaken may remain. Therefore, since we are receiving a kingdom that cannot be shaken, let us be thankful, and so worship God acceptably with reverence and awe" (Heb. 12:26-28; Hag. 2:6; Isa. 13:13; 13:1; also see: Isa. 2:12, 19, 21; Joel 3:15-17). Here we see that this transition and transformation from one covenant world to the other would occur through a "once more" shaking process. So when was the last time "heaven and earth" were shaken? As we saw earlier, it was the destruction of Babylon in 539 B.C. as prophesied by the pre-exilic prophet Isaiah (see again Isa. 13:1, 13). But the writer in this passage is quoting the post-exilic prophet, Haggai. So, once again, I ask you, if the destruction of Babylon is depicted using heaven and earth language, why shouldn't the destruction of Jerusalem also be spoken of in like manner? Furthermore, doesn't this same "removal" scenario perfectly fit with Daniel 12:7's prophecy of "the power of the holy people" being "finally broken?" Speaking of that final act . . .

#5 – Jesus foretold – "Therefore I tell you that the kingdom of God will be taken away from you and given to a people who will produce its fruit. . . . When the chief priests and the Pharisees heard Jesus' parables, they knew he was talking about them" (Matt. 21:43, 45, 40). One of the last parts of the Jewish "power" being "finally broken" (Dan. 12:7) was the kingdom being taken away from them and given to another people. Back then and there, they knew that Jesus was talking about "them" So when was this to happen? In verse 40, Jesus told them it would be "when the owner of the vineyard comes." The Jews also knew from one of their favorite passages, Isaiah 5:1-7, that this owner was God. So, if this coming of God has not happened, even yet today, why doesn't the kingdom still belong to the Jews? Even more poignant, if possible, I know of no verse promising to give the kingdom back to the Jews.

#6 – Jesus further foretold – "When you see Jerusalem surrounded by armies, you will know that its desolation is near. Then let those who are in Judea flee to the mountains, let those in the city get out, and let those in the country not enter the city. For this is the time of punishment in fulfillment of all that has been written. . . . I tell you the truth, this generation will certainly not pass away until all these things have happened" (Luke 21:20-22, 32; also see Matt. 24:15-21; Luke 4:18-19; Isa. 61:1-2). I call this passage of Scripture "the hermeneutic or paradigm of Jesus." Most significantly, in the New Testament, "it is written" means the Old Testament Scriptures. Therefore, "all that has been written" means all of the Old Testament prophecies (see Luke 24:44, for instance). These prophecies would include all of Daniel's end-time prophecies, all of Isaiah's prophecies of the coming of the "new heavens and a new earth" (Isa. 65:17-19; 66:22), and all of "The Song of Moses" about what would happen to Israel in its "latter/last days" (Deut 31:29-32:1-43), and "what their end will be . . . . for they are a perverse generation" (Deut. 32:20, 29, 5), which is exactly what Jesus and Peter called them (see Matt. 17:17; Luke 9:41; 11:50-51; Acts 2:40). So when was all this to happen? Jesus said, within his "this generation" (Luke 21:32; Mark 13:30; Matt. 24:34). The biblical fact is, and as we shall continue to see, this timeframe is the fulfillment context and paradigm the Bible consistently places upon itself—consistently!

#7 – Peter wrote – "But the day of the Lord will come like a thief. The heavens will disappear with a roar; the elements will be destroyed by fire, and the earth and everything in it will be laid bare. Since everything will be destroyed in this way, what kind of people ought you to be? You ought to live holy and godly lives as you look forward to the day of God and speed its coming. That day will bring about the destruction of the heavens by fire, the elements will melt in the heat. But in keeping with his promise we are looking forward to a new heaven and a new earth, the home of righteousness" (2 Pet. 3:10-13). This Bible text is the one most quoted to support a future and universal cataclysm for end of the world / the end of time. But once again, to which "heaven and earth" entity is Peter referring that will be destroyed, disappear, and be made new?

Since I've addressed this passage extensively in a previous book,[17] I'll only ask and address this one aspect here. What are these "elements" that Peter said were to be "destroyed by fire" and "melt in the heat" [or "with fervent heat"– *KJV*]? Most interpreters assume they are either the four physical substances that the ancients believed made up the material world (earth, water, air, and fire) or the modern chemical elements of the universe as they appear on a chemist's periodic table.

Two textual problems, however, are inherent with these assumptions. First, neither reading properly translates the Greek word in question. A quick glance into a Greek concordance—not into an English dictionary—will dispel any doubt as to the primary meaning of this word for those who first received it. The Greek word for "elements" is *stoicheion*. It means something orderly in arrangement, a principle, or a rudiment. It's derived from the verb *stoicheo*, which means to arrange in regular line, to march in (military) rank (keep step), or, figuratively, to conform to virtue and piety or to walk orderly.

The second textual problem is that this word is *never* used to refer to the material creation in any other New Testament occurrence or context. As we compare Scripture with Scripture, we find its uses elsewhere in the New Testament will give us a clearer perspective of its intended meaning here. In Hebrews 5:12 and Colossians 2:8, 20, the same Greek word *stoicheion* is translated as "rudiments," "rudimentary and elemental teachings," "elementary principles" or "truths," and "first" or "basic principles" in various Bible translations (such as the *KJV, AMP, NAS, and NIV*). Paul uses the word twice in his letter to the Galatians (vv. 4:3, 9) to mean elementary teachings, elemental things, or basic principles. He says that under the Law, people were held in bondage to these "elements of the world." Paul certainly didn't mean that these Old Covenant Jews were under bondage to the physical substances of the material creation (earth, water, air, fire, or chemical matter). He meant that they were under bondage to the Law system, its institutions, its priesthood, and its sacrificial rituals. Paul then explains, in verses 4-5, that this was why "God sent his Son, born of a woman, born under the law, to redeem those under the law, that we might receive the full rights

---

[17] Noē, *The Perfect Ending for the World*, 298-306.

of sons." He wasn't saying that they would be freed from the physical world. Peter's meaning for "elements" is the same as Paul's. *It has nothing to do with the physical creation.*[18]

#8 – John in Revelation was shown and instructed to write about – "Mystery Babylon the great the mother of Prostitutes and of the abominations of the earth" (Rev. 17:5ff). The Book of Revelation could have been subtitled "A Tale of Two Cities." That's because the question of "Who is this Babylon?" is one of the contextualizing keys for unlocking all of Revelation's mysteries. But in John's day and time and his receiving of Revelation's prophecy, the ancient city of Babylon no longer existed. It had been abandoned between the 3rd and 2nd centuries B.C. and became a desolate and insignificant pile of rubble. Nor does it exist today.

Nevertheless, the proper identification of the doomed harlot-city Babylon in the Revelation sets the fulfillment and understanding context for the whole of its prophecy. Without this proper contextualizing, however, readers and interpreters are bound to err. And so most have. (We'll cover seven more contextualizing keys in Chapter 14.) They believe the symbol of Babylon in Revelation 17-19 represents Rome, New York City, or any city anywhere, or commercialism in general. But again, by utilizing the basic interpretative principle of letting "Scripture interpret Scripture," we can demonstrate that this Babylon actually represented, first and foremost, 1st-century Jerusalem. Once again, this understanding is in perfect harmony with the seven other scriptural confirmations presented above. This identification can be aptly demonstrated using four simple syllogisms:[19]

---

[18] Reformed scholar, Peter J. Leithart agrees. He writes that *"stoicheia . . .* refers to the life of Israel under the dietary, sacrificial and purity regulations imposed by the Torah . . . . meant adherence to animal sacrifice, the keeping of days, the avoidance of contamination." Peter J. Leithart, *Defending Constantine* (Downers Grove, IL.: IVP Academic, 2010), 324-325.

[19] For more see, Don K. Preston, *Who Is This Babylon* (Ardmore, OK.: n.p. n.d.) 208-210. Also see N.T Wright, *Jesus and the Victory of God*, vol. 2 (London, Great Britain; Society for Promoting Christian Knowledge, 1996) 323, 354.

Major premise #1: Five times this Babylon is called "O great city" (Rev. 18:10, 16, 19; 16:19; 17:18). Twice it is called "great city" (Rev. 18:18, 21).

Minor premise #1: "The great city" is "where also their Lord was crucified . . . which is figuratively called Sodom . . . ." (Rev. 11:8). And Jerusalem is the only city ever metaphorically called Sodom (Deut. 32:32; Isa. 1:10; Ezek. 16:44-58).

Conclusion: Jerusalem is Revelation's Babylon.

~

Major premise #2: Babylon was guilty of "the blood of the prophets" (Rev. 17:6; 18:24; 16:6).

Minor premise #2: According to Jesus and Paul, only Jerusalem killed the prophets (Matt. 23:34-37; Luke 13:33; 11:47-51; 1 Thess. 2:15-16).

Conclusion: Jerusalem is Revelation's Babylon.

~

Major premise #3: John's people are commanded to "Come out of her, my people, so that you will not share in her sins, so that you will not receive any of her plagues" (Rev. 18:4).

Minor premise #3: The only city Jesus ever commanded his followers to flee from is Jerusalem—when they saw two specific signs (Matt. 24:15-16; Luke 21:20-21). Early church Father Eusebius recorded that this departure happened and that no Christians were trapped and destroyed in the siege and destruction of Jerusalem in AD 70.[20]

Conclusion: Jerusalem is Revelation's Babylon.

~

---

[20] Eusebius, *Ecclesiastical History*, Book 3, chapter 5; from Edersheim, *Life and Times of Jesus the Messiah*, p. 138, Peabody, Mass.: Hendrickson; reprint of 1886 ed.

Major premise #4: This Babylon would be destroyed (Rev. 18:2, 8, 10, 11, 17, 19-23).

Minor premise #4: The only city Jesus said would be destroyed was Jerusalem—it would be "left to you desolate" (Matt.23:38) with "not one stone . . . left on another" (Matt. 24:2).

Conclusion: Jerusalem is Revelation's Babylon.

David Chilton concurs and proclaims that "the evidence that the prophetic Babylon was Jerusalem is nothing short of overwhelming."[21] Theologian Donald Guthrie suggests that "the symbol of Babylon was chosen because it stood for the oppressors of God's people."[22] McKenzie agrees and adds that "Harlot Babylon represents those of the old covenant community who rejected Jesus in favor of the temple system."[23]

The bottom line is this. The proper identification of the doomed harlot-city Babylon sets the fulfillment and understanding context for the whole Book of Revelation. In 1st-century Jerusalem, apostate Judaism was persecuting God's emerging Church. And only one city in the world, at only one time in history, ever matched or will match Jesus' instruction to flee and these above descriptions. It was the city in which the "Lord was crucified." That city—and the apostate religious system it represented—was the city God was calling his people, back then and there, to "come out of."[24]

Additionally, and for these and many other reasons, as we shall further see in Chapter 14, I agree with a growing number of reputable scholars who have seriously studied the dating issue (i.e., when was the Book of Revelation was most likely written) that "a date in either AD 65

---

[21] David Chilton, *The Days of Vengeance* (Ft. Worth, TX.: Dominion Press, 1987), 363.
[22] Donald Guthrie, *New Testament Theology* (Downers Grove, IL.: Inter-Varsity Press, 1981) 816.
[23] Duncan W. McKenzie, *The Antichrist and the Second Coming* (n.l., Xulon Press, 2012), 30.
[24] In Chapter 8 of my book *The Greater Jesus*, you will find that the modern-day reality of this symbolic Babylon is universally relevant in today's post-A.D.-70 world.

or early 66 would seem most suitable."[25] In my opinion, the weight of evidence greatly favors a pre-A.D.-70 "early-date" writing.

Consequently, as reformed theologian R.C. Sproul ventures, "if Revelation was written before A.D. 70, then a case could be made that it describes chiefly those events leading up to Jerusalem's fall."[26] And Revelation's city-of-Babylon symbol does not represent a present or future city, *per se*, as the "late-date" (A.D. 95-96) theorists believe it still points to and which is yet to be built and destroyed.

#9 – John's further writing in Revelation 21 and 22 of the coming of "a new heaven and a new earth." I shall defer comment on these passages until we reach Chapter 14 and finish our contextualizing of Revelation's whole prophecy—except for this one, think-about-it tidbit. Six hundred years before Christ, Daniel was instructed to "close up and seal the words of the scroll until the time of the end" (Dan. 12:4, 9). In the Apostle John's time, he is given the opposite instruction for his Book of Revelation: "Do not seal up the words of the prophecy of this book, because the time is near" (Rev. 22:10 [at hand – *KJV*]). Since both Daniel's and Revelation's prophecies speak of the same end, do you now have a better idea for the reason behind these two entirely different instructions?

#10 – Lastly, Jesus clarified – "Heaven and earth will pass away, but My words will never pass away" (Matt. 24:35; Luke 21:33). Given everything we've covered above, I hope you can now grasp a hold of this last confirmation. Surely, it should not be so hard to imagine Jesus sitting on the Mount of Olives a short distance across the small Kidron valley from the Temple, gesturing toward the Jewish Temple complex, and speaking forth these above, prophetic, and most relevant words. The historical fact is, everything from that Old Covenant "heaven and earth" system and world has passed away/disappeared—the Temple, animal sacrifices, the priesthood, the genealogies, the feasts—except for one thing [at this moment in the MPC seminar I'm holding up my Bible and thumb-fanning through its pages as the visual answer]—God's Word,

---

[25] Kenneth L. Gentry, Jr., *Before Jerusalem Fell* (Atlanta, GA.: American Vision, 1998), 336.
[26] Sproul, *The Last Days According to Jesus*, 132.

both Old and New Testaments, and in perfect fulfillment of Jesus' words hereto!

All this divine perfection and much more, which we shall be covering in greater detail in the chapters ahead, is in perfect harmony with Daniel 12:7's "historical setting and defining characteristic of the "time of the end . . . when the power of the holy people is [was] finally broken" and "all these things are [were] completed" (see Chapter 10). And even though this 1st-century, Jewish, and covenantal paradigm is the fulfillment context the Bible consistently places on itself for the divinely "appointed time of the end" as it occurred within human history and not at history's supposed termination, there are two more contending paradigms with which we must deal.

Contending Paradigm #3). What about the distinction between Israel and the Church?

This section will be the second and final section that I've taken almost directly from my dissertation. Again, I do this to give you a more direct feel and hands-on flavor for the confusion and conflict surrounding this highly sensitive paradigm as you hear scholarly interactions from others besides myself, and in their own words.

Classic dispensationalism's unique and sharp distinction between Israel and the Church is a paradigm. It produces two separate peoples of God with two different inheritances and two different destinies. This dualistic paradigm drives their dichotomizing-postponement hermeneutic. As Poythress has noted, this paradigm is the basis for their self-proclaimed "rightly dividing of Scripture" into two categories of passages—one for literal fulfillment for Israel and the other for spiritual fulfillment for the Church.[27] This distinction, as Mathison stresses, "is at the heart of that system of theology" and is its "cornerstone."[28] But he also astutely points out these two facts. It "cannot be found prior to the nineteenth century" and "the early church fathers are almost unanimous in their identification of the church and Israel."[29]

---

[27] Poythress, *Understanding Dispensationalists*, 24.
[28] Mathison, *Dispensationalism*, 8.
[29] Ibid., 13.

The weakness of this third paradigm, like the other two we've covered above, is that it is not revealed from Scripture. Instead, it's imposed upon Scripture from without. This Israel-Church dichotomy is a non-revelational device, a speculative theory, and a human invention. As we saw in Chapter 3, John Nelson Darby has been credited with originating it, or at the least as Kyle underscores, he "systematized" and "spread" its "major principles throughout the English speaking world."[30] Later, Scofield, Chafer, Ryrie, Lindsey, and now LaHaye and many others popularized it.

> ... this paradigm is the basis for their self-proclaimed "rightly dividing of Scripture" into two categories of passages—one for literal fulfillment for Israel and the other for spiritual fulfillment for the Church.

Most revealingly, however, fellow premillennialists recognize the weakness of this paradigm and its consequential dichotomizing hermeneutic. As we've seen, historical premillennialists do not subscribe to this paradigm and progressive dispensationalists are softening their stance and backing away from it.[31] David Turner, again the chairperson of my dissertation committee, perceptively writes: "I would not accept the Darby/Scofield view which overstresses the distinction between Israel and the Church." Turner is also correct in noting that the " antithetical approach which identifies the two is hardly more adequate."[32]

Make no mistake, Scripture does not support two peoples of God, two plans, and two destinies—past, present, or future. This dualistic speculation is a severe departure from the divinely revealed plan of a

---

[30] Richard Kyle, *The Last Days Are Here Again* (Grand Rapids, MI.: Baker Books, 1998), 74.
[31] Darrell L. Bock, "The Kingdom of God in New Testament Theology," in David W. Baker. ed., *Looking into the Future* (Grand Rapids, MI.: Baker Academic, 2001), 29-30.
[32] David L. Turner, "'Dubious Evangelism'? A Response to John Gerstner's Critique of Dispensationalism," *Grace Theological Journal*, 12.2 (1992), 272. We shall cover "replacement theology" shortly.

continuity of oneness (Eph. 2:11-16; 4:4-5; Gal. 3:28; Col. 3:11; also Rom. 11:17-24).[33]

God's Word is emphatic on this matter. From the beginning, there has only been a *oneness*—*one* Garden of Eden, *one* tree of life, *one* Noah's ark, *one* ark of the covenant, *one* Tabernacle, *one* Temple, *one* priesthood, *one* hope, *one* faith, *one* Spirit, *one* baptism, *one* bride, *one* household, *one* flock, *one* body depicted by *one* olive tree into which believing Gentiles were grafted and unbelieving Jews broken off, but can be regrafted in. There is only *one* everlasting New Covenant promised, *one* "time of the end," *one* salvation that is of the Jews, and *one* nation or people of God. This *oneness* has been consistently maintained throughout God's covenants and/or dispensations. It has never been divided or disconnected.

In this manner, believing Jews and Gentiles are united together as equal heirs of God's blessings and equal partakers of God's promises in *one* body through the *one* Messiah. This union of Jew-Gentile *oneness* was the goal of God's *one*, completed program of redemption. That is why "in Christ," the distinction between Jew and Gentile has been utterly done away and *one*, New Covenant people formed (see Rom. 10:12; Gal. 3:26-29; Eph. 2:14-22; 3:6; 4:4; Col. 3:15; John 17:21; 1 Cor. 12:12-13). Jew-Gentile unity was the bottom line.

Who are we to put ethnic division back? There is no such thing as an exempted group of people. God's grand purpose was not to draw more boundaries or to put up or extend another wall of partition between Jews and Gentiles, but to make all *one* in Christ—then, there, and forever (Eph. 1:10). Jews must come to God in exactly the same way as Gentiles do. This Christological unity and *oneness* continuity is the fulfillment of the Abrahamic promise from Genesis to Revelation that "all peoples of earth will be blessed through you" (Gen. 12:3b; also see: 18:18; 22:18; Gal. 3:8; Isa. 49:6; Rev. 21 & 22). It is the mystery Paul made known

---

[33] Ryrie argues that in Ephesians 2:12-15 the "Gentiles are expressly said to be excluded from the blessings peculiar to Israel" and that "Paul does not say that once having believed, these Gentiles now come into the Israelite blessings, but rather that God has brought about a new thing, the new man in Christ Jesus." (Charles C. Ryrie, *The Basis of the Premillennial Faith* (Neptune, NJ.: Loizeaux Bros, 1953), 64). This is an example of his dichotomizing hermeneutic in action. It forces him to reach such conclusions.

(Eph. 3:3-6). Thus, biblical faith became truly universal in the 1st century. All physical Jews and Gentiles are invited to become citizens of that *one* nation and *one* people of God via God's *one* and only way of salvation.

Furthermore, God's *one* inclusive plan of redemption does not await a future millennium or tribulation period. Let us clearly understand that "Christ has become a servant of the Jews on behalf of God's truth, to confirm the promises made to the patriarchs so that the Gentiles may glorify God for his mercy" (Rom. 15:8-9). This understanding saves us from the error that Christianity is separate from the Jewish promises. Perhaps, we would be well-advised in this instance to *apply* the admonition, "What God has joined together, let man not separate [put asunder]" (Matt. 19:6 [*KJV*]).

So even though God chose Israel out of all the nations (Amos 3:2) to be a people for Himself, a witness to the nations, the channel for his revelation, and through whom the Messiah would come, the whole nation of Israel never was "God's Chosen People."[34] In Old Covenant times, only the righteous, faithful remnant in the midst of the greater Israel was "God's Chosen People"—i.e., the Israel within Israel (Rom. 9:6, 27). In the New Covenant, most non-dispensationalists feel that God's faithful people are now called "the Israel of God" (Gal. 6:16).[35] But classic dispensationalists rightly content that "no passage" in the New Testament identifies "Israel with the Church." Unfortunately, they wrongly insist that "in every case, the term is used of the nation Israel or of the believing remnant which has become part of the body of Christ."[36]

Another fact is that the Bible contains six or seven different entities that are literally called "Israel." They are: the man Israel (Jacob), the ten northern tribes, the southern kingdom, the twelve tribes, the nation, the

---

[34] Classic dispensationalists disagree. See Charles C. Ryrie, *The Final Countdown* (Wheaton, IL.: Victor Books, 1982), 44.

[35] Hoch, *All Things New*, 254. Ryrie admits that "the grammar is not definitive" in this verse. The Greek word χαί could be translated as either *even* or *and*. Translating it as *even* "would support the amillennial interpretation." Translating it as *and* "would support the premillennial view." He rightly concludes that "an absolute decision cannot be made from the verse itself." (Ryrie, *The Basis of the Premillennial View*, 68-69).

[36] Ryrie, *The Basis of the Premillennial Faith*, 69-70.

faithful remnant—the true Israel (Rom. 9:6, 27; 11:6; Gal. 4:29),[37] and possibly the Church Israel (Gal. 6:16).

... God's *one* inclusive plan of redemption does not await a future millennium or tribulation period.

Whatever term or terms we use for "God's people,"[38] believing Gentiles were actually grafted into this believing and mostly Jewish remnant. They were not grafted into the unbelieving Israel (Rom. 11:17-24). Moreover, they were grafted in "among the others" (Rom. 11:17) and made *one*—not "one" and a "one(a)" per the modified but still dichotomizing progressive dispensationalist notion.[39] That is why today, neither the modern-day nation nor all ethnic Jews worldwide should be considered "God's Chosen People" or "the Israel of God." Who counts as the true Israel, the children of the promise, was not and is not determined by a blood-line or a race-line, but always and only by a faith-line which transcends the natural descendancy realm. Nowadays, Abraham's real descendants ("seed") are believers in Jesus Christ, whether they are racially Jews or Gentiles. We are all on equal footing. This is the promised and ultimate fulfillment of biblical prophecy. Consequently, there is no other stage of fulfillment needed or to come.

Hence Ladd is correct, therefore, when he cites Jeremiah 4:4 and Deuteronomy 10:15-16 and proclaims that "here plainly is the concept of an Israel within Israel, of a spiritual Israel within national Israel."[40] In another book he identifies the "true people of God" in Old Testament times as those "within the faithless nation a remnant of believers who were the object of God's care."[41] Paul alludes to this same truth in Romans 9:6: "For not all who are descended from Israel are Israel."

---

[37] Hoch, *All Things New*, 253.
[38] Ibid., 254-255.
[39] Ibid., 261.
[40] George Eldon Ladd, *The Presence of the Future* (Grand Rapids., MI.: Eerdmans, 1974), 74.
[41] Ladd, *A Theology of the New Testament*, 106. Also see, Hoch, *All Things New*, 307. But Hoch sees the remnant as exclusively Jewish. He maintains that while this remnant "continued in the Church" through "the Jews . . . who believed the gospel and were added to the church," it will only be "enlarged to

Jesus Christ was an Israelite in the fullest sense. And, as Poythress rightly notes, "the church receives the complete fullness of God's blessings through Christ (Eph. 1:23; Col. 2:10), including being made coheirs with Christ (Rom. 8:17) . . . We are sons of Abraham because he is (Gal. 3:29)."[42] This emphasis of our "union with Christ means being part of one people of God."[43] This *oneness* realization is the biblical strength that must be kept and not diluted, denied, or manipulated. By God's grace, we were and are grafted into the community of God's people as a branch to a tree (Rom. 11:17-18).

Unfortunately, some, like Sailhamer, needlessly wrestle with the notions that "if Israel and the church are the same, then God's promises made to Israel are fulfilled in the church." But then "if they are not the same, then God's promise to Israel of land and blessing are still in effect for them."[44] But neither of his propositions are correct. Of course, a corrective depends on how "Israel" and the "Church" are defined. The political nation of Israel and the "Church" (meaning true believers) are two distinct entities and not unified as one in God's purposes and plans. But, again, it was the by-faith, mostly Jewish remnant within nationalistic Israel in Old Testament times into which Gentile believers were grafted in New Testament times. King appropriately clarifies the

---

include the majority of the nation of Israel at the second advent of Christ (Rom. 11:26)." Therefore, he asserts, this Jewish "remnant of Israel composed of Jewish Christians is present in the church," but it is not the entire Church. (Ibid., 308). One problem with this notion is that Gentiles were added to this Jewish remnant group during OT times. Blaising and Bock, however, seem to equivocate on their concept of this remnant. In one place, they see both Jews and Gentiles as part of this present remnant and with equal blessings (Blaising and Bock, *Progressive Dispensationalism*, 280). But elsewhere, they contend for two remnants—the "remnant of Israel" and "the remnant of the Gentiles" (Ibid., 295).

[42] Poythress, *Understanding Dispensationalists*, 127.
[43] Ibid., 129.
[44] John H. Sailhamer, *Biblical Prophecy* (Grand Rapids, MI.: Zondervan, 1998), 77. Fulfillment of the land promise is contested but beyond the scope of this book. For different non-fulfillment and fulfillment perspectives see: Ryrie, *The Basis of the Premillennial Faith*, 60-61,73-74; Ryrie, *The Final Countdown*, 47. Compare with: Don K. Preston, *Israel: 1948: Countdown to Nowhere* (Ardmore, OK.: n.p., 2002), 7-10; 31-39.

reason why Christ was "a stumblingblock" for the Jew. It was "not because the gospel put Israel's future on hold, but because it opened up the true meaning of Israel's promise."[45]

On the other hand, the amillennial, postmillennial, and historic premillennial idea of replacement theology is also a weakness to be discarded. But even Ladd has fallen for it. While he correctly recognizes the "remnant" and "the concept of an Israel within Israel, of a spiritual Israel within national Israel. As the faithful people within the faithless nation,"[46] he also claims that "the Jewish nation . . . has therefore been set aside as the people of God and is to be replaced by a new people."[47] The fact is that the phrase "replacement theology" is a poor choice of words, a misnomer, as well as an erroneous concept. Better terminology might be "expansion theology." Here are three reasons why:

First, God's promises to Abraham were not only unconditional, they also are "irrevocable" (Rom. 11:29; also 11:1-2) and "everlasting" (Gen. 17:7). But they were not promised to, nor just for, nationalistic Israel. Their scope was for "all nations [families] of the earth" (Gen. 12:3). And even though these promises cannot be disannulled or broken, God has the sovereign right to determine how and for whom his promises are fulfilled (Exod. 33:19; Rom. 9:15-18).

> **. . . the amillennial, postmillennial, and historic premillennial idea of replacement theology is also a weakness to be discarded.**

The Mosaic covenant, on the other hand, was conditional, became obsolete, and disappeared (Heb.8:13). In the New Covenant, God continued what He had been doing all along but further clarified the by-faith criteria for who is "God's chosen people." Consequently, inclusiveness expanded just as He had promised (Isa. 45:22, 25; 54:1-3; Psa. 22:27; Hos. 1:10; 2:23; Luke 13:29; Rom. 9:25-26; 15:8-12). From then on, much greater numbers of Jews and Gentiles, alike, from all nations and ethnic groups entered in, and without the necessity of

---

[45] King, *The Cross and the Parousia of Christ*, 192.
[46] Ladd, *The Presence of the Future*, 73-74.
[47] Ibid., 249.

circumcision, becoming a Jew, or coming under the Law (Rom. 2 & 3; Eph. 2:14-19; 3:6). All barriers, not just some, were removed and the universality of "God's chosen people" was greater and ultimately established.

Secondly, since the New Covenant method of Gentile inclusion was not an entirely new thing, God has always had, and always will have, but one continuous people. Throughout the Abrahamic, Mosaic, and New Covenants, individuals could always be broken off or grafted in. This is the by-faith continuity for God's righteous remnant of all ages (Heb. 11). It is an unbroken legacy of faith. In this regard, the "Church," as an entity, has always existed as the "people of God." This righteous remnant progressed through covenantal history to its fulfillment in Christ. That is why the Jew-Gentile Church was not a totally new and distinct work of God. He had a people before Christ—some were not circumcised in the flesh but all were circumcised in the heart (Deut. 10:16; 30:6; Jer. 4:4; Rom. 2:29)—and an expanded group of people after Christ (Gal. 3:16-18). The transition group was Jesus' 1st-century Jewish disciples. They belonged to both the Old and New Covenants. This remnant continuity and superseding relationship is the proof that God has not abandoned or replaced his people. There was and is no discontinuity to resolve. The fullness and perfection of God's plan of redemption was achieved through this by-faith continuity in which "salvation is of the Jews" (John 4:22).[48]

Thirdly, in the New Testament, many feel the Church is equated with Israel (Gal. 6:16; Rom. 9:6, 24-29) and Israel with the Church (Matt. 18:17; Acts 7:38; Heb. 2:12).[49] This eschatological linkage and covenant-determined title needs to be taken seriously.

---

[48] But Hoch argues for a dichotomy in that "Gentiles share with believing Israel simply by faith alone, while believing Israel enters into the blessing both by faith and by covenant privilege." (Hoch, *All Things New*, 316.)

[49] Hoekema, *The Bible and the Future*, 196-201. But Ryrie argues that the second "Israel" of Romans 9:6 is not spiritual Israel (the Church). I agree. It was the faithful remnant. But then he claims that "Gentile Christians are never included in the designation *Israel*." I disagree. They could become part through the proselyte laws. Finally, he insists that "it means that being an Israelite by natural birth does not assure one of the life and favor promised the true Israelite who approaches God by faith." I agree. (Ryrie, *The Basis of the Premillennial Faith*, 67-68).

In sum, many modern-day interpreters subscribe to "replacement theology" and recognize no distinction between the true Israel of God and the Church today. There is, however, much distinction between the modern-day nation of Israel and the Church, as well as between Jews and Gentiles outside of Christ. But "in Christ" Jews and Gentiles are *one* nation (Deut. 32:21; Rom. 10:19; Matt. 21:43; 1 Pet. 2:9,10), and the continuing covenant community of God's people throughout history. This continuing continuity confirms that God has never abandoned, rejected, or replaced his "Chosen People" (Rom. 11:1). This perspective validates why "God is no respecter of persons." He "accepts men from every nation . . . ." (Acts 10:34-35), not based on birth but on *re*-birth. They are grafted in, added to and among (Rom. 11:16-17), and not a replacement of anyone. Smith has it right: "the identity of the people of God is essentially the same in both Testaments."[50] Thus, "replacement theology's" displacement or transference notion is a weakness and refuted. God is equally interested in all people of all nations, and He always has been.

For these reasons and more, I agree with Mathison that "the dispensational doctrine of two separate bodies of believers is biblically indefensible."[51] Again, not one verse in the Bible validates this claim. Likewise, progressive modifications that rightly "reject . . .radical discontinuity"[52] but still maintain a dualism of sorts are also to be discarded. Similarly, the amillennial, postmillennial, and historic premillennial assertion of replacement theology is also a weakness that must be dropped. Oneness of God's people throughout Old and New Testament history is the strength to be kept.

<u>Kingdom postponement</u>

A related byproduct of this dichotomizing Israel-Church dichotomy is the classic dispensational idea that the kingdom Jesus was bringing was withdrawn and postponed by God when it was rejected by the 1st-century Jews and they crucified Him. Since one's theology of the

---

[50] Ralph L. Smith, *Old Testament Theology* (Nashville, TN.: Broadman & Holman Publishers, 1993), 90.
[51] Mathison, *Dispensationalism*, 37.
[52] Hoch, *All Things New*, 261.

kingdom of God plays a critical role in the eschatological debate and directly relates to one's position on Christ's *parousia*, we must briefly address it.

Please be assured, as Adams affirms, that this "postponement theory" is a "pillar of the dispensational system."[53] Sailhamer describes it this way:

> The Old Testament prophecies of the coming kingdom of God began to be fulfilled in Christ's day, but after his death and resurrection, those fulfillments were 'put on hold' until the days when Christ's return draws near. That is, when Israel rejected Jesus as their Messiah, God cast them off for a while—the "church age"—but he will not cast them off forever. When Christ returns to establish his kingdom here on earth, God will again work through his people Israel, and all the Old Testament prophecies will be fulfilled in the Millennium."[54]

He further stipulates that when the kingdom was withdrawn and postponed, the Church was set up instead as "the 'mystery' form of his coming kingdom."[55] Progressive dispensationalist Turner, on the other hand, sees "a major discontinuity" arising in the arena of "progressive revelation" if "the kingdom announced in the NT is not to be equated with that kingdom promised in the OT." He calls "untenable" the idea of "an emergency 'Plan B' which replaced the original kingdom program" and claims that any "postponement . . . experience" was only "from a human perspective"[56]—whatever that means.

But a withdrawal or postponement of the kingdom has no valid scriptural support.[57] Moreover, this teaching is clearly contradicted by the continuing testimony of Scripture. Below are nine scriptural reasons

---

[53] Jay E. Adams, *The Time Is at Hand* (Phillipsburg, NJ.: Presbyterian and Reformed, 1966), 3.
[54] Sailhamer, *Biblical Prophecy*, 85.
[55] Ibid., 68. Progressives Blaising and Bock also contend for this "mystery form" (Blaising and Bock, *Progressive Dispensationalism*, 262.
[56] David L. Turner, "The Continuity of Scripture and Eschatology: Key Hermeneutical Issues." *Grace Theological Journal*, 6.2 (1985), 285.
[57] We addressed the "delay theory" of Christ's return in Chapter 7, pp-125-127.

to reject this postponement, this paradigm, and this dichotomizing-hermeneutic-producing notion:
1. The New Testament writers know of no such frustration in God's plan. Moreover, Jesus' death was exactly in accordance to plan (John 2:4; 17:1). Guthrie concurs that "there is complete absence of any idea that the death of Jesus would be catastrophic to the fulfillment of his mission, indeed quite the reverse."[58] Peter makes this quite clear in his first sermon when he declared that Jesus "was handed over to you by God's set purpose [i.e., definite plan] and foreknowledge" (Acts 2:23; also see 3:18). Ladd also verifies that Jesus' rejection and death "was not a mere accident but a factor in God's redemptive purpose." God's program did not get knocked off track, postponed, or fail. Nor did He have to settle for a "Plan B" and instigate the Church, instead. Rather, Christ's passion was "the means used by God to bring salvation to the Gentiles."[59]
2. The Apostle Paul, traveling around the Roman Empire on his three missionary journeys, some twenty and thirty years following this supposed withdrawal / postponement event, was "boldly and without hindrance" preaching "the kingdom of God" and "about the Lord Jesus Christ" (Acts 28:3; also see Acts 20:25; Col. 1:12-13). There is absolutely no hint of withdrawal or postponement here.
3. The writer of Hebrews, writing thirty or more years after this supposed kingdom-removal event, says that they were in the process, then and there, of "receiving a kingdom," one that "cannot be shaken," (Heb. 12:28). Furthermore, this unshakable aspect of the kingdom meant that it was to "remain" (Heb. 12:27).
4. In the Revelation, John speaks of the seven 1st-century churches of Asia and Himself as being made "a kingdom" (Rev. 1:6) in the "kingdom" (Rev. 1:9). What kingdom is that?
5. Upon his resurrection, Jesus "appeared to them over a period of forty days and spoke about the kingdom of God" (Acts 1:3). There is no hint of withdrawal or postponement here or anywhere in the New Testament.
6. When Jesus was asked when He was "going to restore the kingdom to Israel?" (Acts 1:6), He did not dignify the question with a

---

[58] Guthrie, *New Testament Theology*, 456.
[59] Ladd, *A Theology of the New Testament*, 607.

direct answer. And why not? It's because this thinking was typical of the "Jewish error"[60] of the 1st century A.D., as well as today—i.e., the false expectation of a visible, political, and future-coming kingdom. But since many Christians today are also expecting this type of a kingdom coming in human history, they, like the Jews of Jesus' time, conclude it has not happened yet and must have been withdrawn and postponed by God. This is a key reason why, in my opinion, we in the Church have had such a long record of confused thinking regarding the kingdom.

7. In dramatic contrast to the notion of the kingdom being restored to Israel someday, Jesus said that it would be taken away from the Jews and given to another people (Matt. 21:43). He did not say it would be "postponed" or "withdrawn," or "given back." Nor did He speak about a restoration of the Jews to the Holy Land.[61] Quite to the contrary, He said their "house" would be "left to you desolate" (Matt. 23:38).

8. Jesus did not come to offer the Jews an earthly political kingdom. He came to offer all peoples of the world a different type of kingdom (Mark 1:14-15; Matt. 6:10, 12:28; Luke 11:20) and to die (Matt. 20:28; Mark 10:45; John 13:3).

9. "Surely the Sovereign Lord does nothing without revealing his plan to his servants the prophets" (Amos 3:7). Once again, the biblical fact is that no Old Testament prophet or New Testament writer ever spoke of a withdrawal or postponement of something as important as the coming of the kingdom of God, and neither should we.

In sum, all the post-cross evidences cited above document that there was no withdrawal or postponement. Furthermore, there is no text in the Bible that validates these removal claims or indicates a mystery form of the kingdom—again, the latter is advocated by both classic and

---

[60] Charles E. Hill, "Why the Early Church Finally Rejected Premillennialism," *Modern Reformation,* Jan/Feb. 1999, 16. From Origen, *de Principiis* .Book 2, Ch. 11. Para. 2, in The Ante-Nicene Fathers, Vol IV (Grand Rapids, MI.: Eerdmans, 1982), 297.

[61] Ryrie defensively argues that "it is the kingdom of God that is taken from them." But this kingdom "is not identified with the millennial kingdom." Therefore, he concludes that "the Lord is *not* saying that the blessings and promises concerning the millennium have been taken from Israel." (Ryrie, *The Basis of the Premillennial Faith,* 70-71). .

progressive dispensationalists.[62] Quite to the contrary, the final and everlasting form of the kingdom of God that Jesus brought into human history was, then and there, present and expanding, and "of its increase . . . there will be no end" (Isa. 9:7a); "his kingdom will never end" (Luke 1:33).

Non-millenarian Waltke agrees that in the New Testament, Christ's kingdom was not withdrawn or postponed but "now transcends the geospatial boundaries of national Israel."[63] Even progressive dispensationalist Bock agrees with this aspect. He draws on the parable of the great banquet in Luke 14:15-24 and claims that "the kingdom is not delayed because of Israel's rejection . . . does not lead to the postponing of the banquet, but to the inviting of others to fill it."[64]

<u>The Church age as an unforeseen parenthesis</u>

Before we leave this third contending paradigm, one other corollary misconception must be dispatched—i.e., the idea that the Church was unforeseen by the Old Testament prophets. Mathison is correct when he argues that "if there were Old Testament prophecies of the church age as Acts 3:24 clearly demonstrates, then it cannot legitimately be argued that this age is a 'parenthesis.'"[65] The biblical truth is that no New Testament writer regards the Church age as an unforeseen parenthesis in God's plan of redemption—i.e., between two ends for national or ethnic Israel— quite to the contrary.

King cites Peter's quotation of the Joel passage in Acts 2:17-21 and later in Acts 3:24 as New Testament evidence that the Church was

---

[62] Blaising and Bock, *Progressive Dispensationalism*, 262. Nor are there any texts supporting the Church as merely "a phase of the eschatological kingdom" (Ibid., 285) or a future kingdom that will be "a worldwide political rule over all nations" (Ibid., 247.) and termed the "intermediate millennial kingdom" (Ibid., 270.). These are contrived terms and concepts that have been imposed upon the text and will not stand up to Scriptural testing, as we shall further see.

[63] Bruce Waltke, "The Kingdom of God in Biblical Theology." In *Looking into the Future*, David W. Baker, ed., *Looking into the Future* (Grand Rapids, MI.: Baker Academic, 2001), 27.

[64] Bock, "The Kingdom of God in New Testament Theology," in David W. Baker, ed., *Looking into the Future*, 42.

[65] Mathison, *Dispensationalists*, 30.

"foreseen by Old Testament prophets" and was "in the original plan of God." Likewise, Paul "justified his turning from the Jews to the Gentiles by an appeal to the Old Testament prophecy (Acts 13:46-47)." Additionally stressed is "throughout the New Testament, appeal is made to the Old Testament to show the things that were taking place in 'the church age' as prophesied by the prophets."[66]

Gentry further notes that we are called the "seed of Abraham" (Rom. 4:13-17, Gal. 3:6-9, 29), the "circumcision" (Rom. 2:28-29; Phil. 3:3; Col. 2:11), "a royal priesthood" (Rom. 15:16; 1 Pet. 2:9; Rev. 1:6; 5:10), "twelve tribes" (Jas. 1:1), "diaspora" (1 Pet. 1:1), the "temple of God" (1 Cor. 3:16-17; 6:19; 2 Cor. 1:16; Eph. 2:21),[67] and the "Israel of God" (Gal. 6:16). Moreover, Gentry correctly understands that "in Christ, all racial distinction has been done away with (Gal. 3:26-28)."[68] He sees the "calling of the Gentiles" in the Old Testament and its confirmation in the New Testament as further evidence against this unforeseen-parenthesis notion.[69]

The biblical truth is that no New Testament writer regards the Church age as an unforeseen parenthesis in God's plan of redemption. . . .

Hence Gentry rightly declares classic dispensationalism's dichotomizing hermeneutic "a fundamental error of the entire system" which "distorts the entire idea of the progressive redemption, the unity of God's people, the fulfillment of prophecy, and the interpretation of Scripture."[70] He terms as "totally erroneous" their view of the kingdom as being literal, political, earthly, and postponed.[71] Notably, Jesus rebuked the two on the road to Emmaus for this same nationalistic notion. Jesus termed it "foolish" (Luke 24:21, 25).

---

[66] King, *The Cross and the Parousia of Christ*, 168.
[67] Gentry, *He Shall Have Dominion*, 166.
[68] Ibid., 167.
[69] Ibid., 170-172.
[70] Ibid., 165.
[71] Ibid., 225.

Gentry further points out that "the entirety of the Temple order and sacrificial system is forever done away with"(John 4:21; Heb. 8:13; 9:10) and "de-centralized" (Matt. 28:18-20). He concludes that "this is very much contrary to dispensationalism's hermeneutic reversal of Christ's economy of redemption back to an Old Testament order."[72]

One simply cannot maintain that the Bible is a hodgepodge—intending different things for two different peoples at two different times—without impugning the Author. Numerous arbitrary decisions must then be made as to what things pertain to Israel and what things pertain to the Church. As Ladd has noted, "this principle has frequently been called 'rightly dividing the Word of Truth.'" He explains that "it is the method of deciding in advance which Scriptures deal with the Church and which Scriptures have to do with Israel, and then to interpret the passages concerned in light of this 'division' of the Word."[73] But it is a faulty and dichotomizing hermeneutic based on an unscriptural and false paradigm. It is a fundamental weakness that must be discarded. Indeed, as Hoekema illustrates, "the church was indeed not an afterthought on God's part, but is the fruit of God's eternal purpose . . . which he accomplished in Christ."[74]

In summary, the idea of an Israel-Church dichotomy, in any form, is a false dichotomy and an unbiblical invention. Likewise, a withdrawn or postponed kingdom, an unforeseen Church age, and replacement theology have no biblical support. There is no scriptural authority for two separate peoples, programs, destinies, or even two separate applications. These dichotomizing ideas do not arise inductively from the text. No text mentions them. Instead, they are imposed from without. Therefore, they are clearly weaknesses that must be rejected and discarded. Unfortunately, these are also notions that are so deeply implanted in some hearts and minds that God's *oneness* may be difficult to accept. But oneness, and the continuance of the kingdom and the Church age, as prophesied by the prophets, are the strengths to be kept for synthesis.

---

[72] Ibid., 470.
[73] Ladd, *The Blessed Hope*, 130.
[74] Hoekema, *The Bible and the Future*, 217.

Contending Paradigm #4). What about A.D. 70 Being the Final Coming?

The insistence by some leading preterists that A.D. 70 was the final coming of Christ—he came "in finality"—creates a *terminus ad quem*, or finality paradigm and another dichotomizing hermeneutic. Hence, Christ's involvement in human affairs is largely viewed as being fulfilled and over. Scriptures and post-A.D.-70 reality are then read through this mindset. Likewise terminated (depending on which preterists you talk to) are intrinsic elements of Christ's kingdom, such as: the functioning of charismatic gifts, the activity of angels, demons, and Satan, water baptism, the Lord's Supper, and even the Church itself. But this dichotomizing paradigm and consequential hermeneutic also fails. Its weaknesses will be covered in chapters 12, 13, and 15 on the many comings of Jesus—past, present, and future.

With the above four false and contending paradigms exposed, deposed, and discarded, let's next explore the need for a more disciplined methodology in the divisive arena of eschatology.

Here again are the four false paradigms contending against God's divinely determined paradigm of the "appointed time . . . of the end:"

Contending Paradigm #1 – "the end of the world" or "end of time."

Contending Paradigm #2 – the "new heaven and a new earth."

Contending Paradigm #3 – the distinction between Israel and the Church.

Contending Paradigm #4 – A.D. 70 being the final coming.

Chapter 9

A More Disciplined Methodology

Paradigm shifts are usually painful. But the hard reality is this. Because of the four contending, traditional, but unscriptural paradigms covered in our last chapter, most Christians throughout Church history have not correctly understood God's Word in regard to eschatology. How can we be so sure this assessment is true? It's because almost every generation since the time of Christ has felt that they were the one who would witness the "the end" and the so-called "second coming" or "return" of Christ. But only one generation in history was or will be that end-time generation to witness God's divinely determined paradigm of the "appointed time . . . of the end."

Another point well worth reemphasizing is that eschatology is not a fringe area or minor issue. As Erickson aptly remarks, "eschatology so interpenetrates the rest of Christianity's themes that one cannot extricate, eliminate, or ignore it without ruining the whole."[1] Consequently, if we are sincere in seeking the intended meaning and making a sound interpretation, we must develop a more disciplined methodology—one that produces a more responsible system of eschatological guidelines that go beyond general hermeneutic (interpretative) principles or rules.

Newcombe captures this quandary of interpretations quite well in writing: "anybody familiar with the subject of Bible prophecies and the end times knows that there's quite a bit of Ben Franklin-type disputes:

---

[1] Erickson, *A Basic Guide to Eschatology*, 51.

Yes, it is! No, it isn't! There are all sorts of opinions out there, and they all claim to base their version of the last days on what the Bible says."[2]

But the major problem is, we tend to violate general hermeneutical principles or rules, which we advocate, whenever we want. Nowhere is this tendency more pronounced than in the field of eschatology. Virkler confirms this tendency in disclosing that "the wide variety of theories concerning the end-times arises not so much from a disagreement concerning principles of prophetic interpretations as from differences in application of those principles."[3] Though our principles may be sound, our applications are not. He also observes that "many great Christians (e.g., Origen, Augustine, Luther) understood and prescribed better hermeneutical principles than they practiced."[4] It seems that factors other than sound hermeneutics have a long track record of take priority.

> **But only one generation in history was or will be that end-time generation to witness God's divinely determined paradigm of the "appointed time... of the end."**

Hence most of us tend to interpret and understand Scripture according to what we have been told and taught, regardless of what really is or is not in the text and its context. Grant astutely recognizes this tendency that too often "theology . . . is interpretation . . . of a religion tradition for the sake of the religious tradition itself."[5] Fee and Stuart add that "our lack of consistency . . . is the great flaw in our common hermeneutics. Without necessarily intending to, we bring our theological heritage, our ecclesiastical traditions, our cultural norms, or our existential concerns to the Epistles as we read them. And this results in all kinds of selectivity or 'getting around' certain texts."[6]

Below are three prominent examples of this abusive tendency:

---

[2] Newcombe, *Coming Again But When?*, 7.
[3] Virkler, *Hermeneutics*, 203.
[4] Ibid., 48.
[5] Grant with Tracy, *A Short History of the Interpretation of the Bible*, 170.
[6] Fee and Stuart, *How to Read the Bible for All Its Worth*, 62.

#1 Literal Vs. Spiritual

Much confusion revolves about the idea of literal versus spiritual interpretation.[7] Seriously, how do we decide what and when a text, or a portion of it, is to be taken literally or spiritually (symbolically/figuratively)? But as Gerstner has noted, "the argument that prophecy must be interpreted literally often has intuitive appeal for many people."[8] So even though "literally" sounds good, isn't it at best unrealistic to assume this totally since biblical writing contains metaphors, similes, figures of speech, parables, allegories, poetry, and symbolism? Therefore, every interpreter uses both literal and figurative exegesis. Nor should we forget that behind every symbolic or figurative expression is an actual literal reality. And, spirit is also literal. So isn't biblical interpretation more of an art, than a science? Or is it both?

Virkler explains that "problems result when readers interpret statements in a mode other than the one intended by the author." But he concedes that "this principle is easier to state than to apply."[9] Hence, pitting literal against spiritual/symbolic/figurative, or imposing an arbitrary insistence on interpreting all prophecy one way or the other, are both overly simplistic errors since prophecy is filled with both literal and figurative language. The real issue is: What did God intend? Unfortunately, no definite guideline(s) prevails. Therefore, many who promote interpreting the Scriptures literally consistently fail to do so, and at some very critical points. Others, who insist certain passages are spiritual, likewise deviate, at whim, when it suites their purposes. What happens is a pick-and-chose hermeneutic. We simply vacillate, whenever and wherever necessary, to comply with the demands of our eschatological system. What becomes obvious is that many, if not most, interpreters are more interested in defending and maintaining their position and holding on to whatever fundamentally flawed, interpretative methodology enables them to do that rather than in finding truth and

---

[7] Literal strictly speaking means to interpret the Bible as it is written—i.e., all forms used are to be interpreted according to normal rules governing those forms—poetry, apocalyptic, figures of speech, etc.
[8] John H. Gerstner, *Wrongly Dividing the Word of Truth* (Brentwood, TN.: Wolgemuth & Hyatt, 1991), 97.
[9] Virkler, *Hermeneutics*, 28.

rightly dividing the word of God. Thus, the basic principles or rules of general hermeneutics are frequently violated and broken whenever and wherever it suits one's purposes.

Astonishingly, nevertheless, Jeffrey claims that "the premillennial return of Christ is the only view consistent with the literal interpretation of the prophecies of the Old and New Testaments."[10] Amillennialist Poythress, of course, disagrees that this one-sided consistency is the correct standard for gauging truth in this matter. He insists that "it becomes relatively easy to harmonize everything *even under the umbrella of an overall system that is not correct.*" Consequently, he charges classic dispensationalism with "artificially generating consistency by the multiplication of distinctions and the doubling of relationships." He concludes, therefore, that "consistency is not a guarantee of truth."[11]

So "what is literal interpretation?", asks Poythress. He answers, "it is a confusing term, capable of being used to beg many of the questions at stake in the interpretation of the Bible." He advises that "we had best not use the phrase but rather speak of grammatical-historical interpretation."[12] Dispensationalist Ryrie agrees that "there is no more basic rule of interpretation than this."[13] But again, the proverbial devil is in the application details.

On the other hand and in defense, Spargimino believes that the literalism charge against dispensationalists is a "straw tiger." While he acknowledges "the existence of symbols, figures of speech, and allegorical language," he also maintains that "when it comes to prophecies regarding God's Kingdom on earth and the nation of Israel, we believe that these prophecies are to be taken literally."[14] But postmillennialist Snowden fires back that "it was the literalizing of the Jewish prophecies concerning the Messiah and his kingdom that led the Jews off into views and hopes of the Messiah that were false and cruelly

---

[10] Jeffrey, *Triumphant Return*, 115.
[11] Poythress, *Understanding Dispensationalists*, 56-57.
[12] Ibid., 96.
[13] Ryrie, *The Basis of the Premillennial Faith*, 36.
[14] Spargimino, *The Anti-Prophets*, 90.

disappointing . . . . It was the literal interpretation of their Scriptures that blinded the Jews to their own Messiah."[15]

Sandwiched in between are historic premillennialists who "see at least some of these prophecies being fulfilled by the church or spiritual Israel."[16] But postmillennialist DeMar holds classic dispensationalists' feet to the fire and asks why they interpret the "horses, bows, and arrows, spears, and clubs in Ezekiel 38 and 39" as modern-day weaponry?[17] He follows up by asserting that this non-literal understanding "does not follow his [their] own interpretive guidelines."[18]

Thus, the basic principles or rules of general hermeneutics are frequently violated and broken whenever and wherever it suits one's purposes.

Amillennialist Hoekema likewise confronts Spargimino's above assertion by noting that classic dispensationalists do not take literally the references to various sacrifices in Ezekiel chapters 40-48 which are to be offered in a future rebuilt temple in Jerusalem during the millennium. These dispensationalists admit that these will only be "memorial sacrifices, without expiatory value." One of the difficult questions he next asks is, "If the sacrifices are not to be taken literally, why should we take the temple literally?" The bottom line for Hoekema in this particular point of argumentation is their reluctant admission that "the principle of literal interpretation . . . is here abandoned, and a crucial foundation stone for the entire dispensational system has here been set aside!"[19] He also cites James' quotation of Amos 9:11-12 in Acts 15:14-15—the Gentiles being gathered into the community of God's people, there in the 1st century—as "a clear example in the Bible itself of figurative, nonliteral interpretation of an Old Testament passage dealing with the

---

[15] James H. Snowden, *The Coming of the Lord* (New York, NY.: Macmillan, 1919), 198-199.
[16] Erickson, *A Basic Guide to Eschatology*, 105.
[17] Gary DeMar, *End Times Fiction* (Nashville, TN.: Thomas Nelson, 2001), 2.
[18] Ibid., 3.
[19] Hoekema, *The Bible and the Future*, 203-204.

restoration of Israel."[20] Later on he claims that "the dispensational understanding of the millennium. . . is not based on a literal interpretation of this most important passage."[21] I would also add to Hoekema's argument Jeremiah's new covenant prophecy of a coming time when the law would be "put in their minds" and written "on their hearts" (Jer. 31:33). Is this prophetic passage to be taken literally?

On the other side of the coin, classic dispensationalists typically eschew the "spiritualizing" hermeneutic as being a weak and flawed exegesis. Far too often they place all non-literal interpretation of Scripture, such as symbolic, figurative, or spiritual under the category of allegorizing. For them, allegorizing is a buzzword, an anathema, and a synonym for error. They use it to "stigmatize" non-literalists.[22] Yet DeMar notes that "even Paul interpreted Scripture 'allegorically'"[23] (see Gal. 4:24 *KJV*).

Progressive dispensationalist Turner judiciously cautions evangelicals to "avoid brash charges of 'allegorizing' or 'hyper-literalism'" and instead to "focus upon issues such as specific NT uses of the OT."[24] Likewise, Guthrie terms this last point "the greatest apologetic element in the NT."[25]

But classic dispensationalists, such as MacArthur, brashly continue to assert that "all the prophecies dealing with the first advent of Christ were fulfilled precisely, literally."[26] Even non-dispensationalist Grenz proclaims that "the prophecies concerning Christ's first coming were fulfilled literally."[27] Jeffrey calls this alleged fact "God's stamp of approval on this literal interpretive system."[28] He deduces, therefore, that all prophecies of his second coming will "be fulfilled in a similar literal manner."[29] Hence, as Ryrie chimes in, "fulfilled prophecy forms the

---

[20] Ibid., 210.
[21] Ibid., 221-222.
[22] Ryrie, *The Basis of the Premillennial Faith*, 39.
[23] DeMar, *End Times Fiction*, 191.
[24] Turner, "The Continuity of Scripture and Eschatology: Key Hermeneutical Issues." *Grace Theological Journal*, 286.
[25] Guthrie, *New Testament Theology*, 59.
[26] MacArthur, *The Second Coming*, 29.
[27] Grenz, *The Millennial Maze*, 100.
[28] Jeffrey, *Triumphant Return*, 45.
[29] Ibid., 28.

pattern."[30] And, "when the principles of literal interpretation . . . are followed, the result is the premillennial system of doctrine."[31]

But Crenshaw and Gunn offer this piece of contradictory evidence. After carefully documenting the prophecies of Christ's first coming that are cited in the New Testament from the Old Testament, they conclude that "out of 97 OT prophecies only 34 were directly or literally fulfilled, which is only 35.05 percent." Most appropriately, they then ask, "Whose concept of fulfillment should be used? Man's or God's?"[32] Postmillennialist Mathison agrees that "the New Testament does not interpret Old Testament prophecy in the same manner as dispensationalism demands."[33]

In view of how the New Testament applies Old Testament prophecy, I concur with Gentry that "the dispensational presumption of a *consistent* literalism is unreasonable." To require that all Old Testament prophecies, especially those that apply to Israel, have to be interpreted literally is to apply a hermeneutic that the New Testament does not apply to itself. Gentry rightly but sarcastically quips, "Is Jesus literally a door (John 10:9)?"[34] And Mathison correctly summarizes that "nobody can be absolutely literal in his interpretation of Scripture. The Bible itself will not allow it."[35]

What we consequently ended up with on both sides of this interpretative issue are arbitrary and selective methodologies. Either one, when carried out consistently, wreaks havoc on biblical interpretation and understanding. Unfortunately, this hermeneutical dilemma has substantially contributed to the self-perpetuating stalemate in the field of eschatology. In the quest to interpret what the Bible says, especially in the field of eschatology, sound hermeneutics have been subordinated to opinions and traditions. This abusive denigration is called passage-picking, cherry-picking, proof-texting, pick and choose, alternate

---

[30] Ryrie, *The Basis of the Premillennial Faith*, 44.
[31] Ibid., 47.
[32] Curtis I. Crenshaw and Grover E. Gunn III, *Dispensationalism: Today, Yesterday, and Tomorrow* (Memphis: Footstool Publications, 1985), 13. – especially see their helpful chart on pages 9-13.
[33] Mathison, *Postmillennialism*, 200.
[34] Gentry, *He Shall Have Dominion*, 148.
[35] Mathison, *Dispensationalism*, 7.

meanings, etc. But these violations of generally accepted hermeneutical principles are rampant and generally accepted. In my opinion, this hermeneutical abuse is the major reason we have so many different and conflicting doctrines and beliefs.

Paradoxically, let's not forget, when the Jews of Jesus' day interpreted the Old Testament passages literally, this led them to reject Him as the Messiah (John 5:39-40; 18:36-37; Luke 17:20-21). Furthermore, why should it strike us as odd, or even absurd, that the Bible truly does speak of spiritual things?

So how are we to avoid substituting one's own subjective opinions and desires ahead and instead of God's intended meaning? Yes, we need a more disciplined methodology.

#2 Tendency to Add

Another common but distorting and disturbing tendency is the blatant importing or adding things to textual content. In Chapter 2 we have already seen a classic example of adding to Revelation 20, even though Revelation specifically warns against this practice and sets out severe consequences for those who violate its warning (Rev. 22:18-19). Yet adding to content is another casually done and accepted practice today.

For instance, again, where in this passage is there any mention of a second coming, a temple, a rebuilt temple, reinstitution of animal sacrifices, or Jesus sitting on an earthly throne? Or where does this passage speak of Israel, an earthly Jerusalem, a gathering of the Jews back to Palestine, a revived Jewish kingdom, an earthly utopian paradise, or material prosperity on the earth? These elements are conspicuously absent. They are also absent from the entire New Testament. But they are vitally important to the most-popular millennial view. Simply and sadly, they have been fabricated and imported into this text.

There is no word for this practice other than accommodation. It is a clear attempt to conform this passage to one's view and make it mean something other than what it says. Fee and Stuart tersely and rightly term this tendency "to make the text mean something God did not intend" an "abuse."[36]

If these first two interpretative examples are not sufficient to convince you of the need for a more disciplined methodology in the field of eschatology, then here is one more to seriously consider.

#3 Contending with Jesus

One week before his crucifixion, Jesus spoke authoritatively and plainly. While sitting on the Mount of Olives, looking across the valley at the beautiful Jewish Temple, Jesus stunned his disciples by prophesying that this entire complex of buildings, an awesome structure "famous throughout the world" (2 Maccabees 2:22 NRSV), would be totally destroyed. "I tell you the truth, not one stone here will be left on another; every one will be thrown down" (Matt. 24:2).

His disciples asked, "When will this happen, and what will be the sign of your coming and of the end of the age?" (Matt. 24:3). He answered, "I tell you the truth, this generation will certainly not pass away until all these things have happened" (Matt. 24:34). As we have seen, included in Jesus' "all these things" were:

- The end of the age and the sign of his coming (*parousia*) (Matt. 24:3)
- The gospel preached in all the world . . . to all nations (Matt. 24:14)
- The end will come (Matt. 24:14)
- The abomination of desolation standing in the holy place (Matt. 24:15)
- The hearers fleeing for their lives (Matt. 24:16-20)
- A great tribulation, unequaled in history before or after (Matt. 24:21)
- False Christs and false prophets appearing, performing great signs and miracles and deceiving even the elect–if that were possible (Matt. 24:24)

---

[36] Fee and Stuart, *How to Read the Bible for All Its Worth*, 21.

- The coming (*parousia*) of the Son of Man (Matt. 24:27-30)
- The sun and the moon darkened, stars falling from the sky and the heavenly bodies shaken (Matt. 24:29)
- The sign of the Son of Man appearing in the sky (Matt. 24:30)
- Them seeing the Son of Man coming on the clouds (Matt. 24:30)

This passage of Scripture is recognized as Jesus' longest, most dramatic, and most problematic teaching. And since Jesus is the prophet "like you [Moses]" (Deut. 18:15, 18), everything He said must "take place or come true" (Deut. 18:22).

We'll have much more to say about this most dramatic passage and its contents in Chapter 13. But the question I now raise is, just how much of Jesus' Olivet Discourse was relevant to his original audience? According to most classic dispensationalists, "little or none of it" was. According to the historic premillennialists, amillennialists, historicists, and some progressive dispensationalists, "some of it" was. According to postmillennialists, "most of it" was. But according to preterists, "all of it" was relevant and fulfilled, right on time.

The problem is, scholars such as Sproul, MacArthur, and even C.S. Lewis have made dogmatic statements representing conflicting positions that seem to equivocate about Jesus' inspiration:

- Sproul: "Though I think some of His [Jesus'] predictions came to pass in A.D. 70, I do not think all of them did."[37]
- MacArthur: "But a closer look at the whole discourse reveals that the most important aspects of His prophecy were *not* fulfilled in the destruction of Jerusalem in A.D. 70.... After all the destruction of the temple foretold in verse 2 was fulfilled by the Roman army in A.D. 70, but the cosmic signs accompanying the return of Christ described in verses 29-31 quite obviously still pertain to the future."[38]
- C.S. Lewis: "It [Matthew 24:34] is certainly the most embarrassing verse in the Bible. Yet how teasing, also, that within fourteen words of it should come the statement, 'but of that day and that hour knoweth no man, no, not the angels

---

[37] Sproul, "... in Like Manner," *Tabletalk*, 7.
[38] MacArthur, *The Second Coming*, 78.

which are in heaven, neither the Son, but the Father.' The one exhibition of error and the one confession of ignorance grow side by side."[39]

What do you say? Your answer will depend on your hermeneutic. One's hermeneutic is the larger context and primary criterion by which end-time prophecy is interpreted. Spykman captured this concept quite well in writing:

> . . . hermeneutics has become increasingly the pivotal point in almost every theological discussion. Every issue, it seems, turns out at bottom to be an hermeneutic issue. Sooner or later the password, "Show me your hermeneutic," rises to the surface as the litmus test in theological decision-making.[40]

It is important here to emphasize, once again, that the point of Jesus' literal time-restriction is not one lost on the liberals or skeptics. The time statements of the New Testament have been and still are the focal point of their attack on the deity of Christ and biblical inerrancy. Sad to say, conservative evangelicals have never been able to mount an effective response. Hence, major portions of the faith have been lost to liberal incursions.

One's hermeneutic is the larger context and primary criterion by which end-time prophecy is interpreted.

Of course, other problematic examples could be cited. But misapplications and abuse of sound hermeneutical principles are critically recognized as being widespread in the field of eschatology. And no view is exempt. I have merely pointed out three of the more significant areas where we find much confusion, difficulty, disagreement, and abuse. Below is an additional sampling of tale-telling comments illustrating the hermeneutical difficulties that many scholars feel they face when approaching this area of eschatology:

---

[39] C.S. Lewis, essay, "The World's Last Night," 385. For the full quote see again pp. 124-125.
[40] Spykman, *Reformational Theology*, 119.

- Fee and Stuart: "The prophetical books are among the most difficult parts of the Bible to interpret or read with understanding."[41]

- VanGemeren: "The process of interpretation of relating prophetic and apocalyptic, promise and fulfillment, and reality and eschatology, is a complex hermeneutic task."[42]

- VanGemeren: "Regrettably, the interpretation of the prophetic legacy has been affected by division, fragmentation, expressions of distrust, and misunderstanding. Disagreements arising from exegetical, theological, or philosophical differences have often been expressed with rigidity and lack of love . . . . An exploration of the prophetic word requires an openness to the whole revelation of God in both the Old Testament and the New Testament . . . ."[43]

- Virkler: "The interpretation of prophecy is a highly complex subject, not so much because of disagreement regarding proper interpretative principles, but because of differences of opinion over how to apply those principles."[44]

- Klein and others: "Apocalyptic probably presents some of the Bible's most difficult passages to interpret."[45]

- Ryken: "In one way or another, visionary literature takes us to a strange world where ordinary rules of reality no longer prevail."[46]

---

[41] Fee and Stuart, *How to Read the Bible for All Its Worth*, 165.
[42] Willem VanGemeren, *Interpreting the Prophetic Word* (Grand Rapids, MI.: Zondervan, 1990), 411.
[43] Ibid., 71.
[44] Virkler, *Hermeneutics*, 190-191.
[45] William W. Klein, Craig L. Blomberg, and Robert L. Hubbard, Jr., *Introduction to Biblical Interpretation* (Dallas, TX.: Word Publishing, 1993), 312.
[46] Leland Ryken, *How to Read the Bible as Literature* (Grand Rapids, MI.: Zondervan, 1984), 166.

The sad reality, once again, is: eschatology is a minefield between armed camps. In a single step or statement, you can get blown away by the opposition. The real casualty, however, is truth and genuine dialogue. It seems that no other field in theology produces the amount of emotion, bitterness, and hostility as does eschatology.

Part of my fourfold premise in undertaking this my doctoral dissertation (see again Chapter 7, p. 116) and now in this book has been that it is not and was not the character or the nature of God to have inspired anything in his Word that would have created this divisive and confusing situation. Surely, we have misconstrued the whole thing.

In this regard Virkler's hermeneutical warning is most relevant:

> ... there are at least two major dangers in accepting a certain system of hypothesis about the nature of divine revelation: First . . . imposing one's system *onto* the biblical data, rather than deriving the system *from* the data . . . . A second and perhaps even greater danger is that of accepting a theory . . . without recognizing it as a theory, or without looking at other theories to see which theory fits the data best.[47]

Like Hollywood, the tabloids, and the media, Christian scholars and believers also seem to be having a hard time getting Christianity right. Nowhere is this tendency more evident than in the field of eschatology. In my opinion, what is needed for a more disciplined methodology are special hermeneutics for addressing eschatological texts. To get there, however, we must first address this key hermeneutical question.

The Key Hermeneutical Question

Literary scholars contend that rules of interpretation are essential and must be properly applied to properly understand the message of any piece of literature. Properly understanding the Bible is no exception. Hence, proponents of all four eschatological views generally agree that the grammatical-historical hermeneutic is preferred—"that a text should be interpreted according to the rules of grammar and the facts of

---

[47] Virkler, *Hermeneutics*, 118-119.

history."[48] As we have seen, agreement here is one thing; application is another. But we shall not take time and space to review common agreed upon principles of biblical interpretation; these are assumed. Instead, we shall focus on relevant issues of special hermeneutics that have a direct bearing on the interpretation of eschatological passages.

The first issue for us to address centers on this key hermeneutical question: "Does time (of fulfillment) determine nature (of fulfillment), or does nature determine time?" Make no mistake, this dichotomy is the root issue. How one answers this question establishes the *controlling* hermeneutic in the interpretation or misinterpretation of eschatology. I further submit that this resultant hermeneutic takes precedence over other classic hermeneutical issues such as: literal vs. spiritual (figurative) meaning, allegorizing, NT use of the OT, the present vs. future aspects of the kingdom, "already but not yet," inaugurated or proleptic, or the continuity of Scripture in progressive revelation.[49] Even the acclaimed historical-grammatical method of interpretation frequently falls victim to this time-versus-nature rubric.

Thus, "time determines nature" or "nature determines time" are the two major competing hermeneutics in the field of eschatology. Every interpreter, knowingly or unknowingly, subscribes to one or the other. Preterists subscribe to the former. They insist that "time determines nature," and that we must honor and take literally and seriously the divinely given time frames and time statements in both the Old and New Testaments. Consequently, a preterist understanding of the nature of fulfillment is subjugated to, disciplined by, and confined within the time-restricting and contextualizing parameters place upon it by Scripture.

. . . the key hermeneutical question: "Does time (of fulfillment) determine nature (of fulfillment), or does nature determine time?"

Most evangelicals, however, have subscribed to the latter hermeneutic that "nature determines time." Their exegesis is driven by it.

---

[48] Ibid., 62.
[49] Turner, "The Continuity of Scripture and Eschatology: Key Hermeneutical Issues," 275-287.

And since they have not seen in history, to date, the nature of fulfillment that they are expecting for any particular text, they deduce that these events have not happened yet. But to do so, they must either ignore or non-literally manipulate the time texts and time-restricted context.

Dispensationalist Spargimino provides a case in point. Consistent with his hermeneutic, he claims that "the most unbelievable aspect of preterism is their . . . treating certain words portending the most stupendous of cataclysmic judgments—falling stars and various heavenly disturbances—and then claiming that such occurred in A.D. 70." He queries, "Since the stars didn't literally fall in A.D. 70 how do they 'explain' their position?"[50] So he insists that "the events leading up to A.D. 70 do not match with the Olivet Discourse."[51] Instead, he suggests a "look at recent developments in technology, and then current events to see if the present time fits God's description."[52] Hence, he is driven by his "nature-determines-time" hermeneutic. It forces him to conclude that "with things like this happening, it is hard to believe that we are now living in the Kingdom age."[53]

Others take a partial approach contending that "the judgment of Israel and of Jerusalem [in A.D. 70] does not supply a full and exhaustive fulfillment to our Lord's words."[54] Jeffrey, for one, totally disagrees. After a review of the Olivet Discourse, he concludes that "none of these detailed prophecies were fulfilled at the destruction of Jerusalem in A.D. 70."[55] Of course, preterists, partial-preterist amillennialists and postmillennialists, and some premillennialists disagree with Jeffrey.

At best, many find it bizarre that anyone could seriously suggest that the millennium is now here. Hence, postmillennialist Kik admits that "all appearances seem to be against the view that we are in the Millennium now." But he counters by arguing that "the trouble is that we have

---

[50] Spargimino, *The Anti-Prophets*, 134.
[51] Ibid., 183.
[52] Ibid., 191.
[53] Ibid., 206.
[54] J. Stuart Russell, *The Parousia* (Grand Rapids, MI.: Baker Book House, 1887, 1985), 47.
[55] Jeffrey, *Triumphant Return*, 138.

altogether a too materialistic concept of the millennial blessings. We fail to see the greatest blessings are spiritual and they are in our midst."[56]

Many other nature-vs.-time examples could be cited, such as Christ's "coming on the clouds," the coming of the "new heaven and a new earth," the fulfillment of other apocalyptic language, or the realization of some specific Old Testament promise. The key hermeneutical question remains: What is the relationship of the time of fulfillment to the nature of fulfillment—particularly, whether a prophecy was completely fulfilled, partially fulfilled, or not fulfilled at all?

Admittedly, the dominant interpretative reality is, preconceived and/or traditional notions of the nature of fulfillment are given precedence over the time hermeneutic. Hence this prevents many from accepting the simple time statements throughout Scripture in a natural, normal, and literal manner. Rather, their interpretations are subjected to speculative subjectivity. This subjectivity manifests itself in the forms of "passage-picking," debates over the "real" meaning of words and phrases, and the common practice of bifurcating a biblical text into two pieces. This is why we hear interpreters say things like, "What Jesus or Paul meant was . . . ." The result has been massive confusion and disagreements. Certainly, this approach is not what rightly dividing of Bible prophecy should be about.

So I ask you, which hermeneutic is right—"time determines nature" or "nature determines time?"

Premillennial postribulationalist Kinman wisely stresses caution. Regarding the Old Testament promises made to Israel, he calls it a "flaw" to assume "that a prophecy not fulfilled in the expected way hasn't really been fulfilled." He petitions that the "New Testament writers occasionally seem to understand prophecy as fulfilled in unexpected or nonliteral ways."[57]

Poythress also wisely counsels that "it is certainly possible to read the Bible looking only for what agrees with preestablished conceptions." But he emphasizes the value of multiple perspectives in his symphonic

---

[56] Kik, *An Eschatology of Victory*, 205.
[57] Brent Kinman, *History, Design, and the End of Time* (Nashville, TN.: Broadman & Holman, 2000), 65.

theology approach as "protection against our tendency to read the Bible only in terms of a preestablished single perspective."[58]

Again, which hermeneutic is right? It cannot be overemphasized that allowing the "nature" of fulfillment to drive one's hermeneutic is dangerous ground. This is the hermeneutic that prevented many 1st-century Jews from receiving Jesus as their Messiah and the error that made them, consequently, miss "the time of thy visitation" (Luke 19:44 *KJV*).

Sproul charges that the "nature-determining-time" hermeneutic leads to "frivolous and superficial attempts to downplay or explain away the force of these [time] references."[59] DeMar chimes in that "the entire thesis of futurism rests on a non-literal reading of the time texts," which he calls "a foundation of sand."[60] Newcombe confirms that "much of the dispute between differing camps on the end times gets down to the timing of the scenes to come."[61] Hence time is important. Even premillennialists dispute among themselves the timing of their rapture (pre-, mid-, pre-wrath-, post-).

Again, which hermeneutic is right? It cannot be overemphasized that allowing the "nature" of fulfillment to drive one's hermeneutic is dangerous ground.

Inevitably, at this point someone may be tempted to ask, "but what about _____? That has not been fulfilled!" The very asking of this question betrays one's hermeneutic. But I submit that this "nature-determines-time" hermeneutic is a major weakness that must be discarded. I further submit that the preterist's "time-determines-nature" hermeneutic is God's intended hermeneutic. That is why God gave us time statements in the first place. Our 19-centuries-removed, personal

---

[58] Vern S. Poythress, *Symphonic Theology* (Phillipsburg, NJ.: P&R Publishing, 1987), 29.
[59] Sproul, *The Last Days According to Jesus*, 202-203.
[60] Gary DeMar, *Last Days Madness* (Smyrna, GA.: American Vision, 1997, 3rd ed.), xiii.
[61] Newcombe, *Coming Again But When?*, 287.

prejudices and presuppositions must become submissive to God's time statements if we truly desire to reach the relevancy goal of hermeneutics—"The goal of hermeneutics is to enable interpreters to arrive at the meaning of the text that the biblical writers or editors intended their readers to understand."[62]

Let us remember that *the* God-stated uniqueness of biblical faith, in contrast to all other religions or ideologies, is this:

> "Bring in your idols to tell us what is going to happen. . . . Or declare to us the things to come, tell us what the future holds, so we may know that you are gods." (Isa. 41:22-23)

> "I am the first and I am the last; Apart from me there is no God. Who then is like me? Let him proclaim it . . . . let him foretell what will come . . . . Did I not proclaim this and foretell it long ago?" (Isa. 44:6-8; also see: 42:8-9; 45:18-24; 46:9-11; 48:3-6)

As we shall see in the chapters ahead, God has proved faithful and "not a man that he should lie" (Num. 23:19). But faithfulness means not only doing *what* was promised, it also means doing it *when* it was promised. This is why Paul tells us that Jesus Christ, the Messiah, came and died for our sins "at just the right time" (Rom. 5:6). Previously, Habakkuk was told there was an "appointed time . . . of the end" (Hab. 2:3). Daniel was given four, Messianic and kingdom-coming time prophecies (see our next chapter). Jesus started his earthly ministry with two time statements (Mark 1:15; Luke 4:18-21).

As we shall continue to see, the God-ordained, time-restriction of fulfillment within human history is the controlling and grounding hermeneutic of Christianity. No other faith or religion has this. We dare not minimize or compromise it. Time is the Bible's constant and reoccurring theme and contextualizing factor of eschatological fulfillment. It is a strength to be kept and synthesized.

The point we cannot overemphasize is this. Time is important to God and He has made it important for us. His decrees and mighty works of power are executed in time. Adherence to God's time contexts will properly guide us in our understanding of the nature of fulfillment.

---

[62] Klein, Blomberg, and Hubbard, Jr., *Introduction to Biblical Interpretation*, 97.

Again, this is why He gave us time frames throughout his Word. What is more, as we shall see, the time statements in the New Testament intensify in imminence as the time for fulfillment steadily approached.

DeMar concurs with this importance in noting that "the key to Bible prophecy is in the *timing* of events." Here's how he dramatically demonstrates the importance of the time-determines-nature hermeneutic:

> For example, if the Bible tells us that forty years had to pass before Israel could enter the promised land, then forty years is the timing key. If God gave Nineveh forty days in which to repent, then forty days is the timing key. If God says seventy years had to pass before the Jews could return to their land after the Babylonian captivity (Jer. 29:10; Dan. 9:2), then seventy years is the timing key. If God says, 'Seventy weeks [of years] have been decreed for your people and your holy city' (Dan. 9:24), then 490 (70 X 7) years is the prophetic timing key. If Jesus says that He will be raised after three days, then three days is the timing key. If Paul tells the Philippians that he will 'send Timothy to [them] shortly' (Phil. 2:19) and that he himself 'shall be coming shortly' (2:24), then shortly is the timing key for both future events. To call these time references into question is to maintain that the Bible is not clear or precise in the way it describes time-sensitive events.[63]

Making this hermeneutical point even stronger, DeMar quotes Pentecost's disparaging comment that "the time element holds a relatively small place in prophecy."[64] He then retorts to the contrary that "'the time element' plays a major role in prophecy. In fact, it plays the defining role. Without precision of meaning for the time texts prophetic pronouncements are meaningless."[65]

Not surprisingly, however, Spargimino complains that "when these 'time texts' are combined with an allegorical interpretation of biblical prophecy, preterists feel scripturally justified in concluding that nothing more than a 1st-century disaster upon Jerusalem is needed to satisfy the

---

[63] Gary DeMar, in Foreword to Francis Gumerlock, *The Day and the Hour* (Powder Springs, GA.: American Vision, 2000), *xvii*.
[64] Dwight J. Pentecost, *Things to Come: A Study in Biblical Eschatology* (Grand Rapids, MI.: Zondervan, 1958), 46.
[65] DeMar, *Last Days Madness*, 3rd ed., 373.

requirements of these predictions."[66] Of course, Spargimino's statement here, once again, illustrates his "nature-determines-time" hermeneutic.

But I contend and will be documenting in the pages ahead that it's only by honoring God's divinely ordained "time-determines-nature" hermeneutic that can we understand God's message as it was contextually intended. Failure to so honor this foundational hermeneutical principle has caused immeasurable confusion and divisiveness. No more. In retrospect, the "nature-determines-time" hermeneutic is employed by the classic dispensationalists to both postpone the kingdom and to denigrate the Church, as unforeseen and a parenthesis, and by the amillennialists and postmillennialists to advance their "end of time" and "end-of-the-world" paradigm. These traditional ideas are tied to "nature-determines-time" understanding of the parousia, and the kingdom of God as well. Consequently, proponents of all three of these views are forced to reject, revise, or manipulate in some manner the time statements, or to bifurcate many passages of Scripture.

> **"'the time element' plays a major role in prophecy. In fact, it plays the defining role. Without precision of meaning for the time texts prophetic pronouncements are meaningless.**

Clifford makes a good point regarding Jesus' teachings of the kingdom of God that is well worth extending to the wider context that we have been addressing:

> The insurmountable difficulties in reconciling the texts with one another have led to all sorts of tortuous attempts to preserve the substantial accuracy and reliability of the Scriptures without being left with a complex of unresolved contradictions.[67]

Likewise, Francis Schaeffer hit it on the head when he wrote: "Sadly we must say in the area of scholarship the evangelical world has not done

---

[66] Spargimino, *The Anti-Prophets*, 126.
[67] Paul Rowntree Clifford, *The Reality of the Kingdom* (Grand Rapids, MI.: Eerdmans,1996), 4.

well. In every academic discipline the temptation and pressure to accommodate is overwhelming."[68]

In sum, the "nature-determines-time" hermeneutic of the futurists is a basic weakness that must be discarded. The "time-determines-nature" hermeneutic of the preterist view is the strength to be kept and synthesized. It is the God-given, grounding, and controlling hermeneutic to which the nature of fulfillment must be subordinated. If we are sincere and desire to preserve the doctrine of biblical authority and inerrancy, the "time-determines-nature" hermeneutic must take precedence and be supported by other special hermeneutics in the field of eschatology. It's to that task we next turn.

Ten Special Hermeneutical Guidelines for Eschatology

To help us transition out of the misleading and false paradigms of Chapter 8, the flawed hermeneutic of "nature determines time," and break through the stalemate of entrenched end-time views that has plagued the field of eschatology throughout Church history, we must produce a more responsible system of eschatological guidelines that goes beyond general hermeneutic (interpretative) principles or rules. Therefore, below I am offering ten special hermeneutical guidelines for the proper study and understanding of eschatology. We shall call them S-H guidelines to distinguish them from our two overall guidelines presented in our Introduction, pp.11-12.

But please be forewarned, as Fee and Stuart have cautioned, "it is difficult to give rules for hermeneutics."[69] That's why I term them guidelines. And while I recognize that it is impossible to address the complexities of debate on every eschatological matter or to resolve all issues with a few guidelines, nonetheless, I offer them for these five fitting reasons.

First, these S-H guidelines are only meant to guide and not to determine interpretation. They are offered as a positive step toward better

---

[68] Schaeffer, *The Great Evangelical Disaster*, 119.
[69] Fee and Stuart, *How to Read the Bible for All Its Worth*, 27.

and more unified understandings and applications of the grammatical-historical method of interpretation.

Secondly, I offer them with the hope that they will make a significant contribution toward the goal of providing a better hermeneutical basis than most Christians have previously had at their disposal.

Thirdly, I pray these S-H guidelines might enable the Church to reach a more unified consensus on how to interpret end-time, prophetic, and apocalyptic Scriptures.

Fourthly, I believe these ten S-H guidelines will demonstrate that the task of properly understanding eschatological issues is not as daunting or formidable as some think.

Fifthly, I agree with Milton Terry, who explained the purpose of special hermeneutics quite succinctly in his classic book, *Biblical Hermeneutics* (1890). Notably, Terry's book "was the textbook of choice for most seminaries through the 1970s."[70] Not only did Terry devote "the larger portion" of his book to "Special Hermeneutics," but he presented numerous preterist interpretative principles for the Bible's "prophetic symbolism" and its "apocalyptic books."[71] In the end, he condensed it all down to this directive: "If Special Hermeneutics serves any useful end, it must cultivate the habit of searching for what the Scripture has to say for itself, not of imposing upon its language the burden of whatever it is able to bear."[72] Terry's directive fits quite well with our agree-on Guideline #1 – *Sola Scriptura*, don't you think?

You may think of other S-H guidelines. If so, please send them to me.

1. ***Time determines nature***. This first guideline is our controlling and grounding hermeneutic. It is the Bible's self-imposed contextualization device and methodology. It provides the temporal boundaries that God has chosen to use and communicate to us. As Spykman observed: "The true meaning of Scripture can only be disclosed contextually. The basic rule for biblical interpretation is

---

[70] Gary DeMar, Product Advertisement, *Biblical Worldview*, March 2001, 24.
[71] Milton S. Terry, *Biblical Hermeneutics* (Eugene, OR.: Wipf and Stock Publishers, 1890, 1999), 5-6.
[72] Ibid., 6.

therefore this: first, last, and always consider the context."[73] Thus, our first guideline stresses audience relevancy. It enables us to narrow down the possibilities of the nature of fulfillment and protects the interpreter from creating overly subjective and forced understandings. Unfortunately, most Christians have employed the opposite hermeneutic and methodology. They subscribe to a nature-determines-time hermeneutic. And since they have not seen in history what they think the nature of fulfillment should be, they are forced to adjust the time factor. There is only one way you can adjust the time factor. And that is out into the future. As we have seen, that's a, if not the, primary reason we are contending with three futuristic end-time views

2. ***The golden rule of biblical interpretation is to be honored and obeyed***. This golden rule truly is one of the best guidelines when honestly followed. LaHaye, who does not honestly follow it, does state it well: "When the plain sense of Scripture makes common sense seek no other sense, but take every word at its primary, literal meaning unless the facts of the immediate context clearly indicate otherwise."[74] As simple as it sounds, this basic guideline is often violated at will. One way for us to test compliance is, as Fee and Stuart suggest, "a text cannot mean what it never could have meant to its author or his or her readers."[75] Secondly, as Virkler posits, "the way one interprets normal human communication."[76] Thirdly, difficult portions are to be interpreted in the light of others that are plain; therefore, obscure passages must yield to passages that are more obvious or plain.

3. ***OT and NT time frames and time statements are to be taken literally, seriously, and consistently***. They were written and/or spoken in the plain, normal, and simple language of the time. The original recipients were mostly uneducated. They were familiar with, could readily comprehend, and easily understand these common words. Hence these words must be honored and understood in their normal grammatical sense. They must not be ignored or their normal meanings

---

[73] Spykman, *Reformational Theology*, 127.
[74] Tim LaHaye, *No Fear of the Storm: Why Christians Will Escape All the Tribulation* (Sisters, OR.: Multnomah, 1992), 240.
[75] Fee and Stuart, *How to Read the Bible for All Its Worth*, 64.
[76] Virkler, *Hermeneutics*, 48.

manipulated or explained away. Even Ryrie concedes that "God is faithful" and "deceives no one."[77]

4. ***God has progressively revealed both the time and nature for the completion of his plan of redemption in history***. Restoring our relationship to the Father is what eschatology is all about. "Eschatology is not a divine afterthought."[78] It is atonement-based, wedded to historical manifestations of divine revelation and power, and, as Klein et al. have written, "God intends that it communicate—not obfuscate."[79]

5. ***The preciseness of fulfillment reflects the nature of the God who inspired it***. Just as the physical creation "proclaim[s] the work of his hands" and "declare[s] the glory of God" (Psa. 19:1), the preciseness of the fulfillment of his plan of redemption, likewise, manifests his work and glory. We simply need to take God at his Word and within the temporal and contextual framework He has determined. Again, I call this attribute of God divine perfection.

6. ***The New Testament writers intended for their original audience to understand.*** They did not write in words, sentences, codes, nuances, or symbols that they would not understand. Fee and Stuart explain that "in many cases the reason the texts are so difficult for us is that, frankly, they were not written to us."[80] Even classic dispensationalist Spargimino teaches that "the interpreter must first know what a scripture meant to the original audience before we can know what it means to us."[81]

7. ***Scripture must be allowed to interpret Scripture***. This basic guideline from the Reformation is often violated. But its comparison methodology must be allowed and followed to provide the determination of meaning for both literal and symbolic passages, and for the time context and nature of fulfillment. Submission to this guideline of the analogy of Scripture is especially significant for passages dealing with the nature of fulfillment, since they utilize both literal and figurative (symbolic) language.

---

[77] Ryrie, *The Basis of the Premillennial Faith*, 83.
[78] Spykman, *Reformational Theology*, 522.
[79] Klein, Blomberg, and Hubbard, Jr., *Introduction to Biblical Interpretation*, 303.
[80] Fee and Stuart, *How to Read the Bible for All Its Worth*, 59.
[81] Spargimino, *The Anti-Prophets*, 132.

8. *"The historically defensible interpretation has greatest authority.* That is, interpreters can have maximum confidence in their understanding of a text when they base that understanding on historically defensible arguments."[82] Klein et al. further advise that we "should seek the most likely *time* for the fulfillment of a prophecy in history."[83] Silva adds that "exegesis must be historical as well as grammatical, and must always seek the meaning intended, not any meaning that can be tortured out of a passage."[84]

9. ***The New Testament must be allowed to interpret the Old Testament.*** Two things that this hermeneutic mean are: first, the inspired expectations of Jesus and the NT writers must take precedence over ours. Secondly, as Klein et al. note, "the NT also indicates that literal OT prophecies may reach fulfillment in non-literal ways."[85]

10. ***There are no double fulfillments, double sense, partial fulfillments, near/far perspectives, or types and antitypes regarding the specific eschatological works of the Messiah, done by Him, in fulfillment of the plan of redemption and any end-time prophecy.*** After all, if we allow a double, why not triple, or quadruple, etc.? No textual warrant exists for resorting to any such claims, speculations, or scenarios. These eschatological works include his virgin birth, his anointing, the cross, his ascension, the sending of the Holy Spirit, and his coming on the clouds in age-ending judgment.[86]

It is my belief that adherence to these ten S-H guidelines will enable us to better follow a strict historical-grammatical-contextual hermeneutical methodology in the arena of eschatology. In the pages that follow, you will be reminded of some of these special S-H guidelines

---

[82] Klein, Blomberg, and Hubbard, Jr., *Introduction to Biblical Interpretation*, 149.

[83] Ibid., 310.

[84] Moisés Silva, *Has the Church Misread the Bible?* (Grand Rapids, MI.: Zondervan, 1987), 8.

[85] Klein, Blomberg, and Hubbard, Jr., *Introduction to Biblical Interpretation*, 307f.

[86] In opposition to this, Ryrie, for one, insists that "sometimes future events are so mingled together in a prophecy that they seem to be peaks in a range of mountains, the valleys being hidden." He also advocates the "law of double reference" (Ryrie, *The Final Countdown*, 18.)

when and where appropriate. My emphasis will always be on the "rightly" and not on "dividing" (2 Tim. 2:15), as we seek to discover the eschatological understanding and substance that best conforms with these S-H guidelines. With adherence to this more disciplined methodology, I also hope to demonstrate that prophetic-apocalyptic Scriptures are no longer "some of the Bible's most difficult passages to interpret."[87] Nor do we have to develop special exegetical devices to circumvent the natural meaning of any text. Their meanings are straightforward, harmoniously fit together, and glorify a God of precision.

In his recent book, *Biblical Hermeneutics*, Gerhard Maier, further highlights our need for "the development of a biblical-historical interpretation" as "the most urgent hermeneutical task facing us in theology today."[88] He calls for an "openness" which "means the constant willingness to be corrected."[89] It is to this task of correction, in regard to bookending the "appointed time . . . of the end" period, that we next turn.

. . . these ten S-H guidelines will enable us to better follow a strict historical-grammatical-contextual hermeneutical methodology in the arena of eschatology.

Please remember, God's attribute of divine perfection is how we humans can and are to know Who the One True God truly is (Isa. 44:6-8; 41:21-24; 42:8-9; 45:20-22; 46:9-11; 48:3-6). It's the God of the Bible Who foretold—many times and in many ways—what was going to happen in the future and when it would happen. As we are about to document, it all has happened, precisely. No other god, faith, religion, or ideology in the world can claim, nor has anything to compare with, the validating evidence of precisely fulfilled prophecy.

---

[87] Ibid., 312.
[88] Gerhard Maier, *Biblical Hermeneutics* (Wheaton, IL.: Crossway Books, 1994), 375.
[89] Ibid., 378.

My Continuing Disclaimer

Before proceeding to our next chapter, I again want to assure you that I have no desire to be in error, in any way, scripturally or historically. If at any time during your reading of this book you feel that I am in error, I want to know about it. My contact information is located in the front of this book, p. vi. I simply ask that you share it with me in the spirit of our two agreed-upon guidelines from the Introduction—#1 *Sola Scriptura* and #2 *In Love*—and in keeping with these scriptural admonishments (1 Thess. 5:21, Acts 17:11, 2 Tim. 2:15; 4:2; 1 Pet. 3:15-16). It would be more than nice if the proponents of each of the four views would extend this same courtesy and openness request to their hearers, readers, and viewers as well.

At this point during the 13-week MPC seminar series and during one of our Q &A times, one of the participants asked me this question: "Is what you are sharing and going to be sharing with us in the rest of this seminar series considered heretical?

"Yes," I answered in the affirmative, "it would be by most Christians." Then I added, "but it's also scriptural. The irony of all ironies, however and in my opinion, is they consider much that is clearly non-and unscriptural to be orthodox." This caveat generated a chuckle from the group.

Please keep in mind, as I additionally reminded them, the definition of "heresy" is: "a belief different from the accepted belief of a church, school, profession, or other group." Also, according to *The World Book Dictionary*, Thomas H. Huxley, a well-known English religious skeptic who invented the term "agnostic" in the mid 19th century, is quoted under the definition of "heresy" thusly, "It is the customary fate of new truths to begin as heresies."

By this above definition and explanation, Jesus was a heretic; so were Peter, Paul, and John, etc. Not bad heretical company to be associated with, are they? So, please keep our two agreed-on guidelines from the Introduction and our ten S-H guidelines from this chapter foremost in mind as we proceed together to test more traditional end-time beliefs and conventions.

Yes, I believe the time is ripe and the climate prime for a more comprehensive approach, a more disciplined methodology, and a significant breakthrough to the long-standing stalemate and divisive tradition of endsaying. Now, after centuries of confusion, thousands of failed predictions, and the recent bombardment of millennial madness (Y2K), you are about to discover what the divinely determined paradigm of the end that Bible consistently proclaims is really all about, that it is past and not future, is behind us and not a head of us, and that we moderns actually are living on the other side of the end—i.e., beyond the end.

. . . Jesus was a heretic, so were Peter, Paul, and John, etc. Not bad heretical company to be associated with, are they?

In our next chapter, let's begin to see if I can demonstrate all of this to you and more. If this is true, it truly is great good news. Its ramifications could change for the better the perspectives of many people and groups, and possibly nations. And it's all part of God's attribute of divine perfection. If you are ready for more, let's begin by delving into God's divinely determined timeline for when all the things concerning the long-proclaimed "appointed time . . . of the end" and "end of all things" were to occur.

Chapter 10

God's Divinely Determined Timeline

We modern-day mortals have not been left to wonder about the timing, duration, or nature of this most important, age-changing, transition, and paradigm-determined, time period that's variously termed the end times, the eschaton,[1] or, biblically, "the last days," "the last time(s)," "the time of the end," or just "the end."

As we have seen, two of several Old Testament prophets who specifically prophesied of "the time of the end" were Habakkuk and Daniel.[2] They are in agreement, and one prophecy gives light to the other. Hence, in the 7th century B.C., God inspired the Old Testament prophet Habakkuk to prophesy:

> For the revelation awaits an appointed time; it speaks of the end and will not prove false. Though it linger, wait for it; it will certainly come and will not delay.
>
> (Hab. 2:3)

---

[1] This term is used in theological circles and is variously defined as: the days of the Messiah, the time of consummation of all last things in salvation history, the time of fulfillment of all God's promises, the end times, the "last days," the coming of the kingdom of God in power, and the "time of the end."

[2] So did Moses (Deut. 31 and 32), Isaiah (Isa. 5:1-7), Zechariah (Zech. 14) and others, but not by using this expression.

At that time, neither Habakkuk nor anyone else had any idea when this "appointed time . . . of the end" (not "end of time"—big difference[3]) would come, or what events would accompany it. All Habakkuk knew was that there was such a thing as an appointed time, that it would "not prove false," that it would "certainly come," and that it would "not delay."

One century later, in the 6th century B.C., and in keeping with Amos 3:7 that God "does nothing without revealing his plan to his servants the prophets," God supernaturally gave another Old Testament prophet, Daniel, the two most spectacular and explicit time prophecies ever given to humankind. They are "Daniel's 70 weeks" and "time of the end." You'll find them in Daniel 9:24-27 and 12:1-13, respectively. Like bookends, these two prophetic time periods pinpointed and bracketed the exact time in history for this coming of the Messiah and Habakkuk's "appointed time . . . of the end." They also foretold the climactic events that would signal the consummation—i.e., the end or goal (Greek word, *telos*) of God's redemptive plan for humankind.

Unfortunately, much disagreement has arisen among both Christian and Jewish scholars over how and when Daniel's prophecy occurred. Some deny its prophetic element and say that Daniel's book was a contemporary forgery composed after-the-fact in the 2nd century B.C. and falsely attributed to a fictitious character of the sixth century B.C. in order to give it prophetic authority. This, they claim, accounts for its accuracy—it was "predicting" events that had already occurred during the persecutions of Antiochus Epiphanes (175-163 B.C.) and the Jewish revolt led by Judas Maccabaeus that defeated Antiochus.[4] This degrading

---

[3] Traditionally and erroneously, Christians have transposed these words to mean that when Jesus returns it will be the end of time, and the end of this material world and universe.

[4] Some liberal scholars have insisted that all or part of this book was written in the 2nd century B.C. in the time of Antiochus Epiphanes (175-163 B.C.). I, however, agree with the majority of biblical scholars who take Daniel at face value. Daniel states that it was written during the time of Babylonian exile, which was in the 6th century B.C. (Dan. 1:1f.). The historical fact that 1st-century B.C. Qumran Jews viewed Daniel's book as inspired, and made more copies of it than any other Old Testament book is the best evidence for its stated date, and for a refutation of the "contemporary forgery" idea. But even if it was written in the 2nd century B.C., that still leaves an approximate two-century

view seems illogical when we note the reverence given to the book of Daniel in Jewish Scripture. It was so prized, revered, and accepted by the 1st-century B.C. scribes in the Qumran community that they made more copies of it than any other Old Testament book. These two factors indicate their regard of Daniel as authoritative. Furthermore, and as we shall soon see, there is no possible way even one of the six purpose statements encapsulated in this prophecy could have been fulfilled during that time of Antiochus (see Dan. 9:24).

Nonetheless, two indisputable facts remain. First, Jesus gave no credence to any kind of a fulfillment or typological "double reference" in Antiochus Epiphanes' time. As we shall see in Chapter 13, He did just the opposite, bypassing Antiochus' time entirely. Secondly, many Jews back in Jesus' day and time were expecting the Messiah. Why was this? They had been reading Daniel's scroll and figuring out its time prophecies. Thus, Messianic fever was running high back then and there.

In a similar degrading fashion, Daniel's two time prophecies, elaborating on Habakkuk's "appointed time . . . of the end," are (it is almost needless to say) some of the most misunderstood and misapplied passages of Scripture. The popular view among Christian evangelicals in our day and time is that this "appointed time" has been delayed (or put on hold), and is yet future. But this is in direct contradiction to Habakkuk's text of "will not delay," and invalidates the very inspiration these proponents seek to uphold.

A word of caution. Over the centuries, many scholars have offered a wide variety of conflicting and manipulative interpretations of Daniel's prophecies. Using questionable techniques and intrusive devises, they have built a wide array of different end-time scenarios and expectations which I am not going to address here.[5] No doubt this methodology is behind the reason many feel that Daniel's time prophecies are "one of the most puzzling prophetic texts to decipher."[6] The problem here is not what or how Daniel prophesied. The problem is with the presuppositions,

---

foretelling factor to explain. Many of these same scholars maintain that all of Daniel was fulfilled in the 2nd century B.C. But they fail to explain how the six purpose clauses in Daniel 9:24 were fulfilled at that time.

[5] Again, for a more extensive treatment in depth and detail, see my book *The Perfect Ending for the World*, 109-133.

[6] Hays, Duvall, and Pate, *Dictionary of Biblical Prophecy and End Times*, 425.

assumptions, and expectations modern-day interpreters bring to this text. Nevertheless, they all recognize that Daniel is the key to the end times— whenever that was or will be.

> **Daniel's two time prophecies . . . are (it is almost needless to say) some of the most misunderstood and misapplied passages of Scripture.**

In my opinion, the understanding outlined in this chapter is the most straightforward, clearest, historically documentable, and inspirationally impressive and defensible. Even a hard-boiled skeptic must be impressed by its unaltered, uninterrupted, chronological exactness, and its historically significant context. As you read, keep in mind that it's not all-important to agree with every detail in order to grasp the totality of what exactly transpired during these two interrelated time periods and the transition in between. Keep in mind that if some aspects were not fulfilled and still lie in the future, as most popular futuristic endsaying views hold, then Habakkuk's "appointed time of the end" failed to arrive on time; it proved false. But such truncated views violate the integrity of Scripture. If it was delayed, then Habakkuk prophesied falsely, for he said it would certainly come, and would not be delayed. We'd be well advised not to monkey with Daniel and his two time prophecies.

In the rest of this chapter, we shall explore how the God of divine perfection throughout his physical creation—macro and micro—applied his order, design, a plan, purpose, and a fixed and specified timeframe into his plan of redemption. We shall see how He foretold it all hundreds of years in advance and fulfilled it with timely and mathematical precision. Thus, everything happened "at just the right time" (Rom. 5:6) and "in its proper time" (1 Tim. 2:6).

Please be assured, that Daniel's two time prophecies can be understood in a straightforward sense and in a fulfillment context that keeps the biblical inspiration intact and proves God is not ambiguous or deceptive. They are his self-imposed boundaries and his divinely determined framework for the end-times. No artificial interpretative devices such as gaps, interruptions, postponements, delays, elongations, twisted dates, flip-flopped segments, symbolic appeals, non-literal tampering, or esoteric qualifying methods of any kind are required to properly understand this fulfillment—which are so commonly employed by others. Nor do they contain hidden or secretly encoded meanings. In other words—God doesn't play word games. Daniel's time prophecies are plainly written. And God intended them to be clearly understood, not confusing and divisive.

So if you're ready, let's now examine, in a highlighted fashion, how Daniel got it exactly right—the literal, exact, chronological, and sequential fulfillment of Daniel's two time prophecies—no interruptions, no gaps, no gimmicks.

Daniel's Time Prophecy of '70 Weeks'

Around the year 538 B.C., some 2,500 years ago, many Jews, along with Daniel, were living in captivity in Babylon. At this time the prophet Daniel prayed to the God of Israel for his people. He knew that God had decreed beforehand, through the prophet Jeremiah, a precise 70-year period of captivity during which no mention was made of any interruptions or gaps of time (Dan. 9:1-2; Jer. 25:11-12; 29:10; also Zech. 1:12; 2 Chron. 36:20-23).[7] Since Daniel and a first group of captives were deported in 605 B.C., he realized that Jeremiah's prophecy was near completion. It was time for their release and return to their homeland.

As he prayed, the angel Gabriel appeared to him. In answer to his petition for the forgiveness and restoration of a repeatedly rebellious Israel, Gabriel gave Daniel a powerful prophetic vision. He was to have clear "insight and understanding" (Dan. 9:22) of the extended future that God had determined for the Jews. Part of that vision was this time prophecy of "seventy sevens" or 70 weeks of years (Dan. 9:24-27 [*KJV*]):

---

[7] It's difficult to fix the exact dates for the beginning and ending of the 70 years of Babylonian captivity. Daniel and some other prominent Jews were taken captive in 605 B.C. Larger groups were deported in 597 and 586 B.C. The final destruction of Jerusalem did not occur until 586 B.C. Likewise, the return from exile was also staggered over a period of years. Contained within this time variance is the actual 70-year period prophesied by Jeremiah.

"Seventy 'sevens' are decreed [determined] for your people and your holy city to finish transgression, to put an end to sin, to atone for wickedness, to bring in everlasting righteousness, to seal up vision and prophecy and to anoint the most holy."

Know and understand this: From the issuing of the decree to restore and rebuild Jerusalem until the Anointed One, the ruler, comes, there will be seven 'sevens,' and sixty-two 'sevens.' It will be rebuilt with streets and a trench, but in times of trouble. After the sixty-two 'sevens,' the Anointed One will be cut off and will have nothing. The people of the ruler who will come will destroy the city and the sanctuary. The end will come like a flood: War will continue until the end, and desolations have been decreed [are determined]. He will confirm a covenant with many for one 'seven,' but in the middle of that 'seven' he will put an end to sacrifice and offering. And one who causes desolation will place abominations on a wing of the temple until the end that is decreed [determined] is poured out on him."

The Hebrew word (*sha bu'a*), translated above as "sevens," or "weeks" in some versions, literally means a unit, a period, or a group of seven of something. It's akin to our English word *dozen*, which means a unit of twelve of something. The word by itself does not tell us what the units are. I agree with the standard interpretation that Daniel's sevens of something was sevens of years.[8] Therefore, seventy times seven *years* equates to a total time span of 490 years.

The angel Gabriel further stated that both the duration and contents of this divinely fixed time period of 490 years were "decreed [or determined] for your people (the Jews) and your holy city (Jerusalem)." It included the achievement of the six purposes stated in Daniel 9:24. But its express purpose was to reveal the exact time and number of years in human history when God would send the "Anointed One, the ruler" or "Messiah the Prince" to Israel to begin his public ministry and confirm a covenant for one week of years (seven years). Thus, Daniel's 70 weeks prophecy historically links the Old Covenant, Judaic period to the New Covenant, Christian period.

This total elapsed time of 490 years further demonstrates that the course of events was already decided. It had a specific starting and

---

[8] For more, see: Noē *The Perfect Ending for the World*, 117.

finishing point, and was subdivided into three time segments: 1) an initial period of "seven sevens" or 49 years, 2) a period of "sixty-two sevens" or 434 years, and 3) a final period of "one seven" or 7 years.

Scripturally and historically, we can examine this prophesied 490-year period and verify its determinism and accuracy. Historically, we can see it transpire as a firm, unbroken sequence of chronological time and events leading to the Christ. For those accustomed to a postponement tradition, the following exposition may be disturbing or even threatening. For others, it will be quite illuminating. For all, it is important validation of the biblical faith that must not be overlooked or truncated. I hope you'll be convinced that this explanation demonstrates that the God of the Bible is the God of divine perfection, exactness, and history told in advance. He definitely is the one, true, and proven God (Isa. 44:6-8; 41:22-23, 26; 42:9; 45:21-22; 46:9-10; 48:3-6; Amos 3:7). And He has spoken through his prophets to all humanity. The sincere seeker of truth will surely recognize and understand the precision and drama of Daniel's prophecy.

Beginning at 457 B.C. and using the ancient dating chronology of Ptolemy,[9] I shall present for your consideration a section-by-section, historic, and mathematically precise fulfillment of Daniel's 70 weeks with no gaps and no gimmicks. As you proceed, please be reminded, once again, of Klein, Blomberg, & Hubbard's counsel that . . .

---

[9] Although Ptolemy's chronology—developed in the 2nd century A.D.—is generally accepted by the majority of scholars, not everyone agrees it is correct. Philip Mauro, in his book, *The Wonders of Bible Chronology* (Reiner Publications, Swengel, PA, 1974) claims that "Ptolemy makes the duration of the Persian Empire more than eighty years too long." Mauro further claims that Ptolemy's chronological statements are "contradicted by the writings of Josephus . . . Persian traditions . . . and by the Jewish National traditions" (p-6). Mauro's chronology is derived from the Bible and recasts the chronology of the last 500 years of the Old Testament era. He, therefore, dates Cyrus' Decree at 457 B.C. Whichever way is correct, both Mauro and this author see 457 B.C. as the appropriate starting date for Daniel's 70 weeks. For readers interested in the details of Mauro's calculations and his proof, I refer you to his book *The Seventy Weeks and the Great Tribulation* (ibid, 1975), and to John C. Whitcomb's book, *Darius the Mede*. All three are well worth one's time and careful consideration.

The historically defensible interpretation has greatest authority. That is, interpreters can have maximum confidence in their understanding of a text when they base that understanding on historically defensible arguments.[10]

And this is exactly what we'll do for both of Daniel's two time prophecies.

The Starting Point

457 B.C. . . . from the issuing of the decree to restore and rebuild Jerusalem . . . (Dan. 9:25).

The Bible records three decrees by Gentile kings that affected the restoration and rebuilding of Jerusalem (Ezra 6:14):

- Cyrus' Decree in 538 B.C. (Ezra 1:2-4).
- Darius' Decree around 520 B.C. (Ezra 6:3-12).
- Artaxerxes' Decree, dated by the majority of historians and Bible scholars at 457 B.C. (Ezra 7:11-26).

Which is the right one?

The decree and date which best begins the grand countdown of 490 years is the last one, Artaxerxes' in 457 B.C., and for a number of reasons.[11] One of these reasons is dating from the first two decrees has no literal, future, or chronological significance or historical prophetic value. For it to work out would require either a time gap or a symbolic reading of the numbers for the time period to come out with any significant meaning. But dating from Artaxerxes' Decree has major significance and covers everything.[12] It is also the latest possible date.

---

[10] Klein and others, *Introduction to Biblical Interpretation*, 149.
[11] See Noē, *The Perfect Ending for the World*, 119.
[12] The 444 B.C. date of Artaxerxes' letters is advocated as the starting point by some Bible scholars. But these "letters" are not accorded decree status in Scripture. These scholars tend to favor the use what is termed "prophetic years" of 360 days each. This notion is taken from the use of the Jewish lunar year and from the idea that the 1,260 days of Revelation 12:6, the "time and times and half a time" of Revelation 12:14, and the 42 months of Revelation 13:5 as all representing a 3½ year period.

First Segment: the Seven Sevens

457 – 408 B.C. . . . *It will be rebuilt with streets and a trench, but in times of trouble* . . . (Dan. 9:25).

The first segment of 49 years spanned the restoring and rebuilding of Jerusalem under the administration of Ezra and Nehemiah. You can read about it in the book of Nehemiah, especially chapters 2-6. Nehemiah records how the Jews returned from captivity and worked "in times of trouble," just as Daniel had prophesied. Carrying materials with one hand and a weapon in the other, returning Jews rebuilt the walls in 52 days (Neh. 4:17-18; 6:15). This was only part of the restoration. They also restored the streets and houses (Neh. 7:4); instituted laws, civil ordinances (Neh. 7:5), and religious reforms (Neh. 13:30); and finished settling in Jerusalem within this 49-year time segment (Neh. 11:1).[13]

Calculation by this method brings scholars close to some of the same 1st-century time dates and events we present. But their explanations are not nearly as descriptive and precise as those presented here. Here's how they figure:

>   444 B.C.
>   +
>   173,880 days (483 Years of 360 days each or
>   approximately 476 solar years of 365¼ days to
>   the Messiah)
>   A.D. 33

Some Jewish scholars begin Daniel's 70 Weeks with God's decree announcement in Jeremiah 29:10, supposedly made in 587 B.C. They end it with the destruction of the Temple in A.D. 70. This raises even more problems since the time span from 587 B.C. to A.D. 70 is 658 years, not 490.

---

[13] Later books in the Old Testament give no information about how long this period of rebuilding took to complete.

"According to Barnes and several other trustworthy Bible commentators, the historian Prideaux declared that Nehemiah's last action in rebuilding the city occurred in the fifteenth year of the Persian ruler Darius Nothus (423-404 B.C.). His fifteenth year was the 49th year from the 457 B.C. (or 458) decree. Josephus seems to support this idea in his remarks about the death of Nehemiah. This can

Second Segment: Sixty-two Sevens

408 B.C. – A.D. 27 *. . . and sixty-two 'sevens'* (Dan. 9:25)
Sixty-two sevens, (i.e., 434 more consecutive years) pass. Note that no interval or interruptive gap between the 7-week and 62-week segments is suggested in the text. Toward the close of this second segment, messianic expectations began running high in the Promised Land, and for good reason. Daniel's time prophecy was well-known, and its fulfillment was being anticipated. In addition, Jesus Christ was born, most probably in 4 B.C., not A.D. 0, as is sometimes assumed. (Mistakes made in transposing dates into the commonly accepted Christian calendar by the 6th-century A.D. Roman monk, Dionysius Exiguus, account for this dating discrepancy.)

Third Segment: One Seven—the First Half

A.D. 27 – 30. *. . . until the Anointed One, the ruler, comes, there will be seven 'sevens' and sixty-two 'sevens' . . .* (Dan. 9:25).
This one week is the most significant and the most misunderstood. It will require special attention. To help our understanding, I have divided it into four sections: first half, middle, second half, and finishing point. An "anointing" event marks both the conclusion of the second 62-week segment and the beginning of Daniel's 70th and final week of unbroken and uninterrupted years.
Again, there is no suggestion in the text of any interval or interruptive gap between the 62-week and 1-week segments. Simple arithmetic shows 483 years (49 + 434 years) had elapsed since Artaxerxes' Decree in 457 B.C. It's now A.D. 27. Jesus Christ, "the

---

be viewed as an indication that the 457 B.C. date is correct. But it is possible that some rebuilding continued after that." From, *The Daniel Papers Discovery Series* by Resources For Biblical Communication, Radio Bible Class (Grand Rapids, Michigan, 1994), 15-16.

In the absence of any better information, it is safe to assume that 49 years after the third decree was issued, the work was completed. Difficulty in reconstructing ancient chronology throughout these weeks means that we have to be satisfied with close but approximate dating in confirming what most probably is absolutely accurate to the very year, if not very day.

Anointed One, the ruler" (or "Messiah the Prince"),[14] who had emptied Himself of his glory, authority, and power to become like other men (Phil. 2:7-8; Heb. 2:17), is hereby publicly identified as the Messiah with his baptism in the Jordan River. At that moment he is *anointed* by the Holy Spirit. No previous or subsequent event in Jesus' earthly life could be taken as the fulfillment of these words of Gabriel to Daniel (see Acts 10:38; Heb. 1:9). Luke reports that Jesus was about 30 years of age at that time (Luke 3:22-23). As was the Jewish custom, the 30th year was the age at which men of Israel were permitted to become active in temple or tabernacle service.

Next, Jesus departed and went into the wilderness for a period of forty days (Luke 4:1-2). Luke 4:13-21 records that after Jesus had been tempted in the wilderness, He went to Nazareth where He had been raised, stood up in the synagogue, and read the messianic prophecy from Isaiah 61:1-2 regarding the coming of an "anointed one" and "the year of the Lord's favor." Then Jesus said, "Today this scripture is fulfilled in your hearing."

Something else, however, is especially noteworthy about Jesus' quotation from Isaiah. He stopped in mid-verse. He did not quote the last half of Isaiah 61:2 concerning "the day of vengeance of our God." Why not? It's because the time period for the fulfillment of that day of judgment was not yet present. Its fulfillment awaited the future time of Daniel's "time of the end," which we'll cover next.

From the day of his anointing, Jesus moved in the power and authority of the New Covenant. During the next 3½ years of his earthly ministry, Jesus taught and demonstrated the new in-breaking kingdom of God (Dan. 2:44; 7:14, 18, 22, 27) and modeled its "powers of the age to come" (Heb. 6:5). Also, He trained and commanded his followers to do likewise. Thus, "Jesus came into Galilee, preaching and manifesting the gospel of the kingdom of God, and saying, the time is fulfilled . . ." (Mark 1:14-15 *KJV*). What time was He talking about? It was the fullness of Daniel's 70 weeks time prophecy.[15] The 70th week was upon them, precisely, right on time.

Next, we must read this verse closely. What is to happen *after* the sixty-two sevens is crucial to our understanding.

---

[14] Anointed" is the Hebrew word *mashiyach* and means "Messiah."
[15] Also, see Daniel 2:44 and 7:15-28.

"After sixty-two' sevens' the Anointed One will be cut off and will have nothing. The people of the ruler who will come will destroy the city and the sanctuary. The end will come like a flood: War will continue until the end, and desolations have been decreed [determined] .... And one who causes desolation will place abominations on a wing of the temple until the end that is decreed [determined] is poured out on him" (Dan. 9:26 [*KJV*]).

The only time restriction here is "after" sixty-two sevens (the 69th week, 483 years). It is not predicting that all this will happen during the 70th week of years. It is simply saying "after" the 69th week. Nor does it say how long after—just after. However, we know that the final week began with Jesus' anointing some 3 years earlier. So, the Messiah being "cut off"[16] so as to "have nothing" meant He was crucified and had nothing befitting the Messiah. Hence, this prophecy foretold the rejection of Jesus by the Jews. This did occur during the middle of that 70th week in A.D. 30. He was without his messianic kingdom. This event is time-restricted in the next verse and will be addressed in our next section on the middle of the 70th week.

Thus we have separated the "cutting off" (the crucifixion), which is time-restricted to the middle of the final week, from the other events of Daniel 9:26, which are not so restricted, but only named as coming "after" the sixty-two weeks. We know from history that these events occurred some thirty-seven years after the crucifixion.

These other events that were to come "after" the sixty-two weeks are the destruction of Jerusalem and the Temple, and desolations and abominations. They were "decreed" or "determined" (meaning fixed and unable to be changed) *within* Daniel's 70th week, when most of Israel did not or would not recognize the time of its visitation by Messiah, just as Jesus had warned (Luke 19:41-44). These latter events did not take place until around A.D. 66 - 73 because they were part of *the end* and were associated with Daniel's other time prophecy, the *time of the end*. In Daniel's last chapter, Gabriel gave Daniel this second and final time

---

[16] Daniel uses the Hebrew word (*Karath*), translated as "cut off." This word was used for the death penalty (Lev. 7:20, 21, 25, 27), and often referred to violent death (1 Sam. 17:51; Obad. 9; Nah. 3:15). In Isaiah 53:8, where it is prophesied of the death of Christ, "He was cut off out of the land of the living," the word is *ghzar* and has a nearly identical meaning.

prophecy for the chronological fulfillment of those "determined," time-of-the-end events. As we shall discover, it has its own separate timeframe, different time parameters, and different terminology.

How can we be so sure these end-time events were only "decreed" or "determined" *within* Daniel's 70th week and not fulfilled in that time segment? The answer is found in the way the Hebrew word is used elsewhere. In Daniel 11:36, the same Hebrew word [*charats*], translated as "decreed" or "determined," is used in a future fulfillment sense, ". . . for what has been determined must take place." Hence, "decreed" or "determined" [past tense] does not require that all events "happen" during that same timeframe, although some did. Others were only set, or locked into motion (determined) for future fulfillment. *This distinction must be understood.* It enables us to maintain the integrity of Daniel's two interrelated and interconnected timeframes without resorting to gaps, interruptions, or other manipulative gimmicks.

Middle of the Final Week

A.D. 30. . . . He will confirm a covenant with many for one 'seven,' but in the middle of that seven, he [Jesus, the Messiah] *shall put an end to sacrifice and offering . . .* (Dan. 9:27).

Please note that this event is in the middle of the last week, the same time as the previous "cutting off." The crucifixion of the Messiah is hereby time restricted to the middle of the 70th week, and so is the end of sacrifice and offering. Even though the Jews continued the practice of animal sacrifices and offerings for another forty years, Christ's death and resurrection ended that Old Covenant obligation. It no longer had value and acceptability. It had been superseded by the "once-for-all . . . sacrifice" of Christ (Heb. 9:26, 10:10; 1 Pet. 3:18). What's more, it sealed or "determined" the fulfillment of all six of the redemptive purposes and promises for Daniel's 70 weeks time prophecy stated in verse 24:

        1. To finish transgression;
        2. To make an end of sin;
        3. To atone for wickedness;
        4. To bring in everlasting righteousness;
        5. To seal up the vision and prophecy;
        6. To anoint the most holy (place).

This listing is restoration language. It is not "Antichrist" or world tribulation language. Nor did any of these six purposes happen during the time of Antiochus Epiphanes (175-163 B.C.). Rather, it speaks of the final portion of God's plan for redeeming humankind from the consequences of sin. With his death on the cross, Jesus set in motion this restorative and consummatory process. But as we shall see throughout this book, the new could not fully come, nor could all six of these purposes and promises be fully brought in and totally fulfilled until the old was completely removed at the "time of the end." That time was still in the future for those living in A.D. 30. But it would "not prove false; it would "certainly come;" and would "not delay," just as Habakkuk had prophesied.

Second Half of the Final Week

A.D. 30 – 34 (3½ Years). After the Messiah was "cut off," or crucified, as the prophet Isaiah had also foretold (Isa. 53:8), his disciples and followers obediently stayed in Jerusalem awaiting and then experiencing the events of Pentecost (Luke 24:49). But after Pentecost they did *not* disperse and "Go . . . and teach all nations" or "make disciples of all nations," as Jesus had commanded (Matt. 28:19 *KJV - NIV*). Why didn't they? It's because the covenant was to be confirmed for "one seven" (one week of years), first and exclusively upon the Jews (Dan. 9:24; Rom. 1:16; John 4:22). The purpose and focus of Daniel's last week of years was to be a 7-year period of covenant confirmation for the Jews—and not a time of world tribulation a la a contrived "Antichrist." Half of this final "one-seven" segment still remained. The covenant to be confirmed was the one promised through the prophet Jeremiah (Jer. 31:31-33). The first half of 3½ years was fulfilled by the earthly ministry of Jesus Christ and his disciples. That meant that 3½ more years were yet to be fulfilled before Jesus' followers would be free to take the Gospel outside the Jewish realm. To this day, most Jews don't recognize that their prophet Isaiah said the Servant (the Messiah) would also be sent to the Gentiles (Isa. 49:6f.).

The biblical fact of Jewish preeminence is frequently emphasized throughout the Gospels. God set it up that way. Remember, Jesus did not minister to the Gentiles (with a few notable foreshadowing exceptions). He had commanded his disciples, "Go not into the way of the Gentiles, and into any city of the Samaritans enter ye not; but go rather to the lost sheep of the house of Israel" (Matt. 10:5-6; 15:24 *KJV*). Is Jesus' command here in contradiction to his Great Commission command to go and teach [make] disciples of all nations (Matt. 28:18-20)? No, it is not. Why not? It's because there was a time-restricted waiting period in which the New Covenant was to be confirmed with the Jews exclusively. That time was during the seven years of Daniel's 70th and final week.

Jesus' disciples knew this. How did they know? Quite simply, Jesus told them. In Luke, Jesus expounded and explained in all the Scriptures the things concerning Himself. He began at Moses and proceeded through all the prophets (Luke 24:27). Jesus' teaching would have most certainly included Daniel, the Jews' most copied book, and Daniel's prophecy of 70 weeks pertaining to the Messiah. Further, "He opened their minds so they could understand the Scriptures" (Luke 24:45). The Bible says that Jesus' teaching caused their hearts to burn within them (Luke 24:32). This is how they knew that they were prohibited in where and to whom they could go until the time restriction ran its course. Consequently, they remained in Jerusalem and preached exclusively to the Jews until the time was up.

Finishing Point of the Final Week

A.D. 34. Toward the end of A.D. 33, Jewish persecution of Christians in Jerusalem reached a climax with the stoning death of Stephen (Acts 7:54-60). The Bible says that all except the apostles were scattered throughout Judea and Samaria (Acts 8:1).

The event that documents the finishing point of Daniel's 70th week occurred when "Philip went down to a city in Samaria, and proclaimed Christ there" (Acts 8:5). How could he do this? Hadn't Christ forbidden it? What's more, the apostles in Jerusalem sent Peter and John to Samaria as a support team to build on what Philip had started (Acts 8:14 ff.). Were they disobeying Jesus' prohibition on going to the Gentiles? The answer is no, because it was now A.D. 34. The time restriction for confirming the New Covenant exclusively for the Jews was now chronologically over.[17]

---

[17] Some scholars feel that Philip's journey to Samaria occurred five to ten years after Christ's death. But the point is the same, the time restriction had expired.

The Gospel of the New Covenant had come first to the Jews, then to the Samaritans, who, as half breeds, were despised by the Jews (Acts 8), and finally to the Gentiles (Acts 10; 11:18-20) and the whole world. In this manner, the mystery of God uniting Jew and Gentile into one body was phased into human history (John 4:22; Eph. 3:3-6, 9; Col. 1:26-27; 2:2; 4:3; Rom. 3:19-31; 15:26-27). God's grand purpose was never to make boundaries between peoples or nations, but to make all one.

In retrospect, then, the prophecy of Daniel's 70 weeks:

- *Commenced* in 457 B.C. with the decree of Artaxerxes.
- Was *determined* in A.D. 30 at the cross.
- Was *confirmed* by the New Covenant for 3½ years before and 3½ years after the cross.
- *Concluded* in A.D. 34 when the Gospel had been preached to the Jews and was now freed to go to the Gentiles.

The entire prophecy transpired over an uninterrupted 490-year period. No valid rationale exists for interrupting the time segments, splitting apart the years, inserting gaps, elongating weeks, or postponing, delaying, minimizing or tampering with the fixed time period in any manner—as so many interpreters have done over the centuries.

The time restriction for confirming the New Covenant exclusively for the Jews was now chronologically over.

Thus, the front bookend of the end-time, age-changing transition period—Daniel's 70th week—certainly came and was perfectly fulfilled. Perfectly! It's a mainstay of messianic authentication, a mathematical demonstration for the divine inspiration of the Bible, and an unanswerable argument for critics of the Christian faith. In other words it's divine perfection.

Even so, all was not completed. More that had been "decreed" or "determined" remained to be accomplished; a fact which brings us to our back bookend, our final time period, and the grand finale of the end that would shortly come to pass. *(See Appendix A for a timeline of the events outlined in this chapter.)*

Daniel's 'Time of the End' Prophecy

Once again, the biblical term is "time of the end," and not "end of time" (Dan. 12:4, 9; 11:35; 8:19). Big difference. The Bible never speaks of an end of time. Changing the order of these words has led many into gross error, resulting in end-of-the-world misconceptions and a false paradigm that we discarded in Chapter 8.

Daniel's second time prophecy is found in his last chapter, Daniel 12:1-13. It serves as the back bookend or boundary of the age-changing transition we call the "end times" and the Bible calls the "last days" (Heb. 1:2).

> "At that time Michael, the great prince who protects your people, will arise. There will be a time of distress such as has not happened from the beginning of nations until then. But at that time your people – everyone whose name is found written in the book – will be delivered. Multitudes who sleep in the dust of the earth will awake: some to everlasting life, others to shame and everlasting contempt. Those who are wise will shine like the brightness of the heavens, and those who lead many to righteousness, like the stars for ever and ever. But you, Daniel, close up and seal the words of the scroll until the time of the end. Many will go here and there to increase knowledge."
>
> Then, I Daniel, looked, and there before me stood two others, one on this bank of the river and one on the opposite bank. One of them said to the man clothed in linen, who was above the waters of the river, "How long will it be before these astonishing things are fulfilled?"
>
> The man clothed in linen, who was above the waters of the river, lifted his right hand and his left hand toward heaven, and I heard him swear by him who lives forever, saying, 'It will be for a time, times and half a time. When the power of the holy people has been finally broken, all these things will be completed.'"
>
> He replied, 'Go your way, Daniel, because the words are closed up and sealed until the time of the end. Many will be purified, made spotless and refined, but the wicked will continue to be wicked. None of the wicked will understand, but those who are wise will understand.

"From the time that the daily sacrifice is abolished and the abomination that causes desolation is set up, there will be 1,290 days. Blessed is the one who waits for and reaches the end of the 1,335 days.

"As for you, go your way till the end. You will rest, and then at the end of the days you will rise to receive your allowed inheritance.'"

In his previous 70-week prophecy, Daniel referred to some of the events that would take place during this "time of the end," including the fall of Jerusalem, the destruction of the Jewish Temple, and many other desolations of war (see Dan. 9:26). But these events were only "decreed" or "determined" within Daniel's 70th week. Their actual occurrence (fulfillment) lies outside that time period. But how can we be sure this interpretation is correct?

In his last vision, Daniel sees two others (angels) standing on the bank of a river and talking. One asks the other, "How long will it be before these astonishing things are fulfilled" (Dan. 12:6b). The asking of this time question subsequent to Daniel receiving his 70 week prophecy strongly suggests that the events of this fulfillment were not included in that previous time period. This is evidently why Daniel is given another time prophecy for another sovereignly determined time period. Note, however, that this one uses different time terminology, which differentiates it from the 490-year time span covered by Daniel's 70 weeks.

This second prophecy speaks in terms of straight days (1,290 and 1,335) instead of "sevens" or "weeks" of years. As we shall see, the two sets of days are not two separate time periods, but rather the shorter period is inclusive within the longer. This can also be legitimately surmised since it was specified that the "time of the end" would be "for a time, times and half a time," or approximately a year, two years, and half a year. This phrase links back to the same terminology used in Daniel 7:25-28 and was the standard Jewish interpretation contained in their rabbinical writings and commentaries. Further, it compares with the 2,300 evenings and mornings (Dan. 8:14) of temporary cessation of Temple services occurring during the three-year and two-month period of occupation by Antiochus Epiphanes in 167-164 B.C.

Daniel's "time of the end" would be a time of intensified trouble and divine judgment. That judgment would be poured out upon Daniel's people (Israel) "in the latter days" (Dan. 10:14 *KJV*) because of their continual breaking of the covenant and rebellion against God and his plan of redemption via the Messiah. The climax would occur "when the power of the holy people (the Jews) has been finally broken." At that time, "all these things" concerning the "time of the end" would "be completed (Dan. 12:7), including the resurrection of the dead (Dan. 12:2, 13).

So, what was this "power of the holy people?" It was the biggest power God had ever given anyone at that time—the power of biblical Judaism (i.e., their exclusive relationship with God as manifested by the Temple complex [Isa. 2:2-5; 56:7]). The final breaking of this power was to be both the *historical setting* and *defining characteristic* for Daniel's "time of the end." Please note, once again, that this distinguishing element was *not* to be the demise of planet Earth, the end of time, the end of human existence, the removal of believers from the world (rapture), a 1,000-year reign of Christ, or any of the other traditional end-time notions.

In Daniel's day, the 6th century B.C., this transitional period of history was still in the "distant future" (Dan. 8:19, 26). So Daniel was told to go his way because "the words are closed up and sealed until the time of the end" (Dan. 12:9). Notably, and in stark contrast, the angel tells John in the 1st-century A.D. book of Revelation, "do not seal up the words of the prophecy of this book, because the time is at hand" (Rev. 22:10). Did you note the significant difference?

The climax would occur "when the power of the holy people (the Jews) has been finally broken." At that time, "all these things" concerning the "time of the end" would "be completed (Dan. 12:7)

Also there is something else significant for us to note. In contrast to the wealth of Scripture supporting the fulfillment of Daniel's 70-weeks time prophecy, none exists for the fulfillment of Daniel's "time of the end." Why not? It's because a strong case can be made that all the books later included in the New Testament canon were written before the "time of the end."[18] However, with the help of Josephus (A.D. 37 - ca.100),[19] the 1st-century Jewish priest and renowned historian for the Romans who was an eyewitness to the end time, we have authentication for the fulfillment of Daniel's final, "time-of-the-end" prophecy—again, no gaps and no gimmicks, but literal, exact, chronological and sequential fulfillment—i.e. divine perfection.

The Starting Point

A.D. 66. (Dan. 12:11) . . . from the time that the daily sacrifice is abolished. . . .

In July of A.D. 66, Josephus records, as part of the Jewish rebellion against Rome, Jewish Zealots stormed Jerusalem and burned the palace of Agrippa and Bernice (the Roman ruler and his sister). They also burned the palace of the Jewish High Priest, Ananias, and killed him in retaliation for his liberal affiliation with the Romans. Next, they massacred a garrison of Roman soldiers. And to top it off, they stopped performing the twice-daily Temple sacrifices for Caesar and the Roman people. Josephus states that this cessation of the daily sacrifice was the true beginning of the Roman-Jewish War.[20] Both the Romans and the revolting Jews viewed it as a formal declaration of war. The total cessation of all sacrifices didn't take place until the Jews ran out of priests and animals in August of A.D. 70, just prior to the fall of Jerusalem and the destruction of the Temple by the Roman army under the command of Titus.

1,290 Days Later *(Dan. 12:11) . . . and the abomination that causes desolation is set up, there will be 1,290 days.*

Earlier, Daniel had referred to "desolations" (note the plural) that had

---

[18] See, for example: Gentry, *Before Jerusalem Fell* and John A.T. Robinson, *Redating the New Testament* (Philadelphia, PA.: Westminster Press, 1976).

[19] Of course, Josephus' historical accounts are not inspired and not as reliable as those in the Bible. He is, nevertheless, considered a very reliable source, and the most accurate and only eye-witness authority of the time for historical information.

[20] Josephus, *The Wars of the Jew,* in William Whiston, trans., *The Works of Josephus* (Peabody, MA.: Hendrickson Publishers, 1987), 2.17.2 (409).

been "decreed" or "determined" (Dan. 9:26b), and stated that "one who causes desolation (note the singular) will place abominations on a wing of the temple until the end that is decreed is poured out on him" (Dan 9:27b).[21] "Wing" refers to a pinnacle or an extremity point of abominations. Again, the determination was done during the 70 weeks, but their fulfillments were not a chronological part of the 70 weeks' timeframe. Remember, the only restriction was "after" the 62-week segment.

Early in the year A.D. 70 (approximately—if not exactly—three years and six months, or 1,290 days, after the cessation of the twice-daily sacrifice for Caesar and Rome), Josephus reports that a major abomination took place in the Temple that all in Jerusalem could see. While the Roman Army (under the leadership of Titus) was encamped in Caesarea on the Mediterranean Sea, approximately fifty-five miles northwest of Jerusalem, and marshaling its forces for the final campaign against Jerusalem, civil strife between three rival, Jewish factions inside the city walls reached a climax. Rival Zealot factions defiled the Temple's innermost courts with murders as fierce fighting raged among the Jews struggling for control. The Temple was their battleground and was defiled with carnage at every corner. Even worshipers were killed while trying to offer their sacrifices.[22] They even burned their own storehouses of grain and corn, which would have supplied and fed them for years under a siege.

There can be little doubt that the warring of the three Jewish factions inside the city walls (and particularly in the Temple area) was one of the many abominations and desolations spoken of by Daniel. But even this was not the worst or the pinnacle one. Josephus details how the Jews frequently and blatantly desecrated their own Temple during the time of the Roman-Jewish War. As a Jewish priest himself, and speaking from a priestly point of view, he felt that these Temple atrocities and their impact on the rest of the Jewish people were what eventually led to the complete desolation of Jerusalem and the Temple by the Roman legions.

A strong argument can be made that the Jews brought the final desolation upon themselves. When all the facts are known, the Jews were

---

[21] The word "temple" is not in the original language. "Wing" means "pinnacle," "height" or "top-most" of the abominations.
[22] Josephus, *Wars*, 5.1.1-3 (1-19).

"the people of the ruler [i.e., the people of Jesus, and not the Roman army under Titus' command or some future Antichrist ruler] who will come and destroy the city and the sanctuary" (Dan. 9:26). The question of who destroyed Jerusalem has been equated with the age-old question of who crucified Christ?" In both cases, the Romans tried to avoid the final action. But the Jews' abominable and self-destructive activities forced the Romans to act. You can read about it in Josephus' eyewitness accounts of the Jewish rebellion and the subsequent Roman-Jewish War in A.D. 66 - 73.[23]

The Finishing Point

1335 Days Later
A.D. 70 (Dan. 12:12) Blessed is the one who waits for and reaches the end of the 1,335 days.

Jesus warned his first followers, "When you see Jerusalem surrounded by armies, you will know that its desolation is near . . . . For this is the time of punishment in fulfillment of all that has been written" (Luke 21:20, 22; see also Luke 19:43-44).

Shortly before Passover in the spring of A.D. 70 (approximately—if not exactly—45 days following the previously-cited Temple desecration), Titus' Roman legions advanced toward Jerusalem from the Northwest through Samaria (just as Antiochus Epiphanes, the king of Syria, had done in 167 B.C. as the invader from the "north" of Ezekiel 38 and 39). He "set up" three encampments within three miles of the walls on the hills surrounding and overlooking Jerusalem. This was the fourth and final encampment of armies around Jerusalem during the Roman-Jewish War period.[24] Although it is not possible to know the final "day or hour" (Matt. 24:36; 25:13), this "setting up" occurred precisely within the 1,335-day time period prophesied to Daniel. The "time of the end" was now at hand. And, as we'll see in Chapter 13, Jesus had given the Jews ample signs and warnings that this end was coming upon them within their lifetime. And come it did.

---

[23] I recommend these commentaries:
Josephus: The Essential Writings, by Paul L. Maier, Kregel Publications, 1988.
The Topical Josephus, by Cleon L. Rogers, Jr., Zondervan, 1992.
[24] See, Noē, *The Perfect Ending for the World,* 175-202.

In April of A.D. 70, the Roman army began the fourth and final siege of the war. In September, it was over. Not only the city and the Temple but the whole of biblical Judaism was utterly destroyed and left desolated. This Roman siege, using 1st-century warfare technology, was precisely the form of judgment Jesus had promised was coming (see Luke 19:41-44). It was also the fulfillment of "the day of vengeance of God." This was the portion of Isaiah 61:1-2 which Jesus, 43 years earlier, auspiciously did not quote while reading the scroll in the synagogue (Luke 4:13-21). Within three years, "every stone" was dismantled in fulfillment of Jesus' most dramatic prophecy (Matt. 24, Mark 13, Luke 21). Therefore, at just the right time, the "appointed time of the end" had "certainly come," it did "not prove false," and did "not delay," just as God's prophet, Habakkuk, had prophesied almost eight centuries earlier.[25]

All the events we've covered so far (and more) as fulfillment of Daniel's two time prophecies (the 70 weeks and "time of the end") took place literally, exactly, chronologically, and sequentially within their two respective time periods, and precisely as foretold, with no gaps or gimmicks. As a result, both the *historical setting* and *defining characteristic* of Daniel's "time of the end" achieved fulfillment in A.D. 66 - 73 when the "the power of the holy people" was "finally broken." The Jews' exclusive relationship with God, as manifested by the Temple complex, was finally terminated. Ever since and yet today, rabbis speak about the destruction of the Temple in A.D. 70 as "the end of biblical Judaism." Even they recognize that something extremely significant had happened back then. Since then, it has not been reversed and, contrary to popular Jewish and Christian views, will never be reversed or restored.

However, we shall miss the greater significance of these events if all we see in them is the destruction of a local city and its Temple. This time of the end involved much more. "All these things," including the accomplishment of Daniel's six purpose clauses (Dan. 9:24), were fully "completed" (Dan 12:7). Additionally, the transition between the two covenantal ages was finished at the fall of Jerusalem circa A.D. 70 - 73.

Thus, the end the Bible proclaims is *past*. Habakkuk's "appointed time . . . of the end" certainly came and is over. It did not demand the

---

[25] For more, see Noē, *The Perfect Ending for the World*, "The End that Was, the Last Days that Were" chapter, 171-202.

end of human history, the end of time, or the destruction of the physical creation—all of which are without end. This end, its end times, and the biblical last days are behind us, not ahead of us. They are in the past, not in the future. Note especially that every New Testament reference to the "last days" or equivalent "last times, last hour," refers to the time its writers were living in—the 1st century. They weren't the last days of planet Earth, or the end of time. They were the last days of the Old Covenant Jewish system and age. There are no exceptions (see Heb 1:2; Acts 2:17; 1 Tim. 4:1; 2 Tim. 3:1; Jas. 5:3; 2 Pet. 3:3; 1 Pet. 1:5, 20; Jude 18; 1 John 2:18).

Like two bookends, Daniel's two time prophecies provide the front and a back for the biblical end-times period. Like a picture frame, they provide the divine and perfect framework in which all end-time events took place and the appointed time of the end certainly came, "at just the right time." This is the one and only end the Bible consistently proclaims.

In our next chapter, we'll see how all this fulfillment of Daniel's two time prophecies perfectly dovetails and harmonizes with Jesus, the early Church, and the New Testament writers. And, we shall address the big question: "What about the Second Coming / the Return of Christ?"

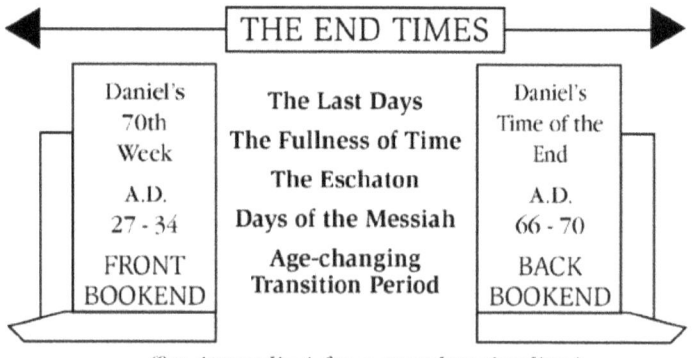

(See Appendix A for a complete timeline.)

Chapter 11

Harmony in the New Testament

If, indeed, Habakkuk's "appointed time . . . of the end" and Daniel's *historical setting* and *defining characteristic* of the "time of the end" perfectly achieved fulfillment as foretold and when the "the power of the holy people" was "finally broken" during the Roman-Jewish War of 66-70 A.D.; and if the end, its end times, and the "last days" the Bible proclaims are all past and not future, behind us and not ahead of us; and if this is and was the one and only end the Bible consistently proclaims— and it was covenantal and not cosmic, arrived timely and precisely, and was not delayed—how does all this fulfillment matchup with Jesus, the early Church and the New Testament writers?

The answer is: *Perfectly!* Scholars of all sorts almost unanimously agree that Jesus, his 1st-century followers, and the New Testament writers all expected Him to come on the clouds in judgment and fulfill "all things" within their lifetime. Why did they believe this way? In the venerable words of the respected Christian apologist C.S. Lewis, "Their Master had told them so."[1]

But where and when did He tell them so?

---

[1] Lewis, Essay "The World's Last Night" (1960), 385. In his made up quotation of a skeptic.

Five Emphatic Time Statements of Jesus

As you read these five time statements, please honestly and sincerely ask yourself how would you have understood these words of Jesus if you had been with Him back then and there, sitting at his feet, and listening, intently?[2]

Matthew 10:23. While talking with his disciples, Jesus promised, *"When you are persecuted in one place, flee to another, I tell you the truth, you will not finish going through the cities of Israel before the Son of man comes."*

Matthew 16:27-28. He informed his disciples, *"For the Son of Man is going to come in his Father's glory with his angels, and then he will reward each person according to what he has done. I tell you the truth, some who are standing here will not taste death before they see the Son of Man coming in his kingdom."*

Matthew 26:64. Quoting from the prophet Daniel, Jesus responded to and forewarned Caiaphas, the high priest, and the Sanhedrin saying, *". . . In the future you will see the Son of Man sitting at the right hand of the Mighty One, and coming on the clouds of heaven."*

Matthew 24:3, 27, 30, 34. Jesus divinely linked the time of his coming to the destruction of the Temple. *"'Tell us,' they said, 'when will this happen, and what will be the sign of your coming and of the end of the age? . . . so will be the coming of the Son of Man. . . . At that time the sign of the Son of Man [Jesus] will appear in the sky, and all the nations of the earth will mourn. They will see the Son of Man coming on the clouds of the sky, with power and great glory. . . . I tell you the truth, this generation will certainly not pass away until all these things have happened."*

---

[2] For a more extensive treatment of these five time statements, see: Noē, *The Perfect Ending for the World*, 219-229.

John 21:22. When Peter asked about John, *"Jesus answered, "If I want him to remain alive until I return, what is that to you? You must follow me."*

For centuries, theologians have tried every way imaginable to get around these "embarrassing," time-restrictive statements of Jesus, while at the same time recognizing that Jesus' first followers understood Jesus' words in a plain, simple, and natural way as applying to them, there and then.

So how would you have understood these words if you were living and hearing them straight from Jesus back then? As we saw in Chapter 1, these time-restrictive statements of Jesus and this event's supposed non-occurrence have been the focal-point of the liberal/skeptic attack on the Bible and deity of Christ.

But here is another reason for the heightened air of expectancy and relevancy back in that 1st century. It's one I think you will find equally compelling. According to the Bible, Jesus' first followers, including the inspired writers of the New Testament books, were guided into all truth and told the things that were yet to come by the Holy Spirit (John 16:13). Obviously, their expectations were formed by this divine guidance.

Here is the rub, however. If their Holy-Spirit-guided expectations for Jesus coming on the clouds and fulfilling "all things" within their lifetime have been proven false by nineteen centuries and counting, how can we trust them to have conveyed other aspects of the faith along to us accurately—such as the requirements for salvation, etc.?

> **For centuries, theologians have tried every way imaginable to get around these "embarrassing," time-restrictive statements of Jesus . . .**

Three other factors worth serious reconsideration are these. 1) If Amos 3:7 is true—that God "does nothing without revealing his plan to his servants the prophets"—then why didn't at least one Holy-Spirit-guided, New Testament writer ever correct these 1st-century-fulfillment expectations? The fact is, none did. Nor did they ever re-explain or contradict Jesus' teachings regarding the timeframe for his coming in judgment—i.e., "this generation." 2) God does not lie (Heb. 6:18; Titus

1:2). 3) He created time and does not purposely mislead or speak to us in words we cannot properly understand. Theologians term this divine attribute the perspicuity of Scripture, meaning clearness and ease in being understood.

Instead, the New Testament writers did the exact opposite. As Jesus' literal, forty-year, "this generation" time period wound down, from A.D. 30 through A.D. 70, the sense of nearness language in the New Testament dramatically picked up.[3] I call this "the intensification of nearness language." This intensification provides further proof that Jesus' first followers understood his words to come on the clouds and fulfill "all things" as applying to them, then and there.

Intensification of Nearness Language

Approximately nineteen years after Jesus delivered his most dramatic prophecy in what is termed his Olivet Discourse (Matthew 24, Mark 13, Luke 21), the writers of the New Testament began writing their epistles, or what we now call the books of the New Testament. The intensification of their nearness language is most evident. To dramatize it, I will provide a recap and countdown by using "T minus" the number of years remaining in Jesus' forty-year, this-generation time period, along with the approximate dates when these works were written.[4] Once again, before you read any further, ask yourself how would you have understood their intensifying words if you had been living back then?[5]

'T *minus* 40 years' (circa A.D. 30) – Jesus said – "*I tell you the truth, this generation will certainly not pass away until all these things have happened*" (Matt. 24:34). According to Deuteronomy 18:22, "If what a prophet proclaims in the name of the Lord does not take place or

---

[3] Theologians prefer the word "imminency" instead of nearness. But they disagree on what this means. Some say it means an event will take place very soon. Others maintain that it only means that it could happen at any moment or is certain to happen someday.

[4] A strong case can be made that every New Testament book was written prior to A.D. 70. See again Robinson, *Redating the New Testament*.

[5] For more, see: Noē, *The Perfect Ending for the World*, 229-276.

come true, that is a message the Lord has not spoken. That prophet has spoken presumptuously. Do not be afraid of him." If Jesus was a true prophet, *what* He said would happen must happen, but also it must happen *when* He said.

Yet C. S. Lewis, the respected Christian apologist and author, termed this verse, "the most embarrassing verse in the Bible" and an "exhibition of error."[6] As we shall continue seeing, the embarrassment rightly belongs to C. S. Lewis. And, as we have seen, Jesus iterated this time-restricted promise to come again in this way several times during his earthly ministry.

'T *minus* 21 years' (circa A.D. 49) – Paul wrote – <u>*"The fullness of time was come"* (Gal. 4:4).</u> What "fullness" of what "time" was Paul talking about nineteen years after Jesus' earthly ministry? If back then was the "fullness," does time ever get more full?

'T *minus* 13 years' (circa A.D. 57) – Paul wrote – <u>*"Time is short"* (1 Cor. 7:29) . . . . *"The world in its present form is passing away"* (1 Cor. 7:31).</u> We hear this first statement a lot nowadays. But whose time was short and what world was passing away back then? The answer to that question is at the *heart* of what all end-time biblical prophecy is all about. One thing is sure; these words distinctly show that a great crisis was near.

'T *minus* 12 years' (circa A.D. 58) – Paul wrote – <u>*"Understand the present time . . . . because our salvation is nearer now than when we first believed. The night is nearly over; the day is almost here"* (Rom. 13:11-12).</u> Paul and some of these Romans first believed twenty to thirty years earlier. Now only twelve years remained until the end of Jesus' literal, forty-year, "this-generation" time period. Something truly significant was about to happen. It doesn't take a modern-day rocket scientist or a high-speed computer to do this simple math.

'T *minus* 12 years' (circa A.D. 58) – Paul wrote – <u>*"The God of peace will soon [shortly] crush Satan under your feet"* (Rom. 16:20).</u> Here is an unmistakable reference to the nearness of a day of deliverance

---

[6] Lewis, essay "The World's Last Night" (1960), 385.

for Christians who were being persecuted by enemies that surrounded them.

'T *minus* 10 years' (circa A.D. 60) – James wrote – *"be patient and stand firm, because the Lord's coming is near (at hand) . . . . The judge is standing at the door!"* (Jas. 5:8-9). James' words are some of the strongest in the Bible indicating the nearness of Jesus' coming in judgment. Jesus had told his disciples in his Olivet Discourse that "when you see all these things, you know it [He] is near, right at the door" (Matt. 24:33), and not nineteen hundred plus years away. Now, with only ten years left in Jesus' forty-year countdown, James writes to real, living, air-breathing, and blood-pumping human beings and admonishes them to have patience as a present-relevant virtue, not a futuristic deception. And then he places Judge Jesus "standing at the door!" James' statements here are unmistakable indications of the nearness of this event, and not just mere expressions of *hope*.

'T *minus* 5 years' (circa A.D. 65) – The writer of Hebrews wrote – *"but in these last days he* [God] *has spoken to us by his Son . . . ."* (Heb. 1:2). By divine inspiration, the writer of Hebrews affixes two specific historical events to the biblical time period known as the "last days": 1) the time of Jesus' earthly ministry and 2) the time in which he was writing. Clearly, he saw himself living in the "last days," back then and there. The question is, those were the "last days" of what? As we have seen, they were the "last days" of the biggest thing that was ending at the time or ever will end on planet Earth and in redemptive and world history.

'T *minus* 5 years' (circa A.D. 65) – The writer of Hebrews wrote – *"In just a very very little while, 'He who is coming will come and will not delay . . . .'"* (Heb. 10:37). In this verse the Greek word translated as a singular "very" in most translations is actually used twice in the original language. Why? It's because, it conveys a double intensification of nearness—"in just a *very very* little while." Thus, the original language is far more expressive and explicit than the English. Even more incredible, and in direct contradiction of this verse, the Church has been preaching delay for nineteen centuries and counting. The question is, who is right— the inspired writer of Hebrews or the uninspired Church and its modern-day, prophecy-postponement experts (also see Hab. 2:3; Ezek. 12:21-28)? Also, when we compare this "little while" phrase with Jesus' seven uses of "a little while" in John 16:16-19, we see that Jesus' "a little while" was only a matter of a week or two before He was arrested, tried, and crucified.

The entire book of Hebrews conveys this same sense of nearness. For example, "as you see the Day approaching" (Heb. 10:25). This and other statements like it, cannot be ignored, twisted, or lightly brushed aside. When Hebrews was written, the early Church was undergoing intense persecution from the Jews and the Roman Emperor Nero. These believers were eagerly awaiting Jesus' promised coming in judgment. Again, ask yourself, how could they "see the Day approaching" if this Day was two millennia in the future?

Let's also note that Jesus said it was the "evil servant" who says "My Lord delayeth his coming" (Matt. 24:48 *KJV*).[7]

'T *minus* 3-5 years' (circa A.D. 65-67) – Peter wrote – *"The end of all things is at hand."* (1 Pet. 4:7 *KJV*). Peter's words are not "the end of *some* things" or "the *middle* of all things," but "the end of all things." "At hand" is the Greek word *engys*. It is the ultimate nearness idiom and means "graspable, seizible, there for the taking, or almost there."

For example, John the Baptist proclaimed "the kingdom of heaven is at hand," referring to the nearness of Jesus' earthly ministry (Matt. 3:2). His ministry began within months. Jesus used it when He said, "behold, the hour is at hand" for his betrayal by Judas (Matt. 26:45 *KJV*), and

---

[7] The evil servant in this parable wasn't "evil" because he said, "My Lord delayeth his coming." He was evil because of what he did during his absence (Matt. 24:49 *KJV*). But he did declare "a delay." That is directly contrary to Scripture (Heb. 10:37; Hab. 2:3). Why shouldn't that statement be considered "evil?" The Church, post A.D. 70, has taken a short period of Jesus' supposed departure and gradually developed it into a longer and longer "delay" idea rather than reexamine its notion of the nature of his Presence and consummating coming. Consequently, every generation except one has wrongly believed that Jesus would "return" in its time. The harm this has done must be "evil." Proverbs 13:12 tells us that "Hope deferred makes the heart sick, but a longing fulfilled is a tree of life." In this chapter, I am contending for the latter portion of this proverb.

"behold, he is at hand that doth betray me" (Matt. 26:46 *KJV*). Jesus also proclaimed "the kingdom of God is at hand" (Mark 1:15) and sent his twelve disciples out to proclaim and minister the same "at hand" kingdom (Matt. 10:7). The Apostle John used it when He said the Jewish Passover was "at hand"—meaning "almost time" (John 11:55). Paul wrote to Timothy, "The time of my departure is at hand" (2 Tim. 4:6). All of them were saying that those events would be soon—certainly within their lifetime or generation.

Neither Peter's nor James' (see again Jas. 5:8 above) hearers and readers understood or interpreted their "at hand" time terminology as meaning a 2,000-years-or-a-longer period, as many of us have been taught today. Neither was Peter nor James deceiving their audience with a different or specialized meaning of known and ordinary words. They issued no disclaimers. Their "at hand" demands the same "right there" or "almost right there" immediacy as its use in other New Testament scriptures, including the Book of Revelation (see Chapter 14). "At hand" means "there" or "real soon," and not centuries later.

Critical Objection: Some similar "near" statements in the Old Testament did not take place shortly, such as: Deuteronomy 32:35; "the day of disaster is near." But if this disaster was speaking of A.D. 70, that was over 1,400 years away.

My Response: Yes, this objection is used by deferment futurists to elasticizes and dismiss all "at hand' and other time statements in Scripture. But in contradistinction, the Book of Numbers, written some 1,400 to 1,440 years before Christ contains a Messianic prophecy that speaks of the Messiah's coming as being "not near" (Num. 24:17). Then, in Deuteronomy 31:14, "The Lord said to Moses, 'Now the day of your death is near." But in Deuteronomy 32 the time for when its events would be "near" was contextualized in that same text to be when in Israel was in her "latter days" (Deut. 31:29; also see: 32:5, 20, 29; Dan. 10:14). Other Old Testaments nearness scriptures are sometimes also cited as precedents (excuses) for elasticizing and dismissing all New Testament time statements. They include: Jeremiah 25:12; 27:16; 29:27-28; Ezekiel 12:21-28, and more. Likewise, these texts, when properly contextualized, can be readily explained. But space limitations prevent an in-depth examination herein.

Let's also not forget that when we read these words of Peter we are reading someone else's mail. Peter's 1st-century letter was addressed

"To God's elect, strangers in the world, scattered throughout Pontus, Galatia, Cappadocia, Asia, and Bithynia" (1 Pet. 1:1). He wasn't writing to them about Christians living in the 21st century. That, again, is taking his words totally out of context. Basic interpretative principles demand audience relevancy. Either "the end of all things" Peter was talking about came upon them back then and there or Peter was mistaken and uninspired.

Furthermore, while Peter was saying "the end of all things is at hand," scoffers present back then (Jude 17-19) were saying, "Where is this 'coming' he promised? Ever since our fathers died, everything goes on as it has . . . ." (2 Pet. 3:4). So, who has history proven was right? The 1st-century scoffers or Peter?

Indeed, something catastrophic was impending, there and then. Ten verses later Peter explains.

'T *minus* 3-5 years' (circa A.D. 65-67) – Peter wrote – *"For it is time for judgment to begin with the family [the house] of God. . ."* (1 Pet. 4:17 [*KJV*]). Peter, like Jesus, was emphatic. He did not say it "might be" or "someday will be." He said, "For it is time!" A catastrophe was now imminent. The time for judgment was to begin at the house of God. There is no other legitimate explanation. Peter further revealed that Jesus was also "ready to judge the living and the dead" (1 Pet. 4:5). What had once been seen as far off by the ancient prophets was now ready to be revealed to Peter's "you" group in that "last time" (1 Pet. 1:5, 12; also see Acts 3:24).

'T *minus* 2-3 years' (circa A.D. 67-68) – John wrote – *"Little children, this is the last hour . . . it is the last hour"* (1 John 2:18). Twice in this one verse John says this. Written on the eve of the destruction of Jerusalem and the Temple,[8] John, like Peter, does not say "might be" or "someday will be" but *"it is* the last hour." Who can deny it? Christian writer Carl F.H. Henry does so. Writing in Billy Graham's *Decision* magazine, Henry claims "the very last hour, remains future."[9] But

---

[8] John A.T. Robinson places the date at A.D. 60-65 (Robinson, *Redating the New Testament*, 352.).
[9] Carl F.H. Henry, "The Very Last Day, The Very Last Hour," *Decision*, September 2000, 27.

according to John in the New Testament, the "last hour" was upon them, back then in the 1st century. Whom should we believe, the inspired writer John or Carl F.H. Henry? Then, it was the "last hour" of what? Theologian Gary DeMar fittingly protests that many, like Dr. Henry, who insist "on interpreting the Bible literally," have literally "turned 'the last hour' . . . into two thousand years of church history."[10]

Next, of course, is the Book of Revelation, which we shall deal with in Chapter 14. But be assured, it, too, perfectly harmonizes with these intensifying expectations and ratcheting-up nearness language.[11]

So why were these inspired, Holy-Spirit-guided writers writing like this back then and there? None of their words are complicated. And the progressive dynamic of their intensifying language cannot be ignored or lightly dismissed. Again, how would you have understood their words if you were living back then?

Many Bible scholars admit that no one reading the New Testament on his own would get the idea that Christ would not come again or that things would not be fulfilled for at least two thousand years. They also agree that the 1st-century Church understood these words in a natural, plain, and literal fashion, and as applying to them, there and then. They expected this coming of Jesus and the fulfillment of "all things" to happen within that first Christian generation.

Clearly, 1st-century expectations of Jesus' coming in judgment were soon and getting sooner. DeMar is right on target again, "No other interpretation is possible if the words are taken in the 'plain, primary, ordinary, usual, or normal' sense, that is they are interpreted literally."[12] And remember, no New Testament writer ever corrected their expectations. Furthermore, a literal interpretation here is in perfect harmony and consistency with a plain, natural, and literal understanding of Jesus' words on this same topic, and with the literal, exact,

---

[10] DeMar, *End Times Fiction*, 141.
[11] For my position on Revelation see my published article – John Noē, "An Exegetical Basis for a Preterist-Idealist Understanding of the Book of Revelation, *Journal of the Evangelical Theological Society*, Vol. 49, No. 4, (December 2006):768-769.
[12] DeMar, in Foreword to Francis X. Gumerlock's, *The Day and the Hour*, 2000), *xxiv*.

chronological, and sequential fulfillment of Daniel's "time of the end" time prophecy.

> **Many Bible scholars admit that no one reading the New Testament on his own would get the idea that Christ would not come again or these things would not be fulfilled for at least two thousand years.**

Is it possible these inspired writers of Scripture were not mistaken and their expectations were the correct ones? Or has time proven them wrong? On the other hand, perhaps God was careless with inspired language and the Church's nineteen centuries of delayed expectations are correct? But how can Christianity maintain credibility in the light of so many plain statements if it continues to argue that Christ has not yet come and fulfilled all things?

Many people in the Church today have been taught that the Lord's coming and other related events (judgment, resurrection, and consummation) are always viewed as being near. Hence church leaders redefine "nearness" to mean "certainty"—i.e., Jesus' so-called "second coming" and "return" are certain and could happen at any time. Or they stipulate that fulfillment was delayed and postponed or that Jesus' and the New Testament writers' words do not really mean what they literally say. If any of this human reasoning (actually excuse-making) is right, then the above-cited time and intensifying nearness statements are meaningless. Fulfillment could still be nineteen centuries away and counting. But how far can we stretch nearness (imminency) before nearness (imminency) loses its value?

Another basic question is, if the New Testament writers *did* want to convey a chronological sense of near and getting nearer, how else could they have said it? How else could they have made it any clearer? Do you think it is possible that these words literally mean what they say and these writers said what they meant? If so, what could have been so monumental and so impending, right there and then and in their lifetime? One thing is for sure. Their intensification of nearness language demonstrates that they understood the New Testament's time statements literally, at face value, and did not seek to mitigate, elasticize, or ignore them.

So how much of the content of these above statements was relevant to its original audience? Most Christians (dispensational premillennialists) say, "none of it was." Some (amillennialists and postmillennialists) say, "some of it was." Only a few (preterists) say, "all of it was" relevant and perfectly fulfilled, right on time, back then and there.

So who's right and what's the scoop? No question about it, the 1st-century followers of Christ lived in expectation of something big about to happen, and happen very soon. But if nothing of radical magnitude did happen—befitting this intensifying nearness language—then these statements were mistaken or misleading, at best. That is exactly the interpretation and understanding that has been given to us by most interpreters. And the liberals and skeptics are certainly aware of this compromising disparity.

But let's consider for a moment the possibility that Jesus and the New Testament writers meant exactly what they said, as they were guided by the Holy Spirit (John 16:13), and that their extreme and growing sense-of-nearness expectations were fulfilled, precisely and right on time. As a matter of fact, the most undeniable aspect of Jesus' Olivet Discourse prophecy is the historical event and reality that Jerusalem and the Temple were totally destroyed exactly *as* and *when* both Daniel and Jesus had perfectly prophesied.

So how much of the content of these above statements was relevant to its original audience?

If so, our next big question becomes, Was this destruction event also Jesus' Second Coming / Return? Most preterists say yes it was—and some of them say there is no other coming or comings to be expecting. Amillennialists and Postmillennialists say no, it was not. But they do concede that it was *a* coming. Premillennialists, for the most part, deny it was a coming at all. Who's right?

The Second Coming / Return of Christ?

It's the central, pivotal, and controlling event that defines and differentiates the four major competing and conflicting end-time views. And the fulfillment of all other end-time events are attached to its occurrence. Again, the four views are in order of proposed fulfillment:

Preterist view – it is past and occurred circa A.D. 70.
Premillennial view – it is future and will occur very soon.
Amillennial view – it is future and no one can know when it will occur.
Postmillennial view – it is future but will not occur any time soon.

Also, as we have seen, and over the course of Church history, these four eschatological and "second coming/return" centered views have evolved, developed, and produced "one of the most divisive elements in recent Christian history. . . . few doctrines unite and separate Christians as much as eschatology."[13]

Therefore, in this section and in keeping with our guideline #1 of *Sola Scriptura*, let's take a fresh look at what the Bible actually says and does not say about this most important and greatly anticipated event of human history. For some, this exposé may be the most threatening part of this book. For others, it will be cathartic and for good reasons.

Try This Little Exercise

One of my favorite ground-breaking exercises before beginning a lecture or a Bible study on this topic is to ask the following question of any group that feels they have above-average knowledge of the Bible. How would you answer it?

QUESTION: IN YOUR OPINION, OVER THE ENTIRE COURSE OF HUMAN HISTORY – PAST, PRESENT AND FUTURE – HOW MANY COMINGS OF JESUS ARE THERE?

---

[13] Kantzer, ed., "Our Future Hope: Eschatology and Its Role in the Church," *Christianity Today*, 1-14 (I).

ANSWERS: A) ONE? B) TWO? C) THREE? D) FOUR? E) MORE?

Circle the answer you believe is correct.

The responses and reactions this survey question elicits are usually quite interesting. Some look offended by just its asking (I am aware of how uncomfortable even the asking of these questions can be). A few others act baffled, become defensive, or sit silent thinking it's a trick question. Almost all, however, are amazed by the variety of answers and reasoning that arises from within their own group. Overall, this little exercise serves as an attention-getter and mind-opener causing the participants to take off their traditional-laden blinders and reconsider with me from the Scriptures just what is and what is not true concerning this important, doctrinal tenet of the Christian faith—the coming of the Lord. After all, the Bible does tell us to "test" and to "prove all things" (1 Thess. 5:21). The coming of Jesus is certainly part of "all things."

What answer did you pick? Most people pick "B) Two," because nothing has been more strongly emphasized throughout Church history than the so-called, "Second Coming" of Jesus Christ and its implied limitation of only two comings. But the biblically correct answer is "E) More." Yes, you may be amazed—I was when I first discovered it—at how little knowledge most of us have about the Bible and the Christian faith in this fundamental area.

Doesn't Fit the Terminology of Scripture[14]

Popular TV evangelists, Bible teachers, and church pastors commonly claim that the Bible "speaks extensively about the Second Coming of Christ," mentioning it many times in the New Testament.

Billy Graham, for instance, in one of his crusades and in a January 2004 article in his *Decision* magazine titled, "The End of the World," claimed, "the Bible speaks extensively about the Second Coming of Christ, mentioning it more than 300 times in the New Testament. By comparison, repentance . . . is mentioned about 70 times, and baptism . . .

---

[14] This and the following sections are taken from my book, *The Greater Jesus*, 24-31.

is mentioned about 20 times." He concluded, "It is obvious, then, that the Holy Spirit, who inspired the Scriptures, places great importance on the return of Jesus Christ."[15]

With all due respect for Dr. Graham, do you know what the Bible actually says (literally mentions) about a "Second Coming?" Nothing! Zero! Zilch! Nada! Nowhere does the Bible use the term *Second Coming*. It's a non-biblical term. Nor does the Bible use the term *Return* in direct association with Jesus.

Actually, the Bible contains many references to many different comings of Jesus, but none to a single "Second Coming." Please be assured that by pointing out this biblical fact, I am not intending to diminish, detract from, or mock the "promise of his coming" in any way. Rather, I'm justifying why the doctrine of a "Second Coming" and "Return" must be faced anew.

Most everyone recognizes that words matter and wording is important. With this in mind, the late-great theologian, George Eldon Ladd, in his highly acclaimed book, *The Blessed Hope*, acknowledged something very important: "The words 'return' and 'second coming' are not properly speaking Biblical words in that the two words do not represent any equivalent Greek words."[16] This is a major admission with huge implications. Another fact is, we Christians have been hamstrung for centuries with these two non-scriptural expressions and mindsets and unscriptural concepts—just like "delay" theory, "end of the world," and "end of time," as we have already seen. They, too, will not stand up to an honest and sincere test of Scripture, which is our *modus operandi* and exactly what we're going to do in this chapter, the next, and Chapter 15.

Actually, the Bible contains many references to many different comings of Jesus, but none to a single "Second Coming."

---

[15] Billy Graham, "The End of the World," *Decision*, January 2004, posted on www.billygraham.org/article.asp?I=396&s=62, January 31, 2004.
[16] Ladd, *The Blessed Hope*, 69. Unfortunately, Ladd ignored his own and valid biblical insight by continuing to use these non-scriptural expressions and unscriptural concepts.

As you will soon discover, the reason the Bible does not use this language is because it's inappropriate. The idea that Jesus is off somewhere waiting to return at some future time, as well as the idea of limiting the comings of Jesus to only two or three times, or to any at all, is man's idea and not God's.

The closest we can come to the phraseology of a "Second Coming" is in Hebrews 9:28: "so Christ was sacrificed once to take away the sins of many people; and he will appear *a second time*, not to bear sin, but to bring salvation to those who are waiting for him" (italics added). Contrary to popular belief, this scripture does not limit, number, or confine Jesus' comings to only two times. Rather, it highlights two specific and significant comings, among many (see a partial list in 1 Cor. 15:5-8 for instance), and for a special salvation-fulfillment purpose. This "second-time" coming follows the typology of Israel's high priest on the Day of Atonement, which occurred every year. And Christ as both our sacrifice and High Priest (see Heb. 7:27-28; 9:11-15) had to come and fulfill this typology, perfectly (see Heb. 8, 9, and 10).[17]

Stop for a moment and ask yourself, Why does the Bible never call Jesus' birth his "first coming?" It's simply because it wasn't (more on this in our next chapter).

But if we persist in limiting the comings of Jesus to only two times and in calling the babe in the manger the "first coming" of Jesus, as so many do, that means the "Second Coming" is over. Chronologically, it happened after Jesus was crucified and ascended to heaven, when He came and appeared to Stephen during his trial before the Jewish Sanhedrin (Acts 7:55-56). Or, it happened when Jesus came and appeared to Saul on the road to Damascus (Acts 9:1-8), or to John in the Revelation (Revelation 1 and John 21:22-23). How do you count or discount those comings of Jesus? And as we shall see in the next chapter, there are many more comings of Jesus.

At this point, you may be feeling a bit perplexed by my last few statements. Or you may be upset. But before you react in a knee-jerk fashion (again, I know how emotional this can be), let me assure you that the coming of Jesus is much more relevant, vital, and greater reality than most of us have been led to believe. Therefore, let's define what we mean by "a coming of Jesus." Then we'll consider the biblical evidence.

---

[17] For more on this aspect, see Noē, *The Perfect Ending for the World*, 243-246.

Please don't dismiss any of this too quickly, and until you've considered it all.

. . . the reason the Bible does not use this language is because it's inappropriate.

My working definition for "a coming of Jesus" is this—It's a personal and bodily intervention and/or manifestation of Jesus into the life of an individual, a group, a church, or a nation on this earth. There are many different types of comings for different purposes, and they occur at different times and places. Some are visible appearances; some are invisible interventions. Some are physical (seen, heard, felt); some are spiritual (an internal illumination or revelation); and some are combinations.

Theologian Henry A. Virkler calls them "a special manifestation of His presence."[18] Also, there may be other types of comings of which I am not aware, if for no other reason than not everything Jesus did was written down (see John 21:25).

He Never Left

While God's Word clearly documents and teaches that the comings (plural) of Jesus run like a thread throughout both the Old and New Testaments, the word "return" is also never used. Like the expression "Second Coming," it is non-scriptural terminology, an unscriptural concept, and a non-event.[19] To this point, I submit that authentic

---

[18] Virkler, *Hermeneutics*, 150.
[19] Jesus did tell a parable once about a nobleman who *returned* after going into a far country to receive a kingdom (Luke 19:12, 15; also see Jesus' parable in Luke 12:36). This nobleman certainly represents Jesus and this parable certainly refers to Jesus' departure and coming again. And this word is correctly translated as "return." However, neither this parable nor any others (see Matt. 25:1-28) can be employed to override Jesus' statements about Himself just because He used this word here, indirectly. Especially note that the object of this parable is a nobleman who is a regular human being and as such is confined

Christianity does not stand for a departed and absent Christ—absent the entire length of the Christian age! Paradoxically, it stands for a departed but still present and active Christ who never left and has truly, wholly, and totally been *with* his Church and people for over nineteen centuries and is still *with* us today. How do I know He never left? He told us so.

Of course, at one point early in his earthly ministry, Jesus also told his disciples that a time would come when He would be "taken from them" (Mark 2:20). Then later, toward the end of his ministry, Jesus said He was "going there [heaven] to prepare a place for you." And He promised to "come again" to "take you to be with me that you also may be where I am." (John 14:2-4). He said his going away (John 16:5, 16) was required and the decisive factor for the coming of the Holy Spirit (John 16:7). But also, in what may seem to be a contradiction, He told them that "I will not leave you as orphans" (John 14:18). And then, at the end of his famous Great Commission in Matthew 28:18-20, He also assured his 1st-century followers that He would be *with* them, "And surely I will be *with you always*, to [until] the very end of the age" (italics added, Matt. 28:20b).

In a similar manner, Jesus previously had promised, "For where two or three come together in my name, there am I *with* them" (Matt. 18:20 – italics added). So how can Jesus both *go* somewhere; i.e., depart, and still be *with* them? Can these two seemingly paradoxical notions be reconciled?

The traditional explanation has been that what Jesus was really saying was He would be *with* them in the future in the Person of the Holy Spirit, Whom He was to send at Pentecost (see Acts 2). The verse, "the Lord is the Spirit," is cited in support (2 Cor. 3:17). But the outpouring of the Holy Spirit was a separately and distinctly prophesied event from the Old Testament (see Ezek. 36:26-27; 37:9-14; 39:29; Joel 2:28-32)

---

within an earthly body. He does not have the same transcendent, omnipresent, and spirit-realm ability as does the ascended Lord and which we will soon discuss further. Imposing that limitation upon the post-resurrected and ascended Jesus, Who is omnipresent, is reductionistic. This parable only foreshadows a period of time that will transpire between Jesus' physical departure (his death) and a special coming again that we shall cover in Chapter 13. Also notable, is the fact that this period of time would be within the lifetime of those mentioned in the parable, and not some future generation two-thousand years or so removed.

and a singular happening in the New Testament (see Acts 2). Furthermore, did Jesus really mean He had to "depart" to send Himself back? No New Testament text written twenty or more years later ever acknowledges this outpouring of the Spirit as a coming again of Jesus. To the contrary, many subsequent, New Testament texts, again written after that event, were still anticipating this coming of Christ as yet future.

Besides, if what Jesus really meant was "the Holy Spirit would be with them always," why be so cryptic? He wasn't cryptic anywhere else when He spoke about the Holy Spirit. In John 14, for instance, Jesus spoke, distinctively and by name, about the Holy Spirit and the Holy Spirit's coming (see John 14:15-29). He clearly differentiated between Himself and the Holy Spirit by using the personal pronouns "I" and "him." Moreover, He spoke, clearly and plainly, in the rest of his Great Commission. So why not here in verse 20 as well?

I believe there is a much better explanation. That is, Jesus did speak, clearly, plainly, and distinctively. He meant exactly what He said. He, Jesus, the second Person of the Godhead, would both leave them to go to heaven *and* yet always be with them, and with us today as well, as opposed to the popular idea that He is currently *absent* from this present world and waiting to unscriptural return.

Howard Clark Kee in his book, *Understanding the New Testament* explains this perplexing conundrum this way:

> Although Jesus' bodily presence among his followers is depicted by Luke as terminating with his ascension, his spiritual presence is vividly described as an ongoing process which obviously did not end with his being taken up . . . ."[20]

Most notably, when we compare different Bible translations with the original and literal Greek language, we find something quite interesting. For instance, in the popular *New International Version (NIV)*, the phrases "when he returns," "I will come back," "I am coming back," "going back," "until I return," and "Jesus . . . will come back" are found in only seven places in the New Testament (see Matt. 24:46; Luke 12:43; John 14:3, 28; 16:28; 21:22-23; and Acts 1:11, respectively). The problem is,

---

[20] Howard Clark Kee, *Understanding the New Testament* (Englewood Cliffs, NJ.: Prentice-Hall, 1983, 1957), 187.

the words "return" and "back" are not in the original language. And the word "back," when added, unfortunately, conveys a nuance of being away and necessitating a "return." But Jesus never said He would "come back" or "return." Correctly translated, his words are "cometh," "come again," "come again," "go to," "till I come," and just "come," respectively. The *King James Version KJV* translates these phrases correctly. Big difference! See this comparison in the table below:

COMPARATIVE

NIV (Incorrect trans.)	Literal Greek	*KJV* (Correct trans.)
"when he returns" (Matt. 24:46)	"coming"	"cometh"
"when he returns" (Luke 12:43)	"coming"	"cometh"
"I will come back" (John 14:3)	"again I come"	"come again"
"I am coming back" (John 14:28)	"I . . . come"	"come ag*ain*"
"going back" (John 16:28)	"go to"	"go to"
"until I return" (John 21:22-23)	"until I come"	"till I come"
"Jesus...will come back" (Acts 1:11)	"will come"	"shall so come"

Also, three of the above phrases (John 14:3, 28; Acts 1:11) are in a future-deponent-indicative verb form. Hence, they convey a dualistic sense of an in-process action of coming and/or a present and continuous activity of coming.

Another revealing tidbit comes from Jesus' unveiling in the Revelation's first chapter. Here, John (and we) see Jesus not off somewhere waiting to return someday, but instead, He's standing "among [in the midst of] the lampstands" (Rev. 1:13, [*KJV*]). Jesus explains that "the seven lampstands are the seven churches" (Rev. 1:20b). This is more evidence that Jesus did not *leave* them but was *with* them; i.e., *with* the churches, in their *midst.*

Also notable, in my opinion, was the question Jesus' disciples asked Him the week before his crucifixion, "what will be the sign of your coming" (the Greek word translated as "coming" here is *parousia* and literally means "presence" as opposed to absence – Matt. 24:3). They did not ask Him "what will be the sign of your return?" or "what will be the return of your presence?" Why not? It is because, in this context, his presence would remain with them and a return was not required. Likewise, why would a sign even be necessary if this coming was going to be so visible that the whole world would see Him, as is customarily taught? Good question don't you think? In Chapter 13, we'll see what the sign was, past tense, and why it was necessary.

Perhaps, the reason so many of us have misunderstood this seeming conundrum and paradox of Jesus' departure and yet remaining *with* them is because of our physical/material mindset. It blinds us to the realities of the spirit realm.[21] However, Scripture makes it clear that both realms are true and real. But still, how can this be? Here's how. By inspiration, the writer of Hebrews not only informs us that "we are surrounded by such a great cloud of witnesses" (Heb. 12:1), but he also tells us who is in this cloud. It contains "thousands upon thousands of angels . . . the church of the firstborn, whose names are written in heaven. . . . God . . . the spirits of righteous men made perfect, to Jesus . . . ." (Heb. 12:22-24; also compare with Psa. 125:1-2). Of course, this revelation is only of the good side of the spirit realm. Quite simply, Jesus would be leaving them in the physical/material realm via his death on the cross and after his resurrection and ascension to heaven. But He would continue being with them in the spirit realm that both surrounded them and would be in them, as it similarly is with us today. Get it?

Consequently and rightly, *Jesus never left*. He remained with them—as He had said, "I will be with you always."[22] Thus, there is no reason for Scripture to speak of a "coming back" or a "return." This terminology would be totally inappropriate and is therefore not used in the Bible. He doesn't have to "come back" from anywhere and "returning" makes no sense. Even Jesus *cannot and will not return* to someplace He *never left*. Get it? He simply promised, "I will come to you" and "you will see me" (John 14:18, 19; also John 16:16). As we will see, He did and they did. Several times after his death Jesus "came" to them and they saw Him (see John 20:24, 26; 21:1, 14).

---

[21] For more on this hindrance, see: Noē, *The Greater Jesus*, 83-93
[22] Jesus' statements in John 7:33-34 cannot be used to lessen or dismiss this assertion.

Likewise, today, we have no scriptural warrant, necessity, or language for a return. It is just as an angel of the Lord told Joseph at Jesus' birth, "'and they will call him Immanuel'—which means, 'God with us'" (Matt. 1:23); and as the Jewish people of that time expected of the Messiah, "We have heard from the Law that the Christ will remain forever, so how can you say, 'The Son of Man must be lifted up'?" (John 12:34). Hence, after Jesus' ascension and as "the disciples went out and preached everywhere . . . the Lord worked *with them* . . . ." (Mark 16:20 – emphasis added).

Consequently and rightly, *Jesus never left*. He remained with them—as He had said, "I will be with you always."

And so it has been ever since. Even after the end of the age (see Chapter 13), He is still here with us! But many of us are impaired by the Church's traditional "Second Coming" and "Return" teachings and our physical/material mindset. Consequently, we have difficulty thinking in terms of spirit and the spirit realm. So we imagine Jesus as being off in some distant place waiting to come back, to return. And we think that He cannot be here with us, at least not totally, unless He has literally and bodily returned in the flesh, and is physically resident and visible someplace on this earth. And yet, as we shall continue to explore, this return terminology and concept is not found in the Bible and is inconsistent with what Jesus actually said—it is totally inappropriate.

When I started studying the presence of Jesus and his many comings several years ago, no one could (or would) answer my questions about why the "Second Coming" wasn't mentioned in the Bible. Most pastors and professors I asked merely beat around the proverbial bush and tried to avoid exposing what they did not know. But each of them assured me the Bible clearly taught it.

More recently, I asked a seminary professor who teaches theology to show me a single scripture to support the idea of a single, future Second Coming. Together, we examined all the classic Second Coming scriptures, one by one. But none of them literally spoke of a "Second Coming." "I agree . . . I agree . . . I agree," he said on each. "But," he lectured me, "I still believe Jesus has left this world, hasn't come back yet, and there will only be one coming—the final Second Coming—at his return."

With all due respect to this precious man of God, such a response is an emotional reaction that grows out of a lifetime of doctrinal conditioning and not from the Word of God. Yet a literal "Second Coming" or a "Return" of Christ is considered a "core" belief that is persistently adhered to, perpetuated, and passed on by learned people with many degrees and much professed wisdom. It is also, once again, the central event around which conflicting and divisive systems of eschatological (end-times) views are conjoined.

Do you see a problem here?

Obviously, old habits are hard to break. But this improved understanding of Jesus' many comings and the fact that He never left us is indispensable to a correct understanding of the New Testament and for grasping the reality of the contemporary Christ, the greater Jesus. As we shall further see, the idea that Jesus is off somewhere waiting to return to planet Earth at some future time is just as erroneous as the notion of limiting the comings of Jesus to only two or three times, or to any at all. It's a classic case of the traditions of men "nullify[ing] the word of God" or making it of "none effect" (Mark 7:13; Matt. 15:6 – *NIV/KJV*).

On Breaking a Bad Habit

I believe it is time for this non-biblical, unbiblical, and yet long-perpetuated tradition to give way to revealed truth. We must not be hamstrung by its artificial terms, human constructs, or preoccupations any longer. Scripture clearly proves that the expressions of "second coming" and "return" of Christ are biblically and historically inappropriate. This invented terminology has only obscured the reality of the greater Jesus and his many comings (plural).[23] Continued use or this terminology is a bad habit we must break; i.e., using the unscriptural phrases and lamenting that *Jesus hasn't come back or returned yet* when the truth truly is, He never left, as He said, and He comes, as He said He would. It's a major piece of unlearning and relearning we must accomplish.

---

[23] See Noē, *The Greater Jesus*.

To help us break this bad and debilitating habit and better grounded us in biblical truth and reality, let us next document and detail some of the many comings of Jesus in both the Old and the New Testaments, as well as the many promises of many different types of comings for many different purposes—some of which you do not want to have happen to you (see Chapter 15). After you read our next chapter, as well as Chapter 15, I believe you will never again be in bondage to a limited, two-advent paradigm and mindset.

I believe it is time for this non-biblical, unbiblical, and yet long-perpetuated tradition to give way to revealed truth. We must not be hamstrung by its artificial terms, human constructs, or preoccupations any longer.

So if you are ready for quite a ride through biblical history, strap on your seatbelt, pull it down tight, and read on.

Chapter 12

The Many Comings of Jesus

Unshackling Christianity from its two-advent paradigm, tradition, and mindset is absolutely essential for unraveling the end and resolving the Great End-Time Fiasco. We've been hamstrung by "second coming" and "return" terminology for too long. Not only is this misleading and debilitating language non-scriptural and unscriptural, but it's a non-event.

Notwithstanding and according to a 2010 Pew Research Center survey, "roughly half (48%) of Christians in the U.S. say they believe that Christ definitely (27%) or probably (20%) will return to earth in the next forty years. Somewhat fewer (38%) say this definitely will not happen (10%) or probably will not happen (28%).[1]

Therefore, let us proclaim the biblical truth loud and clear. The so-called "second coming" or "return" of Christ has not happened already as the preterist view maintains nor is it yet to happen as the three futurist views insist. And yet all four systems of eschatological thought and views are centered upon this pivotal non-event to which all other end-time events are attached. The biblical testimony, however, is many comings of Christ throughout both the Old and New Testaments and promises for countless more comings. As we shall further see in this chapter and Chapter 15, his many comings make a lot of sense. As you

---

[1] "U.S. Christians' Views on the Return of Christ," Pew Forum on Religion & Public Life, posted on www.pewforum.org/Christian/Us-Christians-Views-on-the-Return-of-Christ.aspx, May 8, 2013

will soon be discovering, they are a much more relevant hope than a single future advent and a much greater reality than most of us have been led to believe.

So if you have ever wondered why Jesus' birth and earthly life is never called his "first coming" in Scripture, it's for a good reason—it wasn't. This misconception only leads to the improper limiting and artificial numbering of another coming as his "second coming"—which it wasn't either. Likewise, the idea that Jesus is off somewhere waiting to return to planet Earth at some future time is biblically just as erroneous as the notion of limiting his comings to only two or three or to any at all. These are simply classic examples of the traditions of men "nullify[ing] the word of God" or making it of "none effect" (Mark 7:13; Matt. 15:6 – *NIV/KJV*).

In this chapter, we shall see that God's Word clearly documents, testifies to, and teaches that the comings (plural) of Jesus run like a thread throughout both the Old and New Testament. Again, it's another major piece of unlearning and relearning that we must do if we seriously and properly desire to unravel the end and resolve its maze of conflicting and confusing end-time views. [2]

So if you have ever wondered why Jesus' birth and earthly life is never called his "first coming" in Scripture, it's for a good reason—it wasn't.

As you are about to see, the biblical reality is this. Throughout both the Old and New Testaments Jesus usually came to individuals, but sometimes to groups. He came suddenly, unexpectedly, and usually unannounced. He came to bring aid, to judge, to assign a task, or to proclaim a message. Often his coming and appearing was recognized only by the person for whom it was intended. These comings produced profound, life-altering impacts upon those who received them. And in turn upon other people and nations who were then touched by that person's subsequent life and ministry.

---

[2] Material in this chapter is taken from Noē, *The Greater Jesus,* 32-56.

Jesus' Many Comings in the Old Testament

Consider, for example, several of the Old Testament comings of Jesus that will document and make our point. Theologians technically refer to them as theophanies, meaning "a physical appearance, divine visitation, or vision of God to a person or persons." The word "theophany" is from the Greek *theo* (God) and *phaneia* (to reveal oneself). Some, however, count the times when God spoke to people—such as in the Garden of Eden, or to Moses on Mt. Sinai, or to Noah. Or they count times of other physical manifestations, such as lightning, thunder, a cloud, a consuming fire, fire, a rainbow in the clouds, or radiance, which were the appearance of the glory of the Lord but not a literal, physical, bodily appearance of the Lord Himself.[3]

For our purposes, however, and based upon the following nine reasons, we'll only count and document visible appearances of the person of deity in human form as theophanies of Jesus (with one exception):

1) Since the Bible states that "no one has ever seen God [the Father], but God the only Son, who is at the Father's side, has made him known" (John 1:18; also 1 John 4:12; Matt. 6:6; 1 Tim. 6:16—with the possible exception of Exod. 24:10-11; Isa. 6:1; Heb. 11:27; and "face to face" in Exod. 33:11; Num. 14:14; Deut. 34:10, which is a Hebrew idiom that does not necessitate a visual seeing but rather means "to be in front of, before, to the front of, in the presence of, in the face of, at the face or front of, from the presence of, from before, from before the face of"[4]);

---

[3] For more on this, see Chapter 5 in my book, *The Greater Jesus,* p. 163. But the fact is, "the glory of the Lord" appeared numerous times throughout the Old Testament. And never once was this a literal, bodily, visible, or physical appearance of the Person of God. Rather, the appearance of this "glory" took various forms: as a cloud, a consuming fire, fire, like a rainbow in the clouds, or radiance. (See: Exod. 16:7, 10; 24:16, 17; 40:34, 35; Lev. 9:6, 23, 24; Num. 14:10; 16:19, 42; 20:6; 1 Ki. 8:11; 2 Chron. 5:14; 7:1-3; Ezek. 1:28; 3:12, 23; 10:4, 18; 11:23; 43:5; 44:4; Also see: Psa. 104:31; 138:5; Isa. 35:2; 40:5; 58:8; 60:1; Luke 2:9; 2 Cor. 3:18).
[4] www.biblestudytools.com/lexixons/hebrew/nas/paniym.html, 4/10/12. For another Jewish example, compare how Paul's usage concerning himself in Col.

2) Since the Lord, God the Father, told Moses, "you cannot see my face, for no one may see me and live" (Exod. 33:20, 23; also 19:21; Heb. 11:27);

3) Since there are two Lords in the Old Testament—"The Lord says to my Lord: 'Sit at my right hand until I make your enemies a footstool for your feet'" (Psa. 110:1); the first "Lord" is *Jehovah*—the Jewish national name for God; the second is *Adown*—meaning sovereign;

4) Since Matthew, Mark, and Luke report that Jesus directly applied Psalm 110:1 to Himself (Matt. 22:41-46; Mark 12:35-37; Luke 20:41-44);

5) Since Peter confirms to us in Acts that Jesus has been "exalted to the right hand of God" in fulfillment of Psalm 110:1, which he quotes (Acts 2:32-36; also see Rom. 8:34; Eph. 1:20; Col. 3:1 Heb. 1:13; 8:1; 10:13; 12:21; 1 Cor. 15:25);

6) And since the Holy Spirit has never been seen, as far as we know (John 14:17);

7) These above six reasons leave only one Person in the Godhead (the Trinity) as being the viable candidate Who could have been seen in human or physical form. Therefore, these physical appearances of the Person of God are reckoned by many scholars—including Eusebius, a 4th-century Christian leader and writer, who is often called "the father of Church history" (as we shall see shortly)—to be comings of the preincarnate Son, Jesus. I use the word "reckoned" here advisedly because we cannot be dogmatic about this.

Nevertheless, we also have the physical appearances of one called "the angel of the Lord" in the Old Testament—as opposed to just "an angel of the Lord" in New Testament. Many scholars also reckon this angel to be Jesus for these two additional reasons:

8) This angel receives worship, something regular angels refuse to receive. See, for instance, Revelation 22:8-9 where John falls "down to worship at the feet of the angel" who had been showing him spectacular things. The angel emphatically commands him, "Do not do it! I am a fellow servant with you and with your brothers the prophets and of all

---

2:1 is translated in KJV ("not seen my face in the flesh") and NAS ("not personally seen my face") with NIV ("not met me personally").

who keep the words of this book." Then the angel instructs John about this saying, "Worship God!" This is the second time John made this mistake, for only God is to receive worship (also see Rev. 19:9-10).

9) This angel is called "Lord."

Given these above nine reasons, let's begin our exploration into several prominent Old Testament theophanies and probable comings of Jesus. With only a few possible exceptions, these theophanies were *non-prophesied* comings. Jesus just showed up.

Genesis 17:1-2: Jesus came and appeared to Abram —"When Abram was ninety-nine years old, the Lord appeared to him and said, 'I am God Almighty; walk before me and be blameless. I will confirm my covenant between me and you and will greatly increase your numbers."

Exodus 3:2-15: In a similar encounter, Jesus came and appeared to Moses in the burning bush.

(In verse 2)—"the angel of the Lord appeared to him in flames of fire from within a bush."

(In verse 4)—the angel is called *both* "the Lord" (*Jehovah*—the Jewish national name for God) and "God" (*Elohiym*—a plural form).

(In verse 5)—He commanded Moses "not to come any closer" and to "take off your sandals, for the place where you are standing is holy ground." The taking off of his sandals is an act of worship in the presence of deity.

(In verse 6)—He identified Himself as "I am the God of your father, the God of Abraham, the God of Isaac, and the God of Jacob." Jesus alluded to this identification in John 8:58 when He said, "Before Abraham was, I AM."

(In verse 8)—He stated that He has "come down to rescue them [my people] from the hand of the Egyptians." Therefore, this is certainly a coming.

(In verses 14-15)—He again identified Himself as the eternal "I AM" This is the same identification He gave for both God the Father and Himself in Revelation 1:8 and 21:6, and 22:12, "I AM the Alpha and Omega . . . who is, and who was, and who is to come, the Almighty." (Also see Acts 7:30-34; Rev. 4:8.)

Later, it was said of Moses . . .

>—"whom the Lord knew face to face" (Deut. 34:10; also 5:4).

>—"he [Moses] saw him who is invisible." (Heb. 11:27).

Exodus 17:1-7: Jesus was the rock that Moses struck, and from which life-giving water flowed. That rock was a real, physical, and visible rock. Then how do we know this rock was Jesus? The Apostle Paul by inspiration told us so in 1 Corinthians 10:4, ". . . that rock was Christ." Notice that Paul did not say the rock represented, symbolized, or was a type of Christ. He said it *was Christ*. Two verses later, he states that "these things occurred as examples" (1 Cor. 10:6).

Exodus 24:9-11: "the God of Israel" appears to "Moses and Aaron, Nadab and Abihu and the seventy elders of Israel." That's 74 people at one time. And they visibly and physically "saw" Him for Moses further recorded that "under his feet was something like a pavement made of sapphire, clear as the sky itself" and "they saw God."

Judges 6:11-26: Jesus appeared to Gideon, twice—under an oak and later that night. Here, too, "the angel of the Lord" is equated with being "the Lord" (vss. 14-22) and received worship (vss. 18-19; also see Psa. 34:6-8).

2 Chronicles 7:12f: Jesus, the Lord, came and appeared to Solomon at night and told him, "I have heard your prayer." Then Jesus gave him the famous admonition, "if my people who are called by my name will humble themselves and pray and seek my face and turn from their wicked ways, then will I hear from heaven and will forgive their sin and will heal their land (2 Chron. 7:14) . . . . But if you turn away and forsake the decrees and commands I have given you and go off to serve other gods and worship them, then I will uproot Israel from my land, which I have given them, and will reject this temple I have consecrated for my Name. I will make it a byword and an object of ridicule among all peoples" (2 Chron. 7:19-20).

Twice, this uprooting and rejection happened at another and different coming of the Lord:

1) Solomon's temple was destroyed by the Babylonians in 587-586 B.C. and many Jews were taken into captivity.
2) Herod's temple was destroyed by the Romans circa A.D. 70 and many Jews also taken into captivity. (More on this type of coming in Chapter 13.)

Daniel 3:24-27: Jesus came and appeared in the fiery furnace with the three young Hebrew friends of Daniel. "Did not we cast three men bound into the midst of the fire?" King Nebuchadnezzar asked (v. 24, *KJV*). "Lo, I see four men loose, walking in the midst of the fire . . . and the form of the fourth is like the Son of God" (v. 25, *KJV*). Many Bible scholars believe that fourth man, Who was seen, presents another coming of Jesus.

Daniel 10:1-21; 11:1-2f: More certainly, it was Jesus Who later appeared to Daniel and gave him the prophetic vision and message of his chapters 10-12. This includes "the time of the end" prophecy (Dan. 12). It is argued that this Person could not be the angel Gabriel, who appeared and gave Daniel his prophecy of "70 weeks" in Daniel 9 because Gabriel is not described the way this Man is described (compare the description in Daniel 10:5-12 with similar language describing Jesus' coming and appearing to John in Revelation 1:12-17).

Next, we come to Eusebius, a 4th-century Christian leader and writer who is often called "the father of Church history." Eusebius cited three more Old Testament comings of Christ, Whom he refers to as the "second Lord after the Father" (referencing Psa. 110:1-4; Gen. 19:24). "The Lord says to my Lord: 'Sit at my right hand until I make your enemies a footstool" (Psa. 110:1). Here, the first Lord is "Jehovah" and the second is "adown" meaning sovereign, lord, master, owner (human or divine). But Who do you think that second "Lord" is Who is sitting at the right hand of God? It could be none other than Jesus (see Rom. 8:34; Eph. 1:20; Col. 3:1; Heb 1:13; 8:1; 12:21; Acts 2:33-36). And Who is having "enemies [placed] under his feet" (see 1 Cor. 15:25; Heb. 10:13)?

Genesis 18:1f: Eusebius writes: "Thus the Lord God is said to have appeared as an ordinary man to Abraham as he sat by the oak of Mamre, yet he worshiped him as God, saying, 'O Lord, judge of all the world, will you not do justice?' [Gen. 18:25]. Since reason would never permit that the immutable essence of the Almighty be changed into human form . . . who else could be so described as appearing in human form but the preexistent Word [Jesus], since naming the First Cause of the universe [God the Father] would be inappropriate?"

Genesis 32:30: Eusebius writes: "Then too: 'Jacob called the name of that place 'the Vision of God,' saying, 'For I saw God face-to-face, and my life was spared."

[Author's Note: Jacob not only saw this man but wrestled with Him and had his hip physically wrenched (dislocated) by Him (Gen. 32:22-29). This man also blessed Jacob and changed his name to Israel. This coming of Jesus dramatically altered Jacob's life as well as the course of redemptive history. In confirmation, Hosea 12:3-5 declares that this man was "the angel" and none other than "the Lord God Almighty." Evidently, this is why Jacob/Israel names the place where this happened, "Peniel," which means "the face of God." As he declared, "It is because I saw God face to face, and yet my life was spared" (Gen. 32:30). Don't you think this angel just might have been the same angel of the Lord as appeared to Abraham, Moses, Joshua, and Daniel; i.e., the Lord Jesus? Further notable, God appeared to Jacob again at Bethel (see Gen. 35:9-10).]

Joshua 5:13-15: Eusebius writes: "Joshua too saw him only in human form. For it is written:

> When Joshua was at Jericho, he looked up and saw a man standing before him with a drawn sword in his hand. Joshua approached him and said, 'Are you for us or for our enemies?' He replied, 'It is as commander of the Lord's army that I have come.' Then Joshua fell to the ground, face downward, and asked, 'Master, what do you command your servant?' The commander of the Lord's army replied, 'Take off your shoes, for the place you stand is holy.'"

Eusebius compares this coming and appearing of Jesus to Joshua with a prior coming of Jesus to Moses by writing "the words themselves will show you here too that this was none other than the one who spoke to Moses" in Exodus 3:2-15 (see again above at the burning bush where Moses was also commanded to perform the same act of worship—to take off his shoes).

Eusebius puts down any attempt to diminish these comings with this argument: "to suppose that these recorded theophanies were appearances of subordinate angels and ministers of God cannot be correct, for whenever these appear to people, Scripture distinctly declares in countless passages that they are called angels, not God or Lord"[5]

In conclusion, Eusebius emphatically clarifies his position: "But clearly they knew the Christ of God, since he appeared to Abraham . . . spoke to Israel [Jacob], and conversed with Moses and the later prophets as I have shown."[6]

Space will not permit us to explore in detail other possible Old Testament comings of Jesus. It is likely that there were many more (see also Gen. 12:7; Exod. 33:11, 20-23; Isa. 6:5; and more perhaps not recorded) and as the prophet Micah said, "whose goings forth have been from of old, from everlasting" (Mic. 5:2 *KJV*).[7] Especially note here the use of the plural for Jesus' "goings forth." The more literal Hebrew is "goings out."[8]

I also encourage you to look up these additional Old Testament appearances of "the angel of the Lord" (theophanies), which many interpreters conclude was the "preincarnate Christ" (see for example: Gen. 16:7-14; 21:17ff.; 22:11ff.; 31:11ff.; Exod. 3:2ff; Judg. 6:11ff.; 13:2ff; Zech. 1:10-13; 3:1-2, where this angel either identifies Himself

---

[5] Eusebius, *Eusebius: The Church History*, Book 1.2, Paul L. Maier, trans. and comm. (Grand Rapids, MI.: Kregel, 2007), 24.

[6] Ibid., 31.

[7] Nor shall we have space to consider all the many possible comings of God the Father or of God's glory which are sprinkled throughout the Old Testament (Psa. 68:24).

[8] *NIV* translates this phrase as merely "origins." *Matthew Henry's Commentary (Electronic Database)* says it means Christ's "existence from eternity." But *Adam Clarke's Commentary (Electronic Database)* supports the understanding I am suggesting in commenting, "In every age, from the foundation of the world, there has been some manifestation of the Messiah . . . to his manifestation in the flesh . . . ."

with the Lord and/or those to whom He reveals Himself recognize Him as God).[9]

Please remember, all of these comings serve as examples for us (1 Cor. 10:6). Even back in Old Testament times, Jesus was a frequently present and active God, was He not? Another point I must again emphasize is that none of these above comings were foretold in advance. They were all physical and human incarnations that just happened as and when God the Father and/or Jesus chose. But all this was about to change.

At the tail end of the Old Testament time period, we have the birthing-incarnation event itself—the coming of the promised Messiah born in Bethlehem of Judea. The exact location of his birth was prophesied by the prophet Micah eight centuries earlier (see Micah 5:2). The exact time of his birth in 4 B.C. occurred precisely as prophesied by Daniel six centuries earlier (see Dan. 9:24-27).[10] That's why the Apostle Paul was prompted by God's Spirit to write these time-sensitive words: Jesus Christ was born "when the time had fully come . . . to redeem those under the law" (Gal. 4:4). He also wrote that Jesus died "at just the right time" (Rom. 5:6), and "who gave himself as a ransom for all men – the testimony given in its proper time" (1 Tim. 2:6).

As decisive and significant as the babe-in-the-manger coming of Jesus was, Scripture never terms it his "first coming"—and for good reason, as we have begun to see. Nor would it be his only coming in that same 1st-century A.D. time period.

Jesus' Many Comings in the New Testament

Hundreds witnessed Jesus' death on the cross. But on the third day He arose and during the next forty days hundreds more witnessed his physical presence. As a result, their lives were dramatically changed. They now knew that there is life beyond the grave. After his resurrection,

---

[9] Nor shall we be considering the verses about Melchizedek that some scholars believe was Jesus incarnate.

[10] That is, occurred precisely on the timeline for the sequential unfolding and chronological fulfillment of Daniel's 70 Weeks prophecy covered in Chapter 10. For more on this, see Noē, *The Perfect Ending for the World*, 109-126.

the writers of the New Testament documented many post-Resurrection, pre-Ascension and post-Ascension comings and appearings of Jesus.

Critical Objection: These appearances were not comings.

My Response: Jesus said they were comings: ". . . I will come to you . . . . you will see me" (John 14:18-19). That's good enough for me.

1 Corinthians 15:5-8: "and that He [Christ] appeared to Peter, and then to the Twelve. After that, he appeared to more than five hundred of the brothers at the same time, most of whom are still living, though some have fallen asleep. Then he appeared to James, then to all the apostles, and last of all he appeared to me also, as to one abnormally born." That's a lot of comings/appearances. Some were private; some were public.

Acts 1:3: "After his suffering, he showed himself to these men and gave many convincing proofs that he was alive. He appeared to them over a period of forty days and spoke about the kingdom of God." More documented comings—such as:

1) To the two on the road to Emmaus; "Then their eyes were opened and they recognized him, and he disappeared from their sight" (see Luke 24:13-32).
2) To his disciples on the shore as they saw, talked, and ate with Him (see Luke 24:36-49; also John 21:4-14).
3) To his disciples, and notably Thomas, in the upper room when "Jesus came and stood among them" and talked to them (see John 20:26-29).

Acts 7:55: "But Stephen, full of the Holy Spirit, looked up to heaven and saw the glory of God, and Jesus standing at the right hand of God." This was not a dream. Whether it was a coming or a vision of Jesus, Stephen actually *saw* Him. Perhaps, this was like Elisha's servant in 2 Kings 6:17 whose eyes were opened and saw the angelic army above the hills.

Acts 9:4-5: "He [Saul] fell to the ground and heard a voice say to him, 'Saul, Saul, why do you persecute me?' 'Who are you, Lord?' Saul asked. 'I am Jesus, whom you are persecuting.'" That's a coming and appearance of Jesus, no question about it. See Paul's later account of this event in Acts 26:12-16 for further confirmation that Jesus actually did appear here to him while the others with Saul only witnessed something supernatural—"a light from heaven, brighter than the sun, blazing around me and my companions." And they "all fell to the ground."

Acts 10:13-15: "Then a voice told him, 'Get up, Peter. Kill and eat.' 'Surely not, Lord!' Peter replied. 'I have never eaten anything impure or unclean.' The voice spoke to him a second time, 'Do not call anything impure that God has made clean.'" Again, that's probably a coming of Jesus, even though this text only says this manifestation was a voice.

Acts 22:17-18: "When I [Paul] returned to Jerusalem and was praying at the temple, I fell into a trance and saw the Lord speaking. 'Quick!' He said to me. 'Leave Jerusalem immediately, because they will not accept your testimony about me.'" If your doctrine demands it, you can call that a vision. I'm comfortable calling it a coming of Jesus. (Also see Acts 9:9-16; 18:9-11).

Acts 9:10-16: The Lord appeared to Ananias "in a vision" and gave him instructions to go to Saul. This definitely was a vision, as stated, and not a coming.

Acts 18:9-11: The Lord also spoke to Paul "in a vision" and comforted him. Yes, another vision and not a coming.

Acts 23:11: "The following night the Lord stood near Paul and said, 'Take courage! As you have testified about me in Jerusalem, so you must also testify in Rome!'" This was a visual/physical coming and not a vision.

Matthew 17:1-3: "After six days Jesus took with him Peter, James and John the brother of James, and led them up a high mountain by themselves. There he was transfigured before them. His face shone like the sun, and his clothes became as white as the light. Just then there appeared before them Moses and Elijah, talking with Jesus." Then, Moses and Elijah disappeared leaving only Jesus in his glorified state. Truly, something powerful, glorious, and unveiling happened on that mountain. Peter, who was one of the eyewitnesses to this event, may have referred to this experience as a "coming" (*parousia* – see 2 Pet. 1:16-18). As we shall see in Chapter 13, the presence and then disappearance of Moses and Elijah here was most significant. It was, so to speak, a "preview of coming attractions" that prefigured, foreshadowed, and typified the very essence of the nature of what many people consider to be Jesus' most, or second most, important coming—his *parousia* coming. This transfiguration was also another indigenous component of the expansion of the kingdom of God (Isa. 9:6-7)—the comings of Christ in his kingdom (Matt 16:28b). And as we have already seen, Jesus followers were to witness many of his comings in his kingdom (post-resurrection) some of which, but most likely not all, are recorded for us in the Bible (John 20:30).

Revelation 1:17: "When I saw him, I fell at his feet as though dead. Then he placed his right hand on me and said: 'Do not be afraid. I am the First and the Last.'" In this coming, Jesus not only appeared and spoke to John, He also touched him. This happened on the island of Patmos and for the purpose of giving John the Book of Revelation.

When we consider the symbolic names that refer to Jesus, we shall find other New Testament comings and appearings: to Philip (Acts 8:26), to Cornelius (Acts 10:1-6), and again to Peter (Acts 12:7). With the lone exception of Jesus' birth, none of these other and documented comings in the New Testament were specifically prophesied in terms of time, place, or recipient. At best, they were only generally prophesied (see John 14:18-19; 16:16).

> Question: Which of the above comings of Jesus was or is the "Second Coming?"
>
> Question: So far, how many possible, historical, and biblical comings of Jesus have we identified?

Depending on how we count them, it's between 30 to 40 comings of Jesus. And we're not done. There's much more. But doesn't this listing of up to 40 possible and historical comings of Jesus give you more appreciation for why God's Word never uses the expression "second coming" and why the Church's doctrine of a "second coming" will not stand up to an honest, sincere, and objective test of Scripture?

Surely, by now we can recognize that nowhere do the Scriptures limit the comings of Jesus to a single "Second Coming" event nor to a "First Coming." Instead, both the Old and New Testaments clearly document many comings of Jesus. He came in many different ways, at special and quite unexpected times, and to both those who sought Him and those who did not. All this (and more) happened exactly as Jesus had told them, "You also must be ready, because the Son of Man will come at an hour when you do not expect him" (Luke 12:40).

What's more, innumerably more comings are taught and promised.

Many Promised Comings of Jesus

Sad to say, many Bible interpreters believe that all the New Testament verses speaking of or promising the coming of Jesus refer to a single event. For some, that event is past and over; it happen circa A.D. 70. For most, it's still future and unfulfilled, and to happen at the unscriptural end of the world, the end of time, or before, during, or after a seven-year period of Tribulation.[11] Obviously, someone or ones is/are greatly mistaken.

Of course, it's easy to read Bible passages for years, and given an *a priori* assumption, to never fully realize what's actually being said or not said. And limiting the Lord's coming again to a single event definitely has an appeal of simplicity. On the other hand, why should we assume singularity when the pattern of his coming throughout the Scriptures is just the opposite—many comings? Surely, we need to rise above our preconceived and limiting notions and submit to the authority of Scripture. Therefore, let's see if there is a better way to further sort out the whole thing as we re-explore some of the promised comings of Jesus:

John 14:1-3: "Do not let your hearts be troubled. Trust in God; trust also in me. In my Father's house are many rooms, if it were not so, I would have told you. I am going there to prepare a place for you. And if I

---

[11] I have written on this, extensively. See Noē, *The Perfect Ending for the World*, chapters 1-6 and following.

go and prepare a place for you, I will come [*erchomai*] again [not 'back'] and take you to be with me that you also may be where I am."

This promised coming is often read at funerals as an assurance that Jesus personally comes at the death of each of his saints to receive them into heaven—perhaps angels do, too (see Heb. 1:14). No one can dogmatically deny or prove this one way or the other. But Jesus' promise also bears relevance to his coming to fulfill and finalize all things: "so Christ was sacrificed once to take away the sins of many people; and he will appear a second time, not to bear sin, but to bring salvation to those who are waiting for him" (Heb. 9:28). If, however, Jesus has not come in this way—as He promised in John 14:1-3 above, as was being anticipated by his disciples twenty and thirty years later (see 1 Pet. 1:5; Luke 21:27-28), and as most popular views today still hold—then the unpleasant, inescapable, and present-day consequence is this: heaven must not be prepared and open, even yet. Remember, Jesus also said, "No one has ever gone into heaven except the one who came from heaven – the Son of Man" (John 3:13; also see 13:33, 36). Thus, this supposed "nonoccurrence" poses quite a dilemma for modern-day preachers, if they're honest about it (see again Chapter 1, pp.18-23). There's more.

John 14:18-23:

Verse 18: "I will not leave you as orphans; I will come [*erchomai*, not 'come back'] to you." Come to whom? Who is the "you?" It's not some future, unborn generation. It's his disciples with whom He's talking at the Last Supper.

Verse 19: "Before long, the world will not see me anymore, but you will see me. Because I live, you also will live." The fact is, Jesus came and appeared to them, and they visibly saw Him several times following his resurrection.

Verse 20: "On that day [the day I come to you] you will realize that I am in my Father, and you are in me, and I am in you [in the spirit]."

Verse 21: "Whoever has my commands and obeys them, he is the one who loves me. He who loves me will be loved by my Father, and I too will love him and show [or manifest, *emphanizo*] myself to him." This verse implies an inward illumination and/or a relational coming for an individual. It, too, can be considered part of this coming even though the word "come" is not specifically used here.

Verse 23: is similar ". . . If anyone loves me, he will obey my teaching. My Father will love him, and we will come to him and make our home with him." Here, again, the word "come" (*erchomai*) is used. By the spirit the whole Godhead—not just the Holy Spirit as many have assumed[12]—comes, indwells and manifests perhaps in ways and dimensions beyond our comprehension.

And wow! What a promise this is! It is certainly not a promise of a visible coming or a coming in judgment. This promise is for a spiritual coming. It is addressed to individuals and is unlimited— "whoever . . . if anyone." Jesus fulfilled that promise within a few days; He came to those very same people (see John 20:19-31). Moreover, this promised coming is contingent upon meeting certain conditions of love and obedience—big "ifs." Then, and only then, has He promised to manifest Himself, personally, in this manner. The word "manifest" in the original Greek means: "to exhibit (in Person) or disclose (by words): – appear, declare, inform, show, signify." Although it's true that God does this by his Word, the Bible, that is not the intent of this coming's promise. It's a personal revelation of Jesus Himself, like the type of revelation shared between the closest friends or intimate lovers. Again, some feel this coming is of the Holy Spirit and not the same as a coming of Jesus, *per se.* But that is not what this verse says. Evidently, and since then,

---

[12] Billy Graham, "My Answer," "God lives in us by the Holy Spirit," *The Indianapolis Star*, 4/21/12, E-4 – "The Holy Spirit is God himself, as he comes to live within us when we give our lives to Jesus. . . . when we accept Christ and commit our lives to him, God comes to live within us by his Holy Spirit." Of course, this is true. But this particular coming is over and above and promises more than that.

this coming has occurred many, many times, all over the world, wouldn't you think?

Acts 1:9-11:

Verse 9: "After he had said this, he was taken up before their very eyes, and a cloud hid him from their sight." This cloud may have been an ordinary cloud. Or it could have been the same Shekhinah glory cloud that was in the Temple, the one the Jews followed through the wilderness by day and/or that in which Moses and Elijah appeared in the Transfiguration.

Verse 11: "'Men of Galilee,' they said, 'why do you stand here looking into the sky? This same Jesus, who has been taken from you into heaven, will come in the same way you have seen him go into heaven.'" Again, the Greek word for "will come" is *erchomai*. Remember, biblical Greek is a much more elaborate language than modern English. This word actually means "to come or go (in a great variety of applications, lit. and fig.)."[13] In this instance, it was a going.

The operative phrase we want to focus on here is "in the same way," or, in other translations, "in like manner." Mostly, it has been taught that this means Jesus' return to earth has to be in an identical manner; i.e., identical in every detail, except in reverse order. So since He ascended in a visible resurrected body, He must come back in that same form, physically and visibly. If this is true, then must He also come back to that exact same location on the Mount of Olives? How far do we press this similarity? If we are consistent, doesn't this interpretation methodology require that his so-called return will not be seen by every person on earth since only a handful of disciples saw Him go? Or, must He return to only to those very same people who saw Him ascend and without any fanfare? Obviously, traditional

---

[13] *Strong's Exhaustive Concordance of the Bible*, #2064. W.E. Vine: *An Expository Dictionary of Biblical Words*, New Testament Words, 195. Walter Bauer, F.W. Gingrich, and Frederick Danker, *A Greek Lexicon of the New Testament and Other Early Christian Literature*, 311.

explanations contain numerous problems when you critically think about it. Others, on the other hand, argue for an invisible nature of his return based upon this same account. They reason that since his ascension into heaven was not visible, but hidden from their eyes by the cloud, so shall be his return to earth from heaven; i.e., not visible.

Additionally troubling are these factors. If "in like manner" means "in exactly and literally the same way," how would Jesus come back from heaven riding "a white horse" (Rev. 19:11) and leading "the armies of heaven" (Rev. 19:14, or "with thousands upon thousands of his holy ones" (Jude 14), or "as the lightning comes from the east and flashes to the west" (Matt. 24:27), or "with a loud command, with the voice of the archangel and with the trumpet call of God" (1 Thess. 4:16), or "in blazing fire" (2 Thess. 1:7)? Clearly, these other traditionally taught Second Coming passages in no way resemble Jesus' ascension going and disappearance.

More to the point, the two angels ("two men dressed in white") (v. 10) did not say Jesus would come in a like "body," or the same "body," or to the same "place," or to those witnessing his ascension. The emphasis is on the *manner* of his coming. Contrary to most popular teachings, "in like manner" does not limit Jesus to coming in only a physical/visible mode, nor to that same geographic location from which He ascended, or to a small group. The proper focus here is on *how* He comes. What we can legitimately ascertain from some of his comings we've reviewed so far in this chapter is, Jesus both comes and goes as the Greek word used here (*erchomai*) allows. He comes out of the spirit realm, manifests Himself in the physical realm, then goes back into the spirit realm. That has been the means and manner of his visible and physical comings and goings. They are documented throughout both the Old and New Testaments. With the lone exception of this birth coming, He moves out of one dimension into another and goes back again. His form, the place, the recipients, and the purposes vary. *Erchomai*—comes or (and) goes—is the general, overall manner in which his many visible comings have and do occurred. Angels also have this same capability (Heb. 13:2), do they not?

Jesus Comes in a Variety of Ways

Doesn't the realization of the many past and promised comings of Jesus we have been re-exploring so far give you a new appreciation for Jesus' admonition, "You also must be ready, because the Son of Man will come at an hour when you do not expect him" (Luke 12:40)? It seems ours has been and is a Jesus Who comes. And in my opinion, we dishonor Christ when we limit his comings to only two, three, or to any at all.

Of course, we have much more to cover and expound upon regarding the many past, present, and future comings (plural) of Jesus. The Bible's Book of Revelation is loaded with both past and contemporary relevance in this regard, as well as being the Bible's climactic revelation of other spirit-realm/physical-realm truths and realities.

Unfortunately, the most contested aspect of Jesus' earthly ministry has been his numerous predictions and supposed failure to come again within the lifetime of his contemporaries. These predictions and this supposed "nonoccurrence" charge have troubled Christianity and the world for centuries. No more!

By now, I hope you are beginning to get a glimpse of the big picture. If we sincerely search the Scriptures for what they say and don't say, there is no legitimate, scriptural, or historical way we can limit the comings (plural) of Jesus to a single "Second Coming" event—past or future. This popular, two-advent mindset, clearly and simply, does not fit Scripture's terminology, teaching, or testimony.

> **"You also must be ready, because the Son of Man will come at an hour when you do not expect him" (Luke 12:40).**

Also by now, I trust it's more than evident that the correct, biblical, and historical answer to the question I asked at on pp.249-250 of our previous chapter is "E) MORE." Since the greater Jesus, the contemporary Christ, has shed the hindrance of human limitation, He can come any time He wants and do much more than He could during his earthly ministry. Shouldn't we, therefore, desire for Him to come and do great things in our day and time? As we shall continue to see, He does in many wondrous ways.

So let's now call it like it is. "Second Coming" and "Return" terminology makes no textual, historical, logical, grammatical, or biblical sense. This terminology is totally inappropriate and brings reproach upon the name and integrity of Jesus Christ and his Church. Neither expression is a valid scriptural term or concept.

It is truly amazing when you stop to think about it. Many people, who focus on a single, future Second Coming, support their doctrine by saying that you have to take the Bible literally. Yet, if you take it literally, not one single verse ever makes reference to a "Second Coming" or a "Return," nor do any of the historic creeds of the Church. Perhaps it's our traditions that have led us astray?

Indeed, this is exactly what has happened. "Second Coming" and "Return" expressions are contrived terminology and reductionist ideas that have been read into the Bible and handed down for centuries. They have hamstrung and harmed the Church long enough. The historical and biblical reality of Christ's many comings is a corrective to the limited, misleading, and deceptive idea of a single "Second Coming." And the fact that He never left renders a "Return" totally inappropriate. That is why this language is never used in Scripture. Get it yet?

What's at risk here is plenty and everything! The continued use of this non-biblical terminology is another classic example of the traditions of men dumbing down, diluting, devaluing, and depreciating authentic biblical Christianity (Matt. 15:6; Mark 7:13). And since words mean things and wording is important, we cannot afford to be misinformed or confused about such an important element of our faith. It is paramount, therefore, that we in the Church be clear on and control our word usage; i.e., use Bible names for Bible things. Would you now agree?

Oh, I'm sure Satan and his cohorts would love to keep God's people busy looking for just a single Second Coming and Return, somewhere up in the sky, off in the future. Why? It's because it distracts them from tapping into spiritual dynamite,[14] from worshipping the greater Jesus, the contemporary Christ, in all his unveiled reality, and from doing the

---

[14] See Acts 1:8 and note that the Greek word for "power" is *dunamis*, from which we get our word "dynamite."

kingdom works of and greater works than Jesus (John 14:12) in the full power of his Spirit, today.[15]

In my opinion, the Christian faith cannot and will not progress as quickly, and as effectively as it is capable of doing, until its proponents begin to speak out the biblical truth of what Jesus is like and doing today, especially regarding his presence and many countless comings. Yes, this is a credibility, reliability, relevance, and practical issue. How much so?

Allow me to make a quick fast-forward here. What about your own salvation experience when you became born again? At that time did Christ come into you and the "mystery" of "Christ in you" became a new reality in your life (Col. 1:27)? How did Christ get into you? Is this not another, legitimate, and viable coming of Jesus? Remember spirit is literal, too.

So where am I wrong on this, or on any of it, so far?

My Stronger Recommendation—a Purging

Since Scripture instructs us to "demolish arguments and every pretension that sets itself up against the knowledge of God" (2 Cor. 10:4b-5a), I strongly recommend we demolish this major pretension as the renowned professor Dr. George Eldon Ladd puts it in his classic book, *The Blessed Hope*:

> The second coming of Jesus Christ is an absolutely indispensable doctrine in the Biblical teaching of redemption. Apart from His glorious return, God's work will forever be incomplete.[16]

With all due respect for Dr. Ladd, these two non-scriptural expressions—"second coming" and "return" of Christ—have cast their long shadows for long enough. I am recommending that we'd be well advised to drop the use of both terminologies that is not found in the Scriptures and purge them from our vocabulary and practice of the Christian faith. Let us also cast aside the unscriptural and arbitrary idea of limiting the comings of Jesus in any way at all. It's dishonoring to

---

[15] For more here, see: Noē, *The Greater Jesus*, 339-396.
[16] Ladd, *The Blessed Hope*, 6.

Christ and contradictory of Scripture. Clearly, we serve a God Who comes—Who has come, comes, and will continue coming. So whenever a tradition of men is proven ungrounded in Scripture, it must be purged and no longer allowed to weaken, hinder, or undermine the progress and effectiveness of the faith. All this and much more is what's at risk and at stake.[17]

I further suggest that we seriously consider whether or not we have been "carried away" by "strange doctrine" (Heb. 13:9) that has "deceived even the elect – if that were possible" (Matt. 24:24). The presence of Jesus and his many countless comings are two beautiful truths of Scripture and a long-precedent reality of history. We shall never properly understand or fully appreciate the greatness of our faith and the reality of the greater Jesus, the contemporary Christ, if we are boxed into, or intimidated and brainwashed by, an erroneous and limited mindset and paradigm in this matter.[18]

But if this terminology is non-scriptural, then is this event also non-scriptural? And if non-scriptural, is it unscriptural? And if unscriptural, it is a non-event? Please think long, hard, and seriously about this series of questions. An objective determination is crucial in this case. But not everyone agrees, as some have written to me.

Critical Objection #1: "To me you are quibbling over whether it is called his second (Heb. 9:28) or some other number, is really to miss the important point that all prophecy was fulfilled in A.D. 70."[19]

Critical Objection #2: By setting Jesus' A.D. 70 parousia as just one coming among many (even though you allow for it to be "pretty important"), you delimit the importance and critical nature that Scripture gives for the A.D. 70 parousia. A.D. 70 was the game changer and eternal fulfillment of the soteriological plan of the Godhead. That's the essence of Hebrews 9:24-28. . . . My question to you is, why all this

---

[17] For more on my recommendation, see: Noē, *The Perfect Ending for the World*, 254-257.

[18] I have previously written on this topic of Christ's presence, which I do not plan on duplicating in this book. See Noē, *The Perfect Ending for the World*, 247-252.

[19] From a personal email, 6/23/13.

stress on the "many comings" idea? What is the motivation behind this thesis of many comings that you are pushing?[20]

My Response: I not quibbling or delimiting at all. To the contrary, I'm doing just the opposite. And much is at stake. Please keep in mind that this so-called "second coming" and "return" of Christ is not only the most anticipated event in all of history, it is also the pivotal, central, and controlling event to which the fulfillment of all other end-time events in all four of the competing, conflicting, and divisive end-time views are conjoined. It is the "chief moment" that anchors, defines, and differentiates the four views.

But if we truly desire to reconcile this massive arena of theology termed eschatology, which is what I'm proposing, then we must get at this root cause that has produced "one of the most divisive elements in recent Christian history."[21] It's also the greatest impediment to eschatological reform and unification—i.e., the synthesis of end-time views. Truly and sincerely, I consider the purging of this non-scriptural language and resulting flawed tradition to be a vital part of "the ministry of reconciliation" (2 Cor. 5:18). By eliminating this non-scriptural terminology and unshackling Christianity from its dominance it becomes a non-event (which it is) in peoples' eyes and minds and clears the table of debate and divisiveness for a legitimate and divine solution of synthesis of all four competing and conflicting end-time views into one meaningful, coherent, and cogent view that is more Christ-honoring, Scripture-authenticating, and faith-validating than any one view in and of itself.

By now, I hope this reconciliation direction is beginning to make sense to you. We have been hamstrung by this two-advent tradition of men long enough. It's time to let Jesus out of our man-made, two-advent box. In my opinion, if the Church could get this pivotal, central, and controlling issue properly revolved and removed, what a great stimulus this could be for the advancement of the kingdom of God.

Oh, I can hear the cries of the H-word ("heresy") already arising from those unwilling to honestly and sincerely contemplate the abundant

---

[20] From a Facebook thread discussion, 6/19/13
[21] Kantzer, ed., "Our Future Hope: Eschatology and Its Role in the Church," 1-14 (I).

biblical and historical evidence for the presence and many comings of Jesus, from those who fear such a change would do great damage to the faith of the "fragile," and from those who will not want to give up, for any reason whatsoever, their two- or three-advent hope, mindset, and limited view. But please don't misinterpret my motives. If we are truly sincere about seeking after, knowing, and following Jesus as He now is, that means it's time for serious reflection and further reform. The time has come for us in the Church to honestly reconsider exactly what is heretical, unbiblical, and even anti-biblical in regard to the presence and many comings of Jesus.

> **We have been hamstrung by this two-advent tradition of men long enough. It's time to let Jesus out of our man-made, two-advent box.**

Therefore, dear saints, let us jettison these expressions which are totally foreign to God's Word, as well as to the major creeds. So much is at stake. Again, the presence and many comings of Jesus are such beautiful truths and historical realities. It's time these plain, simple, yet precious truths and realities be proclaimed in scriptural terms. Stop limiting his comings! Amen. Come, Lord Jesus! As we will continue to see, He has; He still does; and He will!

In our next chapter of unlearning and unraveling, let's continue our journey and quest for truth and understanding by revisiting the most contested aspect of Jesus' earthly ministry and his longest and most dramatic prophecy. It's also his most problematic teaching. What's more, it contains the promise of what many consider his "biggest, baddest, and best" coming of all—depending upon your eschatological view, of course. But let's not condescend into calling it his "Second Coming" or "Return" because, as we have seen, Scripture never does.

Chapter 13

Reframing Jesus' Most Dramatic Prophecy

Scholars call it the Olivet Discourse since Jesus gave this prophecy while sitting on the Mount of Olives during the last week of this life. It's also Jesus' most dramatic and longest prophesy. Hence, this chapter will also be our longest. And this prophecy is loaded. Its predictions and promised coming have troubled, baffled, and confused Christianity and the world for centuries, but no more![1]

Something many scholars do not recognize and most Christians do not know is that the Bible contains four slightly different versions of this prophecy. We'll work primarily with Matthew 24's account. It's the most detailed.[2] Luke 21's account contains a few additional items and details well worth consideration. Mark 13's account is the shortest and essentially adds nothing. But then there is a fourth version, and it's not in John's gospel. It's called Book of Revelation and it unveils an amplified account of these same events, and much more. This fourth version will be the subject of our next chapter. For now, however, I suggest you read Jesus' prophetic words for yourself in Matthew 24, Luke 21, and Mark 13. before continuing this chapter.

---

[1] The content of this chapter's first two sections are condensed and taken from Noē, *The Perfect Ending for the World*, 149-164. For a more extensive treatment, see my other book.

[2] The whole prophecy encompasses both Matthew 24 and 25.

But from an overview standpoint, I first want to show you a blatant example of biased interpreting. See if it is contained in your Bible.

The week before He was crucified in A.D. 30, and while walking through the Temple complex and casting seven woes upon the teachers of the law and Pharisees, Jesus made some startling statements about the end, such as:

- "And so upon you will come all the righteous blood that has been shed on earth . . ." (Matt. 23:35a).
- "I tell you the truth, all this will come upon this generation" (Matt. 23:36).
- "Look, your house is left to you desolate" (Matt. 23:38).

A few hours later, while sitting on the Mount of Olives, looking across the valley at the beautiful Jewish Temple, Jesus stunned his disciples by prophesying that this entire complex of buildings, an awesome structure "famous throughout the world" (2 Maccabees 2:22 *NRSV*), would be totally destroyed. "I tell you the truth, not one stone here will be left on another; every one will be thrown down" (Matt. 24:2).

When his disciples asked, "When will this happen?" (Matt. 24:3), He answered, once again with familiar words and using oath language, "I tell you the truth, this generation will certainly not pass away until all these things have happened" (Matt. 24:34). Not only was something significant about to happen, it was to happen in their lifetime, or so they thought. To top it off, He told them about many other end-time events that would take place within that same time period.

Properly understanding Jesus' prophetic words in this passage is paramount to properly understanding all end-time prophecy. Although they have puzzled and perplexed humankind for nearly 2,000 years, they need not. We have only to compare his prophecy with Habakkuk's and Daniel's prophecies—and take Him at this word—to arrive at his proper meaning. Included in Jesus' "all these things" were:

- The end of the age and the sign of his coming (*parousia*) (v. 3)
- The gospel preached in all the world . . . to all nations (v. 14)
- The end will come (v. 14)

- The abomination of desolation standing in the holy place (v. 15)
- The hearers fleeing for their lives (v. 16-20)
- A great tribulation, unequaled in history before or after (v. 21)
- False Christs and false prophets appearing, performing great signs and miracles and deceiving even the elect—if that were possible (v. 24)
- The coming (*parousia*) of the Son of Man (v. 27)
- The sun and the moon darkened, stars falling from the sky and the heavenly bodies shaken (v. 29)
- The sign of the Son of Man appearing in the sky (v. 30)
- Them seeing the Son of Man coming on the clouds (v. 30)
- "This generation" not passing away "until all these things have happened" (v. 34)

He left no doubt that something truly significant was about to happen. But today, millions of Bible readers and scholars continue to be baffled and confused by Jesus' allegedly cryptic words and his emphasis that some of those who were there with Him at the time would witness all these climactic end-time events—i.e., "all these things." Most debate centers on what generation Jesus was really talking about when He referred to "this generation." Let's also note that He emphatically warned his first hearers, "Watch out that no one deceives you" (Matt. 24:4). As we shall see, his warning is just as relevant today as it was back then. So, if we take Jesus at his literal word (as they did) and hold to an authoritative view of Scripture, "all these things" must have occurred within the lifetime of his disciples exactly *as* and *when* He said. Nothing short of the credibility of Jesus Christ is at stake. Surely Jesus didn't make a mistake or intend to mislead his disciples. The only other alternative is that He spoke truly—just as He said He did.

Skeptics, on the other hand, contend that Jesus' Olivet Discourse is an empty prophecy, since neither Jesus' generation, nor any generation since has seen its complete or even any of its fulfillment. However, his prophesied stone-by-stone destruction of the Temple complex is beyond contesting. It's a historical fact. It occurred circa A.D. 70 - 73, precisely within the time period Jesus said. Yet most people of the world have been led to believe that the rest, and most, of Jesus' other prophetic words are still to be fulfilled, or fulfilled completely.

Of course, the historical fact of Jerusalem and the Temple's destruction forty years later is also and exactly in harmony with the fulfillment of Daniel's time-of-the-end prophesy we discussed in Chapter 10. The problem has been that some, many, or most of the other things that were to occur at the same time supposedly failed to happen, have not yet happened, or have not yet fully happened, according to the three most popular and futuristic end-time views in the Church today. But this key issue remains. What generation was Jesus talking about as being the "this generation?"

To sidestep the plain meaning and utmost importance of Jesus' words, prophecy teachers and futuristic theologians have devised every kind of strained exegesis (an explanation or interpretation of a word, sentence, or passage), linguistic gymnastics, and sophisticated arguments imaginable. Not surprisingly, every attempt over the centuries to evade the plain force of this passage and place its fulfillment beyond the 1st-century timeframe Jesus specified has brought nothing but embarrassment and discredit to the Church as well as undermined the deity of Christ and the integrity of the Scriptures (see again Chapter 1, pp. 31-34).

So where is the blatant example of biased interpreting I promised to show you? It's found in footnote inconsistencies in some Bibles (like the *NIV*). Please notice that after Jesus' "this generation" time statement in Matthew 24:34 some Bibles place a footnote clarifying its meaning or possible meaning as being "race." However, *no footnote* is added to the identical usage of this phrase in Matthew 23:36. If, however, Jesus' "this generation" meant "race," then Jesus did not answer his disciples' time question in Matthew 24:3, which proceeded this entire discourse: "Tell us," they said, "when will this happen, and what will be the sign of your coming and of the end of the age?"

As we shortly shall see, Jesus frequently spoke of his contemporaries as *this generation*. And everywhere else in the New Testament, outside of the Olivet Discourse, that the phrase "this generation" is used (17 times), it is not footnoted and does not mean "race." It always means the contemporaries of the writer or person speaking. Stretching out its meaning to mean a race or type of people, or to some future, unborn generation over two-thousand years removed from Jesus' time would, at best, be an interpretation by exception. So how do they justify such an interpretation by exception? Here's one way dispensational premillennialist Thomas Ice justifies it:

> Despite the preterist chorus that "this generation" has to refer to the first century, an alternative *literal* interpretation relates it to the timing of the fulfillment of other events in context. While it is true that other uses of "this generation" refer to Christ's contemporaries, that is because they are *historical* texts. The use of "this generation" in the Olivet discourse in the fig tree passages are *prophetic* texts. In fact when one compares the historical use of "this generation" at the beginning of the Olivet discourse in Matthew 23:36 (which is an undisputed reference to A.D. 70) with the prophetic use in 24:34, a contrast is obvious."[3]

But postmillennialist and partial preterist Kenneth L. Gentry challenges Ice's inconsistent and deferment claims and doesn't let him get away with such a sloppy and despicable handling of Scripture:

> Ice tries to distinguish Jesus' use of "this generation" in Matthew 23:36 from the same phrase in 24:34 on the basis that 23:36 is "historical" while 24:34 is "prophetical" (Matt. 24:34). But note: (1) *Both* are prophetic. In Matthew 23 Jesus prophesies *future* persecution for his own disciples (23:34) and the catastrophic calamity to befall the Pharisees in A.D. 70 (23:35). Declaring future events in advance is by definition, "prophetic." (2) . . . Matthew 24 flows directly from Matthew 23: As Jesus declares Israel's first-century temple "desolate" . . . . the two chapters are interlocked—and so must be the similar time-frame language.[4]

Not surprisingly, most of the debate over the centuries has centered on what generation Jesus was really talking about. But Jesus also warned his first hearers, "Watch out that no one deceives you" (Matt. 24:4). As Ice has demonstrated above, Jesus' warning is just as relevant today. Many today, raised in delay-postponement-futuristic traditions, have attempted to get around the plain, natural, consistent, and literal meaning of Jesus' two words, "this generation." To do so, they have been forced to employ a variety of literary tactics, which I term sidestepping devices.

---

[3] Ice and Gentry, Jr., *The Great Tribulation: Past or Future*, 103-104.
[4] Ibid., 182.

These exegetical gymnastics are necessitated to cover up for Jesus' apparent failure to produce what He promised within the time period He promised.

These interpretive techniques, like that of Ice's above, usually fall under the guise of "traditional explanations." But make no mistake. They are deceptions. You need to know about these devices because many of us naively have been duped by one or more of them. Yet each device is a ploy born of theological necessity. None is textually, exegetically, nor grammatically justifiable. They are simply "necessitated" in order to evade, finesse around, or distort the plain, face-value meaning and clear relevance of Jesus' prophetic words and time restriction of "this generation." Consequently, most Christians (and others) have never considered the possibility that Jesus might have been speaking of events which were *all* to transpire during the lifetime of some of his 1st-century hearers.

These exegetical gymnastics are necessitated to cover up for Jesus' apparent failure to produce what He promised within the time period He promised.

The Four Sidestepping Devices[5]

Sidestepping Device #1: "Generation" must mean "race," "nation," or "a kind of people." As the above blatant example of biased interpreting demonstrated, some Bibles add a footnote following Jesus' word "generation"—but only in its three uses in the three gospel accounts of the Olivet Discourse (Matt. 24:34; Mark 13:30; Luke 21:32)—indicating that the word could mean "race or nation (Israel)."

In essence, this classic sidestepping device stretches Jesus' words "this generation" from being a contemporary group into being a long line of successive generations. As a desired result, all time relevance is lost. Most tellingly, however, in all its other, thirty-three identical uses, for the

---

[5] For a more expansive treatment of "Five Sidestepping Devices," see Noē, *The Perfect Ending for the World*, 151-164,

word "generation" in the New Testament no footnote is attached and no alternative meaning is added, like in Matthew 23:36 for instance and as we saw above. In these other verses, generation is never interpreted as race, nation, Israel, or the Jewish people. Once again, could there be any more blatant evidence of biased interpreting among translators?

Unfortunately, the use of this arbitrary device is a classic example of but one of the desperate measures and inconsistencies to which some will resort to defend their agenda-driven, futuristic, postponing, end-time-scenario schemes. But the biblical fact is, no warrant exits for this intrusive and distortive attempt to make generation mean race or nation.

Others attempt to avoid the temporal meaning of the word "generation" by claiming that it refers to a kind of people possessing similar attributes, such as unbelief and bad character and headed toward judgment. Admittedly, this meaning is one of the secondary meanings in the Greek. Like most words, generation has more than one meaning. Even in English dictionaries today, ten or more possible meanings are listed. This other meaning, however, is not this word's primary meaning.

A simple word study of the Greek word *genea*, translated "generation," should clear things up. The primary meaning is "a people living at the same time." Most scholars agree that *genea's* use in the Bible refers to a chronological association, and not ethnicity or personal characteristics. For example, the Bible says that forty-two "generations" were between Abraham and Christ (Matt. 1:1-17). These obviously are not forty-two races of Israel or forty-two kinds of people carrying Abraham's blood. And Scripture also implies that the length of a biblical generation is forty years (see Heb. 3:9-10,17).

If, however, Jesus had meant to convey any other meaning, the inspired writers of his words could have chosen from several more appropriate Greek words.[6] But in all honesty the phrase "this generation" should cause no difficulty. After all, Jesus was answering a *when* question (Matt. 24:3). These other proposed meanings would be non-answers, or a direct avoidance, and basically leave the disciple's question unanswered. Who are we to add some nineteen centuries and counting to Jesus' time-restrictive phrase?

The truth is, the Bible defines its own limitations. And no interpreter has the freedom or the right to weave in and out of time contexts at will.

---

[6] For these words, see Noē, *The Perfect Ending for the World*, 156.

Jesus' "this generation" must be taken literally, consistently, and within the commonly used and normally understood meaning of this phrase. Outside this historical context the biblical end and its events cannot be properly understood. Therefore, this sidestepping and postponement device must be called for what truly is—unscriptural—and discarded.

Sidestepping Device #2: "Generation" must refer to a future generation. This sidestepping device is probably the most common. Since interpreters in the most popular of the postponing traditions (dispensational premillennialism) can't fathom how "all these things" could possibly have occurred during the lifetime of Jesus' contemporaries or been fulfilled in any subsequent generation, they conclude that they must occur in the lifetime of some future generation almost 2,000 years and counting removed from Jesus' generation.

How do they justify this extrapolation? They maintain that the phrase "this generation" is qualified by the phrase "not pass away until all these things have happened." The latter phrase, they say, governs the timing of the former.

This sidestepping / postponement device was popularized by C.I. Scofield in the 1900s. In the reference notes for Matthew 24:34 in his *Scofield Bible*, he writes:

> The word 'generation' (Gk. *genea*), though commonly used in Scripture of those living at one time, *could not mean* those alive at the time of Christ, as none of 'these things'—i.e. the world-wide preaching of the Kingdom, the tribulation, the return of the Lord in visible glory, and the regathering of the elect—occurred then. The expression 'this generation' here (1) *may mean* that the *future generation* which will endure the tribulation and see the signs, will also see the consummation, the return of the Lord.... (italics mine)

Hal Lindsey, one of the best-known end-time prophecy writers of this same tradition, claims that Jesus' "this generation" began in 1948 with the rebirth of the nation of Israel. In Lindsey's vernacular, our current generation is "the terminal generation." Several red flags wave against this popular but misleading interpretative device. Here are four:

First, it's circular reasoning and double talk to say that whatever generation sees these things happen will be Jesus' "this generation."

Remember, Jesus spoke these words directly to his disciples. Naturally, He used first-person speech and the commonly used, normally understood language of ordinary people of that time. "And the common people heard Him gladly" (Mark 12:37 *KJV*). So how would they have believed He was addressing distant matters and a future, far-removed generation of people? And they were expected to "understand" (see Matt. 24:15).

Second, no other or future generation is mentioned anywhere in this chapter's content or in any of the chapters leading up to or following Jesus' prophecy. That's why the demonstrative pronoun used is *this* and not *that*. And since "this" has no textual antecedent, the generation Jesus was speaking to is its first-person object. To divorce this time-indicator phrase from its most-natural first-person context is both a grammatical abuse and an interpretive violation. Most naturally, Jesus is speaking in the firstperson to his generation.

Third, a simple word study of the seventeen other New Testament uses reveals that the phrase "this generation" always means the same—the generation then living.[7] No textual justification, whatsoever, exists for abandoning its consistent use or its standard, natural, and plain grammatical meaning. Here are a few prominent examples of its consistent usage:

- The same "wicked and adulterous generation" who was asking for a sign (Matt. 12:39; 16:4).
- The same one He calls an "unbelieving and perverse generation" and asks "how long shall I stay with you? How long shall I put up with you?" (Matt. 17:17).
- The same one that would reject God's only Son: "But first he must suffer many things and be rejected by this generation" (Luke 17:25).
- The same one to whom John the Baptist came and about which Jesus lamented, "To what shall I compare this generation?" (Matt. 11:16-24).

---

[7] Matt. 11:16; 12:41, 42, 45; 23:36; Mark 8:12, 38; Luke 7:31; 11:29, 30, 31, 32, 50, 51; 17:25; Acts 2:40. Also see associated uses: Matt. 12:34, 39; 16:4; 17:17; Mark 9:19; 13:30; Luke 1:50; 9:41; 16:8; Acts 8:33; 13:36; Heb. 3:10.

- The same one who would crucify Him: "Therefore, this generation will be held responsible for the blood of all the prophets that has been shed since the beginning of the world . . . Yes, I tell you, this generation will be held responsible for it all" (Luke 11:50, 51b).
- The same one He told, "I tell you the truth, all this will come upon this generation" (Matt. 23:36).
- And the same one Peter warned his contemporaries about: "Save yourselves from this corrupt [perverse] generation" (Acts 2:40; from Deut. 32:5, 20).

So where do you think Jesus and Peter got this terminology of a "corrupt, crooked, wicked, and perverse generation? "Turn to Deuteronomy 32. As far back as the *Song of Moses* in the Old Testament, which prophesied what would happen to Israel in its "last days" (Deut. 31:29 *KJV*) and what its end would be like (Deut. 32:20, 29), God spoke through Moses about this perverse generation to come, thusly:

- "They have acted corruptly toward him [the Rock – Jesus]; to their shame they are no longer his children, but a perverse and crooked generation" (Deut. 32:5).
- "I will hide my face from them . . . and see what their end will be for they are a perverse generation, children who are unfaithful . . . . I will heap calamities upon them and spend my arrows against them" (Deut. 32:20, 23).

Once again, the biblical fact is, Jesus frequently spoke of his contemporaries as *this generation*. Stretching out its meaning to some future, unborn generation over two thousand years removed from Jesus' time or to mean a race or type of people would, at best, be an interpretation by exception.

So what generation were Jesus and Peter talking about? The answer is, the same one intended in all the other uses of the word "generation" and phrase "this generation." There are no exceptions. Even the 1st-century Pharisees knew that Jesus was speaking about them and prophesying an age-ending judgment that was to soon come upon them (Matt. 21:45; 23:29-38; Mark 12:12). They were the ones who would personally experience the horrors of these events. They were the ones upon whom would "come all the righteous blood shed upon the earth . . . ." (Matt. 23:35), not some unborn yet-future generation nor people of the Jewish race in a far distant time. Jesus further prophesied about them, "Look, your house is left to you desolate" (Matt. 23:38).

There is no need to explain anything away. History records that circa A.D. 70-73. exactly forty years and within one generation after Jesus gave his powerful prophecy, Jerusalem, the Temple, and the whole of biblical Judaism were utterly destroyed and left desolated. Only one generation in history was Jesus' "this generation." That generation was a contemporary group who had become the most evil, ungodly, rebellious generation of Jews ever. That generation of Jewish people filled up their cup of iniquity by rejecting and crucifying the promised Messiah and persecuting God's emerging new people (see Matt. 23:32; Isa. 65:6-12). No other generation comes close. No other generation makes sense of the time-limited, time-sensitive, and consistent meaning that Jesus gave it. Consequently, this fulfillment does not pertain to a yet-future generation of Jews—that's certain good news for them, wouldn't you agree?

Only one generation in history was Jesus' "this generation."

Fourth, Jesus' many uses of the personal pronoun "you" always related to the same time period and group of people to whom He was speaking. His plural "yous" consistently refer to the ones living, then and there, and the ones hearing his words. Jesus told then, "*you* will be handed over and put to death. . ." (Matt. 24:9), "*You* will see. . ." (Matt. 24:15), "*Your* flight. . ." (Matt. 24:20), "I have told *you* ahead of time" (Matt. 24:25), "*You* know. . ." (Matt. 24:32, 33), and "I tell *you* the truth . . ." (Matt. 24:34). He used "you" in a personal way. Jesus was not trying to misguide them or keep early Christians in line. They were the "you" He meant. To *them* He applied the fulfillment of his prophecy. Their generation would be the one that would not pass away until "all these things" took place. They would personally witness and experience all these end-time events.

Furthermore, while Jesus' prophetic words were spoken and written *to them* and not to us or some yet-future generation, they were certainly written *for us*. Big difference!

Sidestepping Device #3: Dividing Jesus' prophecy into two sections. This is the sidestepping device is employed mostly (but not exclusively) in amillennial and postmillennial circles. To their credit, most of these scholars agree that Jesus' "this generation" means exactly what it plainly says. But because of their false end-of-time paradigm and resulting dichotomized hermeneutic, they divide his prophetic words into two categories. One category is assigned to events fulfilled circa A.D. 70. The second is for events yet-to-be-fulfilled at the "end of time" (again, a phrase the Bible never uses). Hence the whole of Jesus' predicted events must span two different end-time periods separated by a 19-centuries-and-counting gap of time. But this division is totally unannounced in the text and without any clear biblical authorization. So how can they perform this separation?

It's simply necessitated by their dichotomized hermeneutic—i.e., A.D. 70 vs. end of time. So, some insert an arbitrary dividing line between verses 34 and 35, or 35 and 36, and for *some very strained reasons.*[8] Others go throughout Matthew 24 and 25 and cherry-pick verses to assign to one time category and the rest to the other. A third dividing methodology employs a qualifying of the nature of fulfillment—i.e., saying A.D. 70 was a "partial-in-some-sense-already-but-not-yet" fulfillment, with the "ultimate" fulfillment awaiting the future "end of time." As a result, each of these three methods ends with two ends, two *parousias,* and two returns of Jesus. R.C. Sproul, who subscribes to this device, says it this way: "A.D. 70 . . . was *a* parousia . . . it was not *the* parousia."[9]

Therefore, the word *parousia* in the first section (verse 27) is classified as being metaphorical and occurred in A.D. 70. But the one in the second section (verses 37 and 39) supposedly refers to the final return and final coming of the Lord, again at the end of time. The first one Jesus' disciples could know about. The latter—which wasn't to take place until more than 1,900 years after their deaths—they could not know about.

The biblical truth is, Jesus' Olivet Discourse (Matthew 24 and 25) cannot be divided. He did not jump two millennia in one breath or suddenly change subjects in midstream. Nor did He introduce a different

---

[8] For four reasons see: Noē, *The Perfect Ending for the World,* 159-160.
[9] Sproul, *The Last Days According to Jesus,* 158.

coming, or ambiguously discuss a local minor coming versus a universal major one for twenty-some centuries later. His terminology never changed. And there is no transition verse. Nowhere does the text support any kind of division. It's purely a devised and imaginary dividing line.[10]

Sad to say, this bifurcated solution is akin to that proposed when two women argued over the possession of a baby in 1 Kings 3:16-28. If you remember, king Solomon suggested a division—cutting the baby in half. This solution was unbearable and untenable in that situation. It is also unbearable and untenable here! But let's keep this story and biblical lesson firmly in mind the next time someone suggests dividing Matthew 24 (and 25) into two parts. Likewise, let's honor the scriptural admonition of "rightly dividing the word of truth" (2 Tim. 2:15) with our emphasis on "rightly" and not on arbitrarily "dividing."

In my opinion, there should be no escaping the obvious. The integrity and prophetic unity of Jesus' Olivet Discourse must stand undivided.

Sidestepping Device #4: Jesus was mistaken or never said these words. This device is used by the liberals in the Church and also by atheists, skeptics, and critics of Christianity. To their credit, they do recognize and honor the literal time limitation of Jesus' "this generation" and his pronounced emphasis on the fulfillment of all end-time events within the lifetime of his hearers. Rightly, they also conclude that if "all these things" did not take place *as* and *when* Jesus said, then something is dreadfully amiss.

Remember, C.S. Lewis in 1960 termed Matt. 24:34, "the most embarrassing verse in the Bible" and an "exhibition of error."[11] Yes, this "nonoccurrence" factor is a legitimate criticism and an inescapable dilemma for Christians. Jesus' time statement in his Olivet Discourse, and others like it, was the crack that let the liberals in the door in the 19th century. Once in, they systematically began questioning and dismantling all of Scripture. Their assumption was, and still is, that if the Bible is wrong here, it's surely wrong elsewhere. They even call into question the divinity of Jesus. Even more amazing, is that conservative evangelicals

---

[10] For a graphic illustrating why "The Olivet Discourse Cannot Be Divided," see Noē, *The Perfect Ending for the World,* Appendix B, p, 336.

[11] Lewis, essay, "The World's Last Night," 385. For full quote see pp-124-125.

have had no effective response except to claim that someday Jesus will come back and finish the job. But this only proves the liberals' point.

Consequently and as we saw in Chapter 1, in America over the past 50 to 100 years we have lost seminary after seminary, denomination after denomination, church after church, and believer after believer to the liberal/skeptic attack on the Bible and deity of Christ. They have departed from the conservative faith. Critics have hit Christianity at its weakest point—the embarrassing statements of Jesus to return within the lifetime of his contemporaries and the "failed" Holy-Spirit-guided expectations of the New Testament writers and the early Church that He would do just that (John 16:13).

Rightly, they also conclude that if "all these things" did not take place *as* and *when* Jesus said, then something is dreadfully amiss.

It is called the "battle for the Bible." And the focal point of this battle has been and continues to be the eschatological statements of Jesus and the imminency expectations of the New Testament writers. This is why sidestepping, cover-up, or ignoring devices won't and don't work. Only one credible and effective solution exist for the dilemma of nonoccurrence. It's *occurrence* in the form of the precise, exact, literal, chronological, and sequential fulfillment of God's plan of redemption. In other words, it's contained within the divine perfection that we have been presenting herein.

In sum, the four sidestepping devices are nothing more than exegetical gymnastics designed to evade, explain away, cover up, or undermine the relevance and force of Jesus' prophetic words. They are desperate ploys born of theological necessity and compelled by particular deferment traditions. At best, they are serious errors. At worst, they constitute "handling the word of God deceitfully" (2 Cor. 4:2 *KJV*). These devices have plagued the field of end-time Bible prophecy for far too long. They prevent an honest reader from grasping the true meaning and relevance of Jesus' powerful prophetic words. Instead, we must allow the Bible to speak plainly for itself. Amen?

Why Can't We Take Jesus at His Word?

Any time someone has to create new definitions of familiar words, find exceptions to normal meanings, arbitrarily divide passages, or discount the reliability of Scripture and the deity of Christ, as we've just seen via the above four sidestepping devices, something is very wrong. If allowed to stand, these traditions of men cast aspersions on Jesus and his other sayings, destroy the authenticity, authority, and inerrancy of Scripture, and make the Word of God of little or no effect (Matt. 15:6; Mark 7:13).

So why can't we take Jesus at this word, literally, naturally, and at face value as his first hearers did—the New Testament writers and the early Church? They never imagined He might be talking about events 2,000 years away.

Like the old hymn says . . .

> Tis so sweet to trust in Jesus,
> Just to take Him at His word,
> Just to rest upon His promise,
> Just to know, "Thus saith the Lord."

Why don't we do this here? I can think of two overriding reasons:

- Our allegiance or bondage to a particular postponement tradition.
- Many cannot fathom how "all these things" Jesus' talked about could possibly have occurred during the lifetime of his contemporaries or been fulfilled in any subsequent generation.

It is in response to this second reason we next turn. For our purposes, I suggest you open your Bible and read from Matthew 23:33 through 24:36. As you read, please ask yourself and keep in mind these three questions:

1) If you had been hearing Jesus' teachings, first-hand, how would you have understood his words?

2) Who would you have thought He was talking about that would experience "all these things"?
3) Why should we believe any differently today?

I further suggest that if we do take Jesus at his literal word (as his listeners did) and hold to a high, authoritative, and perhaps inerrant view of Scripture, then "all these things" must have occurred within the lifetime of his disciples exactly *as* and *when* Jesus said. Nothing short of the credibility and deity of Jesus Christ is at stake. Surely, Jesus didn't make a mistake or intend to mislead his disciples. The only other alternative is that He spoke truly just as He said He did.

13 Crucial and Contested Elements

During the Madison Park Church of God seminar series, I identified thirteen crucial and contested elements in Matthew 24:1-36 for our re-exposition. Once again, these have perplexed and confused the Church for over nineteen centuries and counting. But let's see if we can unpack and clear up some of this confusion. Below we shall address these crucial elements of Jesus' prophecy in the order in which they appear. Unfortunately, due to space limitations, we shall only be highlighting a few illuminating particulars for each element. For those of you desiring a fuller treatment, see my book, *The Perfect Ending for the World*.

1) The end of the age (v. 3). What "age" was Jesus talking about that was to end? Foundational to both Judaic and Christian thought in that 1st century was the division of time between two consecutive periods—"this present age" and "the age to come." Back then, they were living in "this present age," the age of Moses, the Old Covenant age of the Temple system. "The age to come" was being anticipated. It was to be a golden age of God in which all of God's promises to Israel would be fully realized and God's power would operate in a new and better way.

This dual concept of time represented the Jewish expectation for God's plan of redemptive history here on earth. They did not view history as a series of unending ages but stressed these two distinct and contrasting periods. No parenthetical age, third age, or interruption between the two ages was ever envisioned. The line of demarcation, or transition between the two ages would be accomplished by a visitation of God. Specifically, "the age to come" was to be ushered in by the coming of the Messiah (Savior) into human history, along with a terrible coming of "the day of the Lord" and the establishment of the eternal kingdom on earth.

Although these two-age expressions are not found in the Old Testament, they are found in the New (Matt. 12:32; Luke 20:35). Jesus equated "The age to come" with eternal life (Mark 10:30; Luke. 18:30). Paul and the Hebrews' writer also spoke of this age division (see Gal. 1:4; Eph. 1:21; Heb. 6:5). These expressions were well known to 1st-century hearers.

The Jewish religious society of that day had been well-schooled and clearly understood that the Messiah, at his coming, would end "this present age" and usher in "the age to come" (the Messianic age). Most rabbis believed that this period of transition between the two ages would last about forty years, like the wilderness wandering, the reigns of David and Solomon, and the three 40-year periods of Moses' life. They further believed it would take place within the confines of history.[12] But Jesus didn't usher in this new age during his earthly ministry, or so most traditions have assumed. Therefore, reasoned the Jews—from that day to the present—Jesus could not be the promised Messiah.

Nevertheless, we know today that the Old Covenant system and its age had been rendered "obsolete" and would soon pass away (Heb. 8:13) at Habakkuk's and Daniel's "appointed time of the end." That time arrived, perfectly and precisely, and right on time! Moreover, the New Covenant age has no end (see Isa. 9:6-7; Dan. 2:44; 7:13-14; Luke 1:32-33; Eph. 3:21; Heb. 12:28; Rev. 11:15).

2) Gospel of the kingdom preached in the whole world . . . to all nations (v. 14). This preaching of the gospel of the kingdom "in the whole world" was a required prerequisite that Jesus stated must take place before the end could come. Many futuristic interpreters, however, cannot fathom how this could have been fulfilled before or in A.D. 70 when the gospel had not yet been preached in the Western Hemisphere, the great missionary movement of the 18th and 19th centuries hadn't

---

[12] See Abraham Cohen, *Everyman's Talmud* (New York, NY.: Schochen Books, 1949), 356.

taken place, worldwide communications hadn't been developed, and many nations and people groups in remote tribes had yet to hear the gospel. These facts alone, critics contend, should stop dead in its tracks any idea that Jesus came and the end was reached circa A.D. 70.

But given our guideline #1—*Sola Scriptura*—and as we've seen before, the Bible must be understood on its own terms and in the context of its original hearers. Only then can we properly understand what any portion really means for us today. So let's do that here, as well.

The Apostle Paul, thirty-one years after Jesus' earthly ministry, confirmed that . . .

- "All over the world this gospel is producing fruit and growing" (Col. 1:6).
- And "the gospel that you heard . . . has been proclaimed to every creature under heaven" (Col. 1:23).
- And "your faith is being reported all over the world" (Rom. 1:8).

This was not Paul's opinion. It is inspired Scripture, using the same or similar words that Jesus used. Thus, he confirmed that Jesus' required prerequisite was accomplished in their day. For more confirmations, read: Rom. 10:18; 16:26; Acts 1:8; 2:5; 24:5; Jude 3; also compare with Dan. 2:39; 4:1, 22; 5:19; 7:23; Luke 2:1, 30-32; 24:47; Rev. 3:10.

Therefore, according to the Bible itself and prior to A.D. 70, the gospel was preached to all nations and to the world. The Greek word translated "world" in Matthew 24:14 is *oikoumene*, meaning land—i.e., the [terrene part of the] globe, specifically the Roman Empire. In this commonly used and restricted sense, the then-known Roman world, or the civilized world of that time, was also the "world" of the Jews into which they had been scattered. If the entire global earth was meant, the Greek word *kosmos* would have been used, as it is in Matthew 24:21. But it wasn't. Hence Jesus' end-coming prerequisite condition had been scripturally met and satisfied.

Also notable, early Church father Eusebius (A.D. 260 – 341) confirmed that both the world-wide preaching of the gospel and this end of biblical Judaism were fulfilled:

Moses had foretold this very thing and in due course Christ sojourned in this life, and the teaching of the new covenant was borne to all nations, and at once the Romans besieged Jerusalem and destroyed it and the Temple there. At once the whole of the Mosaic law was abolished, with all that remained of the Old Covenant . . . .[13]

3) Two prime signs to read and flee (v. 15-20; Luke 21:20-22).[14] Jesus spoke of a whole catalogue of signs (events) which would herald the coming of the end (Matt. 24:5-12, 21-25). Many modern-day interpreters call these "signs of the times" and argue that we are just now seeing them occur, or are seeing them occur with greater intensity and frequency. These signs include: social decay, wars, rumors of wars, famines, diseases, natural catastrophes, earthquakes, false prophets, and apostasy. While it's true that these signs are prevalent in our day, they were also prevalent in A.D. 60 – 69.

In fact, they are continually characteristic of depraved humanity, human history, and/or the earth's physical dynamics. In and of themselves, Jesus said that they do *not* indicate the end. They were only "the beginning of sorrows" or "birth pains" (Matt. 24:8 *KJV – NIV*). So we must not be misled by the presence of these same signs today. Rather, He told his disciples that they should watch for two certain, recognizable, indisputable, and prime signs of the end:

Prime sign #1: The abomination that causes desolation ... standing...."

"So when you see standing in the holy place 'the abomination that causes desolation' spoken of through the prophet Daniel—let the reader understand—then let those who are in Judea flee to the mountains" (Matt. 24:15-16; Mark 13:14).

The Jews of Jesus' time were the "you" group He was warning. They were expected to "understand" without his having to explain to them what He was talking about. Scholars affirm that they understood He was

---

[13] Eusebius, W.J. Ferrar, ed. *The Proof of the Gospel*, book 1, chapter 6, (Grand Rapids, MI.: Baker Books, 1981), 34-35.

[14] This section is also a condensed presented. For a more expansive treatment see: Noē, *The Perfect Ending for the World*, 174-182.

talking about them (Matt. 21:45b). They were the ones for which all Jesus' prophecies applied, and no New Testament writer ever corrected their understanding of this contemporary relevance. As we've seen, they did just the opposite. They intensified their nearness language as Jesus' 40-year, "this-generation" time period neared its end. So, how could they have so understood?

Quite simply, most of them were well-schooled in Jewish history. They knew that the last abomination of desolation that "stood" or had occurred in the holy place was the Temple desecration and temporary cessation of religious rites caused by Antiochus Epiphanes in 167 – 164 B.C. Since that time—during the intertestament period—the Jews were taught that Daniel's prophecy concerning the abomination of desolation had been fulfilled by Antiochus Epiphanes. Jesus, to the contrary, prophesied that all had not yet been fulfilled. Rather, this 2nd-century B.C. abomination, as prophesied in Daniel 8 and 11, was a type and was going to happen again, as prophesied in Daniel 9 and 12. This next time, as before, the very "standing" and presence of pagans in the holy place would be the abominating offense. But unlike before, this next time would bring more than a temporary three-year period of desolation. It would bring the permanent and everlasting desolation (Matt. 23:38). Here's a brief synopsis of abominations that transpired in the Temple.

Early in the decade of A.D. 60 – 69, an unqualified Jew was appointed to the position of high priest. Prior to that time, nothing secular or unholy was allowed in the Temple. This high priest and his staff of other priests failed to properly perform the daily sacrifices and many other required Temple duties. Instead, they made a mockery of the holy ordinances. In A.D. 66, priests and Zealots fought each other in the Temple courts. Josephus reports that the floors swam with the blood of more than eight thousand who stabbed each other. Many more atrocities (abominations) between the Zealots and other Jewish factions occurred in the holy place between A.D. 66–70. The final abomination that caused the final desolation was similar to that of Antiochus Epiphanes. What happened before, happened again when another foreign Gentile army, the Roman army, stood in the Temple, and raised and worshipped its standards, as was their custom. But then the Romans destroyed the Temple and the Temple complex, and tore it down stone-by-stone in fulfillment of Jesus prophecy (Matt. 24:2-3, 34).

Prime sign #2: Jerusalem surrounded by armies.
Luke's parallel account of Jesus' prophecy gave them a second sign.

"When you see Jerusalem surrounded by armies, you will know that its desolation is near. Then let those who are in Judea flee to the mountains, let those in the city get out, and let those in the country not enter the city. For this is the time of punishment in fulfillment of all that has been written" (Luke 21:20-22).

Shortly after the twice-daily sacrifice for Caesar and the Roman people was ceased by Jewish rebels in July of 66 A.D., the die was cast. Then, *four times*, between 66-70 A.D. Jerusalem was surrounded by armies[15] just as Jesus had warned. By the fourth and final time—shortly before Passover in A.D. 70—it was too late to get out. Thus, for Jesus' 1st-century hearers, his warning was not just a matter for a Bible study discussions or fodder for theological debates. It was a matter of life and death.

Eusebius recorded that in obedience to the Lord's instructions 1st-century Christians fled from Jerusalem to Pella in Transjordan around A.D. 68 after the first siege and before the second one,[16] and no Christians were trapped inside Jerusalem and destroyed in the siege that concluded in A.D.70.[17] Others fled to Alexandria in Egypt, and still others to Asia Minor.

Two groups, however, failed to read the signs and did not follow Jesus' instructions. They experienced the horrors of the fall of Jerusalem. They were: 1) The unbelieving Jews. 2) Former followers of Christ who were zealous for the Jewish Law and fearful of being put out of the synagogue. Both groups chose to remain inside Jerusalem and failed or refused to read the signs. Members of both groups suffered the age-ending judgment.

---

[15] The prophecy does say "armies," not army. Why the plural use? Historical accounts reveal that Rome commonly conscripted soldiers from other nations into their fighting ranks. Titus's army below only contained 25,000 Roman soldiers out of approximately 54,000 in the combined armies that came against Jerusalem in A.D. 70.
[16] Eusebius, *Ecclesiastical History*, Book III, V. 86, 138.
[17] Eusebius, *Ecclesiastical History*, Book 3, Ch. 5, 138.

There were also other spectacular warnings and signs, as Jesus had prophesied: "There will be . . . fearful sights and great signs from heaven" (Luke 21:11). Hence, Josephus writes of several strange, if not bizarre, oracles that appeared in the sky and in the city before the first siege in A.D. 66 and foretelling its impending devastation: a star in the shape of a sword that stood over the city; a comet that continued for a year; a brilliant light around the altar at night; a cow that gave birth to a lamb; the sighting of chariots and armed soldiers in the sky above the hills (angelic armies); and the hearing of voices in the inner court of the Temple saying, "We are departing hence."[18] These signs were also reported by the Roman historian Tacitus.[19]

According to Josephus, 1.1 million Jews were killed in the fall and destruction of Jerusalem.[20] Countless more lost their lives in countless skirmishes against the Jews in foreign cities, in the Galilean campaign, or those who died in the Diaspora of disease, famine, and persecution. Ninety-seven thousand more Jews went into foreign captivity. Many of these died in Roman coliseums.

Thus, members of two groups who had held onto false hopes, had rejected Jesus as the Messiah, disregarded his prophetic words, and stayed in the city personally received the judgment of "the time of the end."

Whether you choose to believe this fulfillment or not, one thing is for sure. This explanation is an "historically defensible" explanation. And as Klein, Bloomberg, and Hubbard say in their book, *Introduction to Biblical Interpretation:* "The historically defensible interpretation has greatest authority."[21] Might you now agree?

Whether you agree yet or not, doesn't this explanation stand in stark contrast to the popular and modern-day view that keeps telling us that these signs and warnings apply to a yet-future, time-ending, earth-destroying, great tribulation period? If, however, this latter understanding is correct, then how would Jesus' instruction to "flee to the mountains" be meaningful? Wouldn't it be meaningless and a mishandling of Jesus'

---

[18] *Wars* 6, 289-300.
[19] *The Histories* 1:5-7, 1.2-3.
[20] *Wars* 6, 420.
[21] Klein, Blomberg, and Hubbard, Jr., *Introduction to Biblical Interpretation*, 149.

teachings? Read the signs and flee was what his Jewish and Gentile disciples did in that 1st-century time period. These instructions were given to them and not to us. Dear reader, we are talking audience relevancy here. History records that they properly read the two prime signs and were spared from the horrors of the fall of Jerusalem. Nowadays there is no longer a need to flee to the mountains if Jerusalem becomes surrounded by armies, which, by the way, it is today.

Whether you choose to believe this fulfillment or not, this one thing is for sure. This explanation is an "historically defensible" explanation.

There is more . . .

4) Those days cut short for the elect's sake (v. 21-22). The great tribulation being cut short was for the sake of the elect—i.e., the Church—and not for the unbelieving Jews. God's wrath was upon them. The historical fact is, the Church was never in more danger or more vulnerable to going out of existence than during the time of the Roman-Jewish War of A.D. 66-70. After A.D. 70, the Church never again was so threatened. And never again was it ever considered to be a sect of Judaism. After this war, Christianity was liberated from Judaism and freed up to become its own worldwide movement. It's exactly as Jesus said, "For then there will be great tribulation unequaled from the beginning of the world until now – never to be equaled again."

5) Deception of the elect (v. 23-26). Is it really possible that the elect, or some of them, are deceived? These four verses lay out an urgent and relevant warning. But is it still relevant today?

Most Christians maintain that the coming of Jesus encompassed in Matthew 24 is the so-called "second coming." And it will be very visible, audible, and a worldwide, public event, and appearance of the Person of deity—nothing secretive about it. But as we shall shortly see, this type of coming—"coming on the clouds" in a day of the Lord in judgment—that Jesus was talking about here was never to be a visible appearance of deity. Therefore, the insistence on a visible criterion for this type of coming was and still is part of this deception of the elect. The good news is, those so deceived are still the "elect." But the bad news is, they are deceived, at least on this matter, and, therefore, have been and are still falsely prophesying. How so?

First, by their paralleled misunderstanding of the invisible nature of this type of coming. Today as was true back then, many modern-day saints—the elect—are waiting for a physically visible coming and sighting of Jesus in Person, in the sky in the Israeli desert, in an inner room, inside a rebuilt temple in Jerusalem, or in some other geographic location to which they and everyone living on planet Earth at that time can definitely point to and in like manner exclaim, "There He is!"

Second, by their professing and proclaiming a half-truth faith in a world filled with competing religions and secular ideologies. The truthful half is, the promised Messiah (Jesus) came, lived, died, rose from the dead, and ascended to heaven exactly *as* and *when* prophesied. The untruthful half is, Jesus has not come again in this type of coming to finish the work He started, *as* and *when* He said He would and *as* and *when* He was expected to by his Holy-Spirit-guided, first followers, every New Testament writer, and the early Church (see John 16:13).

Once again, let's recall that other types of comings are visible appearances of Jesus (John 14:18-19)—but not this one.

"Wait a minute!" someone protests. "What about the next verse? Doesn't Jesus' comparison of his coming to lightning demand a visible coming and appearing that will be witnessed by all people everywhere—i.e., "glorious, visible, evident to all?"

As we shall next see, not necessarily.

6) As lightning flashing from East to West (v. 27). From this one verse, many interpreters conclude that this type of coming necessitates a visible and worldwide appearance of Jesus. Why so? It's because you can see lightning, right? Others view this lightning comparison as symbolizing the quickness or suddenness of this coming. Still others focus on the secondary meaning of the Greek word *astrape* as also meaning a "bright shining" and not a quick flash or surge. They argue that it is used this way in Luke 9:29 in a description of Jesus' transfiguration—"and his clothes became as bright as a flash of lightning" (*NIV*); "his raiment was white and glistening" (*KJV*). Furthermore, Jesus described Satan's fall from heaven as being "like lightning" (Luke 10:18).

Hence, this meaning could symbolize sunlight coming out of the east bringing in a new day and setting in the west. Still others see in this symbolism the very march of the Roman army that entered Judah from the east, proceeded westward on their conquest, and approached Jerusalem from the east. Some counsel that lightning in the Old Testament "often signifies the presence of the Lord (Exod. 19:16; 20:18), the manifestation of His power (Ezek. 1:13), and the display of His awesome judgment against His enemies (Deut. 33:2; 2 Sam. 22:15; Psa. 18:14; 144:6)."[22] Please note that in none of these instances was the Person of deity visible to human eyes. Hence, in prophesying of a future coming day of the Lord in judgment, the prophet Zechariah proclaims, "Then the Lord will appear over them; his arrow will flash like lightning" (Zech. 9:14a).

Another possible and interesting aspect of this symbolic lightning language to consider is the fact that physical lightning that "comes from the east and flashes to the west" represents a better argument for invisibility than for visibility. Here are two reasons why:

1) Lightning is associated with a local weather system and is only seen in a specific locale and not everywhere all over the world at once.

2) Lightning that flashes from "east to west" is the intra-cloud variety (within the cloud) or inter-cloud (between two clouds).[23] This is different than cloud-to-ground lightning, which is the kind we "see most often."[24] But it accounts for "only about one-sixth or one-third of all discharges."[25] "Sometimes a very active thundercloud produces hundreds of cloud flashes without a single discharge to the ground."[26] Therefore, "intra-cloud lightning is the most common type. .

---

[22] DeMar, *End Times Fiction*, 94.
[23] Admittedly, the information that follows was not known by Jesus' audience, but could have been known by Him.
[24] Zach's Lightning Page, www.macnexus.org/scds/zachsci/Lightning.html, 5/22/02.
[25] McGraw-Hill Encyclopedia of Science & Technology, vol. 10, 8th ed. (New York, NY., 1997), 73.
[26] D.J. Malan, *Physics of Lightning* (London: The English Universities Press, 1963), 6.

. . Usually the process takes place within the cloud and looks from the outside like a diffused brightening."[27] Consequently, "most (80-90%) is never seen directly"[28] on earth because "it is obscured by the cloud"[29] and the streak or "discharge path is not usually seen"[30] being veiled and muted by clouds.

Perhaps, therefore, by referring to this type of lightning Jesus meant to symbolize the power and suddenness of his coming upon a particular people in a specific locale—Jerusalem; or the darkness of thunderclouds passing in judgment over Israel; or that his presence would only be indirectly "seen" in the attending circumstances and results. In other words, "the sign" of the judgment that fell (see again Matt. 24:3, 30).

Interestingly, two other scriptural passages support the invisibility of this type of coming:

1) Paul's statement in 1 Thessalonians 5:2 that "the day of the Lord will come like a thief in the night" (also see: 1 Thess. 5:4; 2 Pet. 3:10; Rev. 3:3; 16:15). Traditionally, this metaphor is understood to mean suddenly, with surprise, without advance notice, unexpectedly, and in secrecy. Obviously, all of these characterizations apply. But the metaphor can be pursued further—i.e., thieves usually come and do their deeds at night so they will not be seen.

2) Paul's interaction with those who feared that the day of the Lord "has already come" (2 Thess. 2:2), also suggests that an invisible nature is the correct understanding. Notice in this passage that he did not correct their understanding of the nature of this coming. He only corrected the time factor. But if the day of the Lord involves a physically visible Christ

---

[27] Lightning Primer from the GHCC, http://thunder.msfc.nasa.gov/primer/primer2.html., 5/21/02.
[28] Bard Zajac, Colorado State University CIRA, email 5/22/02.
[29] Martin A. Uman, *Understanding Lightning* (Carnegie, PA.: Bek Technical Publications, 1971), 70.
[30] Hans Volland, ed., *Handbook of Atmospheric Electrondynamics* (Boca Raton, FL.: CRC Press, 1995), 127.

and/or a termination or renovation of the physical heavens and earth, how could the Thessalonians have possibly thought it had already come? Likewise, in correcting their false notion, Paul did not appeal to visibility as an argument. If a visible manifestation of deity is the correct nature for this type of coming, he could have closed the case, then and there.[31] But he didn't so appeal.

7) Where the carcass and vultures (eagles) gather (v. 28). This and parallel verses in Luke 17:28 and Revelation 19:21 have also puzzled commentators for centuries. But I believe its meaning can now be ascertained when it's kept within its divinely determined time frame—i.e., in context and consistency with Daniel's "time of the end" and Jesus' "this generation" prophecies.

Perhaps therefore, this verse literally refers to physical vultures that gathered to feast on the mounds of dead bodies piled high during the Jewish-Roman War. Or figuratively to the Roman army who were the vultures as they circled outside the walls of Jerusalem and awaiting their dying prey and as the Jews killed and wore each other out on the inside. Or it could be a reference to the eagles (*KJV* – same Greek word) on the top of the Roman standards, which were literally planted in the soil of a destroyed Jerusalem and inside the Temple itself (which was now a carcass or corpse of itself) and were objects of Roman worship. All three possibilities are quite descriptive of this time and event!

History records that for over fifty years the entire country was left desolate (Matt. 23:38) and devoid of most of its inhabitants. The people had been killed, died, or were sold into slavery. Everything was utterly destroyed—"to the uttermost" (1 Thess. 2:16 *KJV*). Then, sixty-five years after the fall of Jerusalem, the Roman army returned and wiped out the entire state of Judea.

Arguably, no country or people ever suffered the magnitude of God's wrath and judgment than befell Old Covenant Israel. Not only did Israel

---

[31] Detracting from this invisible nature of Christ's coming is the Jehovah's Witnesses claim that Christ returned in 1914 in an invisible way (*Let God Be True* (Brooklyn: Watchtower Bible and Tract Society, 1946; rev. in 1952), 198-99; *Make Sure of All Things* (Brooklyn: Watchtower Bible and Tract Society, 1953; rev. in 1957), 321.

cease being the nation of the living God, it ceased being a nation for nineteen centuries until its rebirth in 1948. However, the world of biblical Judaism perished forever.

It all happened precisely forty years from the time Jesus told his disciples that "not one stone shall be left on another" (Matt. 24:2). This fulfillment in divine perfection is more than coincidence, don't you think?

8) The use of apocalyptic language (v. 29). Falling stars, bloody moons, darkened sun, shaking earth, signs in the sky . . . To our modern minds it sounds like the end of the physical world, which obviously hasn't happened. But was this really what Jesus was teaching here?

Employed throughout the Bible and scattered throughout biblical history, and mostly overlooked or ignored by the popular prophecy writers of today, are numerous uses and fulfillments of this same apocalyptic language. Here, Jesus' is quoting two of those places from the prophet Isaiah (Isa. 13:10; 34:4). However, in all its numerous uses and fulfillments never once was the physical creation ever altered or affected one *iota*.

Arguably, no country or people ever suffered the magnitude of God's wrath and judgment than befell Old Covenant Israel.

Instead, this vivid cosmic-collapsing, earth-shaking imagery type of language has always been associated with another major Old Testament theme—the foretelling of a coming of "the day of the Lord" in divine judgment and destruction of wicked nations, peoples, and cities. Knowing the nature of these previous uses and fulfillments will enable us to make proper sense of Jesus' employment of this biblical and apocalyptic language here. To be ignorant of or to ignore this long biblical precedent of usages and fulfillments simply guarantees you will misunderstand Jesus' intent and meaning of this language in Matthew 24 and elsewhere.

As we shall see, this figurative and apocalyptic language is the language of the prophets. And Jesus gave no indication He was using this language any differently.[32] Therefore, let us look at some of the Bible's apocalyptic prophecies and descriptions of coming cosmic disasters and see how they were actually fulfilled. Again, without this historical perspective we are guaranteed to misinterpret their meaning and commit the error of eisegesis—reading one's own preconceived ideas into the text. Not wise, if one truly desires to know what the text is talking about.

Back then 1st-century Jews were steeped in this scriptural and historical knowledge. Consequently, they expected apocalyptic fulfillments to be quite different from what most of us today have been led to believe. Here are some samples from the Old Testament:

Isaiah 13:10 (Jesus quoted)**,** 13. "The stars of heaven and their constellations will not show their light. The rising sun will be darkened and the moon will not give its light . . . Therefore I will make the heavens tremble; and the earth will shake from its place at the wrath of the Lord Almighty, in the day of his burning anger."

Fulfillment. The prophet was *not* speaking of the end of the world, the final judgment, or a solar or lunar eclipse. He was giving a figurative prediction of the literal destruction of Babylon by the Medes in 539 B.C. (Isa. 13:1). The use of cosmic language means the Presence of God was involved and revealed in this judgment upon these people.

Isaiah 34:4 (Jesus quoted). "All the stars of heaven will be dissolved and the sky rolled up like a scroll; all the starry host will fall like withered leaves from the vine, like shriveled figs from the fig tree."

Fulfillment. This was *not* the end of the world, or the end of the cosmos, but a figurative description of the coming divine destruction of Edom in the late 6th century B.C. (Isa. 34:5).

---

[32] This misconception is nurtured somewhat by the mistranslation of the Matthew 13: 39, 49; 24:3 phrase "the end of the world" in the King James Version of the Bible. The word "world" in the Greek is *aion* and is better translated as "age." Most later translations agree.

Ezekiel 32:7, 8a. ". . . I will cover the heavens and darken their stars; I will cover the sun with a cloud, and the moon will not give its light. All the shining lights in the heavens I will darken over you."
Fulfillment. This prophecy was God's warning to the Pharaoh of Egypt of his impending fall in the mid-6th century B.C. (Ezek. 32:2).

Nahum 1:5. "The mountains quake before him and the hills melt away. The earth trembles at his presence, the world, and all who live in it."
Fulfillment. The subject is God's coming in judgment on the city of Nineveh, and not the physical world, in 612 B.C. (Nahum 1:1).

Isaiah 40:4. "Every valley shall be raised up, every mountain and hill made low; the rough ground shall become level, the rugged places a plain."
Fulfillment. This is not a reference to a giant excavation job, but a description of the 1st-century ministry of John the Baptist (Matt. 3:1-3; Isa. 40:3).

Joel 2:30, 31. "I will show wonders in the heavens and on the earth, blood and fire and billows of smoke. The sun will be turned to darkness and the moon to blood before the coming of the great and dreadful day of the Lord."
Fulfillment. Joel was not describing the end of the world. He was giving a figurative description of the actual events accompanying the coming of the Holy Spirit on the day of Pentecost. Peter said it was fulfilled in their day (Acts 2:16-21). This "day of the Lord" (actually, "the day of Christ") followed less than forty years later.

This Old Testament pattern of figurative language usage and numerous fulfillments by literal, real, momentous, and divine judgments sets the precedent. If the words of these passages were to be taken literally, it would mean that massive changes or destructions of the cosmos and earth occurred numerous times. But this language transcends its literalism and has to be understood figuratively.

So with this same knowledge and perspective in mind, as 1st-century Jews had, let's get back to Jesus' use of this language and his prophesying of another, soon-coming judgment event.

Matthew 24:29. ". . . the sun will be darkened, the moon will not give is light; the stars will fall from the sky, and the heavenly bodies will be shaken."
Fulfillment. Jesus is speaking in a similar fashion and using the same apocalyptic terms drawn from the language of the prophets cited above. Again, this was a language and style very familiar to 1st-century Jews. And Jesus added no disclaimers that He was using it any differently. He was figuratively announcing and describing the coming judgment and destruction of Jerusalem and the Temple and the passing away of the Judaic system and age circa A.D. 70. The imagery and parallel with the Old Testament prophets are far too striking and strong to avoid or ignore. And Peter did the same . . .

2 Peter 3:10, 11a. "But the day of the Lord will come like a thief. The heavens will disappear with a roar; the elements will be destroyed by fire, and the earth and everything in it will be laid bare. Since everything will be destroyed in this way, what kind of people ought you to be?"
Fulfillment. Again, Peter is employing the same common apocalyptic terminology of his day (2 Pet. 3:2). His words are no more to be taken literally/physically than are any of the others above. The figurative fulfillment about which he was warning came upon his contemporaries in a way (nature) totally consistent with all the other apocalyptic fulfillments cited above.

Amazingly, however, in our day and time, a changed meaning has supposedly occurred but without any scriptural justification. Nowadays we are being told that Jesus' descriptive phraseology of the sun and moon darkening, of stars falling from the sky, and heavenly bodies shaken (Matt. 24:29) is declared to mean something entirely different from its time-honored figurative usages and many historical fulfillments.

The popular stream of futuristic end-saying and postponement interpreters has arbitrarily, it seems, assumed that the Bible's apocalyptic language must now be understood literally and physically, and for some strange reason known only to them. Now it's declared to mean something it has never meant before. And since no one has witnessed a literal, cataclysmic, catastrophic, earth-ending event of this nature, its time of fulfillment must lie in the future (a false paradigm and nature-determines-time hermeneutic).

Admittedly, the shock value of earthquakes, exploding stars, cosmic eclipses, and nuclear holocausts is awesome and marketable. Thus, a literal/physical rendering of the Bible's apocalyptic texts serves the popularizing purposes of these endsayers and has become fixed in the minds of millions of Americans and countless others. The obvious problem with this line of thought and methodology of interpretation is, no biblical grounds exist for this assumption. Moreover, it ignores the biblical precedent and pattern of uses and fulfillments. This methodology is not a responsible or credible way to approach the Scriptures. When we fail to give proper attention to the historical fulfillments, we do a grave injustice to understanding the Bible's use of apocalyptic language. On the other hand, as we allow the Bible to shed light on itself, a lot of things become clear.

> **Amazingly, however, in our day and time, a changed meaning has supposedly occurred but without any scriptural justification.**

So what should we learn from the above precedent and perspective? Of course, many more examples could be cited, but that would only belabor the point. Here's the point, plainly and simply. If this apocalyptic language that Jesus directly quoted almost verbatim was appropriate to describe the destructions of Babylon and Edom, etc., why not for the destruction of Jerusalem as well?

I maintain the Bible's use of this collapsing-universe, cosmic-cataclysm, apocalyptic language was consistently employed in the New Testament. No disclaimers, qualifications, or changes are ever recorded or hinted at by Jesus or any New Testament writer. To do so without legitimate textual justification is, at best, a violation of proper and honest interpretation. Where am I wrong on this?

The physical means employed are always those of invading foreign armies or natural disasters. These many biblical judgments were also events of international and/or eschatological importance. In every instance, the "worlds" (social, political, religious) of those receiving this judgment of God were ended or dramatically changed. So complete and comprehensive was each judgment event that it was appropriately spoken of in hyperbolic, world-ending terms. Speaking appropriately does not require that one speak literally. Please note again that in none of these historical fulfillments did the physical nature of literal heavenly bodies or the earth change one *iota*. These scriptural precedents demand that we understand Jesus' usage of this same language in exactly the same way as it was used and fulfilled many times before in Old Testament history.

Critical Objection: What about the possibility that a literal/physical, time-ending, universe-destroying, cosmic-crashing event can be an additional fulfillment? Can't apocalyptic language using symbolism and poetic imagery be taken both figuratively and literally?

My Response: Some theologians argue that it can and term this double fulfillment. But seriously, is this possibility possible here? Certainly, a future cosmic and earthly destruction could be within the sovereignty and capability of a God who many believe spoke the world into existence in the first place (see Gen. 1). But to break the pattern of biblical precedent by suddenly literalizing apocalyptic terms and phrases and reapplying them to the destruction of the physical universe, *and without an expressed biblical warrant to do so*, in my opinion, is to misunderstand the Bible on the Bible's own terms. For all the reasons I've stated above, I suggest this change of meaning in our day is totally arbitrary and reprehensible. It only confuses and leads readers away from what its fulfillment is all about—the change of covenants, not the change of cosmos.

9) Coming on the clouds (v. 30). Twice, Jesus specified exactly *how* He would come in judgment—once in this verse of his most dramatic prophecy and again to Caiaphas and the Sanhedrin (Matt. 26:64). He said He would come "on the clouds." What did He mean?

If you were a 1st-century Jew raised in the synagogue, you would have known exactly what it meant. Why so? Once again, it's because this type of coming of deity had a long biblical precedent. To appreciate the rich Jewish heritage and terminology for cloud-coming, we must again enter the mind of a 1st-century Jew. If we only look at these things through 21st-century eyes, we'll become prisoners of what has become the traditional mindset (paradigm) of misunderstanding and confusion.

Christ's "coming on the clouds" is a common metaphor borrowed from Old Testament portrayals of God (the Father) descending from heaven and coming in power and glory to execute judgment on a nation, people, or city. Again, in all the historic comings of God (the Father) in judgment, He acted through human armies or nature to bring destruction. Hence it is said, "the Lord is a man of war" (Exod. 15:3 *KJV*). Each event was a direct act of God and termed "the day of the Lord." These comings, too, were always described with figurative apocalyptic language as we saw in our last element #8 above. They, too, were empowered by supernatural support and brought historical calamity to Egypt, Edom, Assyria, Babylon, and even on Israel itself.

Stephen, for instance, during his speech at his trial before the Sanhedrin and in quotation of God speaking to Moses stated: "I have indeed seen the oppression of my people in Egypt. I have heard their groaning and have *come down* to set them free . . . ." (Acts 7:34; quoted from Exod. 3:7-8 – italics mine).

As we have seen, the Jews of Jesus' day had studied these "day of the Lord" occurrences and were familiar with this "cloud-coming" phraseology, as well as the application of one with the other.[33] The Hebrew Scriptures are rich in similes and figurative language that poetically portray a heavenly perspective of God literally coming among human beings in judgment and with clouds metaphorically as his mode of transportation. Here are a few:

- See, the Lord rides on a swift *cloud* and is coming to Egypt (Isa. 19:1). (For the earthly fulfillment, see Isa. 20:1-6)
- Look! He advances like the *clouds,* his chariots come like a whirlwind (Jer. 4:13).
- For the day is near, the day of the Lord is near—a day of *clouds*, a time of doom for the nations (Ezek. 30:3).
- Sing to God, sing praise to his name, extol him who rides on the *clouds* . . . (Psa. 68:4).
- . . . He makes the *clouds* his chariots and rides on the wings of the wind. He makes winds his messengers, flames of fire his servants (Psa. 104:3-4).

---

[33] Also, in the Old Testament, God dwelt in, or was present in, a physical and visible Shekhinah glory cloud. This is an entirely different matter and will not be addressed here. Our interest is how cloud phraseology is used in a symbolic manner in both prophetic and apocalyptic eschatology, namely that of swiftness and power of literal judgment.

- Also see Ezek. 30:18; Psa. 18:9-12; 2 Sam. 22:10-12; Nahum 1:3; Joel 2:1-2; Zeph. 1:14-15).

Clouds used in this way are figures of speech and symbolic of God's majesty, power, glory, and elevated position. With familiar cloud-coming imagery Daniel prophesied of the coming of the Son of Man into heaven (Dan. 7:13). Jesus, by deriving his "coming on the clouds" phrase directly from Daniel, was revealing Himself as God and the promised Messiah in his most dramatic prophecy (Matt. 24:30). Likewise, when Jesus used this phrase before the high priest, Caiaphas immediately understood this to be a claim of deity. When Jesus told him that he would "see the Son of Man sitting at the right hand of the Mighty One and coming on the clouds of heaven," Caiaphas responded, "He has spoken blasphemy!" (Matt. 26:64-65). Jesus was also applying his coming in judgment and power of war in the *same* technical way as the Father had come down from heaven many times before in Old Testament times:

> So I have come down to rescue them from the hand
> of the Egyptians and to bring them up out of that land
> into a good and spacious land . . . . (Exod. 3:8)
>
> Look! The Lord is coming from his dwelling place;
> he comes down and treads the high places of the earth (Mic. 1:3).
>
> See, the Lord is coming out of his dwelling to punish
> the people of the earth for their sins (Isa. 26:21).
>
> But your many enemies will become like fine dust,
> the ruthless hordes like blown chaff.
> Suddenly, in an instant the Lord Almighty will come
> with thunder and earthquake and great noise, with
> windstorm and tempest and flames of a devouring fire
> (Isa. 29:5-6).

For more, see: Gen. 11:5; 18:21; Deut. 33:2; Isa. 31:4b; 64:3b; 66:15; Psa. 18:9; 47:5; 50:3; 96:13; 97:5; 144:5; Hos. 8:1; Mic. 1:3-4.

Because of this Jewish background, Jesus' disciples would have understood what He was talking about. The high priest understood it. That was why he was so offended and accused Jesus of blasphemy. Again, let's note that Jesus made no disclaimers to change the meaning or nature of this type of coming, and neither should we. So if God the Father came down to judge nations, cities and people groups and thus shape the course of historical events in human affairs in the Old Testament with his various cloud-comings, why should we be surprised that Jesus is now doing the same thing (see John 5:22)?

Another important factor is that in all these real biblical comings of God the Father in the Old Testament is, God was *never physically visible*; He was unseen by human eyes! Thus, cloud-coming is the language of divine imagery. It denotes divine action. And in every instance, some humans were aware of God's presence and personal intervention in those events of history.

Obviously, this Jewish perspective is quite different from the way we moderns have been conditioned to think of Christ's coming on the clouds. We imagine his coming to be spectacularly visible on the tops of literal fluffy cumulus clouds as they transport Him down to earth. To be consistent, shouldn't we also think of his coming on a white horse (Rev. 19:11), as riding on a literal four-legged steed? Yet every biblical instance of a cloud-coming was a real coming. And Jesus employed the same figure of speech. Thus for Jesus and a 1st-century Jew, coming "on the clouds" was not a claim of deity to come visibly to the human eye.

Because of this Jewish background, Jesus' disciples would have understood what He was talking about. The high priest understood it. That was why he was so offended and accused Jesus of blasphemy.

---

10) The sign of his coming (v. 3) and the sign in the sky (v. 30). Because of the invisible nature of Christ's prophesied *parousia* coming "on the clouds," this coming needed a sign.[34] Thus, a sign was asked for (Matt. 24:3) and given (Matt. 24:30f).

But this sign was not new at that time. It had been prophesied by Ezekiel some six hundred years before Christ in the midst of Babylonian captivity. In Ezekiel 4 and 5, the prophet prophesied of *this sign* when the Lord told him to:

- "Now, son of man, take a clay tablet, put it in front of you and draw the city of Jerusalem on it. Then lay siege to it: Erect siege works against it, build a ramp up to it, set up camps against it and put battering rams around it. Then take an iron pan, place it as an iron wall between you and the city and turn your face toward it. It will be under siege, and you shall besiege it. This will be *a sign* to the house of Israel" (Ezek. 4:1-3 – bold/italics mine).
- "This is Jerusalem, which I have set in the center of the nations, with countries all around her" (Ezek. 5:5). In his wisdom, God had set Jerusalem on a high place (Psa. 48:1-2; Isa. 2:2-3) at the crossroads of the world (three continents)
- "You have been more unruly than the nations around you and have not followed my decrees or kept my laws" (Ezek. 5:7).
- "I myself am against you, Jerusalem, and I will inflict punishment on you in the sight of the nations" (Ezek. 5:8).
- "I will do to you what I have never done before and will never do again" (Ezek. 5:9).
- "I will inflict punishment on you and will scatter all your survivors to the winds" (Ezek. 5:10).
- "because you have defiled my sanctuary with all your vile images and detestable practices, I will withdraw my favor" (Ezek. 5:11).
- "A third of your people will die of the plague or perish by famine inside you; a third will fall by the sword outside your walls; and a third I will scatter to the winds and pursue with drawn sword" (Ezek. 5:12).

---

[34] The Greek noun "parousia" actually means arrival or presence, and not necessarily coming or return. Thus Jesus' disciples were asking "what will be the sign of your arrival/presence."

- "I will make you a ruin and a reproach among the nations around you, in the sight of all who pass by" (Ezek. 5:14).
- "You will be a reproach and a taunt, a warning and an object of horror to the nations around you when I inflict punishment on you in anger and wrath and with stinging rebuke. I the Lord have spoken" (Ezek. 5:15).

Similarly, about that same time and same sign, Daniel prophesied that the defining characteristic and immediate historical setting for the "time of the end" would be "when the power of the holy people has been finally broken, all these things will be completed" (Dan. 12: 4, 7).

Isaiah had also prophesied that the Messiah would come robed "with the garments of vengeance for clothing" (Isa. 59:17f; see also Rom. 12:19), and He would proclaim not only salvation, but also "the day of vengeance of our God" (Isa. 61:2). Jesus' statement in Luke's account of the Olivet Discourse contains this very wording: "When you [Jesus' contemporaries] see Jerusalem surrounded by armies, you will know that its desolation is near . . . flee . . . For this is the time of punishment [*these be the days of vengeance*] in fulfillment of all that has been written" (Luke 21:20-22 [italics above indicated from *KJV*]).

Once again, history records, quite literally, that Jerusalem and the Temple were burned by invading Roman armies in August of A.D. 70. They then began dismantling the entire Temple complex in precise fulfillment of Jesus' prophesy, "not one stone [was] left upon another" (Matt. 24:2).[35]

Undeniably, if we are honest and sincere, Jesus had conjoined his invisible coming "on the clouds" with this dramatically visible and historical event (Matt. 24:1-34). His linkage of time, event, and place cannot be overstated. In this coming, Jesus was not only vindicated in the same arena of his humiliation and his prophesies fulfilled, but He was also revealed as God, not just a man, as He triumphed over those who had slain Him.

That 1st-century apostate Jewish nation with its city and its Temple had become the great enemy of God's emerging new people—the

---

[35] For the reasons the Romans went to this great extent of totally dismantling, see: Noē, *The Perfect Ending for the World*, 182-184.

Church. And the result was just as Isaiah proclaimed it would be. "But the Lord of hosts shall be exalted in judgment . . . . (Isa. 5:16 *KJV*).

Thus, the destruction of Jerusalem and its Temple was the "sign" of Jesus' coming in judgment and his presence (Matt. 24:3). And almost everyone in "the land" of Judea at that time saw this sign. After the fall and burning of the Temple and city in A.D. 70 and their subsequent dismantling, transcontinental traders and travelers from near and far could readily see that something most significant had happened. News of the devastation of God's chosen people, their Temple, and the entire nation spread rapidly throughout the Roman world.

Granted, this sign was not a worldwide sign because it was not a global event, as many over the centuries and yet today have been mistakenly led to expect. But neither were Jesus' birth, anointing, crucifixion, resurrection, or ascension. All were local events with universal significance and relevance.

Scoffers Knew

To their credit, the scoffers of that time correctly recognized something that most Christians still today have failed to recognize. They knew that the destruction of Jerusalem would be the physically visible sign pointing to and corresponding with Christ's invisible, *parousia* coming as they scoffed, "Where is this 'coming' (*parousia*) he promised? Ever since our fathers died, everything [i.e., the Old Covenant system] goes on as it has since the beginning of creation" (2 Peter 3:3-4). Jude confirms that those scoffers were present just before the destruction of Jerusalem (Jude 18-19).

Transfiguration Insight

Even Jesus' transfiguration event prefigured, foreshadowed, and typified this sign when Moses and Elijah appeared and disappeared. They represented the entirety of the Old Covenant since it was Moses who was first given the Ten Commandments of the Law (Exod. 20). And Elijah was the great prophet and precursor of the Messiah (Mal. 4:5-6). Hence, their disappearance depicted the fading glory and passing away the Old Covenant, Mosaic age and world at Jesus' *parousia* coming in judgment. Jesus' glowing and remaining depicted the surpassing and transcending glory of the New Covenant system. This completed change of covenants is exactly what was prophesied and happened with the fall and destruction of Jerusalem and the Temple circa A.D. 70 (see Heb. 8:13; 9:8f, 1 Cor. 7:29a, 31b for instance). All prophecies were fulfilled and the Old Covenant system was "left to you desolate" (Matt. 23:38) within Jesus' time parameter of "this generation" (Matt. 23:36). The biblical and historical fact is, Jesus' coming in judgment circa A.D. 70 ended forever biblical Judaism. Never again would God's people return to a Temple and practice animal sacrifices. That system, depicted by Moses and Elijah's appearance and disappearance at the Mount of Transfiguration, was gone for good—despite dispensational premillennialist insistence that it will return someday.

Sign in the Sky [in heaven] (v. 30)

But what about the "sign in the sky?" Let's recall that the Apostle Paul wrote that Jesus would be "revealed from heaven in blazing fire with his powerful angels" (2 Thess. 1:7). Therefore, this "sign in the sky" [in heaven] could have been the mammoth plumes of smoke arising from the burning debris that rose high into the sky for many days above the mountain plateau on which Jerusalem sat (Mark 10:33).[36]

Regarding these powerful angels, and perhaps even more astonishing, as we have seen, both Josephus, the Jewish/Roman historian and eyewitness, and Tacitus, the Roman historian, reported the sighting of chariots and armed soldiers (angelic armies) riding about in the sky above the hills outside Jerusalem just before the first siege of Jerusalem in A.D. 66. This manifestation certain could be interpreted as "the sign of his coming," since Jesus is the commander of the heavenly hosts and had prophesied of "great signs from heaven" (Luke 21:11).

Therefore, in these above ways and in perfect consistency and harmony of fulfillment, "the Lord Jesus is [was] revealed from heaven in blazing fire with his powerful angels" (2 Thess. 1:7). Josephus and Tacitus also reported a star in the shape of a sword that stood over the

---

[36] Some have suggested that these clouds of rising smoke compare with the cloud that hid Jesus from his disciples' sight upon his Ascension (Acts 1:9-11). Therefore, in a similar manner, Jesus' coming here was hidden from sight. But I think not.

city, a comet that continued for a year before Jerusalem's destruction.[37] Jesus had prophesied of "signs in the sun, moon, and stars" (Luke 21:25).

In a similar manner, the Old Testament prophet Joel had prophesied that God would "show wonders in the heaven above and signs on the earth below . . . . before the coming of the great and glorious day of the Lord" (Acts 2:19-20 in quoting Joel 2:30-31). Correspondingly, Josephus writes of several other strange, if not bizarre, oracles that appeared in the city before the first siege of Jerusalem and foretelling its impending devastation. A brilliant light around the altar at night; a cow that gave birth to a lamb; and the hearing of voices in the inner court of the Temple, saying, "We are departing hence."[38]

Before we leave this element #10, a slight disclaimer is in order regarding Jesus' prophetic statement that "At that time the sign of the Son of Man will appear in the sky [in heaven]" (Matt. 24:30). The better translation in line with the literal Greek is "in heaven." Yet "in heaven" (or "in the sky") does not necessarily modify the sign. Consequently, Jesus may not have been saying that a sign would appear in heaven or in the sky. He may only have been saying that they would see a sign proving He was in heaven, sitting at his Father's right hand (Acts 2:30-36), and now in charge of "all judgment" (John 5:22).

In Sum

I believe the destruction of that city and nation—i.e., Jerusalem and Judea—as with other days of the Lord, was that sign. It confirmed Jesus' enthronement as "King of kings and Lord of lords" (Rev. 19:16), offered proof that He is exactly Whom He claimed to be, and substantiated that Christianity is true. For me, this historical event is the empirical proof of timely, precisely, and completely fulfilled prophecy of our "once for all delivered faith" (Jude 3). Once again, this is how we are to know Who the One True God truly is (see again: Isaiah 41:22-23; 42:9; 44:6-8; 45:21; 46:10-11; 48:4-6).

---

[37] Josephus, *The Wars of the Jews*, book 6, chapter 5, paragraphs 2-3, In William Whiston, trans. *The Works of Josephus,* 741-2. Also see Tacitus, *History*, v, 11ff.
[38] ibid.

The immediate historical setting, the defining characteristic, and explicit end-time framework for these happenings proved to be the Jewish-Roman War of A.D. 66 – 70. After circa A.D. 70, the "last days" were over.

11) Gathering of his elect (v. 31). "And he will send his angels with a loud trumpet call, and they will gather his elect from the four winds, from one end of the heavens to the other." This verse is one of several that refer to the resurrection of the dead ones (plural). I shall defer comment on this element and topic for now. We shall devote our entire last chapter to this exposition.

12) Heaven and earth passing away (v. 35). "Heaven and earth will pass away, but my words will never pass away." As we have seen, there are three different entities in the Bible termed "heaven and earth." The heaven and earth Jesus was talking about in this verse that was soon to pass away and be made new was the covenantal entity. And the rest of this verse is true as well. All that remains from that Old Covenant "heaven and earth" are God's words, the Bible (see again Chapter 8, pp-168-169).

13) No one knows about that day or hour (v. 36, 25:13). Sadly and classically, this verse is misused to extrapolate Jesus' words to mean that no one can ever know the time when all this will happen—i.e., the time is unknowable. But let's especially notice here that the only prohibition against knowing was the "day or hour," and not the week, month, year, or generation. Therefore, knowing was not and is not a futile task, as many teach.

In fact, not knowing was not an excuse for 1st-century Christians to whom these words were originally addressed. They were to know and understand. Their lives depended upon it. But at that time, even Jesus did not know. No one knows the day or hour of the birth of a baby either during a nine-month gestation period.[39] And Jesus compared his coming

---

[39] One can't know the precise day or hour for the birth of a baby, either. This limitation phrase cannot be extrapolated to mean that no one could/can know, as is commonly assumed. Again, the only constraint is "day" and "hour," not week, month, season, year, or generation. The fact is, Jesus never identified a day or

and this end to just that (Matt. 24:8). But, and once again, this is why Jesus gave them two prime signs. By watching for the two prime signs and obeying his instructions to flee, his disciples could know that the tough times of unequalled tribulation were coming, the judgment was very close, and neither would last forever.

In contrast, however, some thirty-seven years later, John knew and twice emphatically proclaimed, "It is the last hour . . . this is how we know it is the last hour" (1 John 2:18)! What was he talking about? How could he know it was "the last hour"? Hadn't Jesus said no one could know the day or hour, not even the angels or Himself? The answer is something significant had changed since Jesus uttered those words a week before his death. That something was Pentecost and the outpouring of the Holy Spirit (Acts 2). And part of the Holy Spirit's ministry was to "guide you into all truth" and "tell you what is yet to come" (John 16:13). That's how John knew "it is the last hour." Understand?

'Tis So Sweet'

No, I cannot absolutely prove that Jesus came "on the clouds" in a day of the Lord and age-ending judgment and in destruction of Jerusalem and the Temple circa A.D. 70. But critics and skeptics also cannot prove that He didn't. Either of these conclusions is a decision. But this decision is important. It should not be made based on presuppositions or compliance to a tradition. It must be informed by biblical precedence, history, and one other thing—"Tis so sweet to trust in Jesus; just to take Him at his word."

Surely by now, and by using the language of the prophets and comparing it with the biblical precedents of fulfillment we've been re-exploring in this chapter for a coming of the "day of the Lord," we can document how Jesus' age-ending coming was accomplished. He came in exactly the same *way* ("on the clouds"), for exactly the same *purpose* (judgment), to accomplish exactly the same *thing* (destruction of a nation).

---

hour. Even He did not know (Matt. 24:36). But that was no excuse for not knowing when it was time to flee.

Just as the cloud-coming Jehovah God came many times in Old Testament times, Jesus came as He said he would, "on the clouds" (Matt. 24:30) and "in the glory of the Father" (Matt. 16:27). From his heavenly perspective, Jesus had witnessed the Father come in the glory of cloud-coming and day-of-the-Lord judgments many times. Therefore, in like manner, Judge Jesus came in that same glory as belonged to the Father, utilizing armies (the armies of Rome), to deliver his people (the Church) from their Jewish persecutors circa A.D. 70. And in keeping with the Old Testament pattern, form, and nature of this type of coming, He was not physically/visibly seen.

> **Surely by now, and by using the language of the prophets and comparing it with the biblical precedents of fulfillment we've been re-exploring . . . for a coming of the "day of the Lord," we can document how Jesus' age-ending coming was accomplished.**

Consequently, "the day of the Lord" (Jehovah) of the Old Testament became "the day of Christ" (*Christos* 2 Thess. 2:2; *kurios* 2 Pet. 3:10) in the New Testament. This change is true because "all judgment" had been turned over to the Son by the Father (John 5:22). As we shall further see in our next two chapters, post-A.D. 70 onward, Jesus now comes and judges as the Father had done many times before. And the purpose of this judgment remains the same—God's glory. Throughout the Old Testament, God's often-stated purpose in acting, intervening, and coming in this manner was to "be a sign and witness to the Lord Almighty" and for the Lord to "make himself known"—i.e., to manifest his sovereignty and majesty as the true God to a particular group, people, city, or nation and among the nations (see Isa. 19:20-21; 37:20; 64:2; and seventy-four times in Ezekiel, and many more). In so doing his name was glorified. Certainly, men and women of discernment could understand Who He is. Hence, the Psalmist admonishes us to this day to "tell of his wonderful acts. Glory in his holy name; . . . Remember the wonders he has done, his miracles, and the judgments he pronounced" (Psa. 105:2-5).

Next, here's how I told of his acts during my trip to Israel.

A True Story in Israel

In 1993 I went on a two-week Christian tour of Israel and Egypt. This tour was sponsored by the Christian Broadcasting Network and hosted by Pat and Shirley Boone. About three hundred of us travelled throughout the "Holy Land" aboard four buses. Each of us was assigned to a bus and each bus had its own Jewish tour guide. Our guide was quite friendly, open, and communicative. But during his first presentation he informed us that even though he had led hundreds of Christian tour groups and knew a lot about the Bible—more than most Christians—he was not a Christian. He also encouraged us numerous times to ask him any questions we might have.

So, here's the irony. As we visited place after place where Jesus had done things recorded in the New Testament, our Jewish and non-Christian guide repeatedly told us, "here was where Jesus did this or that in fulfillment of this or that Old Testament prophecy." After a half dozen or so of these stops and his often-repeated comments about Jesus' fulfilling many Old Testament prophecies, I finally approached him privately as we were walking toward another site.

"Do you really believe that Jesus did these things in fulfillment of Old Testament prophecies?" I asked.

"Yes, I do," he assured me.

"Then why don't you believe Jesus was and is the Messiah?" I followed up.

To which he replied. "I'm asked this question a lot by Christians in the tour groups I lead and I always answer the same way." He looked down at the ground for a moment as I awaited his next few words with baited breath. Looking back up and straight into my eyes, he said.

"It's because Jesus didn't fulfill all the messianic prophecies."

"Oh, yes, He did," I quickly responded shaking my head affirmatively. "He fulfilled everything the prophet Daniel prophesied—exactly, literally, chronologically, sequentially, and Moses prophesied in the Song of Moses – Deut. 32, and Ezekiel, even Isaiah's coming of the new heaven and earth. Everything exactly as and when He said He would and exactly as and when his disciples and every New Testament writer and the early Church expected Him to."

When was that?" he skeptically asked back.

"Within the generation of his contemporaries and in conjunction with the Jewish-Roman War of A.D. 66-70 and destruction of Jerusalem and the Temple circa A.D. 70," I responded. Then he then admitted something I found rather startling at the time.

"You are the first Christian who has ever told me this. Usually, they give me their standard stuff about Jesus coming back someday and finishing the job. But that excuse doesn't cut it with us Jews. When the Messiah comes he will do it all at one time."

"Would you like to know more about how Jesus did do it all during the 1st century?" I queried back.

". . . I always answer the same way . . . It's because Jesus didn't fulfill all the messianic prophecies."

He declined, turned, and walked away over to our assembled group, and once again began telling us about this next place where Jesus did something else in fulfillment of an Old Testament prophecy. Such is the veil that remains over so many faces (see 2 Cor. 3:13-18) and over so many eyes to this very day (see Matt. 13:13-15).

Our next chapter brings us to one of, if not my favorite, book in Scripture. But as you will see, its understanding is in need of revitalization.

Chapter 14

Revitalizing Revelation

Arguably, the Book of Revelation may be the most misread, misunderstood, and mis-taught book in the entire Bible. If this is true, one reason for this continuing fiasco trumps all others.

Real estate agents have a comical but serious saying. They insist that the three most important factors in selling or buying a property are: "Location! Location! Location!" In a similar fashion, what do you think are the three most important factors for properly understanding the meaning of any piece of literature, including books in the Bible?

It's "Context! Context! Context!"

For centuries, however, and today as well, multiple millions have consistently failed to contextualize, or properly contextualize, the whole of this prophecy before trying to read, understand, or teach it. Consequently, they lift it, or major portions of it, out of its divinely determined and stated context, stretch it like a rubber band, nineteen centuries and counting, plop it out into the future. and create a pretext. Whenever you take something out of context, you create a pretext. A pretext allows you to make a text mean almost anything you desire. The result is, the intended and true meaning is distorted or missed entirely. Conflict and confusion thus prevail as pretexts compete for attention and allegiance. Worst of all in Revelation's case, readers don't receive this book's wisdom and promised blessings. We will not be making this mistake.

The purpose of this chapter is to show you how to properly contextualize the whole prophecy of the Book of Revelation. That is:

how to recognize and honor the divinely determined time and nature context this book of prophecy places upon itself. Please be assured that this step of whole-prophecy contextualizing is absolutely essential if we truly desire to grasp its true meaning, unlock its wisdom, and receive its promised blessings for you and me here and now.

It's "Context! Context! Context!"

For your information, much (not all) of the material in this chapter was not only part of my doctoral dissertation, but at the recommendation of Dr. Grant R. Osborn, Professor of New Testament at Trinity Evangelical Divinity School and author of the book *Revelation* (2002) (a part of the Baker Books' *Exegetical Commentary on the New Testament* series) was part of an article written by yours truly and published in the *Journal of the Evangelical Theological Society*. It was titled, "An Exegetical Basis for a Preterist-Idealist Understanding of the Book of Revelation," Vol. 49, No. 4 (Dec. 2006). Next to my doctoral dissertation, this article is most credible piece of scholarly work that I have done because *JETS* is a peer-reviewed publication and one of the world's most respected theological journals.[1]

The Pinnacle of Prophecy

The book of Revelation is not placed last in the Bible for nothing. It is the pinnacle of all of God's progressive and prophetic revelation to humankind (starting with Genesis). If you let it, it will transform not only you but your life. On the other hand, if you disregard or abuse its own contextualization, as so many readers, interpreters, pastors, and so-called prophecy experts have done and are still doing, you will miss out on its wisdom and promised blessings.

---

[1] To read the surprising story of how and why Dr. Osborn's recommendation for publication came about (he's a dispensational premillennialist), see: Noē, *The Greater Jesus*, 413-416. A copy of this article is also posted on PRI's website: www.prophecyrefi.org. Click on "About Us," "In The Media," and "New Academic Journal Article."

So let me ask you a potentially unsettling question. How much of your beliefs about the Book of Revelation are based on your personal search and study of the Scriptures versus how much is based on what others have told you? When I seriously began to study Revelation and other biblical prophecy some twenty-five or so years ago, I quickly discovered that I had picked up most of my beliefs from what other people had told me and not from my direct reading and study of God's Word. Later on I further discovered that much of what I had been told, taught, and had read did not square with its text.

So please be advised, if you have had trouble unraveling the mysteries of the Revelation, you're not alone. Bible scholars over many centuries have been puzzled by this book's strange symbolism and apocalyptic imagery. Martin Luther, for example, felt that it should be dropped from the Canon because it was too different from other New Testament Scriptures. He claimed it neither taught nor acknowledged Jesus Christ. John Calvin, another leading 16th-century reformer, refused to write a commentary on it. Ulrich Zwingli, the 16th-century Swiss reformer and Bible translator, termed it insignificant and refused to concern himself with it.

If you disregard or abuse its own contextualization . . . you will miss out on its wisdom and promised blessings.

In contrast to these disparaging treatments, we shall see that this last book of the Bible is a special and vital book. For over nineteen centuries and counting it has always been God's present-day message to his people. In this chapter, therefore, we'll reexamine seven clear and simple contextualizing keys we can use to begin unlocking the mysteries of this most-misconstrued book and to unlearn many of the popular misconceptions we have been told and taught.

Unfortunately, in this chapter I shall only be able to offer you a highlighted recap of these keys. Much more is contained in the *JETS* article I referenced above.

If you are ready, what we are about to discover is, the Book of Revelation contextualizes and explains itself—if we have eyes to see and hears to hear (Matt. 13:13-16). Do you? Will you?

Seven Contextualizing Keys

Contextualizing Key #1—Revelation's Purpose and Overarching Theme[2]
When you think about Jesus, talk with Him, or sing hymns about Him, how do you picture Him in your mind's eye—such as when you sing this classic hymn?

> *Just a closer walk with Thee,*
> *Grant it, Jesus, is my plea,*
> *Daily, walking close to Thee,*
> *Let it be, dear Lord, let it be.*

If you are like most, your mental image of Jesus is probably based on the historical Jesus of Nazareth. After all, this is the visual impression we read and hear about the most, studied in Sunday school, and see on TV and in the movies. At Christmas time we might picture Jesus as the sleeping baby lying in a manger; at other times as boy growing up, or a young man ministering in Galilee, or as our savior hanging on a cross at Calvary.

Chances are, if you grew up within the past sixty years or so, the image of Jesus most ingrained in your mind's eye is artist Warner Sallman's "Head of Christ" painted in 1941.

Sallman's painting has become "the most popular picture of Jesus of all time," having been reproduced "over 500 million times." Sallman painted Jesus as a young, tender, slender, handsome, meek and mild, sensitive and serene, intelligent-looking, white, Anglo-Saxon man gazing up to heaven with expressive eyes, long brown hair, parted in the middle and flowing over his shoulders. His calm face is full of sweetness and love, without a blemish or wrinkle, and with a faultless nose and mouth and a nicely trimmed beard.

Whether this picture is an accurate representation of the historical Jesus' physical appearance is contestable and highly doubtful. But the Bible offers scant description. Notably, not one New Testament writer provides a physical description of the earthly, historical Jesus. We don't

---

[2] Material in this key #1 is excerpted from and for more, see: Noē, *The Greater Jesus*, 1-18.

even know if He was tall or short. And for more than three hundred years after his crucifixion, church authorities forbid making any images of Jesus for fear they would be idolized. That's why symbols were used like a fish and the Greek letters for fish, *ichthys*—the first letters of an acrostic meaning "Jesus Christ Son of God Savior." Islam to this day allows no images, or even cartoons, of its prophet Muhammad believing this constitutes blasphemy and requires death.

Not surprisingly, some Christians have reacted strongly against Sallman's painting because of its effeminate character, non-Jewish appearance; i.e., pink colored skin and blue eyes, its soft lighting, and retouched commercial studio photograph likeness. Yet this caricature of Jesus appeals to many who long for an intimate and personal relationship with a warm, friendly, and familiar face.

One of the problems this popular image of Jesus creates, as one writer points out is, "a meek and mild Jesus eventually is a bore. He doesn't inspire us." Furthermore, this is "the aspect of church that men find least appealing."[3] Likewise, J.B. Phillips in his appropriately titled book, *Your God Is Too Small*, laments about little nursery rhymes about Jesus that hundreds of thousands learned in their childhood, and which have infected their minds, such as:

> Little Jesus, meek and mild,
> Look upon a little child.
>
> ~
>
> Christian children all must be
> Mild, obedient, good as He.[4]

Phillips aptly criticizes "mild" as "the least appropriate" epithet for Jesus because it conjures up to our minds "someone who is a bit of a nonentity, both uninspired and uninspiring."[5] He sadly concludes that

---

[3] Brandon O'Brien, "A Jesus for Real Men," *Christianity Today*, April 2008, 49-50.
[4] Quoted in J.B. Phillips, *Your God Is Too Small* (New York, NY.: Touchstone Books, Simon & Schuster, 1952, 2004), 26-27.
[5] Ibid., 27-28.

"we can hardly be surprised if children feel fairly soon that they have outgrown the 'tender Shepherd' and find their heroes elsewhere."[6]

Then there are many other visual images of Jesus in today's world, such as: Ancient mosaics, paintings, frescos, drawings, or sculptures created by artists across the centuries, as they imagined Him to have looked. Or, perhaps, it's the handsome and blue-eyed James Caviezel in Mel Gibson's 2004 blockbuster film, *The Passion of the Christ*. If you are a college football fan, there's a somewhat-farcical, arms-raised "Touchdown Jesus" peering over the top of Notre Dame's football stadium from a giant mural painted on the side of a campus building.

With the possible exception of a crucified Jesus, the one thing all these pictures have in common is, they present Jesus in a safe and sanitized manner. And we are comfortable with these "to-Thy-bosom" images. They soothe us even though they may be nothing more than projections of our own escapist piety and wishes.

The world likes these images of Jesus, too. After all, who can object to a baby? Or to a comely and sedentary Jesus relegated to live in the innocuous realm of human hearts and behind church doors? Practically speaking, these images of Jesus fit nicely within societal norms and can easily be taken or left behind by many.

In other parts of the world one can choose from a bewildering array of portraits of Jesus. It seems his physical appearance easily adapts to fit ethnic tastes. So in the Far East, Jesus is seen as an oriental; to the Indians, He's an Indian; to the Africans and some African-Americans, He's a black.

> **The world likes these images of Jesus, too.**
> **After all, who can object to a baby?**

All of us tend to gravitate toward identifiable and non-threatening pictures of Jesus. And since there were no actual paintings, drawings, or renderings of Him, nor were there cameras or video recorders back in Jesus' time, we feel free to impart our own image and/or latch on to whatever non-threatening one appeals to our whims. In spite of these questionable depictions and characterizations of Jesus, as we imagine

---

[6] Ibid.,.28

Him to be, the historical Jesus has still proven to be the most challenging and controversial figure of human history. Therefore, many view the historical Jesus with contempt. Others dismiss Him as an ancient myth, culturally and contemporarily irrelevant. Nonetheless, this Jesus remains important—very important. But what is more important is, *He's not like that* (any of that) *anymore!*

Unveiling and Revealing Jesus Today

If you want to see the latest and only physically descriptive picture of Jesus we have today—one that is sharp, clear, true, authoritative, and more revealing and challenging than any of those above, there is only one place you can go. That is to the greatly misunderstood and abused Book of Revelation.

Unfortunately, this last book of the Bible has both fascinated and frustrated Bible readers for centuries. Its apocalyptic content and symbolic style still confuse and frighten most readers. But its first five words make it perfectly clear that this book's purpose and overarching theme is to unveil and reveal a greater Jesus as He now is, the contemporary Christ, and not to satisfy our intellectual curiosity about distant, future events or the end of the world. (Remember, what my Greek tour guide on the isle of Patmos told us – see again Chapter 8, pp. 146-147.) Those first five words are: "The revelation of Jesus Christ" (Rev. 1:1).

The apostle John, one of Jesus' original apostles, received this revelation from both an angel and from Jesus Christ Himself while he was exiled on the isle of Patmos in the Mediterranean Sea some time during the 1st century. (Although his authorship is contested, this John is the one most widely accepted.)

The Greek word translated "revelation" is *apokalypsis*. It's our word "apocalypse." The kind of imagery that comes to most people's mind in our day when they see or hear the word apocalypse is total devastation, a nuclear holocaust, or an exploding universe. That's why we have books and movies like *The Four Horsemen of the Apocalypse* and *Apocalypse Now*. But that is not what this word meant to John, who wrote down the Revelation, nor what it meant to the Greek-speaking people for whom he wrote it nineteen centuries ago.

The Greek word *apokalypsis* simply means an "unveiling" or "uncovering." And it's *of* Jesus Christ. The Greek preposition translated as *of*, contains two meanings. One meaning is *from*. The other meaning is *about*. Hence, the Bible's last book is not just an unveiling *from* Jesus Christ, which gives it incontestable authority. It is also an unveiling *about* Jesus Christ in his present, ascended, glorified, exalted, transformed, transfigured, and transcendent form. It further reveals his past, present, and future involvement and interactions with humankind and spirit-realm beings.

Yet most current teachings, books, and movies on the Revelation conclude that this book is primarily about Satan, his cohorts, and the supposed Antichrist and what these evil beings are supposedly going to be doing to our world at some future date. A prime example is the runaway mega-best-selling *Left Behind* series. Co-authors Tim LaHaye and Jerry B. Jenkins believe that the Revelation's message is this. Soon, some day in the future "in one cataclysmic moment, millions around the globe [will] disappear" in the Rapture.[7] Then the Antichrist will take over and wreck havoc. Hence, their main character in their sensational series and three movies is the Antichrist.

But one searches in vain to find any mention of an Antichrist in the Book of Revelation.[8] Such interpretations are gross distortions of God's Word, as well as a misrepresentation of the Revelation's stated purpose and content. And yet, the above Antichrist gaffe is the tip of the iceberg of the erroneous ideas many people have imported into this most important and last book of the Bible.

No wonder, however, millions are frightened by Revelation's prophecy and have missed its stated purpose and also miss out on its promised blessings in this life, here and now (Rev. 1:3; 22:7). It seems

---

[7] Tim LaHaye and Jerry B. Jenkins, *Left Behind* (Wheaton, IL.: Tyndale House Publishers, 1995), back cover.

[8] The only two places "antichrist" is mentioned in the Bible are in the New Testament epistles 1 John and 2 John. Here, John puts down the unbiblical idea of only one coming "the antichrist" and replaces it with "many antichrists," which were present back there and then (1 John 2:18). Then he gives descriptions of these people (see 1 John 2:22; 4:2-3; 2 John 7). "Any such person is . . . the antichrist" (2 John 7). This is the biblical position regarding antichrist(s)—there are many (past, today, and future) who fit these descriptions, and not just one.

the very trap the Revelation warns about—adding to or taking away from the prophecy of this book (Rev. 22:18-19)—has ensnared millions of people and thousands of churches. The consequence has been to strip the Apocalypse of its present reality and life-giving power.

But one searches in vain to find any mention of an Antichrist in the Book of Revelation.

But this fact remains. If you really want to know and follow Jesus as He is today—what He's like and what He is doing—you must come, expectantly, to the last book of the Bible. Again, the Book of Revelation is the pinnacle of prophecy and the climax and completion of God's progressive revelation to humankind. It is the only source that unveils and reveals Jesus in his present-day, pertinent, and full reality. This is *the Jesus of the Apocalypse, the contemporary Christ.* And He's a much greater Jesus than most of us have been led to believe! But this is the Jesus each of us needs to meet, know, and take seriously.

Notwithstanding, however, He is also the same Jesus Who was born of a virgin, raised as a boy, ministered throughout Judea, and died on a cross. Without this historical Jesus we would still be lost in our sins (1 Cor. 15:17). So we must stay grounded in this Jesus Who was "made a little lower than the angels" (Heb. 2:7, 9) and "made Himself nothing, taking the very nature [form] of a servant, being made in human likeness" (Phil. 2:7). But at the same time we also must understand that this same Jesus is no longer confined in an earthly human body. Nowadays, He is both the same and a greater Jesus. Why is this so? It's because after his birth, earthly life, death, burial, resurrection, and ascension, "God exalted him to the highest place and gave him the name that is above every name that at the name of Jesus every knee should bow, in heaven and on earth, and every tongue confess that Jesus Christ is Lord, to the glory of God the Father" (Phil. 2:8-11; also Eph. 1:20-23). "So he became as much superior to the angels as the name he has inherited is superior to theirs" (Heb. 1:4).

Consequently, we must recognize that the mission of Jesus—his leaving heaven, coming to earth, and going back to heaven—was a change in his bodily form and ministerial capacity. That's why Revelation's last revealed form of Jesus is a more complex Jesus than during his earthly ministry. Whether you agreed or disagreed, this same Jesus has changed from before creation to cradle to cross to coronation. One thing perhaps that we can agree upon now, and, hopefully more so, if you have the time and inclination to read my book *The Greater Jesus*, is this Jesus of today is a much greater Jesus than has been and is generally being presented, preached, and perceived.

In my opinion, one of the great tragedies of today is so many people in most churches don't know Jesus in the greater way in which the Book of Revelation unveils and reveals Him. This deficiency accounts for much of the lack of faith, power, and effectiveness in the Church today. Yet every year we joyously present to Christians and the world the image of Jesus as a baby—so tiny, so adorable, and so helpless.

Again in my opinion, the whole message of Christ must include an accurate and up-to-date presentation of Jesus as He is today, not only during Christmas time to the masses, but all year long to the regulars as well. A change of this magnitude would change many things for the better. For one, the Bible's last book teaches that the more you know and follow Him as He now is, the more blessings and power will be unleashed in and through your life (Rev. 1:3; 22:7). Therefore, my prayer for you during the rest of this chapter and book is, your heart will be stirred, your mind challenged, your faith awaken, your emotions fired, and your intentions refueled to know and follow Jesus, the contemporary Christ as He is today, and to worship Him more devotedly and serve Him more obediently, faithfully, and effectively—so help you God.

If you are ready, let's next take an introductory look at Jesus as He is today, a much greater Jesus than most of us have been led to believe!

The Latest Picture of Jesus

The first chapter of the Book of Revelation unveils and reveals the latest and most physically descriptive picture of Jesus in the entire Bible. By inspiration, John records what he heard and saw:

> *I, John, your brother and companion in the suffering and kingdom and patient endurance that are ours in Jesus, was on the island of Patmos because of the word of God and the testimony of Jesus. On the Lord's Day I was in the Spirit, and I*

heard behind me a loud voice like a trumpet, which said: "Write on a scroll what you see and send it to the seven churches: to Ephesus, Smyrna, Pergamum, Thyatira, Sardis, Philadelphia, and Laodicea.

I turned around to see the voice that was speaking to me. And when I turned I saw seven golden lampstands, and among the lampstands was someone "like a son of man," dressed in a robe reaching down to his feet and with a golden sash around his chest. His head and hair were white like wool, as white as snow, and his eyes were like blazing fire. His feet were like bronze glowing in a furnace, and his voice was like the sound of rushing waters. In his right hand he held seven stars, and out of his mouth came a sharp double-edged sword. His face was like the sun shining in all its brilliance.

(Revelation 1:9-16)

Yes, this is Jesus *as He is right now!* We are not told here the meaning of the sword coming out of his mouth or why his hair is white and his eyes like blazing fire, etc. Nor are we told why a crown of thorns no longer encircles his head. But one thing is sure. He is no longer the historical Jesus of popular thought and tradition. Nor does He look the way most people today picture Jesus in their mind's eye. He is still that, of course, but He is also now much more. He is the ascended, glorified, exalted, transformed, transfigured, and transcendent *Jesus of the Apocalypse, the contemporary Christ!*

Let me also assure you of one other thing. Grasping the full reality of this divinely revealed Jesus and knowing and serving Him as He is today are essential if we hope to hear the words from Him someday, "Well done, good and faithful servant" (Matt. 25:21, 23). Anything less is less. But where is this Jesus being preached and presented, nowadays? Where is this picture of Jesus hanging on a wall? Where is this present-day and pertinent perspective being taught, studied, and worshiped?

Since John saw the contemporary Christ like this over nineteen hundred years ago, this Jesus has not changed. For sure, "Jesus Christ is the same yesterday and today and forever" (Heb. 13:8). That is, however, He is the same in his Personhood and divinity—the second Person of the

Trinity. Some theologians, though, contend that what is meant by the word "yesterday" is that Jesus has never changed from his preexistence before creation. And that assertion is partially true. But a partial truth parading as a whole truth is a lie!

The testimony of Scripture is, Jesus has changed, and in some major ways from his preexistent form into a babe, into a boy, into a man, into a dead man, into a resurrected body, and onto being the ascended, glorified, exalted, transformed, transfigured, and transcendent Lord of the Apocalypse.

Another factor these theologians tend to overlook is this. How many literal "yesterdays" have transpired between Jesus' ascension and glorification in A.D. 30 (see Dan. 7:13-14) and the time of the writing of this verse in the book of Hebrews (A.D. 65-67)? The answer is: around 12,000. Thus, we can both affirm that Jesus "is the same yesterday and today and forever" and yet He has changed.

So how did John respond after seeing and hearing Jesus this way in the Revelation? Remember, John had personally known and served Jesus, had stood at the foot of the cross, and even saw Jesus after his death in his post-resurrected form. Yet this Jesus of the Apocalypse was so different, so awesome, and so much greater than John had previously known that he reports, "When I saw him, I fell at his feet as though dead" (Rev. 1:17a).

So, ask yourself, how would you react if this Jesus suddenly came, appeared to you like this, face-to-face, and in this form? Well, if you have the eyes of faith—i.e., spiritual eyes to see, He just did. Otherwise, these words in the first chapter of the Revelation are only ink on a page.

One of the blessings the Book of Revelation offers is for Jesus to appear to you, personally, face-to-face, here and now, as He is today through these inspired words. Prior to being exiled on the isle of Patmos, John had written, "But we know that when he appears [is made known / is manifested] . . . we shall see him as he is" (1 John 3:2). Once again, the primary purpose and over-arching theme of the Revelation is to show us the contemporary Christ. And when we let Jesus appear to us this way, by what we might call "spiritual reading," we can come to know and communion with Him as He is today, and not just know about Him some 2,000 years ago. With this insight, we shall no longer be limited to view Christ only from an earthly perspective. But rather, we shall see Him in an apocalyptic, heavenly light (see 2 Cor. 5:16).

> **So, ask yourself, how would you react if this Jesus suddenly came, appeared to you like this, face-to-face, and in this form?**

Not everyone, however, will accept or can receive this visionary experience of Jesus. And why not? It's for the same reason Jesus pointed out when his first disciples asked Him, "why do you speak to the people in parables?" (Matt. 13:10). Jesus responded:

> *'Though seeing, they do not see;*
> *though hearing, they do not hear or understand.'*
> *In them is fulfilled the prophecy of Isaiah:*
> *'You will be ever hearing but never understanding;*
> *you will be ever seeing but never perceiving.*
> *For this people's heart has become calloused;*
> *they hardly hear with their ears,*
> *and they have closed their eyes.*
> *Otherwise they might see with their eyes,*
> *hear with their ears,*
> *understand with their hearts*
> *and turn, and I would heal them.'*
>
> (Matthew 13:13-15, from Isaiah 6:9-10; also see Ezekiel 40:4; John 12:39-41; Acts 28:25-27)

So, can you see Jesus now? Is this different from the way you have pictured Him before? Later in the Revelation, John will see him again as a slain lamb with seven horns and seven eyes (chapter 5); then perhaps as a mighty angel holding a little scroll (chapter 10); then as a male child Who was to rule all nations with a rod of iron (chapter 12); then sitting on a white cloud wearing a golden crown and holding a sharp sickle (chapter 14); then as a rider on a white horse with the armies of heaven following Him (chapter 19); then on a great white throne from whose face the earth and the heaven fled (chapter 20); and, lastly, as the Alpha and Omega [the first and last letters of the Greek alphabet], the Root and Offspring of David, and the bright Morning Star (chapter 22).

Each of these pictures gives us a different description of the contemporary Christ—i.e., portraying via metaphors the broad range of what He's like and doing today. The fact is, we have no other language with which to convey present-day realities of a transcendent God in human terms. And there is much more in this awesome last book of the Bible waiting for us to unveil and reveal regarding this same but greater Jesus.[9]

Admittedly, these picturesque glimpses of Jesus of the Apocalypse are symbolic. But they do reveal some wonderful truths about what Jesus is like now, his glory and power, and what He is doing. Please keep in mind that behind every biblical symbol is a practical and relevant reality—more practical, more relevant, and more powerful than if these images were merely understood literally and futuristically. So what do they mean? One thing they mean, when they are correctly understood is, Jesus of Nazareth has changed, and yet He is still the same Person.

After John saw Him like this, Jesus placed his right hand on John, comforted and commissioned him to "Write, therefore, what you have seen, what is now and what will take place later" (Rev. 1:19). This is how and why we have the Book of Revelation today. It unveils and reveals a lot more pertinent, here-and-now truths and realities than most postponement, Christian prophecy teachers, Bible commentators, and preachers have conveyed.

Revelation's first chapter sets the stage. But there is much more to be unveiled and revealed about this Jesus of the Apocalypse, the contemporary Christ. Truly, truly, He is a much greater Jesus than we have been led to believe. So if this climactic prophecy is all about revealing Jesus as He is today, why does it use such bizarre creatures, descriptions, and symbols to deliver its message? If God had something important to tell us, why didn't He just come right out and say it in simple, everyday language?

In fact, God does have something very important to tell us and He did say it clearly and simply in the Book of Revelation. The problem is, most readers and interpreters have garbled his message by attaching their own meanings to it.

---

[9] Again see Noē, *The Greater Jesus*.

Contextualizing Key #2—The Revelation Uses Figurative Language and Symbols to Reveal Spiritual/Physical Events and Realities

The reason Revelation uses these types of language is because we humans have no frame of reference to enable us to understand the realities of the spirit realm. And we can only relate from what we know to what we do not know.

Hence, this strange imagery is not God's way of keeping us confused. Rather, it represents the efforts of an infinite God to communicate with finite human beings about truth and reality in both the spiritual and physical realms. In other words, it's a behind-the-scenes peek at the reality behind the reality, the unseen world behind the seen natural world, the great things taking place in the invisible spirit realm, and how these interact with and manifest themselves in the visible physical world. Hence, Revelation informs us that this unseen world is just as real, has a powerful effect on the seen world, and plays an active role in individual lives and in human history.[10]

The trouble lies not with the way God has chosen to convey his message, but with the way we humans try to grasp it. We simply cannot grasp invisible spiritual reality in the same way we ingest scientific or historical knowledge. Spiritual reality can only be grasped by faith through spiritual ears (see 1 Cor. 1:18-25; 3:19; Rev. 2:7; 2:11; 2:17; 2:29; 3:6; 3:13; 3:22) and eyes (Matt.13:13-15, from Isaiah 6:9-10). But we try to understand his meanings in purely physical/material terms[11] because of our physical/material mindset.

For example, when Jesus explained the most basic spirit-realm/physical-realm reality—the new birth—to a searching Pharisee named Nicodemus, he was unable to grasp Jesus' message. Instead, he asked about reentering his mother's womb. Jesus exclaimed back to him, "I have spoken to you of earthly things and you do not believe; how then will you believe if I speak of heavenly things?" (see John 3:1-13).

---

[10] Some assume that a book written in a more "straightforward" form would have attracted more persecution from the authorities.

[11] Throughout my *The Greater Jesus* book I use "spiritual" and "spirit-realm" interchangeably. Too often in today's usage, "spiritual" is restricted to mean only a moral or ethical condition of the heart. This is true but much more is involved—specifically, the interaction of spirit beings in our physical universe.

Therefore, Revelation's very first verse stipulates its communication style, "and he [God] sent and signified it by his angel unto his servant John" (Rev. 1:1 *KJV*). The word "signified" (Greek word, *semaino*) most literally and graphically means "sign – ified"—i.e., making known or communicating with signs and symbols.[12] Hence, if we take the Revelation precisely for what it is—visual parables of spiritual/physical reality—any sincere believer can understand it. But the physical/material mindset, the so-called scientific approach denies or ignores the dimension of the spirit and blinds us to the spirit-world realities of the Revelation. Once, however, we accept that God is speaking in spirit-realm/physical-realm terms and using signs and symbols, the Revelation begins to open up its treasures to us.

The trouble lies not with the way God has chosen to convey his message, but with the way we humans try to grasp it.

The fact is, we shall never be able to understand the physical world and live victoriously and rule and reign in it with Christ effectively until we understand the world of the spirit. It is crucial that we recognize how spirit-realm beings and forces influence the behavior of both individuals and nations and shape events in the material world.

Likewise, John's prophetic message explains that the horrors the original recipients of that book were experiencing in the material/physical realm—as well as some of us today, perhaps—directly result from spirit-realm activities. Thus, it uses visual parables to show these spiritual/physical realities. And Revelation makes it clear that no matter what the situation might look like at any moment in the visible world, God is in charge, Jesus Christ is the King of kings and Lord of lords (Rev. 1:5; 17:14, 19:16), and his kingdom belongs to those who have experienced the new birth and follow Him (see Rev. 1:6). Further, it shows that those who obey and remain faithful in the midst of great

---

[12] The Greek verb here is "semaino." W.E. Vine's *An Expository Dictionary of Biblical Words* provides this definition: "to give a sign, indicate." In specific reference to its use in Rev. 1:1, Vine's adds: "where perhaps the suggestion is that of expressing by signs."

troubles will receive the power to overcome the worst that Satan and his cohorts can do to them (see Rev. 12:10-12).

What a glorious reality! It's the kind of message that produces good fruit if we have ears to hear and eyes to see. Do we? Do you?

Next we shall see that not only have interpreters attached their own meanings to Revelation's message—because of their physical/material mindset—they have also taken it out of its original divinely determined time and relevancy context.

Contextualizing Key #3—Revelation Most Likely Was Written Prior to Jerusalem's Destruction in A.D. 70

Also of critical importance for unlocking Revelation's mysteries is the question of when the book was actually given to John on the isle of Patmos. Sorry to say, scholars have reached different conclusions after assessing the dating evidence.

The majority contends for a date around A.D. 95 or 96. This is termed the "late date." But a sizeable and growing minority feels that Revelation was written prior to the Jerusalem and the Temple's destruction in A.D. 70. This is termed the "early date." Adherence to the late date effectively rules out any contemporary and significant historical event as the soon-coming fulfillment, or any relevance to the original and named recipients. But acceptance of the early date opens the possibility that it describes those events leading up to and including Jerusalem's fall and the destruction of the Temple in A.D. 70. This understanding is, of course, in complete harmony with Daniel's "time of the end" and Jesus' "this generation," as we have seen earlier in this book.

Without getting bogged down in the scholarly debate—see my *JETS* article for more on this—here are two points well worth considering:

1) Philip Schaff, who wrote *History of the Christian Church* in eight volumes, and in the preface to his Revised Edition, admits that "on two points I have changed my opinion – the second Roman captivity of Paul . . . and the date of the Apocalypse (which I now assign, with the majority of modern critics, to the year 68 or 69 instead of 95, as before)."[13]

---

[13] Philip Schaff, *History of the Christian Church*, Vol. 1, (Grand Rapids, MI.: Eerdmans, 1910 [third revision]) *vi*, also 420, 834n.

2) The major piece of dating evidence cited for the popular late date is an ambiguous and questionable passage written by Irenaeus, one of the early church fathers who wrote around A.D. 180-190. The problem with Irenaeus, however, is his credibility. For instance, he claimed that Jesus' earthly ministry lasted approximately fifteen years and Jesus lived to be almost fifty years of age.

On the other hand, and in my opinion, the arguments for the early date are superior, both quantitatively and qualitatively. In this field of study, two types of dating evidence are presentable: 1) Internal evidence, which is contained inside a document and precedence over. . . . 2) External evidence, which is what others have said about a document, like Irenaeus. In Chapter 8, pp. 166-167, we presented a major piece of internal dating evidence in the form of four simple syllogisms demonstrating that Revelation's symbol of Babylon was, first and foremost, 1st-century Jerusalem, which was yet but soon-to-be destroyed.[14] But this Babylon was more than just 1st-century, apostate Jerusalem, for reasons we shall see shortly.[15]

But a sizeable and growing minority feels that Revelation was written prior to the Jerusalem's and the Temple's destruction in A.D. 70.

For these and many other reasons, I agree with a growing number of reputable scholars that "a date in either AD 65 or early 66 would seem most suitable." Again, in my opinion, the weight of evidence greatly favors a pre-A.D.-70 writing. Therefore, as Reformed theologian R.C. Sproul has suggested, "if Revelation was

---

[14] Others expand this 1st-century identification beyond the literal city of Jerusalem to being a community of Temple-oriented, Jerusalem-centered, Christ-denying, and unfaithful Jews throughout the Roman Empire who were persecuting Christians.
[15] But this ongoing revelation and application is beyond and outside the scope and space of this book. I have addressed it in Noē, *The Greater Jesus*, 251-289.

written before A.D. 70, then a case could be made that it describes chiefly those events leading up to Jerusalem's fall."[16]

Contextualizing Key #4—The Revelation Is Time Restricted
Like bookends at the beginning and the end, direct time statements in the first and last chapters using plain, simple, literal terms establish the immediate historical context for the soon and now past-fulfillment of the whole prophecy of the Book of Revelation. They are:

- "what must soon [shortly] take place" (Rev. 1:1; 22:6 [*KJV*]).
- "Blessed is the one who reads the words of this prophecy . . . who hear it and take to heart [obey] what is written in it" (Rev. 1:3; 22:7 [*KJV*])
- "the time is near [at hand]" (Rev. 1:3; 22:10 [*KJV*]).
- "Do not seal up the words of the prophecy of this book" (Rev. 22:10). As we have seen, Daniel was told to "close up and seal the words" of his book "until the time of the end" (Dan. 12:4). In Revelation, that time was now "near" or "at hand."
- "Behold, I am coming soon [quickly]!" (Rev. 22:7, 12 [*KJV*]).
- "Yes, I am coming soon [quickly]." (Rev 22:20 [*KJV*]).

Thus, to look for a distant, future fulfillment two thousand years removed from its writing for all or even part of this prophecy, as most modern-day prophecy teachers still do, requires that one either ignore or try to explain away this book's plainest teaching and to engage in a pretext. This common trait demands a manipulation and bifurcation of the text and ensures misconception and misunderstanding. But the reader, teacher, or interpreter who does not hold fast to the Revelation's own contextual parameters at both its start and finish, which encompass the *whole* its prophecy, will infallibly lose himself in a labyrinth of conjecture and wild pretext speculations—as each of the three futurist end-time views have so done.

Consequently, dispensational premillennialists divide Revelation's prophecy between the past and the future between chapters 3 and 4. Amillennialists and postmillennialist do this in chapter 20. But

---

[16] Sproul, *The Last Days According to Jesus*, 132.

bifurcation anywhere is arbitrary and a violation of the time-sensitive parameters this Book of Revelation places upon itself. Its fulfillment unity is self-imposed and must be honored. The *whole* of this prophecy stands together.

Other sidestepping tactics utilized to support deferment views of portions of this prophecy declare and take these above simple words and time-restricting phrases figuratively in order to undermine their literal and intended meaning. Or, they just ignore them entirely and jump straight into fancy and fearful futuristic charts and timelines. Second Peter 3:8 is frequently cited as a dismissal justification: "But do not forget this one thing, dear friends: With the Lord a day is like a thousand years, and a thousand years are like a day." It is then concluded that we can "get around" or dismiss not only Revelation's time statements but all New Testament time statements with the same and flawed human logic that God is not bound by time the same as are we humans, and/or that He measures time differently than we do. Once again, these deceptive tactics come from those who know that God created time—the sun, moon, and rotation of the earth—"to serve as signs to mark seasons and days and years" (Gen. 1:14) and should know that God speaks to us in time language we can understand.

This common trait demands a manipulation and bifurcation of the text and ensures misconception and misunderstanding.

These scriptural abuses perpetrated upon time statements are then further abused with the insistence that time must be seen from God's perspective—i.e., "soon" in God's sight, is *not* "soon" from our human viewpoint. The bottom-line result is, these time statements are relativized, elasticized, or otherwise distorted and made obscure in meaning, dismissed, and ignored.

Practically speaking, however, not one scripture supports this dismissive treatment. Quite to the contrary, the Book of Revelation was clearly written to man "to show his servants what must soon take place" (Rev. 1:1). What could be more plain, simple, and natural than that? Sadly, many gullible Christians are coerced by their tradition and its intimidating leadership to change, ignore, or deny what the Bible clearly says. Others explain that these words really refer to the speed with which these events will be carried out once they begin—i.e., speedily. Or these words merely convey certainty that someday all these things are certain to happen, or that those prophetic events are always viewed as being near. In other words, the meaning of biblical time statements is rendered meaningless. Hence, the time of fulfillment is stretched out like a rubber band far into the future, and fulfillment pretexts abound.

Once again, these sidestepping devices and tactics are classic examples of the non-literal tinkering, tampering, or demolishing that has been perpetuated upon the time texts in Revelation (and other similar time texts in both the Old and New Testaments) by those driven to find a meaning in keeping with their delayed, yet-to-be fulfilled interpretations. This is the type of manipulations that has produced the incredible amount of conflict, anxiety, and confusion in the field of eschatology. It's the reason Revelation's prophecy only becomes difficult, if not impossible to understand, when it is lifted out of its self-declared, 1st-century time context and bifurcated like the solution of splitting the baby in half (see 1 Ki. 3:16-28).

But conspicuously, one fact nearly all nearness-evading and word-manipulating theorists rightly recognize is Revelation's original recipients did not understand these simple, plain, and time-restrictive words and phrases in the way these theorists are proposing. They were expecting the occurrence and fulfillment of all these things within their lifetime. And who can blame them?

Postmillennialist and partial preterist DeMar is right on target about these nearness-avoidance tactics when he appropriately quips, "this is surprising since this line of argument is most often put forth by those who insist on a literal interpretation of Scripture."[17] He further condemns this abusive treatment of the time statements because it "calls into question the reliability of the Bible and makes nonsense of clear statements of Scripture."[18]

On the other hand, if the Book of Revelation was given and written prior to the destruction of Jerusalem in A.D. 70, these time statements make perfect sense and a distant fulfillment untenable. This is the time

---

[17] DeMar, *Last Days Madness*, 214.
[18] Ibid., 215.

context Revelation places upon itself. Who are we to ignore it, deny it, or remove it?

What is needed, as elsewhere, is a careful, honest, and more disciplined methodology, one that preserves the integrity and harmony of the *whole* of the prophecy and its associated events. Arbitrary divisions and specialized or alternative meanings of common and ordinarily used words have no part in this process. The simplest and most natural solution is to recognize that the *whole* of the prophecy was written, first and foremost, to 1st-century Christians. Its book-ending and full-content-bracketing time statements must be taken, literally and plainly, and honored seriously. They make perfect sense and bear witness to this book's unity and original audience relevancy.

However, if this relevancy was not true, ask yourself this pertinent question. Why weren't this book's original recipients ever informed of this fact? (Remember Amos 3:7?) This non-mentioned omission, if true, would give the Book of Revelation the character of deception rather than of revelation. I think not. But what do you now think?

In sum, the original recipients were plainly told the time was "at hand" and this Jewish apocalypse would "soon take place." The practical reality is this. Only the preterist view, as one of its major strengths, recognizes and honors these contextualizing parameters for the *whole*-prophecy and that this book places upon itself.

Contextualizing Key #5—The Revelation Is Fulfilled
Under his attribute of "divine perfection," all that God has created He created in perfect harmony with literal, exact, chronological, and sequential fulfillment—no gaps, no gimmicks, and no delays. Therefore, in perfect harmony with Daniel's "time of the end" and Jesus' "this generation," the Book of Revelation is, first and foremost, a fourth version of Jesus' longest and most dramatic prophecy, the Olivet Discourse.

We simply must accept the Revelation on its own terms as a prophecy for its own time and original audience. Its fulfillment does not await an unscriptural "end of the world" or "end of time," as is commonly held. It fully and accurately predicted and described, using signs and symbols, the events leading up to and including the fall of Jerusalem in a coming day of the Lord in judgment and the completion of the change of covenants (not cosmos), circa A.D. 70.

All these events and more occurred "soon" and "shortly"—i.e., within two to seven years, depending upon the exact date of this book's writing. Any interpretation of its fulfillment or partial fulfillment that lies beyond the time frame of its original hearers and readers is, at best, suspect. And, once again, just like Jesus' birth, life, death, resurrection, and ascension, Revelation's fulfillment was accomplished via a series of local events with universal applications, implications, and significance. Locally is just how God chose to fulfill it and his plan of redemption. These events ended, forever, the Old Covenant system and age of biblical Judaism, which had previously been rendered "obsolete" (see Heb. 8:13; 9:10).

Reluctantly, the late, renowned, and futuristic theologian George Eldon Ladd was forced to concede that "there must be an element of truth in this approach for surely the Revelation was intended to speak to its own generation."[19] Mistakenly, however, he and many others feel that if this prophecy was totally fulfilled, a la the preterist view, then this makes it meaningless to modern-day Christians. This impression could not be farther from the truth.

As we shall see in our next contextualizing key, Revelation's past fulfillment does not exhaust its meaning, relevance, and symbolism. In fact, past fulfillment makes this prophecy *more meaningful and relevant* beyond its fulfillment circa A.D. 70. Why is this so, you may ask? It's because Revelation itself shows us that it is more than a tract for its own time—much more! This unique aspect brings us to one of the major weakness of the preterist view and a contextualizing key that many preterists have not recognized or honored.

Key #6—Revelation Is Also Timeless and Universal in Its Relevance

In the middle of the unfolding apocalyptic drama of the breaking of the seven seals, the sounding of seven trumpets, and the pouring out of seven vials (bowls), John is given a drastic instruction. Sadly, most commentators downplay it. In Revelation 10:9, the angel instructs John to *eat the scroll*. This is the same sealed scroll previously handed to the

---

[19] Ladd, *A Theology of the New Testament*, 672.

lamb to open in Revelation chapter 5.[20] Why was John told to perform such a graphic and grotesque act—have you eaten any good books lately? Here's what the angel told him:

> So I went to the angel and asked him to give me the little scroll. He said to me, "Take it and eat it. It will turn your stomach sour, but in your mouth it will be as sweet as honey." I took the little scroll from the angel's hand and ate it. It tasted as sweet as honey in my mouth, but when I had eaten it, my stomach turned sour. Then I was told, "You must prophesy again about many peoples, nations, languages and kings." (Rev. 10:8-11)

Let's recall that this instruction is contained in a book filled with signs and symbols. So it is not unreasonable to assume that John's eating of the scroll was also a sign and symbol of something far more literal and significant. Here's my explanation. See if you agree.

The physical act of eating, ingesting, and digesting something always transforms the substance of what has been eaten. So I suggest that by this imagery the whole of the prophecy of the Book of Revelation, which is contained in that little scroll, is transformed from its fulfillment context into greater applications.

Please note that immediately after John ate the little scroll, he was commanded to regurgitate it, if you will. That's why the angel told him, "You must prophesy again about many peoples, nations, languages, and kings" (Rev. 10:11). This list lays out an entirely different audience from the book's original recipients—i.e., "the seven churches in the province of Asia" (Rev. 1:4, 11, 20). When you couple the angel's "prophesy again" statement with his later instructions to John, "do not seal up the words of the prophecy of this book, because the time is at hand" (Rev. 22:10), this provides the exegetical basis for why I further suggest that the relevance of Revelation's prophecy was not exhausted in its circa A.D. 70 fulfillment. Rather, its relevancy was broadened from its

---

[20] So argues Ian Boxall, *The Revelation of St. John* (Peabody, MA.: Hendrickson Publishers, 2006), 25; Grant R. Osborn, *Revelation* (Grand Rapids, MI.: Baker Academic, 2002), 401; and many others. For other scriptures about eating scrolls and other scrolls, see: Ezek. 2:8-3:7; Zech. 5:1-4; Isa. 29:11-18; Dan. 12:4.

primary fulfillment audience and focus to a different, timeless, and universalized audience and focus.

Let's next take a look at six additional insights supporting my suggested universal application and timeless relevance of this *whole* prophecy beyond its circa A.D. 70 fulfillment. Theologians call this extension of relevancy a *sensus plenior*—i.e. "a fuller sense .... the possibility of more significance to . . . [a] passage than was consciously apparent to the original author . . . ."[21]

Why was John told to perform such a graphic and grotesque act—have you eaten any good books lately?

First and foremost, we cannot overemphasize that the *whole* of this prophecy from first to last was written to encourage its original audience. They were under severe persecution and in need of relief. This fulfillment is Revelation's primary focus. The *whole* of it, therefore, is rooted, time-restricted, and fulfilled in one, immediate, specific, and real coming of Jesus Christ in judgment and consummation circa A.D. 70. As Russell rightly recognizes, "the coming of the Lord is its grand theme."[22] That contemporary and historical setting was Revelation's one and only fulfillment. And it "must play a controlling role"[23] as we explore a *sensus plenior*.

Secondly, John's prophesying "again about many peoples, nations, languages and kings" (Rev 10:9-11), is clearly a different audience of recipients and wider application of this prophecy than John's original area and audience of the seven churches (Rev 1:4, 11, 20). Traditionally, however, commentators have tried to minimize the meaning of this dramatic symbolism of John's eating the scroll and prophesying again. Employing various but flawed devices, they contend that it only meant a personal application for John. In my opinion, this sidestepping tactic is so ridiculous that I'm not going to take up space in this book with

---

[21] Virkler, *Hermeneutics*, 1981) 25.
[22] Russell, *The Parousia*, 531.
[23] Klein, Blomberg, and Hubbard, Jr., *Introduction to Biblical Interpretation*, 125.

presenting their arguments. For those of you interested in these arguments, please see my *JETS* article.

Thirdly, similar expressions are found five other times in Revelation 5:9; 7:9; 13:7; 14:6; and 17:15 (also see Rev. 22:9 and Dan. 4:1; 7:14). In Revelation 5:9, for instance, we read: "And they sang a new song; 'You [Jesus] are worthy to take the scroll and to open its seals, because you were slain, and with your blood you purchased men [and women] for God from every tribe and language and people and nation." This includes you and me, does it not? If you agree, then this expression universalizes the application of Jesus' sacrifice.

Fourthly, if this expression's use in Revelation 10:11 is consistent with this book's other five uses, and we employ the interpretative principle of letting "Scripture interpret Scripture," then it must carry the same universalized and timeless meaning here as well. Thus, this widening of application is the textual rational for reapplying the relevancy of the *whole* prophecy beyond its circa A.D. 70 fulfillment. As a result, the words of this climactic prophecy now refer and pertain to all peoples and nations throughout the world from that time on and forever. Where am I wrong on this?

We must also specially note that in Revelation 10:11, "kings" replaced "tribes' as the fourth element in the list. In Revelation 1:6 and 5:10, believers are called "kings." If this correspondence is correct, then the Apocalypse is concerned with the entirety of humankind from both a corporate and an individual sense. This exegetical evidence is why I suggest to you that the universal relevance and timeless application of Revelation's *whole* prophecy goes beyond its fulfillment and is the most natural way to understand a consistent use of this multi-used terminology.

Fifthly, Revelation's relevance—its realities, blessings, judgments, principles, and portrayals, which cannot be limited to a one-time, historic, and static eschatological fulfillment for its own day (which it was), nor postponed to someday still out in the future—serves in a typological and controlling manner.

Thus, Revelation's fulfillment becomes a type for repeating patterns of Christ's ongoing involvement and activity in history and in individual lives. In other words, John's prophecy now transcends its fulfillment in time and context and into new historical and personal applications, worldwide. Post A.D. 70, this prophecy is not only timeless, but also multifaceted.

This ongoing relevancy and these timeless and universal applications are part of the Revelation's uniqueness. This ongoing aspect further differentiates it from only being consider a fourth version of Jesus' Olivet Discourse (Matthew 24, Mark 13, and Luke 21, which cover the same fulfillment timeframe and events). Nevertheless, Revelation's ongoing aspects resist predictability because John's prophesying "again" was general and not time-sensitive or place-specific.

Hence, the Revelation is still an open book and meant to be forever kept open. From the time of its writing forward, Revelation's exciting message proclaims the ongoing involvement of Jesus Christ in the struggles of the spirit realm and the physical/material realm for all ages and peoples. Such a reformed and widened application may help us better understand the rise and fall of empires, the history of nations, the lives of people, and the comings and goings of groups, institutions, and other corporate bodies. Indeed, they are controlled by God through Jesus, the contemporary Christ (also see Dan. 2:21).

Of course, there is more to be considered. But this textual understanding of Revelation's ongoing relevance and timeless and universal applications secures its meaningfulness from the time of its fulfillment through all periods of Church and world history, does it not?

The Revelation also warns that "If anyone adds anything to them, God will add to him the plagues described in this book. And if anyone takes away from this book of prophecy, God will take away from him his share in the tree of life and in the holy city, which are described in this book" (Rev. 22:18-19).

This ongoing relevancy and timeless, universal applications are part of the Revelation's uniqueness.

For this reason, I urge you to constantly make sure that no message you read, hear, believe, or present adds to or takes away from the content and the relevancy of this Apocalypse. These two dire warnings and consequences are just as relevant for us today as they were for the Revelation's original audience. If not, they are toothless.

In my opinion, any modern-day interpretation and/or teacher of this prophecy who relegates the relevance of all or any portion solely to the past or mostly to the future is at risk of violating these warnings and possibly suffering their consequences. I may have personally known of one such pastor who died mysteriously after doing just this.[24]

Taking communion in an "unworthy manner" also contains another similar warning, which might involve the same plagues mentioned in the Book of Revelation (see 1 Cor. 11:27-30). Surely, there is something to these warnings and to the ongoing relevancy of all of Revelation's prophecy. After all, this ongoing relevancy does perfectly correspond with God's redemptive grace and purpose. While totally local in fulfillment, all aspects are universal and timeless in goal, scope, and application, are they not? Seen in this manner, the Revelation is truly a prophecy of "the eternal gospel to proclaim to those who live on the earth – to every nation, tribe, language and people" (Rev. 14:6).

Sixthly, there is no suggestion of a termination of these applications. The popular terminology of a "final" or "last judgment," a "final blessing," a "final coming," a "final day of the Lord," or a "final Antichrist" is non-scriptural language and unscriptural concepts. Therefore, in the prophecy of the Book of Revelation, we moderns have real, ongoing blessings, warnings, comings, judgments, and interactions with Christ to be personally involved and concerned about (Rev. 1:3; 22:7, 14-19).

Please make no mistake; this realization of the Revelation's ongoing relevancy is not a lesser reality or a second-rate option. In comparison with solely past, mostly future, or partly future fulfillment views, it is more significant and meaningful than any single eschatological view has yet to present. Through "the revelation of Jesus Christ" (Rev. 1:1), God is equipping believers of all generations with an understanding of how the world of the spirit operates and interacts with the physical/material realm. This revelation is the highest form of knowledge and wisdom. It is also just as pertinent today as it was in the past and will be in the future.

Thus, nowadays, the entire vision of the Revelation is past, present, and future and the timeless unveiling of Jesus Christ as He now is. It is not a timetable of yet-future events. To see and comprehend both its

---

[24] See Noē, *The Greater Jesus*, 75-76.

fulfillment and ongoing relevance is to understand the Revelation as it was intended and to qualify to receive one of its blessings. Not to realize this significance is to miss its richest meaning, for in this same but greater Jesus Christ "are hidden all the treasures of wisdom and knowledge" (Col. 2:3).

In my opinion, this revitalized understanding should create a greater sense of responsibility, a greater motivation for obedience, and a greater desire to worship than the traditional deferment views, past or future. God through Jesus, the contemporary Christ, continues to act in history and in the lives of his saints in an apocalyptically revealed manner.

Key #7—Let the Bible Interpret Itself

We don't need a dictionary, an encyclopedia, tomorrow's newspaper, "googling," or "the-Lord-told-me-so" claims to properly interpret and understand Bible prophecy. We simply must let the Bible interpret itself and study it diligently enough to know what it says.

True prophetic revelation is always anchored solidly in Scripture. As we study the Book of Revelation in poverty of spirit, the Holy Spirit and "the spirit of prophecy" (Rev. 19:10) will reveal to us the spirit-realm/physical-realm realities it contains. Sometimes these realities are straightforward. Revelation's "at hand" time-restrictive theme, for example and which spans the entire prophecy, is stated in simple terms. These terms cannot be tortured to mean nineteen centuries away and counting.

In other instances, Revelation contains direct statements made in the context that interpret many of the strange symbols of the Revelation. Consider these simple explanations:

- "The seven stars are the angels [literally, messengers] of the seven churches, and the seven lampstands are the seven churches" (Rev. 1:20).
- "Each one [of the four living creatures] had a harp and they were holding golden bowls of incense, which are the prayers of the saints" (Rev. 5:8).

- "The great dragon was hurled down—that ancient serpent called the devil, or Satan, who leads the whole world astray. He was hurled to earth, and his angels with him" (Rev. 12:9).

If a symbol is not explained in its context, you can be sure it refers to something that is explained elsewhere in Scripture.

Summing Up Revelation

With these above seven contextualizing keys for the Book of Revelation firmly in hand and mind, you will be well-grounded to reread and re-explore the whole prophecy anew.

Key #1—Purpose and Overarching Theme.

Key #2—Uses Figurative Language and Symbols to Reveal Spiritual/Physical Events and Realities.

Key #3—Most Likely Written Prior to Jerusalem's Destruction in A.D. 70.

Key #4—Is Time Restricted.

Key #5—Is Fulfilled.

Key #6—Is Also Timeless and Universal in Its Relevance.

Key #7—Let the Bible Interpret Itself

Truly, truly, the Book of Revelation explains itself. By honoring and following these seven keys you can be assured you are properly contextualizing the *whole* of this prophecy.

But before we move on to our next chapter, let's address one more point. At the very end of the Revelation, Jesus issues a very personal invitation. "Come!" and "take the free gift of the water of life" (Rev. 22:17). Most Christians have been told and believe that this free gift of the water of life is available and accessible in their lives, here and now. But notice that this water of life is located in the New Jerusalem, the central city of the new heaven and new earth. It was "at hand" and present back, then and there, as part of everything in the Revelation that was to "soon/shortly take place." It is present, here and now, and it will continue to be present in the future. Why so? It's because the time and nature of its prophetic fulfillment was covenantal, not cosmic.

Also, this invitation to partake comes from the unveiled Jesus Who proclaims Himself to be "the Alpha and Omega, the First and the Last, the Beginning and the End" (Rev. 1:8; 22:13). The ancient Greeks used the idiom *alpha to omega* to express completeness. The Hebrews expressed completeness as *from aleph to tau*, or *the first to the last*. These parallel our expression *from A to Z*, meaning everything or all. Just as we do not mean to drop all that represent the letters between *A* and *Z*, Jesus is not implying that He was active at the beginning and will someday show up and be active at the end, but is inactive in between. He is both complete (needing nothing) and eternally present. He has been, He is now, and He always will be involved with humanity.

This is the final reality of God's plan of redemption. The Book of Revelation conveys it via powerful signs and symbols. It's the wonderful truth of Who Jesus is today and what He is literally doing. Yes, this Jesus, the contemporary Christ, is much greater and more awesome than most of us have been led to believe.

Truly, truly, the Book of Revelation explains itself. By honoring and following these seven keys you can be assured you are properly contextualizing the *whole* of this prophecy.

Throughout the centuries, and in spite of flawed interpretations, many Christians have drawn strength, faith, and courage from Revelation's prophecy as a message and vision that was within reach for their times. To limit its symbolic imagery to speculation about single historical events that have either already occurred or are yet to occur someday out in the future is to rob this vital book of its pertinent reality and practical guidance for our daily lives.

Remember and use this chapter's seven contextualizing keys to unlock the mysteries of this last book of the Bible and unravel the unveiling of Jesus contained therein.[25] And if you ever again happen to sit under someone's teaching of this book who does not contextualize the *whole* of this prophecy before wading into it and tries to tell you what they think some of this prophecy means, I suggest you advise them of the importance of contextualizing and warn them of the consequences of adding to or subtracting from it. If your advice goes unheeded, which is likely, sad to say, I suggest you get up and leave or change the channel. Amen?

With these seven contextualizing keys firmly in mind, let's next look at many more, countless, and different type of comings of Jesus, the contemporary Christ, that this prophecy also promises—some of which you do not want to happen to you.

---

[25] For more, check out Noē, *The Greater Jesus* on Amazon.com. (yes, this is a shameless commercial).

Chapter 15
More Countless Comings

To further unshackle Christianity from its two-advent paradigm, tradition of men, and delimiting mindset and to help us better appreciate and present our faith, it is absolutely essential that we re-explore many more countless comings promised within the pages of the Bible's Book of Revelation. And given the textual justification for the ongoing, universal, and timeless applications of Revelation's *whole* prophecy covered in our last chapter, these comings certainly take on more relevance and significance for our here and now. Let's see if you agree or not.

Revelation's Many Comings of Jesus

Revelation 1:7: "Look, he is coming [*erchomai*] with the clouds, and every eye will see him, even those who pierced him; and all the peoples of the earth will mourn because of him. So shall it be! Amen."

The declaration, "Look, he is coming" or "cometh" [*KJV – King James Version*], is explicitly descriptive and revealing. In the original Greek language the verb "is coming" is a present deponent indicative. Since Greek is a more elaborate language than English, this verb tense is used to convey either an in-process action or a present and continuous action. In other words, it expresses Jesus as either in the process of getting ready to come at a specific and future time and place and/or many ongoing, present, and future comings—i.e., "Look, he is coming, and coming, and coming, again, and again, and again!" Moreover, and twice more in the Revelation's last chapter, Jesus uses this same verb form and sense of meaning: "Behold, I am coming soon! [suddenly or quickly]" (Rev. 22:7, 12).[1] In light of all that's promised herein and revealed elsewhere, both meanings are supportable, scripturally and historically—an in process of coming and/or a continuous activity of coming.

And since we have seen that the future comings of Jesus cannot be limited to a single historical event close to or far removed from Revelation's writing, nor can his comings (plural) be confined to a single geographic location or restricted to a single time frame, then what are we to do with the two phrases "every eye will see" and "all peoples of the earth will mourn"? What do they fully mean?

Literally, these phrases mean exactly what they say. But they have been differently interpreted and understood for centuries as a single, worldwide coming visible only to those people living on planet Earth at that moment. Especially singled out, however, are the 1st-century, Roman guards who physically "pierced" Jesus during his crucifixion in A.D. 30 (John 19:34-37; Psa. 22:16). Others must also be included in this piercing: those who "pierced" Him by their participation in his sentencing and the Jews who accused Him in the first place (Matt. 27:25; Acts 2:36). Therefore, the full realization of this promised and universal coming for "every eye" and "all peoples of the earth," must have started in the 1st century and continues from there.

"Look, he is coming, and coming, and coming, again, and again, and again!"

Let us also note that "every eye" is comparable with "every knee" bowing "in heaven and on earth and under the earth" and "every tongue" confessing (Phil. 2:10-11). Somehow in some way, at some time or times, in life, in death, or after death "every eye" of every person who has ever lived, lives now, or will live, literally sees Jesus, at least once. But this verse does not stipulate that everyone has to see Him at the same time, in the same manner, at the same place, or with the same results.

---

[1] For more on these two verses, see: Noē, *The Greater Jesus*, 52.

Verse 1:8: "'I am the Alpha and the Omega,' says the Lord God, 'who is, and who was, and who is to come [*erchomai*], the Almighty.'"

Just as God the Father comes [notice the similarity with verse 4] so comes Jesus, the contemporary Christ. Perhaps, the "is" is the present coming of Jesus to John on the Isle of Patmos; the "was" are his many past comings; and the "is to come" are his many and countless future comings. Please read on.

Revelation 2 & 3: The focus of these two chapters is obviously not on a Christ who is away and waiting to come back. Rather, they are focused on Christ Who is in the midst of these churches (Rev. 1:13, 20) and comes.

Interestingly, in these two chapters we find a collection of different types of comings of Christ. First, of course, they apply to Revelation's seven churches and their individual members. But because of Revelation's ongoing, timeless, and universalized relevance (Contextualizing Key #6 in our last chapter), these comings are still relevant and happening today around the world. Some of them you would not want to have happen to you. That's why after each message Jesus said to the individual in each of the seven churches, and to us today as well, "He who has an ear, let him hear what the Spirit says to the churches" (note the plural – "churches"). Also, let's make note that these churches were located throughout Asia Minor (the modern-day country of Turkey). They were not in Jerusalem. So, these comings must not be confused with Jesus' coming "on the clouds" in age-ending judgment of that city and its Temple. Nor are these promised but conditional comings directed toward the world at-large or the ungodly. They are addressed to believers!

Verse 2:5: "Remember the height from which you have fallen! Repent and do the things you did at first. If you do not repent, I will come [*erchomai*] to you and remove your lampstand from its place." Here Jesus threatened this special coming/comings in judgment to this particular church in Ephesus and to the individuals in it (the "he" who has an ear) and, again, to all of the seven churches (plural) (Rev. 2:7).

Verse 2:16: "Repent therefore! Otherwise, I will soon come [*erchomai*] to you and will fight against them with the sword of my mouth." It's another promised and conditional coming/comings of Jesus to that church, persons, and to the other six churches and people therein.

Verse 2:25-26: "Only hold on to what you have until I come [*heko*]. To him who overcomes and does my will to the end, I will give authority over the nations." An individual coming(s) of reward for faithfulness. (Also Rev. 22:12).

Verse 3:3: "Remember, therefore, what you have received and heard; obey it, and repent. But if you do not wake up, I will come [*heko*] like a thief, and you will not know at what time I will come to you." It's another unexpected coming(s) in judgment and with consequences best to avoid.

Verse 3:11: "I am coming [*erchomai*] soon. Hold on to what you have, so that no one will take your crown." Crowns in Scripture are only given to individuals. It's another imminent coming(s) of reward for perseverance.

Verse 3:20: "Here I am! I stand at the door and knock. If anyone hears my voice and opens the door, I will go in [*eiserchomai*] and eat with him, and he with me." What a wonderful promise of his coming(s). This coming is not, however, a salvation promise because it is being made to those who are already believers.

In sum, these descriptions in Revelation 2 and 3 of Jesus' corporate and individual comings in judgment, reward, or the continuance or withdrawal of his presence are not the subject of a single and universal event. They are a pertinent and conditional reality in the lives of his saints at that time and onward.

Revelation 19 – Rider on the White Horse

Another way we see Jesus coming in the Apocalypse is as an awesome, conquering warrior wearing many crowns and riding on a white horse. Once again, we see Him with his eyes blazing like fire and a sharp sword is coming out of his mouth. But there is more:

I saw heaven standing open and there before me was a white horse, whose rider is called Faithful and True. With justice he judges and makes war. His eyes are like blazing fire, and on this head are many crowns. He has a name written on him that no one but he himself knows. He is dressed in a robe dipped in blood, and his name is the Word of God. The armies of heaven were following him, riding on white horses and dressed in fine linen, white and clean. Out of his mouth comes a sharp sword with which to strike down the nations. "He will rule them with an iron scepter" [from Psa. 2:9]. *He treads the winepress of the fury of the wrath of God Almighty. On his robe and on his thigh he has this name written:*
    KING OF KINGS AND LORD OF LORDS

Make no mistake; this is the revelation of a crowned Jesus Christ coming in judgment. He is riding atop a white horse of war and coming to do battle on the earth. The symbol of a white horse has been used before in this prophetic book to represent a conqueror (Rev. 6:12). But no one else in history has ever been, or will ever be, like this Rider on the white horse. The names and descriptions make it clear: "Faithful and true" witness (Jer. 42:5; Rev. 1:5; 3:14) and "Word of God" (John 1:1-5). There can be no doubt that this is Jesus Christ the Conqueror in all his spirit-realm reality and apocalyptic glory.

Another way we see Jesus coming . . . is as an awesome, conquering warrior wearing many crowns and riding on a white horse.

And yet He is not alone. He leads the armies of heaven against the nations. These armies are riding white horses as well and are wearing "fine linen white and clean." But heaven does not contain stables or house horses. Therefore, these white horses are symbolic of God's victorious armies conquering via the word of God. Some feel these armies are comprised of angels. Others believe they are earthly saints because of the fine linen they are wearing. Previously, in Revelation we are told that "the bride has made herself ready. Fine linen bright and clean, was given her to wear," which is symbolic of "the righteous acts of the saints" (Rev. 19:7-8).

Let's also recall that early in his earthly ministry Jesus told his disciples that God the Father "has entrusted all judgment to the Son" and "has given him authority to judge" (John 5:22, 27). This is why "on his robe and on his thigh he has this name written: KING OF KINGS AND LORD OF LORDS" (Rev. 19:16). We can understand why He might have a monogram on his robe. But why would the same name be engraved on his thigh? One possibility is that, in the thick of 1st-century battle foot soldiers might confuse the identity of a rider on a horse. Hence, the name on his thigh would be at eye level and easily recognizable.

Once again, we are not told the meaning of the sword coming out of Jesus' mouth and his eyes blazing like fire (see again Rev. 1:14-16). We do know, however, from other scriptures that "the sword of the spirit" is symbolic of "the word of God" (see Eph. 6:17), which "is living and active. Sharper than any double-edged sword, it penetrates even to dividing soul and spirit, joints and marrow; it judges the thoughts and attitudes of the heart." (Heb. 4:12). Hence, this is no ordinary sword. It also kills "the flesh of kings, generals, and mighty men, of horses and their riders, and the flesh of all people, free and slave, small and great" (Rev. 19:18, 21.)

Likewise, his blazing eyes are not ordinary eyes for "nothing in all creation is hidden from God's sight. Everything is uncovered and laid bare before the eyes of him to whom we must give account" (Heb. 4:13).

Bottom line, and once again, Jesus is being revealed as both God and man. And once again, this symbolic representation of Who He now is, is more powerful than a mere literal interpretation. Nor is this Jesus an easy-going, meek-and-mild Jesus everyone wants to buddy up to, talk with, or love. This Jesus is a far different Jesus from his portrayals in the Gospels. Here, He's the conquering Son of God Who sovereignly rules the world from behind the scenes in the spirit realm.

Interestingly, Jesus' first followers were accused of turning the world of their day "upside down" as they were doing battle and "defying Caesar's decrees, saying that there is another king, one called Jesus" (Acts 17:6-7). Perhaps, their vision of Jesus was in stark contrast to our popular, modern-day image of Jesus as painted by Warner Sallman in 1941, or the prevalent, modern-day notion that Jesus is not yet King.

Yes, I'm sorry to report that Tim LaHaye, the co-author and creator of the Left Behind series, insists Jesus has not ridden this horse yet. But some day very soon He will. In LaHaye's own words, "When Jesus comes, He is going to be 'King of kings and Lord of lords . . . to say Christ is ruler now is a statement that reaches almost blasphemous proportions."[2] Even the much-revered Billy Graham doesn't believe Jesus is ruling yet. He writes that "someday wars will cease and we'll all live in harmony and peace. But unfortunately, we never will until God's Messiah comes to establish his rule over all the earth."[3]

To the contrary, the book of Revelation and many other scriptures refute LaHaye's and Graham's futuristic-deferment contention. In its most uncontested portion, John writes that Jesus Christ "*is* [not someday will be] the faithful witness, the firstborn from the dead, and the *ruler of the kings of the earth*" (Rev. 1:5; also see: 1 Tim. 6:15; Rom. 8:34; Heb. 2:9; 10:13; Matt. 28:18; 1 Cor. 15:25; and many more).

Moreover, if Jesus was not then and is not now ruler and King, as LaHaye and Graham would have their rapture-ready followers believe, what is the meaning of: Jesus sitting at the right hand of God (Rom. 8:34; Eph. 1:20; Col. 3:1; Heb. 1:13; 8:1; 12:2l; Acts 2:33-36; Psa. 110), Who is seated on his heavenly throne (Psa. 2:4; 11:4; 22:28; 47:2, 8; 103:19; Prov. 8:13; Isa. 66:1)? And is Jesus "now crowned with glory and honor" (Heb. 2:9)? Or is Jesus merely sitting around passively up in heaven waiting to reign someday? And what about the meaning of these verses:

- Peter's declaration that Jesus is sitting there "at God's right hand – with angels, authorities and powers in submission to him" (1 Pet. 3:22)?
- Jesus' Great Commission and past-tense statement that "all authority in heaven and on earth has been given to me" (Matt. 28:18)?
- Paul's present-tense statement that "he must reign until he has put all his enemies under his feet" (1 Cor. 15:25; Heb. 10:13)?
- Jesus presently "sustaining all things by his powerful word" (Heb. 1:3)?

---

[2] LaHaye and Ice, *The End Times Controversy*, 11.
[3] Billy Graham, "My Answer," *The Indianapolis Star*, 7/23/13, E-4.

Perhaps it is LaHaye whose contention is "almost blasphemous" if not outright blasphemy! It is my opinion that both LaHaye and Graham have succumbed to "the deception of the elect" about which Jesus warned (see Matt. 24:23-26). Furthermore, anybody buying into LaHaye's "Left-Behind" theology is likewise buying into this deception of the elect.

So why don't more Christians confront this popular view? Why do we just stand by shaking our heads and letting them "rule the roost?" But what can we refute it with, you ask? How about with something of substance like divine perfection in the mathematically precise physical creation and in precise and timely fulfillment of God's plan of redemption! After all, isn't that what "contend for the faith that was once for all delivered to the saints" (Jude 3) is all about?

In contradistinction to LaHaye and Graham, theologian A.A. Hodge offers a scripturally sound conclusion on this matter in writing, "In the strictest sense we must date the actual and formal assumption of [Christ's] kingly office, in the full and visible exercise thereof, from the moment of His ascension into heaven from this earth and His session at the right hand of the Father."[4]

Perhaps it is LaHaye whose contention is "almost blasphemous" if not outright blasphemy!

Another respected theologian, Arthur F. Glasser, concurs that after Jesus completed his atoning work, ascended, and was seated at the right hand of the Father, "the reign of the risen Christ had now begun."[5]

Tragically, as we continue to see, LaHaye's contention is only the tip of the iceberg of unscriptural understandings and sidestepping tactics, devices, and attempts employed to explain away and dumb down "the revelation of Jesus Christ" and other related end-time prophecy from its intended meaning and relevance. Most appropriately, DeMar fires a shot directly into LaHaye's theology as he poignantly laments that while "a

---

[4] A.A. Hodge, *Evangelical Theology* (Edinburgh: Banner of Truth, [1980] 1976), 227.
[5] Arthur F. Glasser, *Announcing the Kingdom* (Grand Rapids, MI.: Baker Academic, 2003), 253.

majority of evangelicals believe LaHaye based on the millions of copies of Left Behind sold . . . . It's a shame that this type of nonsense is continually promoted by Christian publishers that know better..."[6]

Let's also reemphasize that Jesus' riding this white horse of war and coming in judgment was part of the *whole* of the Revelation's prophecy. It was "near," "at hand," and part of the "things that would shortly take place" (Rev. 1:1, 3; 22:6, 10). Another aspect of these happenings is the vision of Jesus in Revelation 14:14—"seated on a white cloud with a crown of gold on his head and a sharp sickle in his hand." Then John sees an angel come out of the Temple and calls to Him saying, "Take your sickle and reap, because the time to reap has come . . ." (Rev. 14:15). Given the high likelihood that the Book of Revelation was written prior to A.D. 70, there can be little doubt as to the fulfillment of this historical judgment and how it was delivered. Additionally, given Revelation's ongoing timelessness and universal relevance, Jesus likely still rides this white horse of war occasionally (Rev. 10:9-11). Would you agree?

But since we live in a day and time in which most people have been told and taught that Jesus' "second coming" has not yet happened, the burden of proof lies on those of us who proclaim past fulfillment and ongoing relevance. This is why we reviewed of some of the similar comings of a "day of the Lord" in judgment of other nations, peoples, cites, and on Israel itself in the Old Testament (see again Chapter 13, pp. 312-317).

Really a Present Reality?

Pragmatically, how can we know, that Jesus' many different types of comings are still a present and ongoing spirit-realm/physical realm reality and not some solitary event waiting to happen out in the future? Or, a la the preterist view, that they are not just a single coming that happened almost two millennia ago after which all comings of Christ ceased? In other words, is Jesus still the God Who comes in many or all the ways we have documented so far in this book (over 40) and in

---

[6] Gary DeMar, "Giving Aid and Comfort to the Enemies of the Gospel," *Biblical Worldview* (December 2006), 23.

countless more ways we have seen promised? In concluding this chapter let's re-scrutinize five scriptural perspectives and two continuing and pertinent questions that further bear on this matter of the many countless comings of Jesus.

1) Revelation's Timeless and Universal Relevance

Seriously, do you really believe that Jesus, after coming and going many times in the Old Testament, having gone to the additional trouble of lowering Himself to come down to this earth, to being born into human flesh, to getting sacrificed on a cross, and to coming and going many times after his resurrection, then leaves "Dodge" for two millennia and counting? For example, after A.D. 70, did Jesus dismount, hitch that white horse to a post up in heaven never to ride it again? And is/are the only value of his past coming(s) merely a history lesson? And if He really did come circa A.D. 70, does this rob us of our "blessed hope" (Titus 2:13)?

But if the entire prophecy of the Book of Revelation is timelessly relevant and universal in scope and application, none of these concerns has any merit. He still rides that horse and comes in many different ways—some of which you do not want to have happen to you.

2) His Continuing Presence Insures Many More Comings

"Men of Galilee, why do you stand here looking into the sky?" (Acts 1:11). It's still an appropriate question for today. What saddens and troubles me deeply is the popular idea that Jesus is off somewhere waiting to come back/return when, in fact, He never left, as He said! Equally troubling, is the preterist idea that A.D. 70 was his coming in finality, after which there are no more comings.

But surely his active and omnipresence presence with us facilitates the likelihood of the continuance of his many comings found in the Scriptures. And there may be other types of comings not so found, if for no other reason than John tells us that Jesus did many other things that were not recorded (see John 20:30; 21:25). Moreover, nothing I know of in Scripture precludes this continuance in similar fashions and for similar purposes.

3) A Character and Nature of God Issue

Conceivably, the best scriptural rationale for ongoing comings of Jesus is rooted in the revealed character and nature of God. As far back as the pre-Fall garden and throughout redemptive history, both the Father and the Son have chosen to have direct and supernatural involvement with some earthly people. As theologian, George Eldon Ladd affirms, "there is a God in heaven who visits human beings in history."[7] In another book, he adds, "this idea of 'the God who comes' is one of the central characteristics of the Old Testament teaching about God."[8]

But surely his active and omnipresence presence with us facilitate the likelihood of the continuance of his many comings found in the Scriptures.

So when this demonstrated desire of the Godhead to commune and intervene is coupled with these two other revealed aspects of God's character and nature 1) Immutability – "I the Lord do not change" (Mal. 3:6a; Heb. 13:8) and 2) Continuity – The Father and the Son always being at their work (John 5:17), don't we have a strong scriptural inference for advocating the continuance of divine comings of many different types and for many different reasons beyond Jesus' A.D. 70 coming on the clouds in judgment?[9]

Furthermore, and twice in Revelation, we are told that He is the God "who is [present], and who was [past], and is to come [future]" (Rev. 1:4, 8). No hint of termination, a deistic departure, or withdrawal of this divine attribute and activity is presented anywhere in Revelation or in the rest of Scripture. Moreover, as we saw in Chapter 11, pp. 341-342, Hebrews 13:8 definitely affirms that "Jesus Christ is the same yesterday and today and forever." Since his ascension to and glorification at the

---

[7] Ladd, *A Theology of the New Testament*, 272.
[8] Ladd, *The Presence of the Future*, 48.
[9] For non-eschatological, non-revelatory, and non-redemptive purposes. By non-revelatory I mean not to reveal more Scripture. The canon is closed. Yet God can still reveal more from his revealed Word. By non-redemptive I mean not to fulfill his plan of redemption. It is fulfilled. Yet God can and does bring people to salvation in many ways.

right hand of God the Father in A.D. 30 and his coming "on the clouds" in age-ending judgment circa A.D. 70, there have been over 12,000 literal "yesterdays." During those many yesterdays, there were many comings. Therefore, if He's still "the same . . . forever," after circa A.D. 70, this intrinsic element of the Godhead's character and nature remains steadfastly in place. Would you now agree?

4) We Need a Fuller Realization of His Presence

Some may question if Christ's many comings in and out of the spirit realm is a second-rate option to the ever-so-popular "second coming" notion. No! A thousand times, no! The spirit realm is as real as this book in your hands. In fact, it's even more real because it is eternal. And the personal and bodily presence of Jesus Himself in that spirit realm, as well as his many comings into and out of the physical realm, are precisely what I am suggesting continues to happen, occasionally and/or frequently, from his abiding and omnipresent presence with humankind all around this earth.

In my opinion, these many comings of Jesus are a past, present, and future reality, some of which we Christians should be celebrating, wanting to experience more fully, and exuberantly communicating to others. Sadly, we're not. Hence, for most Christians, who fill pews on Sundays or stay at home and snooze, Jesus' coming remains a someday and singular hope.

Like it or not, the degree to which we are or are not conscious of his abiding presence and many countless comings will have a direct bearing on the way each of us leads our individual Christian life, on our confidence and boldness to witness of Him, or our lack thereof.

Notably, a number of people in recent history have testified and/or written about having personal coming-encounters with the risen, glorified, and greater Jesus. Some were visual, some audible, some revelational, and some were all three. Some may have been illusions or wishful thinking. But for those comings that were genuine, there is plenty of scriptural precedent and support.[10]

---

[10] For more and examples, see: Noē, *The Greater Jesus*, 155-188.

5) Jesus Comes When, Where, How, and to Whom He Pleases

Please also note and understand that Jesus' comings are totally beyond human control. There is absolutely nothing we can do in our own strength to bring about one of his comings. We can't meditate or pray Him down from heaven or visualize his coming into a reality. And we cannot predict or prophesy when and if He will come. He is free to come or not come at any time and utilize whatever means He desires to commune and communicate with us human beings, and/or intervene in the course of individual lives, groups, and nations in history.

Consequently, and post-A.D.-70, Christ's many countless comings are part of his continuing rule and his post-redemptive work in all aspects of his creation as He sustains "all things by his powerful word" (Heb. 1:3; Col. 1:17). The one exception is his spiritual and inward illumination coming, which is promised and conditional (see again Chapter 12, p-276 and John 14:21, 23). But one thing we can do is to ask or invite Him to come. "Amen. Come, Lord Jesus" (Rev. 22:20b).

Like it or not, the degree to which we are or are not conscious of his abiding presence and many comings will have a direct bearing on the way each of us leads our individual Christian life, on our confidence and boldness to witness of Him , or our lack thereof.

In my opinion, the possibility that Jesus the contemporary Christ can come and visit us, or come for us, or come against us, personally and at any moment, should undergird our need to always be ready. Let's remember what Jesus told us, "You also must be ready, because the Son of Man will come at an hour when you do not expect him" (Luke 12:40). Traditionally, of course, this verse has been misunderstood, lessened, and deferred to only be referring to one still-future coming that hasn't happened for almost two-thousand years. But now we know better. The witness and testimony of Scripture is indisputable. He comes, unexpectedly and suddenly! This is true of all his comings. The reality that He might come to you or me at any moment, and in a number of different ways for different purposes, is no doubt intended by Jesus to be a most pressing motivation and powerful incentive for righteous living and bold and aggressive ministry—not only for individual Christians, but for the churches, as well. Indeed, this ongoing relevance should be more of a motivator than a one-time occurrence that hasn't taken place for almost two-thousand years. Would you agree?

It is also my opinion that the contemporary and practical realization of Christ's many, countless, and continuing comings would make a huge difference in the preaching of any pastor and in the life of any Christian. After all, who would want to miss out on his or her "day of visitation?" (1 Pet. 2:12). Or who would want to have some of the not-so-pleasant comings happen to you? So do you "long for his appearing" to you (2 Tim. 4:8)? According to Scripture, "Everyone who has this hope in him purifies himself, just as he is pure" (1 John 2:3).

The best way to prepare for this personal possibility is to never forget Christ's presence and his many, countless, and continuing comings, and to be "pure in heart, for they will see God" (Matt. 5:8). On the other hand, let's also not overlook Jesus' words to Thomas after Jesus had come and appeared to him and the others, "Blessed are those who have not seen and yet have believed" (John 20:29).

6) Is There a Final Coming after Which No More?

To answer this question, we must continue to submit ourselves to Scripture. And no scripture uses this terminology or even hints at a termination. At best, a so-called "final coming" is an assumption that's read into the Bible. The bottom line is: there is no scriptural justification for a discontinuance of the long precedence and pattern of his various many comings.

Quite to the contrary, Scripture states and the Nicene Creed affirms that his kingdom on this earth is "without end" (Isa. 9:7; Dan. 2:44; 7:14; Luke 1:33). And, as we've seen, our world and age are also without end. Then why should his comings in his kingdom (Matt. 16:28) on this earth have an end?

7) Do His Many Comings Rob Us of Our 'Blessed Hope?'

"The Blessed Hope" spoken of in Titus 2:13 is another widely misunderstood verse because it is mistranslated in most Bibles—"while we wait for the blessed hope – the glorious appearing of our great God and Savior, Jesus Christ . . ." (*NIV, KJV*). Grammatically, the correct translation (as rendered from the original Greek and in the *NAS*) is, "looking for the blessed hope and the appearing of the glory of our great God and Savior, Christ Jesus;" Did you catch the difference? The key word here is "glory." It's a noun and not an adjective. Hence, it should not be translated as the adjective "glorious" to modify the noun "appearing." This "glory" is the object that was to appear and not the visible Person.[11] Big difference!

Most notably and quite appropriately, in every instance of the appearance of "the glory of the Lord" throughout the Old Testament, major optical and/or physical manifestations were present—manna and quail dropping out of the sky, a cloud, consuming fire, thunder, a voice, the ground splitting open, a plague, etc. These were signs of Yahweh/Jehovah God's presence.[12] But never once was the Person of deity visibly seen. (See for example: Exodus 16:7, 10; 24:16, 17; 40:34, 35, and many more.[13]) Again, the noun "glory" and not the Person was what would appear as "the blessed hope" in Titus 2:13. And it did, as Jesus came "in the glory of the Father" (Matt. 16:27) circa A.D. 70, along with many optical and physical manifestations as we saw in Chapter 13, pp. 306, 324-325.

Please Don't Miss Our Main Point

Let's wrap up our discussion of Jesus' many, countless, and continuing comings—past, present, and future—this way. Our main point has not so much been *how* Jesus comes but *that* He comes, and mostly to individuals. Once again, I encourage you to break the

---

[11] According to Ron Allen, my friend, Greek consultant, and Professor of Preaching and Second Testament at Christian Theological Seminary, under certain circumstances a noun in a genitive construction can function as an adjective. But it usually functions as a noun. Therefore, the normal function of this noun in this verse is the more probable understanding of this expression.
[12] Yahweh and Jehovah are both phonetic transliterations of the four-consonant name of God in the Old Testament, YHWH, which was never pronounced by observant Jew out of deep respect.
[13] For other notable appearances of "the glory of the Lord" see: Lev. 9:6, 23; Num. 14:10, 21; 16:19, 42; 20:6; 1 Ki. 8:11; 2 Chron. 5:14; 7:1-3; Psa. 104:31; 138:5; Isa. 35:2; 40:5; 58:8; 60:1; Ezek. 1:28; 3:12, 23; 10:4, 18; 11:23; 43:5; 44:4; Hab. 2:14. Also see: Luke 2:9; 2 Cor. 3:18; 8:19; and more.

unscriptural shackles of traditional "second-coming" and "return" teachings and receive Jesus, the contemporary Christ, as He chooses to come. As I've written elsewhere: *He still comes in many wondrous ways.*[14] Jesus' many countless comings is the main point not to miss.

In our next and last chapter, before we go into a synthesis of the four end-time views, we shall tackle the last of the four chief moments/events of end-time prophecy—resurrection reality.

Our main point has not so much been *how* Jesus comes but *that* He comes, and mostly to individuals.

---

[14] See Noē, *The Greater Jesus*, 155-188.

Chapter 16

Resurrection Reality

Biblical resurrection is a complex and multi-faceted reality. Therefore, in this chapter we shall only be discussing and documenting the fulfillment and ongoing reality of the bodily resurrection of deceased believers in Christ. That means we shall not be addressing the resurrection and eternal destiny of unbelievers, which I've partially covered in another book.[1] Nor shall we explore the spiritual resurrection of alive believers, which I've covered in a different book.[2]

At My Parents' Funeral

In 2005, both of my parents passed away within ten days of each other. Therefore, within a one-month period, my brother and I eulogized them four times during two funerals in Indiana and two memorial services in Florida where they lived. Neither he nor I were going to let some pastor who never or hardly knew them give the eulogy. Moreover, we were bound and determined that these services would be a time of celebration and presentation of a strong Christian witness for the benefit of our five children, my thirteen grandchildren, our spouses, and everybody else attending.

---

[1] For these discussions see: John Noē, *Hell Yes / Hell No: What really is the extent of God's grace . . . and wrath?*
[2] For this discussion see: Noē, *The Greater Jesus*, 316-337.

Below is an excerpt from my eulogy for my father, who died first. Ten days later, I reused this same part at my mother's funeral. Two weeks later I used it again at the two joint memorial services in Florida.

> In that casket lies my dad's 85-year-old body. But he's not there in that body, anymore. Our family's solace and comfort is in knowing that he has entered heaven and is with the Lord Jesus Christ. And just as he enjoyed trading cars when he was here with us, he has now traded in that old body for a new resurrection "spiritual body," which God "gives," according to 1 Corinthians 15:35-44.
>
> For as it was also written and fulfilled more than 1,900 years ago:
>
>> "Then I heard a voice from heaven say, 'Write: Blessed are the dead who die in the Lord from now on.' 'Yes,' says the Spirit, 'they will rest from their labor, for their deeds will follow them.'" (Rev. 14:13)

Next, I presented a somewhat humorous recap of Dad's life before turning the service over to my brother for his eulogy.

The critical eschatological point in my above eulogy was Revelation 14:13's phrase, "from now on"—i.e., from back then in the 1st century. Please recall that this verse is part of the *whole* prophecy of the Book of Revelation. And that whole prophecy was fulfilled and its delivered realities made timelessly relevant and ongoingly available as we covered in Chapter 14.

But here's the rub. Christians today are told that "when we die, we are consciously and immediately in the presence of our Savior in heaven."[3] Yet Jesus proclaimed that "no one" was in heaven and his disciples could not go there (see John 3:13; 13:33, 36) until He had gone there, prepared that place, come, and "take[n] you to be with me that you also may be where I am" (John 14:3). Therefore, if these three prerequisite events of Jesus' preparing that place and this coming to receive his disciples to where He is have not yet taken place, as we also have been and still are traditionally told and taught, you cannot reach this conclusion and proclaim this realized reality that heaven is now open. Would you agree?

---

[3] Daniel R. Lockwood, "Until We Meet Again, *Christianity Today,* October 2007, 98.

Then, there is this fourth prerequisite event—the dead had to have been raised, first (1 Thess. 4:15). The Apostle Paul taught: "we who are still alive, who are left till the coming (*parousia*) of the Lord, will certainly not precede those who have fallen asleep" (1 Thess. 4:15b). So where were the dead located at that time? Their disembodied souls were in Hades, Abraham's bosom, or Sheol, that afterlife and temporary holding place of both the righteous and unrighteous. They were confined in Hades and awaiting the resurrection of the dead (see Luke 16:19-31; Matt. 12:40; 16:18; 1 Pet. 3:18-20; 4:6; Eph. 4:9; Rev. 1:18; 6:8; 20:13-14; Ezek. 26:20; 31:14, 16; 32:18-30; Job 3:13-19; Isa. 53:8-9; 24:21-22; 25:8; 28:18; Hos. 13:14; Psa. 49:15).

Once again, here's the rub. If you were to die tonight and if these four scriptural and prerequisite events have still not happened, you would not go to heaven and you would not yet be receiving your new resurrection "spiritual body." The Scriptures are that clear and plain about this most important matter. But if the dead ones have been raised and Jesus has come after finishing his preparation of heaven, you can reach this conclusion and credibly proclaim this fulfilled and ongoing reality as I did during my four eulogies for my parents.

For far too long, in my opinion, the scriptural and historically documentable truths we shall be addressing in this chapter have been ignored or covered up. As a result, multiple millions of Christians have fallen for a new and seductive teaching called "the Rapture." As we shall soon see, it's an invented human idea that directly contradicts Scripture:

1) Jesus specifically prayed against it in John 14:15, 20. In this his prayer for "all believers," He prayed that they and we would not be removed from the world, but for their and our preservation in this world.
2) Hebrews 9:27 states that it is "appointed unto men once to die, but after this judgment." At best, the so-called "Rapture" would be an exception. But I'll contend that it's an outright contradiction.

Nonetheless, multiple millions of Christians worldwide fervently want to believe this relatively new teaching that someday, real soon, and in their lifetime they will escape this Hebrews 9:27 death, be delivered from the difficulties of this life, and removed, alive and well from the literal surface of planet Earth as they are taken away from all their earthly problems and responsibilities and up into heaven. This novel view was first and possibly invented in 1788 by an American, Southern Baptist preacher, Morgan Edwards. Later, from 1830-1880s, it was further developed and popularized by a Scottish, Plymouth Brethren leader, John Nelson Darby, who made many speaking trips to America during this time period.

If you were to die tonight and if these four scriptural and prerequisite events have still not happened, you would not go to heaven . . .

Sadly, this compelling but unscriptural end-time view (based on a mistaken reading of the texts) is the predominant view in conservative, evangelical Christianity today. It is termed the dispensational premillennial view, which we presented in Chapter 3. But beliefs have consequences. In this case, they are highly negative and significant. Unfortunately, we don't have the time and space to get into these aspects of the "Rapture" business in this book.[4]

However, we shall be re-exploring several Bible passages that are used to support a so-called "rapture of the Church." As you will discover, all the scriptures used by popular "rapture" teachers were actually fulfilled by real bodily resurrections. And these all occurred within the 1st-century time frame of Jesus' "this generation" and in complete harmony with the end-time expectations of every New Testament writer (see John 16:13) and Daniel's two time prophecies covered in Chapter 10. In addition, we'll see how the biblical concept of resurrection is another eternally relevant and totally applicable reality for us today.

Most assuredly, the resurrection of the dead is one of the central truths of the Christian faith, as well as one of eschatology's four chief moments. Also, please make no mistake; resurrection reality is totally contingent and based upon Jesus' bodily resurrection in A.D. 30. Of course, his bodily resurrection is largely uncontested in conservative evangelicalism. But the *how* and *when* an individual believer participates

---

[4] For more on this topic, see: Noē, *The Greater Jesus*, 291-309, 330-337 and Noē, *Off Target*, 101-108.

in Christ's bodily resurrection has been one of the most distorted, confused, and misunderstood concepts in the Christian Church. No more!

In this chapter, we shall document the fulfilled and ongoing reality of post-mortem, bodily resurrection for believers in a clear and concise manner and under these two topical headings:

> Order and Time of Fulfillment
> The Nature of Bodily Resurrection Reality

Order and Time of Fulfillment

To set the stage, please turn to Daniel 12. Verses 2 and 13 state that the resurrection of the dead, including Daniel's own resurrection would take place at the "time of the end" (Dan. 12:4, 7). The prophet Ezekiel also deals with this same future-coming resurrection. It is termed "the Valley of Dry Bones" (Ezek. 37). Likewise, Jesus prophesied about this same resurrection event, ". . . for a time is coming when all who are in their graves will hear his voice and come out . . ." (John 5:28-29).

So given this resurrection background, what do you think the Apostle Paul meant, by inspiration, when he penned these perplexing words?

> "Brothers, we do not want you to be ignorant about those who fall asleep, or to grieve like the rest of men, who have no hope. We believe that Jesus died and rose again and so we believe that God will bring with Jesus those who have fallen asleep in him. ***According to the Lord's own word***, we tell you that we who are still alive, who are left till the coming of the Lord, will certainly not precede those who have fallen asleep. For the Lord himself will come down from heaven, with a loud command, with the voice of the archangel and with the trumpet call of God, and the dead in Christ will rise first. After that, we who are still alive and are left will be caught up with them in the clouds to meet the Lord in the air. And so we will be with the Lord forever. Therefore encourage each other with these words."
>
> (1 Thessalonians 4:13-18 – bold/italics mine)

Besides in John 5:28-29, where else did Jesus (i.e., "According to the Lord's own word") speak of this resurrection event? In his longest and more dramatic prophecy Jesus proclaimed, "And he [Jesus] will send his angels with a loud trumpet call, and they will gather his elect from the four winds, from one end of the heavens to the other" (Matt. 24:31). Three verses later, he specified that this event (and all other elements He mentioned) will take place within "this generation" (Matt. 24:34).

All of which brings us to the Apostle Paul's other major writing about this event in 1 Corinthians 15. Here he tells us more about the realization of resurrection's fulfillment and ongoing reality.

> "But Christ has indeed been raised from the dead, the firstfruits of those who have fallen asleep. For since death came through a man, the resurrection of the dead comes also through a man. For as in Adam all die, so in Christ all will be made alive. ***BUT EACH [every man] IN HIS OWN TURN [order]***: Christ, the firstfruits; then, when he comes [at his coming], those who belong to him."
>
> (1 Corinthians 15:20-23 – caps, bold, italics mine)

In this short passage, Paul assured God's people, then and there and us here and now, of our future resurrection and that it would be based upon Jesus' resurrection. He also revealed an order, or a sequencing, for resurrection occurrences. First in Paul's sequence was Jesus' resurrection. Second is the "firstfruits." Third is the rest of the dead to be raised at Christ's *parousia* coming. And fourthly, there is the "each" or "every man in his own turn/order."

The Greek word translated "turn" or "order" is *tagma*. This is the only place in the New Testament where it's used. It was a military term that means "a series or succession." The thought is of soldiers marching or of a parade in which others follow along individually. As we shall see, this ordering beautifully harmonizes with what happened historically and with all the other fulfillments we've been presenting and documenting in this book. But there is more Paul has to tell us in this second crucial passage:

"Listen, I tell you a mystery: We will not all sleep, but we will all be changed – in a flash, in the twinkling of an eye, at the last trumpet; For the trumpet will sound, the dead will be raised imperishable, and we will be changed – in a flash, in the twinkling of an eye, at the last trumpet. For the trumpet will sound, the dead will be raised imperishable, and we will be changed. For the perishable must clothe itself with the imperishable, and the mortal with immortality. When the perishable has been clothed with the imperishable, and the mortal with immortality, then the saying that is written will come true: 'Death has been swallowed up in victory.'

'Where, O death, is your victory?
Where, O death, is your sting?'

The sting of death is sin, and the power of sin is the law. But thanks be to God! He gives us the victory through Our Lord Jesus Christ. Therefore, my dear brothers, stand firm. Let nothing move you. Always give yourselves fully to the work of the Lord, because you know that your labor in the Lord is not in vain."

(1 Corinthians 15:51-58)

If it's true, however, as the "left-behind" people insist, that these inspired words of Paul have not been fulfilled for over nineteen centuries and counting, then the nonoccurrence of this event presents a highly problematic dilemma:

1) Paul's words of encouragement turned out to be a cruel misrepresentation in the lives of his original readers.
2) 1st-century believers actually ended up deceiving "each other with these words," rather than encouraging. And they died "in vain" not having received what they expected in their lifetime.
3) If Paul's Holy-Spirit-guided imminency expectations proved false (John 16:13), how can we trust him to have conveyed other aspects of the faith along to us correctly?

But in this chapter we are going to take a higher road and different approach. Let's see, therefore, if we can arrive at a better understanding, from a *Sola Scriptura* standpoint, of the order and time of fulfillment and then the nature of biblical bodily resurrection reality.

Before we wade in, I want to remind you, once again, that we are going to be exploring a scriptural and historically defensible interpretation. So please keep in mind the words of Klein, Blomberg, and Hubbard as they remind us in their book, *Introduction to Biblical Interpretation* that . . . *"The historically defensible interpretation has greatest authority.* That is, interpreters can have maximum confidence in their understanding of a text when they base that understanding on historically defensible arguments."[5]

By my referencing this quote once again, I'm not dogmatically saying that the interpretation we shall be exploring is right. But if it is not right, I am saying that John 3:13 is still in effect; and if you were to die tonight, you would *not* go to heaven . . . yet. This consequence of non-fulfillment is scripturally that clear and inescapable. That said, here are our four stages of bodily resurrection fulfillment and reality.

Four Stages

> **Stage 1.** Jesus' Resurrection—the first physical evidence.
> **Stage 2.** Resurrection of Many (not all) Old Testament Saints from Their Graves—the second physical evidence.
> **Stage 3.** The Harvest—Resurrection Day for the Rest of the Dead—the third physical evidence.
> **Stage 4.** The Ongoing Reality.

STAGE 1. Jesus' Resurrection—the first physical evidence.
The bodily resurrection of Jesus Christ from the tomb is one of the most well-attested and well-known facts of human history. No other event has such overwhelming weight of evidence and has left such an impact on the world.[6]

---

[5] Klein, Blomberg & Hubbard, *Introduction to Biblical Interpretation*, 149.
[6] I recommend Josh McDowell's two books, *Evidence That Demands a Verdict* and *More Than a Carpenter*.

What is not well-known is that the resurrection of Jesus Christ marked the beginning of the eschatological general resurrection of the dead ones (plural). Why so? It's because other bodily resurrections out of real graves also occurred in that 1st century period. Therefore, Jesus' resurrection was not an isolated event separated by centuries of time from a future resurrection. Here are two reasons why:

First, Jesus was/is the "firstborn from the dead" or "the first to rise from the dead" (Col 1:18; Rev 1:5; Acts 26:23). Of course, both the Old and New Testaments document other instances of people raised from biological death, prior to Jesus' resurrection.[7] But each of these resurrected recipients succumbed to death again.

In contrast, the Hebrews writer alluded to a coming "better resurrection" (Heb 11:35). That was to be the resurrection to which Jesus attained—to die no more (Rom. 6:9). "On the third day," as prophesied in Old Testament Scripture (Hos. 6:2), and as Jesus Himself declared (Matt. 12:39-40; 16:21; 17:23; 20:19; 27:63; also Acts 10:40; 1 Cor. 15:4), Jesus rose from the dead. Then, over a period of forty days He came and appeared to many and offered "many convincing proofs that He was alive" (Acts 1:3). Hence, Jesus' post-resurrection comings and appearances were the first physical evidence and a "living" proof that He had conquered death, the grave (Acts 2:29-32), and the realm of the dead, Hades.

Second, Jesus also was and is the "firstfruits" or the first portion of those being raised from the dead (1 Cor. 15:20, 23). Paul's inspired usage of this "firstfruits" metaphor and agricultural imagery is no accident. It's taken from Leviticus 23 and was a common, agricultural procedure in Bible times.

... the resurrection of Jesus Christ marked the beginning of the eschatological general resurrection.

---

[7] The widow's son raised by Elijah (1 Ki. 17:17-24); the Shunammite's son raised by Elisha (2 Ki. 4:18-37); a dead man whose body touched Elisha's bones after Elisha had been dead for some time (2 Ki. 13:20-21). Also, at the Mount of Transfiguration, Moses and Elijah were raised but did not receive their new spiritual bodies. Also see, Heb. 11:35.

The idea of firstfruits means a standing and full harvest is ripe and ready. The firstfruits were the first portion of a harvest of grain, corn, wine, oil, meat, fruit, bread, etc., and not just a single stalk or piece, but a small bunch. It was cut from and representative of a whole harvest ready to get underway (Exod. 23:16, 19; 34:26), was physically paraded through the streets of Jerusalem, taken into the Temple, and waved as an offering to God before the rest could be harvested. The cutting of the firstfruits signaled the beginning of the gathering process in that same season of time.

Thus, the metaphor of "firstfruits" does not suggest or convey a postponement, delay, or gap between this initial first portion and the rest of the harvest. But with the firstfruits cut, paraded, waved, and dedicated, the harvest proceeds. The eschatological harvest of the resurrection of the dead was to occur in a similar manner. It had begun with Jesus, who was not only the "firstborn" and the "firstfruits," but in keeping with Jewish typology, He was also the "first of the firstfruits" (Exod. 23:19; 34:26; Ezek. 44:30 *KJV*). Therefore, after his resurrection, the "firstfruits" group was not complete. More resurrections were imminent.

STAGE 2. Resurrection of Many (not all) Old Testament Saints from Their Graves—the second physical evidence.

> "And behold, the veil of the temple was torn in two from top to bottom, and the earth shook; and the rocks split, and the tombs were opened; and many bodies of the saints who had fallen asleep were raised; and coming out of the tombs (graves), and *after* His [Jesus'] resurrection they entered the holy city [Jerusalem] and appeared to many."
>
> (Matthew 27:51-53 (Caps, bold, italics mine)

Many interpreters have tried to ignore, sidestep or downplay this biblically recorded and collective event that took place just *after* Jesus' death and resurrection.[8] And, yes, this account is only found in

---

[8] Some interpreters claim this resurrection took place *before* Jesus' resurrection (Kee, *Understanding the New Testament*, 134). The literal Greek here regarding

Matthew's gospel. But, obviously, some kind of literal bodily resurrection was taking place. This second physical evidence and "living" proof demonstrates that the eschatological and general resurrection of the dead ones was underway and expanding.

The Greek word for "bodies" here is *soma* and means the human body as a whole, and not a soul or a disembodied spirit. And there were "many" but not all Old Testament saints who were raised and seen as they paraded through Jerusalem. They had been physically dead (the "fallen asleep in Christ" – 1 Thess. 4:13, 15). By faith, they had placed their trust in God's Messianic plan of redemption (Gen. 15:6) but had died before the gospel was preached to them and before the consummation of the age was reached. But in this resurrection they were thereby emancipated from the powers of death.

Thus, this eschatological event, immediately followed "after" Jesus' resurrection. It was in partial but literal fulfillment of Jesus' prophetic words: "Do not be amazed at this, for a time [the hour] is coming when all who are in their graves will hear his voice and come out – those who have done good will rise to live, and those who have done evil will rise to be condemned." (John 5:28, 29).

So ask yourself this question. What better explanation could there be for some in those times who were "saying that the resurrection is past already" (2 Tim. 2:18; 2 Thess. 2: 1-2)? Notice that Paul never challenged their concept of the nature of resurrection. He only corrected their timing (2 Thess. 2:1-12). And at *that* time the consummatory resurrection event was not "past already." But what a sight and a news-making event that parade of the dead-now-alive bodies walking through the streets of Jerusalem must have been!

No doubt, this was also why Paul, during his defense before King Agrippa, remarked, "Why should any of you consider it incredible that God raises the dead?" (Acts 26:8). The Greek word translated "dead" here is actually in the plural. It's "dead ones" or "dead persons." Paul also used this plural form several other times: in Acts 17:32; 23:6; 24:21;

---

the placement and context for the word "after" is somewhat obscure. It reads: "And behold the veil of the shrine was rent from above to below in two and the earth was shaken and the rocks were rent and the tombs were opened and many bodies of the having fallen asleep saints were raised and coming forth out of the tombs after the rising of him entered into the holy city and appeared to many."

1 Cor. 15:12, 13, 15, 16. Please note that he did not use a collective term in these verses, such as "raises the dead," as he did in 2 Cor. 1:9; Acts 4:2, for instance. Nor did he say, raised Jesus from the (collective) dead, as he did in Romans 6:9; Acts 17:31.

What undoubtedly grieved many unbelieving Jews the most, back then and there, was not only the preaching of "through Jesus the resurrection from the dead" (Acts 4:2), but this abundance of resurrection evidence paraded right before their eyes.

"Why should any of you consider it incredible that God raises the dead?" (Acts 26:8).

Hence Jesus' resurrection could not have been and cannot be perceived as an isolated event. Rather, the long-expected and general resurrection of the dead was now underway. Still, many other faithful saints remained to be raised out of the hadean realm as part of the resurrection harvest then underway. But that completion awaited the consummation and Resurrection Day for the rest of the dead and alive "in Christ." This day was still being anticipated as the New Testament was being penned (Rom. 8:23-35; 2 Cor. 3:18; Phil. 3:20-21; 1 John 3:1-3). Its awaited fulfillment and realization accounts for the use of future-tense language and explains why Paul so strongly opposed any doctrine teaching a completed general resurrection prior to Christ's *parousia* coming at the end of the age.

Then, almost thirty years after these two resurrection events that we've just discussed, Paul at his trial before Felix stated: "I believe everything that agrees with the Law and that is written in the Prophets, and I have the same hope in God as these men, that there **WILL BE *[to be about to be]*** a resurrection of both the righteous and the wicked" (Acts 24:15 (Caps, bold, italics mine).

Two of Paul's pivotal Greek words in this passage are *mellein esesthai*. Traditionally, they have been translated as "will be" or "shall be." In the literal Greek, however, they are: "to be about to be" (these words are also used in Acts 11:28 and 27:10). This double-intensified force of imminency is missed in all major English translations. Not only was Paul's future resurrection hope grounded in the fulfillment of the Law and the Prophets—i.e., the Old Testament promises and in a "firstfruits" typology—it was a very imminent and pending event back then and there.

The bottom line at this time was this. The die was cast and the nature set. The bodily resurrection harvest had begun with Jesus and the Matthew 27:51-53 group. All that awaited was the proper time for the rest of the harvest to come out of the hadean realm. That time would come.

Critical Objection #1: It is often argued that Paul's pre-*parousia* (A.D. 70) statements in A.D. 58 – "I *desire* to depart and be with Christ, which is far better" (Phil. 1:23) and in A.D. 56 – "absent from the body; i.e. a human body, present with the Lord" (2 Cor. 5:8) teach that heaven was open back then and there when Paul was writing. Dr. Billy Graham, for instance, who does not believe that any end-time resurrection event has taken place (expect for Jesus', of course), confidently assures his readers today, "The Bible doesn't answer all our questions about life after death – but it does tell us very clearly that when we die we go immediately into the presence of the Lord if we know Christ. Paul's great hope was 'to be away from the body and at home with the Lord' (2 Corinthians 5:8)."[9]

My Response: Then was Paul contradicting Jesus' statements in John 3:13; 13:33, 36; 14:1-3 that "no one" had gone into heaven yet?[10]

---

[9] Billy Graham, "If we know Christ, we go straight to heaven," "My Answer," *The Indianapolis Star*, May 2, 2005, E-2.

[10] Two possible exceptions or seemingly contradictory examples are commonly cited: 1) Enoch, who may or may not have seen death, was taken away by God (Gen. 5:24, Heb 11:5). To where he was taken is not stated. 2) Elijah who "went up to [into] Heaven in a whirlwind" (2 Ki. 2:11). The preposition "to" does not exist in the original Hebrew. It's only implied and is rendered as either "to" or "into." If its meaning was "to," that doesn't necessitate going "into." If it was "into," then it may only refer to a temporary experience like the man Paul said he knew who was caught up to the third heaven (2 Cor. 12:2-4). Or it could mean "into" the outer courts of the heavenly realm and not into the Presence of God in the Holy of Holies, if we follow Jewish temple typology. Or the Hebrew word *shamayim*, which is translated as "heaven," also means "to be *lofty*; the *sky* (as *aloft*); alluding to the visible arch in which the clouds move, as well as to the higher ether where the celestial bodies revolve): – air, astrologer, Heaven" (-s) [#8064 – *Strong's Exhaustive Concordance of the Bible*]. Or lastly, this is the only scripturally cited exception to Jesus' John 3:13 statement. We'll stick with

Let's take a closer look. In Philippians 1:21-24, Paul was only expressing his desire, a yearning, or a preference about dying and being present with the Lord. He only said, "I *desire* to depart and be with Christ," not "I *know* I can depart and be with Christ." Likewise in 2 Corinthians 5:8, he only said "would *prefer*," not that he "could." So let's not make more of this than what Paul did. Furthermore, his words here must be understood within his previously stated and futuristic context of "a deposit, guaranteeing what is to come" (2 Cor. 5:5). Hence, and at best it's a stretch to claim that Paul was teaching a then-present reality in conflict with Jesus' John 3:13; 13:33, 36, and 14:1-3 statements and that if he died, he would immediately go to heaven to be with the Lord.

Critical Objection #2: Ephesians 4:8 is also cited. Here Paul wrote: "When he ascended up on high, he led captives in his train . . . " [in *KJV* ". . . he led captivity captive . . ."]. This then is falsely viewed as the total emptying out of the paradise side (the righteous side) of Hades at Christ's ascension in A.D. 30. The presence of "souls" in heaven "under the altar . . . of those who had been slain" and the "great multitude" pictured in the Book of Revelation (Rev. 6:9-11; Rev 7, respectively, and written pre-A.D. 70) is next cited as evidence that this group is in heaven.

My Response: When Jesus told the dying thief on the cross that "Today, you will be with me in paradise (Luke 23:43), He was not saying you'll be with me in heaven. First of all, on the very day that both Jesus and the thief died, Jesus did not go to heaven. He went to the hadean realm for three days and three nights and preached to the disembodied spirits of the dead held captive there (1 Pet. 3:18-20; 4:6; Eph. 4:9). Secondly, we further know He hadn't gone to heaven yet because after his resurrection and many appearances around Galilee, when Jesus came and appeared to Mary of Magdala, He told her so. "Do not hold on to me, for I have not yet returned to the Father" (John 20:17a).

The phrase "he led captivity captive" (Eph. 4:8; from Psa. 68:18) does not necessitate that *all* the righteous held captive in Hades were taken out and up to heaven upon Christ's ascension. This language is quite abstract. Literally, the Greek reads, "He led captive captivity."

---

what Jesus said, "no one."

Seriously, what does that mean? We must be careful not to put too much interpretative weight or deductive reasoning upon this rather obscure and short statement.

STAGE 3. The Harvest—Resurrection Day for the Rest of the Dead—a third physical evidence.

Question: So when would or were the rest of the dead to be resurrected? From Scripture we know that this harvest of the resurrection would happen at "the end of the age" (Matt. 13:39-40) and on the long-anticipated "last day" (John 6:39, 40, 44, 54). Martha also understood this "last day" focus when she answered Jesus saying, "I know he [Lazarus] will rise on the last day" (John 11:24). In response, Jesus did not correct her understanding of the time of Lazarus' resurrection. He only added, "I am the resurrection and the life" (John 11:25).

Amazingly, most Bible scholars agree with this timing for the eschatological resurrection of the dead being on "the last day." But on the last day of what? Traditionalists assume it means the last day of the world, of human history, the Church age, a future millennium, or at the end of time. This preconceived idea and false paradigm is deeply entrenched. Additionally, most think this time terminology literally means that after this "last day" there will be no more days. But as we have seen, the world, the universe, the kingdom, and the Church age, biblically have no end (Eph. 3:21; Eccl. 1:4; Psa. 78:69; 89:36-37; 119:90; 148:4, 6; Isa. 9:7; Dan. 2:44; 7:14, 18, 27). Therefore, they have no last day in which to place a resurrection.

The explicitness of the time expression "the last day" and its use in pinpointing the time of resurrection consummation must be understood within the historical context of that 1st century. Nor can we divorce the biblical "last day" (singular) from the biblical "last days" (plural). By inspiration, the writer of Hebrews placed both Jesus' earthly ministry and the time he was writing in the timeframe biblically termed as "these last days:"

> "In the past God spoke to our forefathers through the prophets at many times and in various ways, but ***IN THESE LAST DAYS*** He has spoken to us by his Son . . ."
> (Hebrews 1:1-2a – caps, bold, italics mine)

And "these last days" were the "last days" of the biggest thing in the process of "passing away" (1 Cor. 7:31) and ending at that time, there and then.

The relationship between "the last day" (singular) to "the last days" (plural) should be more than obvious for those of you having read this far into this book. "These last days" perfectly coincided with the days and work of the Messiah in destroying, removing, and ending the Old Covenant Jewish age. Emphatically as Jesus had prophesied, all this and much more would happen within the "this generation" of his hearers (Matt. 24:3-34). Likewise, the prophet Daniel had precisely pinpointed this same timing and nature at "the time of the end . . . .when the power of the holy people [the Jews] has been finally broken, all these things will be completed" (Dan. 12:1-4, 7b). Furthermore, Daniel was promised that this time would also be the time of his own personal resurrection, "at the end of the days you will rise . . ." (Dan. 12:13). At the end of what days? Again, the most important days of human and redemptive history—"the last days."

Perfectly and precisely, on "the last day" (singular) of the "last days" (plural), Resurrection Day happened. At some point in the late summer or early fall of A.D. 70, or two to three years later when the last stone was removed from the Temple complex and the field plowed over in fulfillment of Micah's Old Testament prophecy (Mic. 3:12), the remaining disembodied souls of the righteous dead ones were raised out of the hadean realm. Of course, no one back then, not even Jesus or the angels, could literally know "that day or hour" (Matt. 24:36, 44; 25:13). Still today we cannot go back and reconstruct this exact time.

But unlike before, no resurrection bodies were seen rising out of earthly graves, or parading around Jerusalem, or showing up in groups, unexpectedly. That physical evidence had already been provided, *twice* before. And in keeping with the applied metaphor, only the firstfruits of harvested grain each year were visibly paraded through Jerusalem and distinctly dedicated to God. The rest of the harvest never received this special treatment. Likewise, the rest of the dead on their resurrection-harvest day did not receive the same visual treatment as did the firstfruits group. Instead, their resurrection took place in the invisible spirit realm.

But there was visible and tangible evidence for this "last day" event. As we've seen, the destruction of the Old Covenant Jewish system was the physical "sign" for this occurrence (Matt. 24:3, 30), as well as the historical setting and the defining characteristic for the one and only end the Bible consistently proclaims (Dan. 12:7). This end is history. It's behind us, not ahead. And it was covenantal, not cosmic in nature.

This "time of the end" of the Jewish age was also prophetically connected to Christ's *parousia* coming on the clouds (Matt. 24:3, 27, 30, 34). And Christ's *parousia* was divinely connected with this resurrection harvest of the dead (1 Thess. 4:15; 1 Cor. 15:23). These verses and many more, as we have seen, refer to that same 1st-century time period in human and redemptive history.

Then, on that "last day" and within the time span of Jesus' "this generation"—the one that had rejected Him—Christ came in a "day of the Lord" judgment and similar to those judgments recorded in the Old Testament. All other eschatological and conjoined events took place "at that time" (Dan. 12:1) at the close of the Jewish age—sometime circa A.D. 70-73.

Perfectly and precisely, on "the last day" (singular) of the "last days" (plural) Resurrection Day happened.

This 1st-century time factor for Resurrection Day is further reinforced by a consistency and convergence of all prophetic time indicators in the Bible. It is in perfect harmony with the exact, literal, sequential, and chronological fulfillment of Daniel's two specific time prophecies (in Dan. 9, and 12)—no gaps, no interruptions—and with the imminency expectations of every New Testament writer and the early Christian community. Their Holy-Spirit-led expectations were not mistaken and did not prove false (John 16:13). Their expectations were the correct ones.

Let's also recall that Jesus established that not "one jot or one tittle" (the smallest letter or stroke) would pass away from the law "till all be fulfilled (Matt. 5:18, *KJV*). And the resurrection of the dead was an eschatological promise rooted in the Law and the Prophets (Acts 24:14-15). Moreover, more than a "jot or tittle" of the Law was fulfilled and passed away back then at the sounding of the last trumpet.

At the Last Trumpet
Paul wrote this exposition to living believers in Corinth:

"Listen, I tell you a mystery. We [them, then and there] will not all sleep [die like before], but we will all [all believers] be changed – in a flash, in the twinkling of an eye, at the last trumpet. For the trumpet will sound, the dead will be raised imperishable, and we will be ***CHANGED***."

(1 Corinthians 15:51-52 (Caps, bold, italics mine)

What a highly significant change this was in Paul's day, as well as for us today! Yet none of it could be assessed by any of their five natural senses. Nonetheless, this change was real. It involved the whole person—spirit, soul and body. Hopefully, what we shall cover next will greatly broaden and revitalize your concept and appreciation of fulfilled and ongoing resurrection reality.

The Message of the Last Trumpet
In the words of an old hymn, "When the trumpet shall sound, and the dead shall arise . . ." Twice, Paul declared that the eschatological resurrection of the dead and the changing of those alive would take place at the sounding of "the last trumpet" (1 Cor. 15:52; also 1 Thess. 4:16).

Most Christians today have been led to believe that this trumpet is a literal, physical, and brass instrument, and its sounding will be audible throughout the earth. Whereupon, millions of living Christians, worldwide, will suddenly and mysteriously disappear up into thin air. But circa A.D. 70-73 and following, nothing of this nature occurred in the physical/material realm. Why not? It's because the dead in Christ were not located on the surface of the earth.

On the other hand, can you imagine the excitement the sounding of this trumpet must have produced in the hadean realm? The disembodied souls of some saints had been held in this holding place for centuries, and others for millennia. Forty years earlier Jesus had descended into this temporary abode of the departed and preached to the spirits of the dead held captive there (1 Pet. 3:18-20; 4:6; Eph. 4:9)—call it post-mortem evangelism.[11]

He no doubt informed them that He would come again for them on the "last day" of the "last days." And since He has "the keys of death and Hades" (Rev. 1:18), He then took the "firstfruits" group out, brought them into Jerusalem, paraded them through its streets and into the Temple, and finally lifted them up into heaven with Him. Possibly, this was the Ephesians 4:8 group.

Next, some forty years or so years later, the trumpet sounds, perhaps even audibly, but in the hadean realm. Jesus then unlocks its gates and it's time to go. Their departure only awaited the literal "shout" and the "voice of the archangel" (1 Thess. 4:16). He shouts. They're gone. The righteous side or compartment of Hades is emptied out and locked up, forever.

But on earth, no audible sounds were heard and no visible sights were seen. Why not? Once again, it's because this end-time event took place in the invisible spiritual realm—a realm that earthly spectators normally cannot hear or see. Yet this sounding of the trumpet and shout of the archangel were real and highly meaningful for both the remaining "dead in Christ" and also those alive.

Another historical fact is, any devout, 1st-century Jew alive at that time would have been well-schooled in the Old Testament history and symbolism of trumpets. He would have known that the sounding of a trumpet always communicated a very important message. In those days before modern forms of mass communication trumpets were commonly used to call people into assembly, relay warnings, and direct mass-people movements, especially in battle (see Exod. 19:10-20; Lev. 25:8; Num. 10:1-10; Josh. 6; Judg. 7; Psa. 81:3-5; Isa. 27:13; 58:1; Jer. 4:19-21; Ezek. 33:3-6; Joel 2:1,15; Zeph. 1:14-16; Zech. 9:14; Amos 3:6). Notably, at the start of John's historical encounter with Jesus recorded in the Book of Revelation, John heard a great voice "like a trumpet, which said . . ." (Rev. 1:10).

Likewise, the sounding of Paul's "last trumpet" is a message, actually a twofold message. One message for the dead in the hadean realm. The other for those alive on the earth. This sounding of this "last trumpet" is consistent with "the last days," "the last day," the "last time,"

---

[11] For more, see: Noē, *Hell Yes / Hell No*, 257-261, 329-363.

and Daniel's "the time of the end." It's the same trumpet Jesus said would sound before his "this generation" passed away (Matt. 24:31, 34).

Furthermore, Paul's phraseology "at the last trumpet" implies that more than one trumpet is involved. Some feel we can identify this "last trumpet" with the seven trumpets found in the Book of Revelation. All are trumpets of judgment. But none are literal, physical, brass instruments. All, however, sound literal messages which were "at hand," "obeyable," and not to be sealed up (Rev 1:3; 22:7, 10), back then and there in the 1st century.

> **... this end-time event took place in the invisible spiritual realm—a realm that earthly spectators normally cannot hear or see.**

Therefore, and contrary to what most postponement theologians teach, Paul's "last trumpet" is, most likely, Revelation's seventh trumpet. For sure, this seventh trumpet is the last trumpet in Scripture. And its message was part of John's 1st-century vision of things that "must shortly come to pass" (Rev 1:1; 22:6).

With this possibility in mind, here is the message of Revelation's seventh and last trumpet for both those dead and those alive in Christ:

> "The seventh angel sounded his trumpet [message],
>   and there were loud voices in heaven which said:
>
> [Here's the message for those alive]
> 'The kingdom of the world has
> become the kingdom of our
> Lord and of his Christ,
> and he will reign for ever and ever.'
>
> And the twenty-four elders, who were seated on
>   their thrones before God, fell on their faces and
>   worshiped God, saying [elaborating on this
>   message of the seventh trumpet]:

> We give thanks to you, Lord God Almighty
> who is and who was
> because you have taken your great power
> and have begun to reign.
> The nations were angry;
> and your wrath has come.
>
> [Here's the message for those dead and alive]
> The time has come for judging the dead,
> and for rewarding your servants the prophets
> and your saints and those who reverence your
> name, both small and great –
> and for destroying those who destroy the earth."
>
> (Revelation 11:15-18)

This seventh-trumpet message is the past-tense yet ongoing message of eschatological consummation. And according to Revelation 10:6-7, there was to be "no further [more] delay! For in the *days* [note the plural] when the seventh angel is about to sound his trumpet, the mystery of God will be accomplished, just as he [Jesus] announced to his servants the prophets" (Rev 10:6b-7).

Once again, the timing and fulfillment of these events are not future for us today. They, too, were part of the "things which must shortly come to pass" in that 1st century (Rev 1:1; 22:6). Therefore, please be assured that "the last trumpet" did sound circa A.D. 70-73. It sounded the death knell of Old Testament Judaism. And it announced the amazing positional truth that "the kingdom of the world has become the kingdom of our Lord and of his Christ."

This powerful message relates to Christ's kingdom and needs to be systematically unpacked and presented. This task, however, is not our present topic and will have to await a future book.[12] It also signaled the judgment of the dead, the rewarding of believers, the accomplishment of the mystery, and the completion of God's plan of redemption.

---

[12] John Noē, *A Once-Mighty Faith: What have we done to Christianity?* scheduled for release in 2014-2015.

Unfortunately, most of the Church has never "heard" this trumpet nor understood its fulfilled, ongoing, and relevant message. And why not? One prime reason is postponement theologies with their unscriptural notions of the time and nature of the fulfillments of "the end of all things" (1 Peter 4:7, also see 17).

STAGE 4. The Ongoing Reality
In this fourth and final stage we shall address the question of "how were the alive changed?" The facts are that after the "last-day," alive Christians have a tremendous advantage over pre-"last-day" Christians. Post circa A.D. 70-73, we have the fullness of salvation and resurrection reality. No longer is consummation a future hope. Post this fulfillment, it's now our heritage.

After "the last trumpet" sounded, one of the changes for those alive Christians back then and there was, whenever they physically died they would no longer go to Hades, that temporary holding place of the dead and of separation from God, to await resurrection and judgment. After Resurrection Day on the "last day," that time of waiting and anticipation was over. Jesus, Who holds "the keys to death and Hades"(Rev. 1:18; 20:13-14) had emptied out and locked up Hades forever. So from then on at death, it's straight to heaven, to our individual judgment (Heb. 9:27), and the receiving of our new "spiritual body" (1 Cor. 15:44)!

Therefore, if you were to die tonight, you can now be sure that it's straight into God's Presence in heaven and into the Holy of Holies, directly and immediately, upon physical death. Heaven's door was then and is now wide open. Hence, "Blessed are the dead who die in the Lord from now on " (Rev. 14:13)—the verse I quoted during my four eulogies at my parents' two funerals and two memorial services.

But don't forget, this resultant reality is only true if Christ has completed his high priestly atonement duties, finished preparing heaven (John 14:1-3), come, and appeared "a second time, not to bear sin, but to bring salvation" (Heb 9:28; 1 Pet 1:3-7). In other words, He completed the redemptive process and raised all the dead. I solidly affirm that He has accomplished all this and more. Would you now agree?

As a result, the last great and remaining obstacle to eternal life with God was eliminated. The hadean realm was the "last enemy" (1Cor. 15:26) and final power of Satan over God's people (Heb. 2:14-15). It was destroyed. Hence these words are fulfilled, "death has been swallowed up in victory" (1 Cor. 15:54; Isa. 25:8) and "we shall not all sleep" (1 Cor. 15:51; also 1 Thess. 4:14). With God's plan of redemption now complete, the victory over death was fully accomplished. No more would the gates of Hades prevail against Christ's Church (Matt. 16:18).[13] And it all happened "in a flash, in the twinkling of an eye, at the last trumpet." When that trumpet sounded, it permanently changed the destiny of all believers. From that time on, it's only one step from this life to the resurrection state in heaven. Isn't that great, good news!

> **But don't forget, this resultant reality is only true if Christ has completed his high priestly atonement duties . . .**

Let me also emphasize that physical death was not eliminated. Jesus Himself did not conquer death by not dying, and neither shall we. He died physically, and so shall we. All human beings die in terms of biological demise (Heb 9:27). That doesn't change, nor will it in the future. This death is a fixed part of being born human no matter how much we might desire to escape it.

But, and once again, we can solidly affirm the greater good news is: "Blessed are the dead who die in the Lord from now on" (Rev 14:13). It's a done deal! Truly, fulfilled resurrection reality is no longer our hope but part of our heritage. "Therefore encourage each other with these words" (1 Thess. 4:18).[14] Amen?

---

[13] This verse has been greatly misconstrued and misused to mean that someday "hell" or evil will not prevail against Christ's Church in this life and on the earth. Again, Hades was the afterlife and temporary holding place of all dead, departed, and disembodied souls prior to the general resurrection we are discussing. Thus, this verse is a resurrection verse and not an evil-ending or defeating verse.

[14] Some preterists do not agree with these four stages. They subscribe to another concept of spiritual resurrection called the "collective body view," which was presented in Chapter 6. This collective body is then defined as 'the church,' which is raised out of the dead "body" of biblical Judaism and into the new "body" of Christ. While I affirm that this perspective is another aspect of the multi-faceted nature of resurrection reality, it is not its primary focus.

Summary of four stages

>   **Stage 1**. Jesus' Resurrection—the first physical evidence.
>
>   **Stage 2**. Resurrection of Many [not all] Old Testament Saints from Their Graves—the second physical evidence.
>
>   **Stage 3**. The Harvest—Resurrection Day for the Rest of the Dead—the third physical evidence.
>
>   **Stage 4**. The Ongoing Reality.

First in this ordering or sequence was Jesus' resurrection as the "first of the firstfruits."

Second was the company of many Old Testament saints who joined with Him as part of that initial portion of "firstfruits."

Third was the rest of the dead, raised forty or so years later out of Hades at his *parousia* coming on "the last day." And while Jesus' resurrection was individual, these latter two stages were corporate resurrections—a whole group resurrected, simultaneously.

Fourth, after the "last day, " it's "each" or "every man in his own turn or order" with resurrection reality repeated, over and over again in the lives of individual believers being born, saved, dying, going to heaven, and experiencing death and resurrection at different times—again, "each in his or her own turn or order."

That's the beauty of bodily resurrection fulfillment and its ongoing reality. Then what kind of body do we get?

The Nature of Bodily Resurrection Reality

For centuries, Christians have wrestled with these two profound questions:

1) "What bodily form do the saints currently in heaven possess?

2) "What will it be like for me?"

As far as I have been able to ascertain, only three viable options exist in answer to both of these questions:

Option #1 – As disembodied, or bodiless, spirits/souls.
Option #2 – In temporary bodies of unknown type, awaiting the traditionally posited physical, selfsame-body resurrection.
Option #3 – In new and eternal, resurrection bodies.

In support of Option #1, a bodiless existence, some interpreters cite the "souls under the altar" mentioned in Revelation 6:9 and 20:4. Coupling this option with the traditional, yet-future, selfsame-body resurrection, this reference to "souls" seems to indicate that these martyrs, and by extension all others, did not and still do not have bodies. But in Acts 27:37, Paul used the same Greek word, *psuche*, to literally refer to himself and his living, air-breathing, blood-pumping shipmates as "276 souls." They all possessed physical human bodies.

Others who also favor Option #1 advance the Greek belief in bodiless soul immortality. They claim that those who believe in Jesus never die, so they have no need to be raised from physical death. For them, a future bodily resurrection is nonessential and serves no purpose. They conclude that Jesus' physical resurrection was like his other miracles and only a type to call attention to a greater spiritual reality. Therefore, when a believer physically dies, he or she continues living spiritually in the Presence of God, except without a body. They employ the verse "absent from the body . . . present with the Lord" (2 Cor. 5:8) as support for their eternal, bodiless position.

A few other Option #1 supporters claim the souls of departed believers are currently asleep in a state of unconsciousness called "soul sleep." Whether they are located in Hades, heaven, or somewhere else is inconsequential. They will remain in their disembodied and unaware state until Jesus calls them to life on Resurrection Day.

Option #2, however, is the dominant view today. It is the one I'm going to argue that most Christians have been forced to settle for, by default. It's termed the "intermediate state." Under this option, all departed believers are now in heaven with the Lord and are conscious. But they are not in possession of their permanent resurrected bodies, which are still in graves, water, etc. Instead, they are clothed with some other kind of temporary body.

Admittedly, this intermediate state is *not* the hope of the Christian faith. That hope is the eternal resurrection body, which they supposedly won't receive until some end-of-history, end-of-time, second-coming event. At that future time, millions upon billions of old human corpses will come out of their earthly or watery graves, be reunited with the disembodied souls of their original tenants, and be transformed into glorified, selfsame, resurrected bodies. What happens to all the old temporary bodies is unknown and usually not addressed.

This second option is so deeply ingrained that many worry about being cremated and some are hesitant to donate body parts. "If we are going to experience a reunion with our physical bodies, shouldn't they be kept intact at death?" the thinking goes. They also wonder if they'll get back the same age-racked, scarred, or variously damaged body in which they died. Or if someone dies in infancy, would that person be resurrected and live throughout eternity as a baby?

To his credit, Dr. Billy Graham handles these concerns quite well with this insight. "This is not a problem, because God is able to bring about the miracle of resurrection regardless of our former state."[15] Yes, I agree with Dr. Graham here and finally, as we'll see momentarily.

In my opinion, however, nothing in Scripture precludes Option #3 from being the current bodily status of those saints now in heaven, as well as for those who die today, tomorrow, and in the future. This third option should not be lightly dismissed or pejoratively labeled as unbiblical or unorthodox. It perfectly squares with all resurrection texts and is in complete harmony with the prophetic and divinely determined timeframe we've been discussing. Nevertheless, this is not an area for dogmatism.

If, however, our faith was truly "once for all delivered to the saints" (Jude 3); and if "the end of all things" was truly "at hand" and fulfilled in the same 1st-century context in which these words were penned; and if Jesus' "this generation" didn't pass away until "all these things" He talked about had happened; then there is no scriptural reason why Option #3 cannot be correct. So what kind of body do we get and when?

---

[15] "My Answer" column by Billy Graham, Indianapolis Star, October 7, 1992.

Curiously, the Bible never uses the terms "resurrected body," "resurrection of the body," "resurrection of the flesh," or "physical resurrection." Consequently, these traditional expressions do not accurately describe resurrection. Instead, the Bible uses two inspired phrases: "the resurrection of the dead" (Matt. 22:31; Acts 17:32; 23:6; 24:15, 21; 1 Cor. 15:12, 13, 21, 42; Heb. 6:2) and "resurrection from the dead" (Luke 20:35; Acts 4:2; Rom. 1:4; Phil. 3:11). That is it! Big difference!

Nonetheless, the non-inspired Apostles' Creed, for example, does use the phrase "the resurrection of the body." This has been taken to mean the physical body. In my opinion, this portion of the creed needs revision to one of the two biblical expressions cited above. And yet no "bodiless resurrection" is ever mentioned in Scripture. How can this be?

Biblically, the nature of the resurrection body is mysterious and miraculous. Nevertheless, we have not been left totally in the dark. Scripture does provide three descriptions.

1. A "Spiritual Body."

In the 1 Corinthians 15:35-49 passage, the Apostle Paul by inspiration calls the resurrection body, which God "gives" a believer in heaven, a "spiritual body" (1 Cor. 15:38, 44). He does not call it a "resurrected (physical) body." In verse 44, Paul also does not say it is sown a natural body and *changed* into a spiritual body. He simply says there are two bodies. Yet this spiritual body is a real body that is produced via a real bodily resurrection.

Initially, this resurrection realization may be hard for an "orthodox traditionalist" to believe. So think of it this way. Wasn't your spiritual birth a real birth? Then why can't a spiritual body be a real, actual body and in perfect harmony with the spiritual process began in you at your new birth? As it is written, "Flesh gives birth to flesh, but the Spirit gives birth to spirit." (John 3:6).

Here's how the Apostle Paul further described and assured his contemporaries about what was soon to come:

> "For we know that if the earthly tent (house) we live in is destroyed [physical death], we have a building from God, an eternal house in heaven, not built by human hands. Meanwhile, we groan, longing to be clothed with our heavenly dwelling,

because when we are clothed, we will not be found naked. For while we are in this tent, we groan and are burdened, because we do not wish to be unclothed but to be clothed with our heavenly dwelling, so that what is mortal may be swallowed up by life. Now it is God who has made us for this very purpose and has given us the Spirit as a deposit, guaranteeing what is to come.

(2 Corinthians 5:1-5)

2. Like Jesus' Resurrected Body.

The terminology "spiritual body" does not necessarily define its substance nor does it necessarily mean this body is composed purely of spirit, as opposed to physical matter. Perhaps, the best and only indication of what our new spiritual bodies may be like; i.e., nature, can be gleaned from Philippians 3:20-21: "But our citizenship is in heaven. And we eagerly await a Savior from there, the Lord Jesus Christ, who, by the power that enables him to bring everything under his control, will transform our lowly bodies so that they will be like his glorious body." Whatever Jesus' glorified body is like (nature), ours will be like his body. But "like" does not necessarily mean "same" or "identical," as we shall further discover.

3. Paul's Seed Analogy.

For me, Paul's seed analogy in 1 Corinthians 15:35-38 is most enlightening. See if you agree. Here Paul uses this analogy to compare the sowing of the natural body and the raising of the spiritual body to the sowing of "a seed . . . of wheat, or of something else" and the coming forth of its new plant.

Analogies, as well as metaphors and similes, are frequently used in the Bible as familiar ways to communicate complex spiritual concepts and truths. For example, Jesus frequently taught using earthly objects and activities, such as living water, bread of life, a living vine, even the born-again experience. The danger, however, in interpreting and applying an analogy, metaphor or simile is twofold—1) pressing the illustration too far; 2) not pressing it far enough. Conveying bodily resurrection reality by this seed analogy is no exception.

With these two cautions in mind, let's explore three straightforward and reasonable insights I believe we should be able to draw from this agricultural analogy and illustration. After all, that's what an analogy is for. In so doing, we'll focus on both the degree of continuity and discontinuity between the seed and its resulting new plant to help us see the application between our present physical body and our future new, resurrection, spiritual body.

a) The new comes from inside the old.
The life ingredients of a new plant are contained inside its seed. They are called the endosperm and germ and begin to grow within the seed. When the seed germinates, these growing ingredients break out of the shell and into the fabric of the new plant. This natural process happens all the time all around us. But it is still an amazing reality of God's physical creation.

In a like manner, I'm suggesting that the ingredients of a believer's new spiritual body are contained inside our natural body. How so? Here's how. At our new birth our spirit is indwelled by God. Then, our spirit begins to grow, develop, and rise up within us. One day it will break out of its shell (our earthly body) and into the fabric of our new spiritual body. That's a continuity. But the new body is different from the seed body. That's a discontinuity. Thus, Paul taught, "when you sow, you do not plant the body that will be, but just a seed . . . " (1 Cor. 15:37). Still, many today and traditionally take this verse to mean that our outer shell—i.e., our physical earthly body—is what will be transformed. But this popular notion does not follow from nor is compatible with Paul's seed analogy.

This same pattern can also be seen in the Spirit's progressive work of forming and quickening, and of being "a deposit guaranteeing our inheritance until the redemption of those who are God's possession" (Eph 1:14; also 2 Cor. 1:22; 5:5). Likewise, it follows the pattern of "Whoever believes in me, as the Scripture has said, streams of living water will flow from within him [out of his belly]. By this he meant the Spirit, whom those who believed in him were later to receive . . ." (John 7:38-39a [*KJV*]).

If this application, as I have deduced from Paul's seed analogy, is valid, those alive who have been indwelled by God's spirit, now have inside them, in their "inner man," the ingredients for some or all of their future resurrection, spiritual body. What a metamorphosis that will be! This also means that your new spiritual body is not created from nothing, *ex nihilo*. Rather, it's already being formed inside your "inner man" (2 Cor. 4:16) and is the fulfillment and culmination of a spiritual process begun in you at your new birth.

Thus, it is written, first comes "the natural, after that the spiritual" (1 Cor. 15:46). Our personal and future bodily resurrection is directly and intrinsically related to and in a continuity with the spiritual substance inside us now. But it's also in a discontinuity with the matter composing our physical body. Why is that? It's because . . .

b) Not all the old ends up in the new.

When a seed germinates, not all of its physical substance rises above ground and becomes part of the new plant. The shell or outer coat remains in the ground and decomposes. What lesson do you think we should draw from this aspect of Paul's seed analogy?

This lesson should be obvious. God does not need or use the old natural body in creating the new spiritual body. Hence, when we die we leave that old body behind, forever. Like a seed's shell, it stays in the ground and decomposes. What we put on is the new spiritual body that God gives. This means that the continuity is the spiritual and not the physical. Again, the new emanates out from inside of the old. Get it?

c) Different in appearance.

Another analogous factor is, full-grown plants look entirely different from their original seeds. This is discontinuity. So how will our heavenly spiritual bodies compare in appearance and substance to our earthly bodies? And how will we be able to recognize one another, especially our loved ones? Only God knows. All we can know is our spiritual body, we will be "like his glorious body"(Phil. 3:21; also see 1 John 3:2), Who is the "firstfruits." Perhaps, that is a reason believers in Christ are also called "a kind of firstfruits" (Jas. 1:18). Yes, that's a continuity. But let's also note that John says, "it has not yet been revealed what we shall be . . . for we shall see Him as He is" (1 John 3:2a). This verse certainly implies that at that time, neither they nor John had seen Jesus as He now is, even though they had seen the resurrected Lord several times during the forty-day period following his resurrection and prior to his ascension.

McRay concurs that "when the body of Jesus was raised from the dead, it did not immediately undergo complete transformation."[16]

Brian L. Martin nails down this perplexity quite nicely. "The nature of Christ's body prior to His ascension wasn't to demonstrate to us the *nature* of our resurrected body, but to show that He had conquered death, and thereby demonstrated the *guarantee* of our resurrection body."[17] Once again, for the latest description of what Jesus looks like today, see Revelation 1:12-16. Then what is that post-ascension glorious body like? McRay answers, "Paul gives us no answer, perhaps because it lies beyond the understanding of mortal beings. It is enough to know that we shall be like him and 'like his glorious body.'"[18]

Before we move on, there is more major discontinuity between our new spiritual bodies and Christ's resurrected body that we have not yet addressed. This scriptural tidbit brings us to the classic objection of all postponement and delayed resurrection traditions.

'The Bones-Are-Still-in-the-Graves'

Despite a straightforward application of Paul's seed analogy and the fact that the Bible never mentions a "resurrection of the body," "resurrection of the flesh," "resurrected body," or "physical resurrection," the popular consensus in evangelical Christianity is looking forward to a rather bizarre scene. One day earthly graves in graveyards all around the world will crack open and old physically decayed corpses will begin coming out, be supernaturally reconstituted, and transported onto and ushered into heaven.

These futurists further reason that the nature of our resurrection on that day must be precisely identical to that of Jesus—i.e., a selfsame and reconstituted physical body. And since his body and bones weren't left in the tomb, it's assumed that those of believers won't be left there either. What's more, since He arose in his earthly, physical body, so will we.

---

[16] John McRay, *Paul: His Life and Teaching* (Grand Rapids, MI.: Baker Academic, 2003), 416.
[17] Brian L. Martin, *Behind the Veil of Moses* (Napa, CA.: The Veil of Moses Project, 2004), 390.
[18] McRay, *Paul*, 417.

Therefore, in their opinion, every grave still occupied by a dead Christian body, not to mention the unrighteous, is evidence to the contrary that the resurrection of the dead has already occurred, as we have been presenting.

"When the resurrection does occur," they confidently assure us, "everybody will know it. Those graves will split open and be left empty. You can count on it, brother!"

It's called the "bones-are-still-in-the-graves" objection. It's based on the idea that decomposed physical bodies will come forth, be physically reunited with their departed souls, and physically transformed to be like Jesus' body. Then these revived and regenerated physical bodies of both dead and alive believers will be lifted off the surface of planet Earth to meet the Lord in the clouds in the air (a la 1 Thess. 4:17).[19]

But below are three scriptural counterpoints well worthy of careful consideration before one buys into this "bones-are-still-in-the-graves" notion:

1. Jesus' Body Was the Only One Promised Not to See Decay.

> *"David said about him* [Jesus]*: . . . nor will you* [God] *let your Holy One see decay."*
> (Acts 2:25, 27, also see 31; 13:35; from Psa. 16:10; 49:9)

That promise was made for no one else, not even to the rest of the firstfruits group. The resurrection of Jesus' selfsame body, even with its identifying and remaining nail scars, was only made to and for the Messiah. Why so? It's because Jesus' human body was the only body ever born of a virgin, without sin, and as God in the flesh. And He never sinned. The Scriptures declare that every other human body inherits a sin state from Adam and, therefore, dies a physical death (Rom. 5:18-19;

---

[19] Two different Greek words are used in the New Testament to refer to two different locations of "air." One is the air where birds fly sky or higher: above the mountain tops, in the atmosphere, outer space or heaven itself. That air, however, is not the word used in this verse. The Greek word used here means the internal breathing "air" inside and in the immediate proximity of human beings. Big difference. For an academic excursus on this significant distinction, see: Noē, *The Greater Jesus*, 302-303, 330-337.

1 Cor. 15:21-22; Heb. 9:27; Eccl. 7:2) and returns to dust—"for dust you are and to dust you will return" (Gen. 2:7; 3:19; 1 Ki. 2:2; Psa. 90:3).

If, however, the physical resurrection of human corpses is required to match up with Jesus' self-same resurrected body, why isn't a physical death of scourging and crucifixion on a cross also required, as well as leaving nail scars in our hands and on our feet or other personal scars of this life? If the one, why not the other?

2. The Re-gathering Problem.

At the heart of "the-bones-are-still-in-the-graves" classic objection, is the human assumption that God will or must reuse and transform the physical composition of our old, selfsame, and earthly bodies in order to produce our new resurrected bodies. If this assumption is true (and it's not), God has quite a reclamation task on his hands. Somehow He will need to re-gather, reassemble, and revive countless and scattered atoms and molecules, which have composed billions of individual earthly bodies at the time of death. For bodies decomposed in earthen graves, lost at sea, or cremated, this will be quite a retrieval challenge since no intact body exists to be raised. M.C. Tenney in his book, *The Reality of the Resurrection*, raises another significant problem:

> When the body of Roger Williams, founder of the Rhode Island colony, was exhumed for reburial, it was found that the root of an apple tree had penetrated the head of the coffin and had followed down Williams' spine, dividing into a fork at the legs. The tree had absorbed the chemicals of the decaying body and had transmuted them into its wood and fruit. The apples, in turn, had been eaten by people, quite unconscious of the fact that they were indirectly taking into their systems part of the long-dead Williams. The objection may therefore be raised: How, out of the complex sequence of decay, absorption, and new formation, will it be possible to resurrect believers of past ages, and to reconstitute them as separate entities?[20]

This problem of joint ownership or shared composition of atoms and molecules is no doubt the case for the vast majority of long-decomposed,

---

[20] M.C. Tenny, *The Reality of the Resurrection* (New York: Harper, 1963/Chicago: Moody, 1972, 170-71.

physical bodies of believers over the eons of time. After they died, their various body particles returned to dust, were dispersed, reentered the food chain, became assimilated into plants, eaten by animals, animals eaten by humans, and digested into countless other human bodies. So at the so-called future physical resurrection, who gets which atoms and molecules back?

Of course, "nothing" is too great, too hard, or "impossible for God" (Luke 1:37). We readily admit that (with some cynicism). The crux issue, however, is not what God can or cannot do, nor how He may or may not do it. Since God created the universe out of nothing; He could obviously re-gather, reassemble, split up, and transform human atoms and molecules. The real issue is, what is the nature of bodily resurrection? And God has not promised in his revealed Word to resurrect old physical bodies. Once again, please remember, only Jesus' human body received that promise. Instead, He has promised to give the believer a new spiritual body. Therefore, a recovery of decomposed body parts and particles is a moot point.

Is God's creation of a new spiritual body so hard to fathom? Think about this. Not only has God created the physical universe and all life from nothing. He has also demonstrated four different ways of making a human body:

1) Without the agency of either a man or woman—Adam was created from dust.
2) From only a man—Eve was formed from Adam's side.
3) Through the union of a man and a woman—how we entered the world.
4) Through only a woman—how Jesus received his human body.

It bears repeating that the traditional view of old, decayed, and decomposed physical bodies being raised out of the ground, water, etc. is totally absent in Paul's seed analogy. That's why he used this common, familiar, and agricultural illustration—to illuminate something entirely different from our popular but "over-physicalized" idea.

The plain fact is, God has no need of and is not required to reuse old earthly bodies or body parts in creating our new spiritual body. Nor is God limited or bound by our human understanding or assumptions of how this happens. Since we don't have any idea how He created everything that is in the first place, why should we expect to understand how resurrection works? It's that simple, that profound, in my opinion.

3. Loosening Our Attachment to the Body Sown.
"You do not sow the body that will be, but just a seed" (1 Cor. 15:37). That's it. It is the main point in Paul's seed analogy. The outer shell of a seed always stays in the ground and does not become part of the new plant. How else could Paul have been any more clear? This is also why Jesus said, "fear not the one who can kill the body, but the one who can kill the soul" (Matt. 10:28). It's also why Scripture never speaks of us receiving "a resurrected body." Again, for God, raising up new spiritual bodies without using old and original atoms and molecules probably isn't any more difficult than "in the beginning God created the heavens and the earth" (Gen. 1:1).

Critical Objection: But the first reference in the Old Testament to the resurrection of individuals is Job 19:26, which states that "And after my skin has been destroyed, yet in my flesh I will see God."

My Response: The Hebrew preposition translated as "in" here is obscure and uncertain. A more literal and perhaps better rendering is "apart from," "out of my flesh," or "without my flesh."

Closing Our Case on Resurrection Reality

Of course, much more is involved with resurrection—for the righteous, the unrighteous, the dead, and the alive. That's because resurrection in the Bible is a complex and multi-faceted reality. I have written more on this in some of my other books.[21] But please be assured, there is nothing we have not covered that conflicts with or contradicts in any way what we have presented in this chapter.

Yet in countless churches and seminaries and in Christian books and magazines the reality of resurrection and life in Christ is ambiguously described as a somewhat present but incomplete element of Christ's redemptive work. They are telling us that we don't get the "best" until we get our old physical and decayed bodies back.

---

[21] See Noē, *The Greater Jesus*, 291-337, John Noē, *Off Target*, 101-112, and Noē, *Shattering the 'Left Behind' Delusion* (out of print).

To the contrary, the bottom line and greater good news is this. There is no scriptural reason why departed Christians now in heaven are not embodied in their new resurrection spiritual bodies. Jesus has come *as* and *when* He said He would and the dead have been raised *as* and *when* they were expected to be. However, if these two prerequisite events have not occurred, then these two conclusions cannot be reached. Scripture is that straightforward, that inescapable, and that profound.

Likewise, there is no scriptural reason the graves of old decayed bodies and bones need be emptied out, transformed, and transported up to heaven in order for the resurrection of the dead ones to have taken place and continue taking place each and every day. To the contrary, the beauty of "divine perfection" in the precise foretelling and timely fulfilling of all end-time promises and prophecies is strong and compelling evidence that these two events have happened exactly *as* and *when* they were supposed to happen and continue to happen.

Therefore, if you, or someone you love or know and who is a Christian were to die tonight, you or they will go directly to heaven, receive your judgment of rewards (Heb. 9:27), and put on your new, eternal, resurrection, spiritual body (1 Cor. 15:44). Remember, it's "each [every man] in his own turn/order" (1 Cor. 15:23). Count on it. I am!

Yet in countless churches and seminaries and in Christian books and magazines the reality of resurrection and life in Christ is ambiguously described as a somewhat present but incomplete element of Christ's redemptive work.

"Now you know the rest of the story"—the late radio commentator Paul Harvey's signature sign-off line—and why I said what I said during my four eulogies at my Dad and Mother's two funerals and two joint memorial services. Resurrection reality is fully part of our "once-for-all-delivered faith" (Jude3). So where am I wrong on this?

Well, that's enough for this book. It is now time for the climactic conclusion as we recap the strengths and weaknesses of the four competing and conflicting end-time views in the historic Church, discard their weaknesses, and synthesize their strengths.

Part IV – Reconciliation of Views

"There has been little attempt to synthesize the whole field of prophecy . . . and there is a great need for a synthetic study and presentation of Biblical prophecy."[1]

J. Dwight Pentecost

"It may be . . . we have now reached that point in the history of dogma in which the doctrine of the last things will receive greater attention and be brought to further development[2] . . . . "eschatology is even now the least developed of all the loci of dogmatics." [3]

Louis Berkhof

"The history of theology is all too often a long exhibition of a desire to win. But we should understand that what we are working for in the midst of our difference is a solution—a solution that will give God the glory, that will be true to the Bible, but will exhibit the love of God simultaneously with his holiness."[4]

Frances A. Schaeffer

---

[1] Payne, *Encyclopedia of Biblical Prophecy*, vi. From Pentecost, *Things to Come*, viii.
[2] Berkhof, *The History of Christian Doctrines*, 267.
[3] Berkhof, *Systematic Theology*, 664.
[4] Schaeffer, *The Great Evangelical Disaster*, 176-177.

"the easiest approach . . . is to follow one's own particular tradition as the true view and ignore all others, but intelligent interpreters must familiarize themselves with the various methods of interpretation that they may criticize their own views."[5]

George Eldon Ladd

"the search for truth can never be limited to the categories of a single modern school of thought."[6]

John Warwick Montgomery

"The Structure and Sequence of Matthew 24:1-41 . . . . some combination of the two (preterist-futurist views)" offers "the most promising solution to the exegetical difficulties of this passage."[7]

David L. Turner

"Both the futurist and preterist views have their strengths and weaknesses. Instead of choosing only one or the other, a 'both/and' approach that applies the strengths of each is a better option. . . . Combining the preterist and futurist views allows us to understand both that the message of Revelation spoke directly to John's own age and that it represents the consummation of redemptive history. . . . The preterist position by itself fails to understand that Revelation confronts the modern reader with promises, challenges, and choices that are similar, if not identical to those faced by the book's original readers. The futurist position by itself is prone to see Revelation as a crystal ball with a literal timetable of events that will happen in the future."[8]

David S. Dockery

"we would be mistaken if we merely weighed the evidence, chose one, and ignored the other two. The Spirit has something important to tell us in each of the three traditional views of the millennium."[9]

Stanley J. Grenz

---

[5] Ladd, *A Theology of the New Testament*, 670.
[6] Montgomery, *The Suicide of Christian Theology*, 177.
[7] Turner, "The Structure and Sequence of Matthew 24:1-41: Interaction with Evangelical Treatments," 3, 26.
[8] Dockery, "Is Revelation Prophecy or History?" 86.
[9] Grenz, "The 1,000-year Question: Timeless truths behind the debates over Christ's return," 35.

Conclusion
Recaps & Synthesis

Throughout this book we have been conducting an honest and sincere inquiry into the principle strengths and weaknesses in each of the four end-time views. If you hold to one of those views, I hope you did not find it offensive or threatening when we pointed out some of its problems. Rather, I hope you were open to be challenged and to reevaluate and reshape your beliefs based on the scriptural and historical evidence presented.

In my opinion, the biggest problem in the divisive arena we call eschatology is the many non-scriptural expressions and unscriptural concepts that are vying for attention and allegiance. Most certainly, this book has exposed these issues as well as challenged traditional paradigms that will not stand up to an honest and sincere test of Scripture. All these must be rejected and discarded. Unshackling Christianity from these inventions, false paradigms, traditions of men, and limiting mindsets is absolutely necessary if we hope to reform and reconcile "one of the most divisive elements in recent Christian history."[1]

Yes, all four end-time views have captured a portion of the truth. But each has also added a portion of error. Therefore, no one view has all the right answers. Below are recaps of the strengths and weaknesses of each view and a synthesis of their strengths into one meaningful, coherent, and

---

[1] Kantzer, ed., "Our Future Hope: Eschatology and Its Role in the Church," 1-14 (I).

cogent view that is more Christ-honoring, Scripture-authenticating, and faith-validating than any one view in and of itself.

Perhaps the greatest benefit this synthesis will offer is, it will allow one's beliefs in this area of theology to be more defensible and not as easily disparaged and disregarded by thinking people. Hence, a Christianity based on the divine perfection of precise fulfillment and ongoing relevance must be taken more seriously by everyone—sincere believers, seekers, scoffers, skeptics, and critics, alike. Yes, I hope, this recap and synthesis approach will open wide the dialogue within and without of the church about issues previously closed or stalemated to discussion. It is my further hope that the synthesis foundation that this book has laid down will be refined and expanded as colleagues from other theological persuasions enter into this dialogue.

Assuredly, the followers of Jesus during this third millennium of Christianity really do have a faith solidly based on divine perfection and practical relevancy. Therefore, we can and should be doing a much better job of responding to criticism. We also can do a much better job of relating to one another and to our culture and bearing a more effective and fruitful witness to Christ's lordship in this world and in the afterlife. This, in my opinion, should be our main purpose in life.

The difficulty is, we live in a world where the majority of people do not share our faith. Our response, however, should not be to give up on this world and want out of it. Our response must be to overcome our ignorance and strengthen our faith into a more powerful countercultural and revolutionary movement. Then, we must take this rejuvenated and reenergized faith to the world as it was divinely, effectively, and boldly intended to be taken. Yes, we have the numbers. What we've been lacking is the will. Where am I wrong on this?

Possibly, the most germane question I can leave you with, as we prepare to enter this book's recaps of the strengths and weaknesses for each view and our synthesis, was astutely and succinctly asked by Hank Hanegraaff, who is known as "The Bible Answer Man." "Are we willing to sacrifice our treasured traditions on the altar of biblical fidelity, or has tradition become our god?"[2]

---

[2] Hank Hanegraaff, *The Apocalypse Code* (Nashville, TN.: ThomasNelson, 2007), 236.

Recaps of Strengths and Weaknesses by View

Dispensational Premillennial View

Strengths:
- Strong interest in end-time prophecy.
- Emphasis on the dynamic role of Christ in the present and future affairs of humankind.
- Recognizes that eschatology is connected to Israel and pertains to the end of the Jewish age.
- Realization that at least one coming of Christ is not visible.

Weaknesses:
- Positing the time of Christ's "Second Coming" and "Return" as being very soon.
- Interrupting divine time frames without clear textual justification.
- Arbitrary use of gaps of time.
- Bifurcating passages of Scripture, including the Book of Revelation.
- Interpreting by exception and specialized meanings—i.e., ignoring or changing the meaning of commonly used and normally understood words in the time statements.
- Postulating postponement of the kingdom of God.
- Postulating delay theory.
- Advocating a future 7-year period of tribulation.
- Inventing the "Rapture" idea in direct contradiction of Scripture.
- Identifying Daniel's 70th week with Jesus' Olivet Discourse.
- Advocating separate redemptive plans for Israel and the Church.
- Denigrating the Church as unforeseen and a parenthesis in God's redemptive plan.
- Advocating a future restoration of the old and inferior Judaic order.
- A dichotomizing hermeneutic based upon a false paradigm—i.e., the Israel-Church distinctive.
- Advocating an incomplete salvation and resurrection reality.
- Positing a negative worldview and short-term outlook for our present time.

Amillennial View

Strengths:
- Idealist interpretation of the Book of Revelation.
- Emphasis on the literal/unseen realities behind symbolic fulfillment.
- Recognition that the "last days" existed in the first century.
- The present reality of the kingdom of Christ.
- Rejection of the idea of a future kingdom.
- Attempts to honor both literal and figurative language.

Weaknesses:
- Positing the time of Christ's "Second Coming" and "Return" as being unknowable.
- Advocating ambiguity and uncertainty re: the understanding of eschatological prophecies.
- Insistence that the time of fulfillment cannot be known.
- Little interest in end-time prophecy.
- Reliance on delay theory.
- Adherence to an unscriptural "end-of-time" paradigm.
- Use of a dichotomizing hermeneutic based upon that paradigm.
- Bifurcating passages of Scripture, including the Book of Revelation.
- Advocating a final return, final consummation (how many are there?).
- Advocating an incomplete salvation and resurrection reality.
- Numerous partial-preterist inconsistencies from failure to fully honor the time statements.
- Belief that the Jewish age, the Old Covenant order, and the law were completely fulfilled and removed, and that all Old Testament promises/prophecies were fulfilled, accomplished, and completed at the Cross.
- The New Covenant began and was fully in force at Pentecost—i.e., the full establishment of the kingdom/Church/New Covenant order was given, perfected, and fulfilled.
- The Church as the replacement of Israel.
- Claim that eschatology pertains to the end of the Christian age and to a split fulfillment in time and disposition (Jewish age/Christian age) with a gap of thousands of years in between.

- Advocating a current intermediate state of disembodied existence in heaven.
- Advocating a future evil-less, utopian, and eternal state on earth for believers and not in heaven.
- Equating the "age to come" to being heaven or yet future.
- A mixed positive-negative worldview.

Postmillennial View

Strengths:
- Strong kingdom-society orientation.
- Positive emphasis and motivation for human effort to expand God's kingdom on earth as it is in heaven.
- Positive worldview, long-term outlook.
- Recognition of many comings of Christ.
- Many valid preterist understandings.

Weaknesses:
- Positing the time of Christ's "Second Coming" and "Return" as being far away.
- Insistence the world must be "Christianized" to a significant degree before Christ can return.
- Adherence to an unscriptural "end-of-time" paradigm.
- Use of a dichotomizing hermeneutic based on that paradigm.
- Claim that eschatology pertains to the end of the Christian age.
- Postulating two or more *parousia* returns of Christ.
- Postulating a final coming and last judgment, after which no more.
- Numerous partial-preterist inconsistencies from failure to fully honor the time statements.
- Bifurcating passages of Scripture, including the Book of Revelation.
- Reliance on delay theory.
- Insistence that the time of fulfillment cannot be known.
- Advocating an incomplete salvation and resurrection reality.
- Advocating a future evil-less, utopian, and eternal state on earth.
- Overdependence on creedal authority.
- The "age to come" is yet future

Preterist View

Strengths:
- Fully accepts the natural reading and understanding of eschatological timeframes and NT time and imminency statements, including those bracketing the entire prophecy of Revelation.
- Supports the 1st-century Holy-Spirit-guided expectations as the correct ones.
- Balances literal and figurative language for nature of fulfillment.
- Uses biblical precedent to explain the nature of fulfillment.
- Harmonizes time convergence of OT time prophecies with NT time statements and Holy-Spirit-led expectations.
- Recognizes that eschatology is connected to Israel and pertains to the end of the Jewish age.
- Affirms that God has always had only one, continuous, by-faith people.
- Posits a positive worldview, long-term outlook.
- Acknowledges that God's material creation is without end.
- Answers the liberal/skeptic attack on the Bible and on Christ, effectively.

Weaknesses:
- Positing A.D. 70 as the time of Christ's "Second Coming" and "Return."
- A finality paradigm that limits the comings of Jesus to only two.
- Thus, A.D. 70 was Christ's final coming.
- Overly spiritualizes and diminishes the kingdom and resurrection.
- Enormous exegetical and historical burden for documenting fulfillment.
- Lack of attention in writings to the nature of post-A.D. 70 reality and implications for Christian living.
- Gross cessationism—some preterists advocate the annihilation of Satan, his kingdom, and of demons, and/or the cessation of the operation of angels, the ministry of the Holy Spirit, the miraculous charismatic gifts, water baptism, the Lord's Supper, and even the Church itself in A.D. 70.

A Synthesis of Views

First and foremost, the central, pivotal, and controlling end-time event contained in each of the four views—the "second coming" or "return" of Christ—is taken off the table of synthesis. It is a weakness to be discarded for the following reasons:

- "The words 'return' and 'second coming' are not properly speaking Biblical words in that the two words do not represent any equivalent Greek words."[3]
- These two non-scriptural expressions are also unscriptural concepts that will not stand up to an honest and sincere test of Scripture.
- They are to be replaced by the many comings of Jesus and the biblical fact that He never left as He said (Matt. 28:20).
- Hence, these two traditional expressions and concepts are inappropriate and that's why the Bible (properly translated) never uses them.

Secondly, while viewed as a threat to established futuristic paradigms, the **preterist view** is simple, profound, and superior, but not sufficient. On the positive side, it is the only view that fully accepts and honors the natural reading and understanding of Jesus' time-restrictive words and the intensifying imminency declarations of the New Testament writers. No other view can legitimately make this claim. It also documents how Jesus came "on the clouds" in age-ending judgment exactly *as* and *when* He said He would and exactly *as* and *when* every New Testament writer and the early Church expected—as they were led into all truth and shown the things that were to come by the Holy Spirit (John 16:13; 14:26). It emphasizes the harmony of this precise past fulfillment with the literal, exact, chronological, and sequential fulfillment of Daniel's two specific time prophecies—no interruptive gaps, no exegetical devices. These prophecies frame the end times and establish its historical setting and defining characteristic (Dan. 12:7).

---

[3] Ladd, *The Blessed Hope*, 69.

Thus, everything happened perfectly, "at just the *right* time" (Rom. 5:6) and "in its *proper* time" (1 Tim. 2:6)—including the individual bodily resurrection of the dead ones. This amazing harmony and perfection of timely past fulfillment is God's stamp or fingerprint of divinity. Or as I have chosen to call it, divine perfection—not only in creation and in Bible times—but also in the end times. Hence, the proverb is true. "Hope deferred makes the heart sick, but a longing fulfilled is a tree of life" (Prov. 13:12). To believe in a "hope deferred" is also to concede to a sick heart of discouragement and incompleteness that Jesus, his predictions, and the Holy-Spirit-guide expectations of the New Testament writers and the early Church proved false. No more.

The **preterist view**, however, was found to be insufficient with two major weaknesses. These are: 1) the destruction of Jerusalem and the Temple was the "final coming" of Christ. 2) The prophecy of the Book of Revelation was exhausted in the events of A.D. 70. Therefore, the strengths of the other three views must also be incorporated with the strengths of the preterist view.

From the **amillennial view** was kept the idealist interpretation of the Book of Revelation, with its ongoing and timeless relevancy and countless applications in human history. But these now follow, rather than precede, Christ's historic and literal coming in judgment and consummation circa A.D. 70.

From the **postmillennial view** was incorporated but reapplied its strong kingdom-society orientation, positive worldview, long-term outlook, and many comings of Christ—past, present, and future.

From the **dispensational premillennial view** was retained its strong interest in prophecy and the current dynamic role of Christ in the present and future affairs of humankind (although this must now be reapplied per this synthesis).

Discarded were the identified weaknesses from each of the four views that did not stand up to an honest, sincere, and objective test of Scripture.

In sum, this book has presented a new foundation, groundwork, and break-through initiative for eschatological reform, consensus, and unity. Others can now build on these findings as we more readily come together to build a fuller and deeper understanding of our "once for all delivered faith" (Jude 3) and God's once-again demonstrated attribute of divine perfection in *foretelling* and *fulfilling* his plan of redemption.

Delimitations

Due to space limitations and other considerations, I have not addressed or synthesized every item, issue, nuance, or possible question regarding end-time prophecy, its fulfillment, and ongoing reality in the pages of this book. But please be assured, all these omissions can be perfectly positioned, readily harmonized, and adequately explained within the prophetic and divinely determined timeframe for fulfillment we've laid out and discussed herein. These include: spiritual resurrection of alive believers and the resurrection and eternal destiny of unbelievers, which I have previously addressed, respectively, in my two books, *The Greater Jesus: His glorious unveiling* and *Hell Yes / Hell No: What really is the extent of God's grace . . . and wrath?*

Also, I plan to address the strengths and weaknesses of different views of the millennium (the 1,000 years) spoken of only in Revelation 20:1-10 in my future kingdom book.

So below are some other significant areas and topics of delimitation from this book that deserve a future book of their own:

- The continuance or future elimination of evil from this world—future book tentatively titled—*The Divine Origin of Evil: Casting light into the purpose of darkness / Solving the problem of the presence of evil* (est. pub. date: 2013-2014).

- The kingdom of God, which was the central teaching of Jesus—future book tentatively titled—*A Once-Mighty Faith: What have we done to Christianity?* (est. pub. date: 2014-2015)

- The future role or non-role of Israel in Bible prophecy—future book tentatively titled—*The Israel Illusion: Pulling back the curtain on the 'land of God'* (est. pub. date: 2016).

- A preterist-idealist commentary on the Book of Revelation historically documenting and explaining the fulfillment and ongoing relevance (past, present, and future) of the entire prophecy—future book tentatively titled—*The Scene Behind the Seen* (est. pub. date: 2017-2018).

What Shall We Call This Synthesis View?

"Your view has to have a name," several colleagues over the years have insisted. So what shall we call it?

I'm open and welcome your suggestions. For lack of anything better and as I mentioned at the end of Chapter 6, I have been simply calling it P.I.P.S. No, it's not related to Gladys Knight, known as the "Empress of Soul," and her backup group of 60s and 70s fame known as "the Pips." Rather, it's an acronym for Preterist / Idealist / Postmillennial Synthesis.

Or, perhaps, something generic like "the synthesis view."

What do you think?

Finally, I'll close this book with four summarizing and bottom-line questions: 1) How much end-time biblical prophecy has been fulfilled?

- Full preterists say 100%.
- Partial preterist amillennialists say "some."
- Partial preterist postmillennialists say "most."
- Dispensational premillennialists say "none."
- But from a P.I.P.S. standpoint, I say 100% plus.

And since you are now in possession of a much better way to present and explain the timely and precise fulfillment and ongoing relevancy of our "once for all delivered faith" (Jude 3; also 1 Pet. 1:5, 9; Luke 21:28), my last three questions are: 2) What will you do with this greater knowledge? 3) Will you take on this new responsibility and help us straighten out our Christian faith in the Church and the world?

Truly, I hope you will partner with us in this next reformation regarding the covenantal completion of God's plan of redemption.

4) What say you now?

Again, to listen to the podcasts from the MPC seminar series, go to PRI's website at www.prophecyrefi.org. Click on "About Us," "In the Media," and "Unraveling the End Teaching Series."

Appendix A

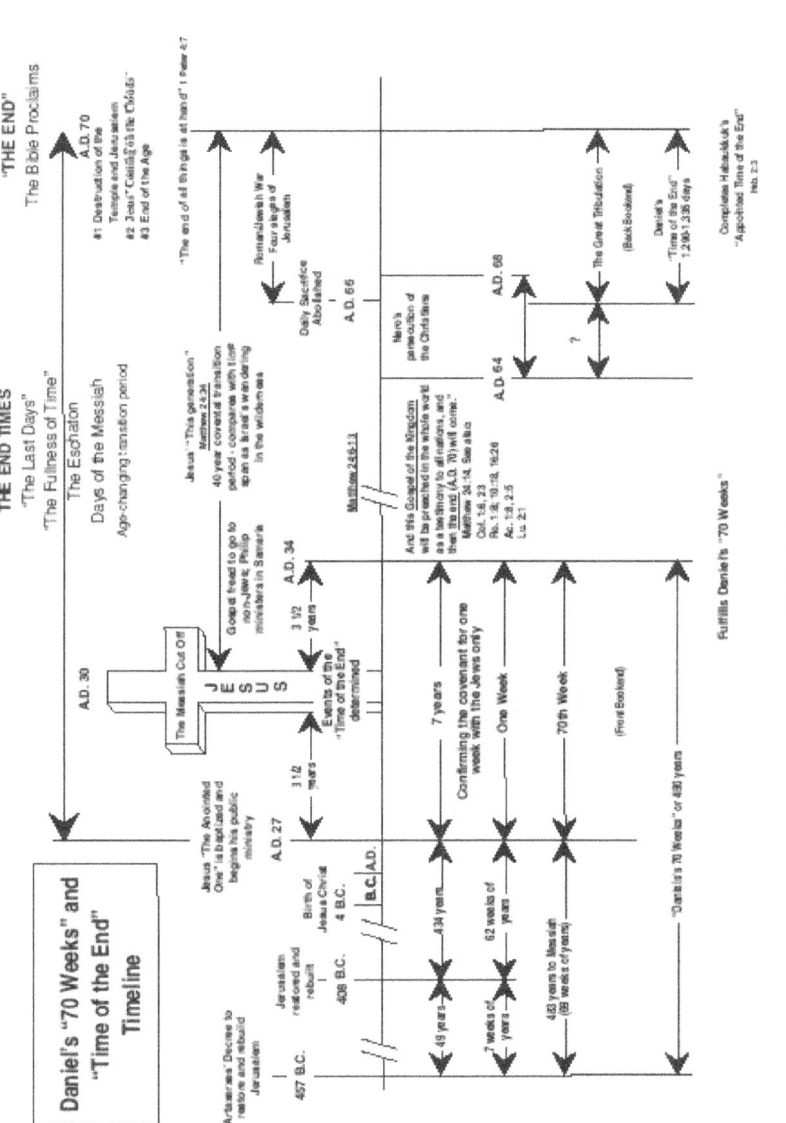

Contending ... "for the faith that was once for all delivered (entrusted) to the saints"
(Jude 3)

More Books from John Noē

(Available on Amazon.com)

Which Jesus Is the Jesus You Follow?

No longer is Jesus the earth-bound, historical Jesus of Nazareth we have come to know and love in churches around the world every week. No longer is He the sleeping babe in a manger we celebrate every Christmas, or the boy who played in Galilee, or the man they hung at Calvary, or even the lamb who died for you and me. Those traditional views are simply out-of-date and inadequate. Why so? It's because *He's not like that anymore.*

Yes, the Jesus of the Gospels has changed since his birth and earthly ministry. Yet He's still the same Person. Most people today, however, remain unaware and uninformed about this same but more glorious, greater Jesus.

In this book you will discover:

- He looks different than the way we usually picture Him.
- He rides a horse on the clouds.
- He hosts a grand banquet.
- He's not sitting around (up in heaven) waiting to come back.
- He comes in many wondrous ways.
- He fights the battle of Armageddon.
- He plagues the great prostitute.
- He raptures a remnant.
- He wants you to live in the city.
- And much more.

". . . a terrific and timely read. I enjoyed the hell (whoops!) out of it. . . . This his fourth and longest book in a new series may just be Noē's most dynamic and challenging. — **John S. Evans, Ph.D., Amazon.com Review**

"This looks like a book that we have needed for a long time. I am excited to read it!" — **Edward J. Hassertt, JD**

"This book is of great interest to me, because I am developing a new course for Bible 10: 'Christ from Creation to Consummation.'" — **Robert Preston, M.A., M.Div., Bible Teacher at Liberty Christian School**

"This book is needed. I wish you well and much success in getting this out to thousands . . . hopefully millions." — **Jerry Bernard, BM, Ph.D., Phil.D., Litt.D.; Director of Research at Library in the Palms Research Center; VP of Scripture Research**

"It really and truly sounds very interesting and hopefully compelling . . . . Am looking forward to reading it." — **Miller Houghton, President, Houghton Oil Co.**

What are millions worldwide looking for today?

That's right! The perfect ending! Here it is!

Why All 'End-of-the-World' Prophets Will <u>Always</u> Be Wrong!

The perennial prophets of doom have failed to recognize that our world is without end and "the end" the Bible consistently proclaims *for* the world is behind us and not ahead of us; is past and not future. This is the perfect ending! It's also the climax of the rest of the greatest story ever foretold. In this book you'll discover:

- ~ WHY THE WORLD WILL NEVER END.
- ~ HOW THE PERFECT ENDING FOR THE WORLD CAME RIGHT ON TIME.
- ~ DIVINE PERFECTION IN GOD'S END-TIME PLAN.
- ~ A NEW & GREATER PARADIGM OF THOUGHT AND FAITH.
- ~ OUR GREATER RESPONSIBILITIES HEREIN.
- ~ WHY THE FUTURE IS BRIGHT AND PROMISING.
- ~ THE BASIS FOR THE NEXT REFORMATION OF CHRISTIANITY.

"Noē's book just could be the spark that ignites the next reformation of Christianity." – Dr. James Earl Massey, Former Sr. Editor, *Christianity Today* Dean Emeritus, School of Theology, Anderson University & Distinguished Professor-at-Large

"Your treatment of the 'end of the world' is the best treatment of this idea . . . . Your book could really open the eyes of a lot of people." – Walter C. Hibbard, Former Chairman, Great Christian Books

"Noē . . . argues, with no little energy, against traditional views . . . [it] does have an internal logic that makes for exegetically interesting reading." – Mark Galli, Book Review Editor, *Christianity Today*

'Hell Yes / Hell No: What really is the extent of God's grace . . . and wrath?' –

This compelling and controversial book strikes at the heart of Christian theology and Christianity itself. It presents a balanced and scholarly re-exploration of "one of Christianity's most offensive doctrines"—Hell and the greater issue of the extent of God's grace (mercy, love, compassion, justice) and wrath in the eternal, afterlife destiny for all people. Inside, conflicting views are reevaluated, their strengths and weaknesses reassessed, and all the demands of Scripture are reconciled into one coherent and consistent synthesized view. The author further suggests that our limited earthly view has been the problem, rediscovers the ultimate mystery of God's expressed desire, will, and purpose, and transcends troubling traditions as never before. The bottom line is, God's plan of salvation and condemnation may be far different and greater than we've been led to believe. In a clear and straightforward manner, this book lays out the historical and scriptural evidence as never before.

Can We Really Be So Sure Anymore?

Battle lines are drawn. Sides are fixed. Arguments are exhausted. The majority proclaim, "Hell yes!" But growing numbers are protesting, "Hell no!" After nineteen centuries of church history, no effective resolution or scriptural reconciliation has been offered—until now!

So what really is the true Christian doctrine on this matter of hell and the greater issue of the extent of God's grace (mercy, love, compassion, justice) and wrath in the eternal, afterlife destiny for all people? The answer goes to the heart of Christian theology and Christianity itself. Has our limited earthly view been the problem? Could God's plan of salvation be far different than and from what we've been led to believe?

In this book you'll discover:

- A balanced scholarly re-exploration of the mystery of God's desire, will, and purpose in the eternal afterlife destiny for all people.
- Reevaluation of conflicting views.
- Reassessment of the strengths and weaknesses of pro and con arguments.
- Synthesis of the strengths into one coherent and consistent view that meets all scriptural demands.
- Reconciliation of the greatest debate of 'all.'
- Transcending troubling traditions as never before!

(Available on Amazon.com)

More Books from John Noē

Today's Dumbed-down Dilemma

Truly, have we Christians been led astray by our own leaders; dumbed down in our theology by ideas, interpretations, teachings, doctrines of men, and traditions that will not stand up to an honest and sincere test of Scripture; and consequently drawn off target in the practice of our faith?

This on-target, bull's-eye-aimed book re-explores what authentic Christianity really is versus today's institutionalized and substandard versions that we've comfortably come to know and accept. As you'll discover, beliefs do have consequences. This is why our modern-day versions pale in comparison with vibrancy and effectiveness of the Christianity that was preached, practiced, and perceived in the 1st century and turned that hostile world "upside down" (Acts 17:6). They also pale in contrast with the faith that brought our forefathers to America to found this country and establish its great institutions—most of which we moderns have given away to the ungodly crowd and without a fight. Bottom line is, we Christians are paying an awful price for our self-inflicted deficiencies.

Inside these pages we will reassess today's dumbed-down dilemma in these key 18 exposé areas:

- Divine Perfection in Two Creations
- The Kingdom of God
- The Gospel
- Hell
- The 'Last Days'
- Second Coming / Return
- Rapture
- Antichrist
- The Contemporary Christ
- Book of Revelation
- Battle of Armageddon
- Israel
- Conflicting End-time Views
- Doing the Works of Jesus
- Doing Greater Works than Jesus
- Origin of Evil
- Eternal Rewards and Punishment for Believers
- Your Worldview

Revised edition – PEAK PERFORMANCE PRINICIPLES FOR HIGH ACHIEVERS *is a dynamic story of how one man transformed himself, sedentary and out-of-shape in his mid-thirties, into a dynamic leader – and how you can too.*

John R. Noē is using his mountain-climbing adventures as an allegory for the challenge of goal setting and the thrill of high achievement. He shows you how to choose accurate goals, how to reach them, how to remain committed to the accomplishment of a goal whether earthly or spiritual, and—in short—how to become a high achiever. To help you succeed, Noē offers a unique philosophy of reaching "beyond self-motivation" to the spiritual motivation that comes from God.

In this revised edition, Noē adds further insights and updates his reader on how these principles have fared in his life since the book's original writing in 1984—which was named one of Amway Corporation's "top ten recommended books."

Noē shows you how to learn the six essential attitudes of a high achiever:

1. High Achievers make no small plans.
2. Are willing to do what they fear.
3. Are willing to prepare.
4. To risk failure.
5. To be taught.
6. And must have heart.

"After reading this marvelous book I realized how little I have accomplished with my life . . . compared to what I could have done. But, it's not too late."

Og Mandino, Author of:
The Greatest Salesman in the World

"So many Christians are going through life settling for mediocre, settling for second best, and choosing the path of least resistance. Not Dr. John R. Noē, author of this old (1984) and new (2006) book, *Peak Performance Principles for High Achievers – Revised Edition*. He reminds us that the first mountain we need to conquer is that of ourselves and that God wants us to accomplish great things for His glory."

Dr. D. James Kennedy, Ph.D.
Senior Minister
Coral Ridge Presbyterian Church

What's Next?

More pioneering and next-reformation titles are in development and forthcoming from John Noē and East2West Press. Tentatively titles and subtitles and their estimated publication year are:

THE DIVINE ORIGIN OF EVIL
Casting light into the purpose of darkness / Solving the problem of the presence of evil
  (Est. 2013-14)

A ONCE-MIGHTY FAITH
What Have We done to Christianity?/ Restoring the central teaching of Jesus—the kingdom of God
  (Est. 2014-2015)

GOD THE ULTIMATE COMPETITIVE EDGE
Transcending the limits of self / Why settle for anything less?
  (Est. 2015)

THE ISRAEL ILLUSION
Pulling back the curtain on the 'land of God' (Oz) / Major theological misconceptions about this modern-day nation
  (Est. 2016)

THE SCENE BEHIND THE SEEN
A Preterist-Idealist commentary of the Book of Revelation—unveiling its fulfillment and ongoing relevance—past, present & future
  (Est. 2017)

LIFE'S LAST & GREATEST ADVENTURE
What really happens today immediately after you die?—you may be surprised!
  (Est. 2018)

'WARRIORS OF THE LAST TEMPLE'
The back story, theology, and script behind the movie (Est. ?)

Books Out-of-Print
BEYOND THE END TIMES
SHATTERING THE 'LEFT BEHIND' DELUSION
DEAD IN THEIR TRACKS
TOP TEN MISCONCEPTIONS ABOUT JESUS' SECOND COMING AND THE END TIMES
PEOPLE POWER
THE APOCALYPSE CONSPIRACY

Scripture Index

OLD TESTAMENT

Genesis

1	317
1:1	135, 155, 413
1:1-2:3	136
1:14	139, 350
1:16	139
1:28	75
2:7	411
3:19	411
5:24	19, 391
8:21-22	151
9:7	75
9:11	152
11:5	319
12:3	29, 171, 175
12:7	269
13:16	157
15:5	157
15:6	389
16:7-14	269
18:21	319
17:1-2	265
17:7	175
18:1f	267
18:18	171
18:21	319
18:25	268
19:24	267
21:17ff	269
22:11ff	269
22:17	157
22:18	171
31:11ff	269
32:22-29	268
32:30	268, 268
35:9-10	268

Exodus

3:2ff	269
3:2-15	265, 269
3:7-8	318
3:8	319
15:3	318
16:7,10	263, 377
17:1-7	266
19:10-20	397
19:16	309
19:21	264
20	323
20:18	309
23:16, 19	388
23:19	388
24:9-11	266
24:10-11	263
24:16, 17	263, 377
33:11	263
33:11, 20-23	269
33:20, 23	264
34:26	388, 388
40:34, 35	263, 377

Leviticus

7:20, 21, 25, 27	244
9:6, 23	377
9:6, 23, 24	263
23	387
25:8	397

Numbers

10:1-10	397
14:10	263
14:10, 21	377
14:14	263
16:19, 42	263, 377
20:6	263, 377
23:19	100, 202
24:17	244

Deuteronomy		7	397	6:3-12	220
		13:2ff	269	6:14	220
5:4	266			7:11-26	220
7:9	154	*1 Samuel*			
10:15-16	173			*Nehemiah*	
10:16	176	17:51	224		
17:6	156			4:17-18	221
18:15, 18	194	*2 Samuel*		6:15	221
18:18-22	100			7:4	221
18:22	194, 240	22:10-12	319	7:5	221
19:15	156	22:15	309	11:1	221
29:29	124			13:30	221
30:6	176	*1 Kings*			
31 & 32	213			*Job*	
31:14	244	2:2	411		
31:28	156	3:16-28	297, 351	3:13-19	381
31:29	156, 244, 294	8:11	263, 377	19:26	413
31:29-32:1-43	163	17:17-24	387		
32	244, 294, 329			*Psalms*	
32:1	156, 156	*2 Kings*			
32:1-43	156			2:4	369
32:5	294	2:11	19, 391	2:9	367
32:5, 20	294	4:18-37	387	11:4	369
32:5, 20, 29	244	6:17	271	14:1	136
32:20, 23	294	13:20-21	387	16:10	410
32:20, 29	294			18:9	319
32:20, 29, 5	163	*1 Chronicles*		18:9-12	319
32:21	177			18:14	309
32:32	166	16:15-17	154	19:1	129, 151
32:35	244			22:16	364
33:2	309, 319	*2 Chronicles*		22:27	175
34:10	263, 266			22:28	369
		5:14	263, 377	24:1	87, 136
Joshua		7:1-3	263, 377	47:2, 8	369
		7:12f	266	47:5	319
5:13-15	268	7:14	266	48:1-2	321
6	397	7:19-20	266	49:9	410
		36:20-23	217	49:15	381
Judges				50:3	319
		Ezra		68:4	318
6:11ff	269			68:18	392
6:11-26	266	1:2-4	220	68:24	269

78:69	151, 393	
81:3-5	397	
89:36-37	151, 393	
90:3	411	
93:1	151	
96:10	151	
96:13	319	
97:5	319	
103:19	369	
104:3-4	318	
104:5	151	
104:31	263, 377	
105:2-5	328	
105:7-10	154	
110	369	
110:1	264, 264, 264, 267	
110:1-4	267	
119:90	151, 154, 393	
125:1-2	257	
138:5	263, 377	
144:5	319	
144:6	309	
148:4, 6	151, 393	

Proverbs

8:13	369
13:12	243, 422

Ecclesiastes

1:4	151, 153, 393
3:2	158
7:2	411

Isaiah

1	156
1:2	156
1:2-3	156, 156
1:10	166
1:18	xii
2:2-3	321
2:2-5	145, 231
2:12, 19, 21	162
5:1-7	27, 162, 213
5:16	323
6:1	263
6:5	269
6:9-10	343, 345
9:6-7	25, 75, 273, 301
9:7	181, 376, 393
13:1	155, 156, 162, 162
13:10	312, 313
13:13	155, 156, 162, 162, 313
13:19-22	155
19:1	318
19:20-21	328
20:1-6	318
24:21-22	381
25:8	381
26:21	319
27:13	397
28:18	109, 381
29:5-6	319
29:11-18	354
31:4	319
34:4	312, 313
34:5	313
35:2	263, 377
37:20	328
40:3	314
40:4	314
40:5	263, 377
40:26-28	135
41:21-24	138, 202, 210, 219, 325
41:22-23	202
42:8-9	138, 202, 210, 219, 325
44:6-8	138, 202, 210, 219, 325
45:17	150
45:20-22	138, 202, 210, 219, 325
45:22, 25	175
46:9-11	138, 202, 210, 219, 325
48:3-6	138, 202, 210, 219, 325
49:6	171
49:6f	226
51:13	156
51:13-16	157
51:15-16	156, 158
53:1	136
53:8	224, 226
53:8-9	381
54:1-3	175
56:7	145, 231
58:1	397
58:8	263, 377
59:17f	322
60:1	263, 377
61:1-2	163, 223, 235
61:2	223, 322
64:2	328
64:3	319
65:6-12	295
65:17-19	163
66:1	369
66:15	319
66:22	163

Jeremiah

1:10	158
4:4	173, 176
4:13	318
4:19-21	397
18:9	158

25:11-12	217	32:2	314	8	304
25:12	244	32:7, 8	314	8:14	230
27:16	244	32:18-30	381	8:19	229
29:10	203, 217, 221	33:3-6	397	8:19, 26	231
29:27-28	244	36:26-27	254	9	267, 304, 395
31:31-33	226	37	383	9:1-2	217
31:33	190	37:1-14	108	9:2	203
42:5	367	37:9-14	254	9:22	217

Lamentations

		37:11	108	9:24	203, 215, 215, 218, 226, 235
3:22-23	154	37:14	108	9:24-27	100, 105, 214, 217, 270
		38 & 39	189, 234		
		39:29	254	9:25	220, 221, 222, 222
		40-48	189		

Ezekiel

		40:4	343	9:26	106, 224, 224, 230, 233, 234
		43:5	263, 377		
1:13	309	44:4	263, 375	9:27	103, 225, 233
1:28	263, 377	44:30	388	10:1-21	267
2:8-3:7	354	47:1-12	75	10:5-12	267
3:12, 23	263, 377			10:14	145, 231, 244
4	321	**Daniel**		11	304
4:1-3	321			11:1-2f	267
5	321	1:1f	214	11:35	229
5:5	321	2	395	11:36	225
5:7	321	2:21	357	12	267, 304, 383, 395
5:8	321	2:35	75		
5:9	321	2:39	302	12:1	145, 395
5:10	321	2:44	75, 223, 223, 301, 376, 393	12:1-4, 7	394
5:11	321			12:1-13	143, 214, 229
5:12	321	3:24-27	267		
5:14	321	4:1	356	12:2	145, 383
5:15	321	4:1, 22	302	12:2, 13	231
10:4, 18	263, 377	5:19	302	12:3	157
11:23	263, 377	7	395	12:4	100, 349, 354
12:21-25	127	7:13	319	12:4, 7	322, 383
12:21-28	34, 243, 244	7:13-14	301, 342	12:4, 9	168, 229
		7:14	356, 376	12:6	230
16:8	109	7:14, 18, 22, 27	223	12:7	145, 145, 162, 162, 169, 231, 231, 235, 395, 421
16:44-58	166	7:14, 18, 27	393		
26:20	381	7:15-28	223		
30:3	318	7:23	302	12:9	231
30:18	319	7:25-28	230		
31:14, 16	381	7:27-28	75	12:10	146

12:11	232, 232	*Nahum*		**_APOCRYPHA_**	
12:12	234				
12:13	383, 394	1:1	314	*2 Maccabees*	
		1:3	319		
Hosea		1:5	314	2:22	193, 286
		3:15	224		
1:10	175			**_NEW_**	
2:23	175	*Habakkuk*		**_TESTAMENT_**	
6:2	387				
8:1	319	2:3	34, 100, 126,	*Matthew*	
12:3-5	268	139, 141, 141, 202,			
13:14	381	213, 243, 243		1:1-17	291
		2:14	377	1:23	258
Joel				3:1-3	314
		Zephaniah		3:2	243
2:1-2	319			5:8	376
2:1, 15	397	1:14-15	319	5:17-18	159
2:28-32	108, 254	1:14-16	397	5:18	395
3:15-17	162			6:6	263
		Haggai		6:10	180
Amos				6:22	109
		2:6	162, 162	6:33	6, 27
3:2	172			7:13-14	82
3:6	397	*Zechariah*		10:5-6	227
3:7	126, 139, 139,			10:5-15	76
141, 180, 214, 219,		1:10-13	269	10:7	244
239, 352		1:12	217	10:7-8	76
9:11-12	189	2:8-9	29	10:23	238
		3:1-2	269	10:28	109, 413
Obadiah		5:1-4	354	11:16	293
		9:14	309, 397	11:16-24	293
9	224	14	213	12:28	180
		14:4	97	12:32	149, 301
Micah				12:34, 39	293
		Malachi		12:39	293
1:3	319			12:39-40	387
1:3-4	319	3:6	373	12:40	21, 381
3:12	394	4:5-6	323	12:41, 42, 45	293
5:2	269, 270			13:10	343
				13:13-15	330, 343, 345

13:13-16 333	289, 289, 291, 293, 294, 324	24:21-30 82, 145
13:22, 39, 40, 49 149	23:38 145, 180, 286, 295, 304, 311, 324	24:23-26 307, 370
13:24-30 83		24:24 193, 282, 287
13:31-32 75		24:25 295
13:33 75	23:44 91	24:27 278, 287, 296, 308
13:36-43 83	24 82, 235, 240, 285, 285, 285, 289, 296, 296, 297, 312, 357	
13:39-40 393		24:27-30 194
13:39, 49 313		24:28 311
15:6 259, 262, 280, 299		24:29 194, 287, 312, 315, 315
	24:1-34 322	
15:24 227	24:1-36 300	24:29-31 194
16:4 293, 293	24:1-41 119	24:30 194, 194, 287, 287, 317, 319, 320, 325, 328
16:18 381, 401	24:2 145, 167, 193, 194, 286, 312, 322	
16:21 328, 387		
16:27 377	24:2-3, 34 304	24:30f 321
16:27-28 238	24:3 149, 193, 193, 257, 286, 286, 288, 291. 300, 313, 320, 321, 323	24:31 326, 384
16:28 273, 376		24:31, 34 398
17:1-3 272		24:32, 33 295
17:17 163, 293, 293		24:33 242
17:23 387	24:3, 27, 30, 34 238 395	24:34 92, 100, 103, 145, 163, 193, 194, 240, 286, 287, 288, 289, 289, 289, 289, 290, 292, 295, 297, 384
18:16 156		
18:17 176	24:3, 30 310, 394	
18:20 254	24:3-34 394	
18:32 127	24:4 287, 289	
19:6 172	24:5-12, 21-25 303	
20:19 387	24:8 303, 327	24:34-35 296
20:28 180	24:9 295	24:35 155, 168, 326
21:40 27	24:9-14 83	24:35-36 296
21:43 27, 177, 180	24:13 92	24:36 64, 91, 234, 288, 299, 326, 327
21:43, 40, 45 162	24:14 77, 78, 193, 193, 286, 286, 301, 302	
21:45 27, 294, 304		24:36, 44 394
22:31 405		24:37 296
22:41-46 264	24:15 287, 293, 295	24:39 296
23 289, 289	24:15-16 166, 193, 303	24:42-51 127
23:29-38 294		24:44 64
23:32 295	24:15-20 303	24:46 255, 256
23:33 299	24:15-21 163	24:48 127, 243
23:34 289	24:16-20 193, 287	24:49 243
23:34-37 166	24:20 295	25 285, 296, 296, 297
23:35 286, 289, 295	24:21 193, 287, 302	
23:36 286, 289,	24:21-22 307	25:1-28 253
		25:13 64, 91, 234,

Scripture Index

	326, 394
25:21, 23	341
25:26	127
26:12	109
26:45	243
26:46	244
26:64	238, 317
26:64-65	319
27:25	364
27:51-53	388, 391
27:52-53	145
27:63	387
28:18	369, 369
28:18-20	76, 183, 227, 254
28:19	226
28:20	76, 76, 149, 254, 421

Mark

1:14-15	180, 223
1:15	75, 202, 244
2:20	254
4:26-29	75
4:30-32	75
7:13	259, 262, 280, 299
8:12	293
8:38	293
9:19	293
10:30	301
10:33	324
10:45	180
12:12	294
12:35-37	264
12:37	293
13	235, 240, 285, 285, 357
13:14	303
13:30	163, 290, 293
16:20	258

Luke

1:32-33	301
1:33	25, 75, 181, 376
1:37	412
1:50	293
2:1	92, 92
2:1, 30-32	302
2:9	264, 377
3:22-23	223
4:1-2	223
4:13-21	223, 235
4:18-19	163
4:18-21	202
7:31	293
9:29	308
9:41	163, 293
10:1-12	76
10:18	308
11:20	180
11:29, 30, 31, 32, 50, 51	293
11:47-51	166
11:50-51	163, 294
12:36	253
12:40	274, 279, 279, 375
12:43	255, 256
13:18-19	75
13:20-21	75
13:29	175
13:33	166
14:15-24	181
16:8	293
16:19-31	381
17:20-21	192
17:25	293, 293
17:28	311
18:8	82
18:30	301
19:12, 15	253
19:22	127
19:41-44	224, 235
19:43-44	234
20:35	301, 405
20:41-44	264
21	235, 240, 285, 285, 357
21:11	306, 324
21:20-21	30, 166
21:20-22	303, 305, 322
21:20, 22	234
21: 20-22, 32	163
21:25	325
21:27-28	275
21:28	21, 426
21:32	163, 290
21:33	155, 168
23:43	21, 392
24:13-32	271
24:21, 25	182
24:27	227
24:32	227
24:36-49	271
24:44	163
24:45	227
24:47	302
24:49	226

John

1:1-5	367
1:18	263
2:4	179
3:1-13	345
3:6	109, 405
3:13	19, 20, 20, 20, 20, 275, 380, 386, 391, 392
3:16	20

3:16, 17	154	14:18-23	275	1:11	255 256, 256, 372
4:21	183	14:20	255	2	254, 255, 327
4:22	176, 226, 228	14:21, 23	375	2:1-21	108
5:17	373	14:26	421	2:5	92, 302
5:22	27, 320, 325, 328	14:28	256	2:16-21	314
5:22, 27	368	16:5, 16	254	2:17	6, 236
5:28-29	383, 384, 389	16:7	254	2:17-21	181
5:39-40	192	16:13	99, 100, 101, 149, 239, 248, 298, 308, 327, 382, 385, 395, 421	2:19-20	325
6:39, 40, 44, 54	393			2:23	179
7:33-34	257			2:25, 27	410
7:38-39	407	16:16	257, 273	2:29-32	387
8:17	156	16:16-19	243	2:30-36	325
8:21-22	20	16:28	255, 256	2:31	21, 410
8:32	121	16:33	54	2:32-36	264
8:58	265	17:1	179	2:33-36	267, 369
11:24	393	17:15	54	2:36	364
11:25	393	17:20	54	2:40	163, 293, 294
11:55	244	17:21	171	3:18	179
12:34	258	18:36-37	192	3:24	181, 245
12:39-41	343	19:34-37	364	4:2	390, 390, 405
13:3	180	20:17	21, 392	4:24	155
13:33	22, 275, 380, 391, 392	20:19-31	276	7:30-34	265
		20:24, 26	257	7:34	318
13:36	22, 275, 380, 391, 392	20:26-29	271	7:38	176
		20:29	376	7:54-60	227
14	255	20:30	273, 372	7:55	271
14:1-3	21, 22, 274, 275, 391, 392, 400	21:1, 14	257	7:55-56	252
		21:4-14	271	8	228
		21:22	239	8:1	227
14:2-3	20	21:22-23	252, 255, 256	8:5	227
14:2-4	254			8:12	24
14:3	256, 380	21:25	253, 372	8:14ff	227
14:3, 28	255, 256			8:26	273
14:12	281	**Acts**		8:33	293
14:15, 20	381			9:1-8	252
14:15-29	255	1:3	6, 24, 179, 271, 387	9:4-5	271
14:17	264			9:9-16	272
14:18	254	1:6	24, 180	9:10-16	272
14:18-19	257, 271, 273, 308	1:7	64	10	228
		1:8	92, 302	10:1-6	273
		1:9-11	277, 324	10:13-15	272

10:34-35	177	**Romans**		11:11-24	67
10:38	223			11:16-17	177
10:40	387	1:4	405	11:17	173
11:18-20	228	1:8	92, 302	11:17-18	174
11:28	390	1:16	150, 226	11:17-24	171, 173
12:7	273	1:20	136	11:26	174
13:35	410	2 & 3	176	11:29	175
13:36	293	2:28-29	182	12:19	322
13:46-47	182	2:29	176	13:11	21
14:15-17	155	3:4	xii	13:11-12	241
14:22	24	3:19-31	228	14:17	24
		4:13-17	182	15:8-9	172
15:14-15	189	5:6	100, 138, 139,	15:8-12	175
17:6-7	368		202, 216, 270, 422	15:16	182
17:11	xii, xii, 6, 10,	5:18-19	410	15:26-27	228
	121, 211	6-8	109	16:20	241
17:31	390	6:6	109	16:26	92, 302
17:32	389, 405	6:7-9	110		
18:9-11	272, 272	6:9	387, 390	**1 Corinthians**	
19:8	6, 24	6:12	109		
19:20	24	7:4	109, 109, 110	1:18-25	345
20:25	24, 179	7:24	109, 110	3:16-17	182
22:17-18	272	8:2	109, 110	3:19	345
23:6	389, 405	8:6	110	4:20	24
23:11	272	8:12	109	6:18	109
24:5	92, 302	8:17	174	6:19	109, 182
24:14-15	395	8:18-23	109	7:4	109
24:15	53, 390	8:23	109	7:29	161, 241, 324
24:15, 21	405	8:23-35	390	7:31	161, 241, 324,
24:21	389	8:34	264 267, 369,		394
26:8	389, 390		369	10:4	266
26:12-16	272	9:6, 24-29	176	10:6	266, 270
26:23	387	9:6, 27	172, 173	11:24	109
27:10	390	9:15-18	175	11:27-30	358
27:37	403	9:25-26	175	12:12-13	171
28:3	179	10:12	171	12:12-27	109, 109
28:23	24	10:18	92, 302	14:33	116
28:25-27	343	10:19	177	15	384
28:31	6, 24	11	110	15:4	387
		11:1	177	15:5-8	252, 271
		11:1-2	175	15:12, 13, 15, 16	
		11:6	173		390

15:12, 13, 21, 42 405	5:6 109	2:14-22 171
15:17 339	5:8 21, 22, 109,	2:21 182
15:20-23 384	391, 391, 392, 403	3:3-6 172
15:20, 23 387	5:16 342	3:3-6, 9 228
15:21-22 411	5:18 xii, 283	3:6 171, 176
15:23 395, 414	7:1 109	3:9 149
15:24 24	8:19 377	3:21 149, 301, 393
15:25 264, 267,	10:4-5 281	4:4 109, 109, 171
369, 369	12:2-4 19, 391	4:4-5 171
15:26 400	13:1 156	4:8 392, 392, 397
15:35 109		4:9 21, 381, 397,
15:35-38 406	**Galatians**	392
15:35-44 380		5:23 109, 109
15:35-49 405	1:4 301	5:30 109, 109
15:37 109, 407, 413	3:6-9, 29 182	6:17 368
15:38 109	3:8 171	
15:38, 44 405	3:16-18 176	**Philippians**
15:44 109, 400, 405	3:26-28 182	
15:46 408	3:26-29 171	1:20 109
15:51 401	3:28 171	1:21-24 21, 392
15:51-52 396	3:29 174	1:23 391
15:51-58 385	4:3 164	2:7 339
15:52 396	4:4 137, 241, 270	2:7-8 223
15:54 401	4:9 164	2:8-11 339
	4:21-31 109	2:10-11 364
2 Corinthians	4:24 190	2:19 203
	6:16 172, 173, 176,	2:24 203
1:9 390	182	3 23
1:16 182		3:3 182
1:22 407	**Ephesians**	3:11 405
3-6 110		3:20-21 390, 406
3:6 110	1:4 139	3:21 109, 408
3:7-9 108, 109	1:10 171	
3:13-18 330	1:14 407	**Colossians**
3:17 254	1:17 124	
3:18 263, 377, 390	1:20 264, 267, 369	1:6 92, 302
4:2 298	1:20-23 339	1:12-13 179
4:16 408	1:21 301	1:13 24
5:1-5 406	1:23 174	1:17 375
5:2-4 109	2:11-16 171	1:18 109, 109, 387
5:5 22, 392, 407	2:12-15 171	1:23 92, 302
	2:14-19 176	1:24 109

1:26-27	228	**1 Timothy**		3:2-6	109
1:27	281			3:9-10, 17	291
2:1	264	2:6	138, 216, 270,	3:10	293
2:2	228		422	4:12	368
2:3	359	4:1	236	4:13	368
2:8	164	6:15	369	5:12	164
2:10	173	6:16	263	6:2	405
2:11	182			6:5	108, 223, 301
2:20	164	**2 Timothy**		6:18	239
3:1	264, 267, 369			7:27-28	252
3:11	171	2:15	210, 211, 297	8, 9, 10	252
3:15	171	2:18	389	8:1	264, 267, 369
4:3	228	3:1	236	8:13	161, 175, 183,
4:11	24	3:1-5	82		301, 324, 353
		3:12-13	82	9:8f	324
1 Thessalonians		3:16	151	9:8-10	161
		4:2	211	9:10	110, 183, 353
2:12	24	4:3-4	82	9:11-15	252
2:15-16	166	4:6	244	9:24-28	282
2:16	311	4:8	376	9:26	225
4:13, 15	389			9:27	381, 382, 400,
4:13-18	383	**Titus**			401, 411, 414
4:14	401			9:28	21, 252, 275,
4:15	381, 381, 395	1:2	240		282, 400
4:16	278, 396, 397	2:13	372, 376, 377	10:10	225
4:17	410			10:13	264, 267,
4:18	401	**Hebrews**			369, 369
5:2	310			10:25	243
5:4	310	1:1-2	5, 393	10:36-37	21
5:21	xxi, 9, 17, 42,	1:2	63 146, 229,	10:37	34, 127, 242,
	121, 148, 211, 250		236, 242		243
5:23	109	1:3	369, 375	11	176
		1:4	339	11:5	19, 391
2 Thessalonians		1:8	150	11:27	263, 264, 266
		1:9	223	11:35	387, 387
1:5	24	1:13	264, 267, 369	12:1	257
1:7	278, 324, 324	1:14	275	12:21	264, 267, 369
2:1-2	389	2:7, 9	339	12:22-24	257
2:1-11	82	2:9	369, 369	12:26-28	162
2:1-12	389	2:12	176	12:27	179
2:2	310, 328	2:14-15	400	12:28	6, 24, 179,
		2:17	223		301

13:2	278	3:8	350		387
13:8	341, 373, 373	3:9	100	1:6	179, 182, 346, 356
13:9	282	3:10	310, 328	1:7	363
		3:10-11	315	1:8	265, 361, 365
		3:10-13	163	1:9	179

James

1 John

1:1	182			1:9-16	341
1:18	408			1:10	397
2:26	109	2:3	376	1:12-16	409
5:3	236	2:18	55, 100, 236, 245, 327, 338	1:12-17	267
5:8	244	2:22	55, 338	1:13	256
5:8-9	242	3:1-3	390	1:13, 20	365
		3:2	342, 408, 408	1:14-16	368
		3:14	110	1:17	273

1 Peter

		4:2-3	55, 338	1:18	381, 397, 400
1:1	182, 245	4:12	263	1:19	344
1:3-7	400			1:20	256, 359
1:5	21, 275			2 and 3	365, 366

2 John

1:5, 9	426			2:5	365
1:5, 12	245	7	55, 338, 338	2:7	345, 365
1:5, 20	236			2:11	345

Jude

1:20	139			2:16	365
2:9	182			2:17	345
2:9, 10	177	3	100, 302, 404, 414, 422, 426	2:25-26	366
2:12	376	14	278	2:29	345
3:15-16	211	17-19	245	3	349
3:18	225	18	236	3:3	310, 366
3:18-20	381, 392, 397	18-19	323	3:6	345
				3:10	302
3:22	369	**Revelation**		3:11	366
4:5	245			3:13	345
4:6	381, 392, 397			3:14	367
4:7	100, 243, 400	1	252	3:20	366
4:17	100, 245, 400	1:1	337, 346, 346, 349, 350, 358, 398, 399	3:22	345
				4	349

2 Peter

				4:8	265
		1:1, 3	371	5:8	359
1:16-18	273	1:3	338, 340, 349, 349, 358, 398	5:9	356, 356
3:2	315			5:10	182, 356
3:3	236	1:4, 11, 20	354, 355	6:8	381
3:3-4	323	1:5	346, 367 369,	6:9	19, 403
3:4	245			6:9-11	392

6:12	367	19:11	278, 320
7	392	19:14	278
7:9	356	19:16	325, 346, 368
10:6-7	399, 399	19:18, 21	368
10:8-11	354	19:21	311
10:9	353	20	27, 43, 192, 349
10:9-11	355, 371	20:1-10	40, 42, 45
10:11	354, 356, 356	20:4	403
11:8	166	20:13-14	381, 400
11:15	150, 301	21 & 22	155, 168, 171
11:15-18	399	21:1-4	22
12:6	220	21:4	110
12:9	360	21:6	265
12:10-12	347	22:6	349, 398, 399
12:14	220	22:6, 10	371
13:5	220	22:7	338, 340, 349
13:7	356	22:7, 10	398
13:8	139	22:7, 12	349, 364
14:6	356, 358	22:7, 14-19	358
14:13	380, 380, 400, 401	22:8-9	264
14:14	371	22:9	356
14:15	371	22:10	168, 231, 349, 349. 354
16:6	166	22:12	265
16:15	310	22:13	361
16:19	166	22:17	360
17-19	165	22:18-19	43, 192, 339, 357
17:5ff	165	22:20	349, 375
17:6	166		
17:14	346		
17:15	356		
17:18	166		
18:2, 10, 11, 17, 19-23	167		
18:4	166		
18:10, 16, 19	166		
18:18, 21	166		
18:24	166		
19	366		
19:7-8	368		
19:9-10	265		
19:10	359		

www.ingramcontent.com/pod-product-compliance
Lightning Source LLC
Chambersburg PA
CBHW020728160426
43192CB00006B/148